Dispute Resolution in Electronic Commerce

Studies and Materials on the Settlement of International Disputes

VOLUME 9

Dispute Resolution in Electronic Commerce

by

Yun Zhao

MARTINUS NIJHOFF PUBLISHERS
LEIDEN / BOSTON

Library of Congress Cataloging-in-Publication Data

Zhao, Yun
Dispute resolution in electronic commerce / by Yun Zhao.
p. cm. — (Studies and materials on the settlement of international disputes ; v. 9)
Includes bibliographical references and index.
ISBN 90-04-14383-1
1. Electronic commerce—Law and legislation. 2. Dispute resolution (Law) I. Title. II. Series.
K1005.Z47 2005
343.09'944—dc22

2005041687

Printed on acid-free paper.

ISBN 90-04-14383-1

Koninklijke Brill NV incorporates the imprints Brill Academic Publishers, Martinus Nijhoff Publishers and VSP.

Printed and bound in The Netherlands.

CONTENTS

ABBREVIATIONS

AAA	American Arbitration Association
ABA	American Bar Association
ACH	Automated Clearing House
ADR	Alternative Dispute Resolution
AJIL	American Journal of International Law
AOL	American Online
ARPANET	Advanced Research Project Agency Network
ASP	Application Service Provider
B2B	Business to Business
B2C	Business to Consumer
BBB	Best Business Bureau
CDA	Communications and Decency Act
CHM	Common Heritage of Mankind
CI	Consumer International
CIC	Computer Integration Courtroom
CLI	Cyberspace Law Institute
CRDP	Center de Recherche an Driot Public
DART	Dispute Avoidance and Resolution Team
DISH	Data Interchange on Shipping
DNS	Domain Name System
ECU	European Currency Unit
EDI	Electronic Data Interchange
EEC	European Economic Community
EEF	Electronic Frontier Foundation
EFTA	European Free Trade Association
EJIL	European Journal of International Law
EU	European Union
EuroISPA	European Internet Services Providers Association
FAQ	Frequently Asked Questions
FEDMA	Federation of European Direct Marketing
FNC	Federal Networking Council
FTC	Federal Trade Commission
GATS	General Agreement on Trade in Services
GBDe	Global Business Dialogue for Electronic commerce

GII-GIS	Global Information Infrastructure—Global Information Society
GUIDEC	General Usage for International Digitally Ensured Commerce
IAB	Internet Architecture Board
IAHC	Ad Hoc Committee
IANA	Internet Assigned Numbers Authority
ICANN	Internet Corporation for Assigned Names and Numbers
ICC	International Chamber of Commerce
ILPF	Internet Law and Policy Forum
INTA	International Trademark Association
IP	Internet Protocol
IPWG	Internet Privacy Working Group
ISOC	Internet Society
ISP	Internet Service Provider
ITU	International Telecommunications Union
JWT	Journal of World Trade
MUD	Multi-User Dimension
NAF	National Arbitration Forum
NCAIR	National Center for Automated Information Research
NCCUSL	National Conference of Commissioners on Uniform State Laws
NSI	Network Solutions, Inc.
NTIA	National Telecommunications and Information Administration
OECD	Organization for Electronic Cooperation and Development
SLD	Second Level Domain
TACD	Trans Atlantic Consumer Dialogue
TOS	Terms of Service
TRIPs	Trade Related Aspects of Intellectual Property
TLD	Top Level Domain
UCITA	Uniform Computer Information Transactions Act
UDRP	Uniform Domain Name Dispute Resolution Policy
UETA	Uniform Electronic Transactions Act
UNCITRAL	United Nations Commission on International Trade Law
UPS	United Parcel Services
US	United States
USAA	United States Arbitration Act

USCIB	United States Council for International Business
WELL	Whole Earth 'Lectronic Link
WIPO	World Intellectual Property Organization
WTO	World Trade Organization
WWW	World Wide Web

CHAPTER ONE

INTRODUCTION

1. *The Setting*

One of the most spectacular events approaching the end of the last century was the wide acceptance and use of electronic commerce.[1] Never before had people imagined obtaining all sorts of information without stepping out of home or doing business in an invisible world. But with the result of several innovations that came together in the 1980's involving computerization, telecommunications, miniaturization, compression technology, and digitalization, these fantasies became truths and signaled an irreversible trend for the future. By sitting in front of a computer and surfing through the Internet, you can accomplish a lot of tasks, which still sounds amazing to some people.

Actually, forms of electronic commerce emerged much earlier than what we call electric commerce today. When we use telephones, fax machines, or other familiar electronic communication tools, we are involved in electronic commerce in the broadest sense of the word.[2] However, people only realized the possibilities of electronic commerce after the Internet came into the arena. It is the open, multifunctional and international nature of the Internet, in particular, which has galvanized the potential for electronic commerce, revealing the revolutionary effect the Internet can exert on modern business.[3] It is changing the way businesses of all sizes interact with their customers and suppliers; it is also affecting individuals who will increasingly communicate with businesses and other individuals through computers. One leading authority has described the change as being "so startling in its economic implications that it may reasonably be

[1] A. Goldstein & D. O'Connor, *E-Commerce for Development: Prospects and Policy Issues*, OECD Development Center, at <http://www.oecd.org/dev>; R. Perez-Esteve & L. Schuknecht, *A Quantitative Assessment of Electronic Commerce, Economic Research and Analysis Division*, WTO, Staff Working Paper ERAD-99-01, September, 1999, at 2.

[2] K.W. Grewlich, *Governance in 'Cyberspace': Access and Public Interest in Global Communications*, 47, 383 (Kluwer, 1999).

[3] See *Electronic Commerce*, OECD Policy Brief No. 1-1997, at 1-3.

considered a watershed in the way we do business . . . an abrupt and irrevocable turning point, one that signals a shift in historical direction by obliterating an established set of business practices and replacing them with a new commercial paradigm."[4] It is because of this consideration that electronic commerce based on the Internet is the topic for the present study.

Doing business through the Internet, which was a rather exotic fantasy until recently, has been undergoing exponential development.[5] Everyday we are confronted with additional statistics that reflect the rapid expansion of electronic commerce. The electronic trading boom is in full swing and the Internet offers unlimited opportunities to transform the way business is conducted.[6]

While there were only some 4.5 million Internet users in 1991[7] and commercial use of the Internet was even invisible at that time, new means of exchanging information have since transformed many aspects of social and economic structures.[8] When extended to the commercial world, the strong influence of the Internet was soon obvious to the public. Businesses, organizations, institutions, governments, and individuals can use computer networks to sell products, share information, converse, and develop communities across borders of space and time to deal with virtually every subject.[9] Within only several years, electronic commerce has developed dramatically. It is estimated that by now there are as many as 300 million or more Internet users,[10] and business through the Internet captured from virtually

[4] T.M. Siebel & P. House, *Cyber Rules, Strategies for Excelling at E-Business*, 1 (1999).

[5] M.M. Waldrop, Culture Shock on the Networks, 265 Science 879–880 (12 August 1994).

[6] T. Melville-Ross, The Changing Face of Business, in T. Nash (Ed.), *Electronic Commerce: Directors and Opportunities for Electronic Business*, 5 (1998).

[7] On the dramatic growth of the Internet, see K.S. Byford, Privacy in Cyberspace: Constructing a Model of Privacy for the Electronic Communications Environment, 24 *Rutgers Computer & Tech. L.J.* 1–38 (1998). The Internet is conservatively estimated to connect well over twenty million people in 1994. See G.P. Long, III, Comment, Who are You?: Identity and Anonymity in Cyberspace, 55 *U. Pitt L. Rev.* 1177–1178 (1994).

[8] For further discussion, see generally R. Wiley & R. Butler, National Information Infrastructure: Preserving Personal Space in Cyberspace, 12 *Communications Lawyer*, No. 3, 1 (Fall 1994).

[9] See G. Friedman & R. Gellman, An Information Superhighway "On Ramp" for Alternative Dispute Resolution, 68 *N.Y. St. Bus. J.*, 38–39 (May–June 1996).

[10] The Internet is growing at the rate of five to eight percent per month. J. Clark, The Online Universe: Find Out Why Some 30 Million People Count Themselves as Citizens of this Mysterious World, *Toronto Star*, October 20, 1994, at J1; Internet Crimes Soars, *Information Week*, October 10, 1994, at 20.

zero to a predicted US$300 billion in the ten years up to the turn of the 20th century.[11] Another study predicts that the number of users making transactions over the Internet will jump to over 183 million in 2003 and the amount of commerce through the Internet will top a staggering US$1 trillion.[12] Internet-based business might still be a minor player compared with the traditional business, but considering that the paper-based businesses have been in existence for hundreds of years, the results of electronic commerce have been rather fantastic and, more importantly, electronic commerce is presently developing at an even more rapid pace. It is expected that Internet-based business will account for 2 percent of all commercial transactions in industrialized countries by the year of 2003,[13] and by 2004 it should account for 8.6 percent of worldwide goods and services.[14]

As the leader in information technology, The United States (US) has been even more active in Internet-based business and is showing the way for other regions. About 70 percent of Internet web sites are located in the US, and in 1996/1997 over 85 percent of the world revenue in Internet-based electronic commerce was generated there.[15] By the year of 2003, the value of business-to-business electronic commerce[16] is expected to amount to US$1300 billion in the US alone.[17]

---

[11] See M. Bachetta, P. Low, A. Matto, L. Schuknecht, H. Wager & M. Wehrens, *Electronic Commerce and the Role of the WTO*, 1 (1998). According to another resource, the number shall be US$200 billion. See Opening remarks by B. Munder on *Customer Privacy on the Web—Self-Regulation or Government?* March 4, 1998, at <http://mcgraw-hill.govservices.com/speech/forum1.html>. The number of Internet users is still growing at an exponential rate every day. See Web News & Views: *Internet Marketing 101*, Basics, at <http://www.cincymart.com/webnews/market.html>. Currently, traffic on the Internet is doubling every 100 days. See R.I.R. Abeyratne, Auctions on the Internet of Airline Tickets, *Communications Lawyer*, No. 1, 22 (1999).

[12] The Global Market Forecast for Internet Usage and Commerce, International Data Corporation, June 1999. Similarly, Forrester's Research estimates that e-commerce just among businesses for all types of goods and services will reach US$1.33 trillion world-wide by 2003. See R. Holleyman, *The Impact on Intellectual Property: Jurisdiction, Enforcement and Dispute Resolution,* International Conference on Electronic Commerce and Intellectual Property, Geneva, September 14 to 16, 1999, WIPO/EC/CONF/99/SPK/6–C

[13] See further Bachetta, *supra* note 11, at 23.

[14] Forrester, *supra* note 12.

[15] See further Bachetta, *supra* note 11, at 25.

[16] Electronic commerce can be divided into several types. Business-to-business transaction is an important one that shall be described further in Chapter Two.

[17] *Financial Times*, 12 April 1999.

Having realized the advantages of electronic commerce, other regions are trying to catch up with the US. The European Commission agreed on an ambitious agenda to push through all remaining electronic commerce legislation by the end of year 2000 in an effort to help the European Union (EU) improve its Internet-based economy.[18] Meanwhile, Africa, Asia, and Latin America reported the highest growth rates in Internet hosts for the period between 1993 and 1996, and even more rapid developments are expected out of those regions later on.[19]

Looking forward, the potential for electronic commerce to gain a sizeable share of consumer and business purchases appears to be large, although it is difficult to quantify.[20] The developments in communications infrastructure, digital networks, and graphic-based Internet applications have made and will continue to make transmission of information much faster, cheaper, and simpler. With further technological improvements, communication shall become much more reliable and thus more applicants shall be attracted to this splendid field. This shall inevitably increase productivity and efficiency in a number of industries and businesses. Increased productivity will theoretically yield higher profit margins and a more stable economic system.[21] Accordingly, commercial use of the Internet, more specifically, electronic commerce, should have a magnificent future.

Emerging numbers of online consumer transactions foreshadow this bright future for electronic commerce. The Internet encourages the entry of consumers into electronic commerce by way of facilitating direct interaction between consumers and merchants. Although the volume of business-to-business electronic commerce currently far exceeds that of consumer transactions,[22] the large-scale entry of con-

---

[18] *Financial Times*, 26 June 2000. Commissioners wanted to pass seven remaining directives and pieces of legislation, which include directives on copyright, distance selling of financial services, electronic money, etc.

[19] ITU, World Telecommunications Indicators Database, 1997 b.

[20] J. Coppel, E-commerce: Impacts and Policy Challenges, Economics Department Working Papers No. 252, OECD, ECO/WKP (2000) 25. Electronic commerce is harder to measure than the industry itself. Tracking the exchange of goods and information across electronic networks and between businesses is impossible. How many Internet users there are and for what purpose they use the Internet are also mysteries.

[21] See further *USA Today*, December 8, 1995.

[22] See *Measuring Electronic Commerce, Committee for Information, Computer and Communications Policy*, OECD/GD (97) 185, at 13, which is available at <http://www.oecd.org/dsti/sti/it/ec/prod/e_97-85.htm>.

sumers into electronic commerce is believed to be a simple matter of time.[23] Business transactions shall be made between merchants and users while they simply sit before computers connected to the Internet, which could fundamentally change the normal commercial world. The potential profitability entailed in such transactions has already enticed merchants.

2. *The Problem*

Recognising the efficiency and convenience brought by the Internet, the business world is trying to modify traditional business to accommodate new forms of communication. To be successful, businesses must develop integrated strategies addressing their commercial, technical, security and legal requirements to better serve their customers and avoid potential liabilities. Thus, this new phenomenon has brought with it new challenges in various areas, which demand fast and efficient responses.[24]

The need to address legal issues is urgent.[25] Controversy has arisen over whether or not existing law offers clear enough guidelines to promote the development of Internet business;[26] whether or not certain barriers must be removed; how contractual requirements, such as those for a "writing," a "signature," and an "original" shall be reconsidered in the context of electronic commerce; and so forth.

Actually, much work has been done to fill in the possible loopholes.[27] For example, the United Nations Commission on International

---

[23] The Emerging Digital Economy, U.S. Department of Commerce report, April 1998, at 5–6, at <http://www.ecommerce.gov/whatsnew.htm>.

[24] See, for example, M.I. Meyerson, Virtual Constitutions: The Creation of Rules for Governing Private Networks, 8 *Harvard Journal of Law and Technology*, 129 (1994); see also I.K. Gotts & A.D. Rutenberg, Navigating the Global Information Superhighway: A Bumpy Road Lies Ahead, 8 *Harvard Journal of Law and Technology* 275 (1995).

[25] See, for example, P.H. Schuck, Legal Complexity: Some Causes, Consequences, and Cures, *42 Duke L.J.* 1, 18 (1992).

[26] See, for example J.K. Winn, Open Systems, Free Markets and Regulation of Internet Commerce, 72 *Tul. L. Rev.*, 1177(1998); R.J. Robertson, Electronic Commerce on the Internet and the Statute of Frauds, 49 *S.C. L. Rev.* 787(1998); H.K. Towle, Electronic Transactions and Contracting, 520 PLI/Pat, 515 (1998); K.S. Haw, E-Commerce: Technology Can Bypass the Legal Pitfalls, *Bus. Times* (Singapore), October 14, 1996, at 16.

[27] For example, the International Chamber of Commerce (ICC) formulated General Usage for International Digitally Ensured Commerce (GUIDEC); this document

Trade Law (UNCITRAL) took the initiative to draft Model Law on Electronic Commerce, which was adopted on December 16, 1996.[28] Other legislation is also well underway at international and national levels.[29]

However, attention has only recently been paid to the area of dispute resolution.[30] With more and more electronic commerce taking place on a daily basis, disputes arising from misunderstanding, conflicting interests, or malicious actions are inevitable.[31] For example,

---

can be found at <http://www.iccwbo.org/guidec2.htm>. For general discussion, see Survey of International Electronic and Digital Signature Initiatives, Internet Law & Policy Forum at <http://www.ilpf.org/digsig/survey.htm>.

[28] United Nations, UNCITRAL Model Law on Electronic Commerce, 36 I.L.M. 197 (1997); see also the Report of UNCITRAL on the work of its 29th Session, UN General Assembly Official Records Supplement No. 17 (A/51/17), Annex I; A.H. Boss & J.K. Winn, The Emerging Law of Electronic Commerce, 52 *Bus. Law.* 1469 (1997); J.Y. Gliniecki & C.G. Ogada, The Legal Acceptance of Electronic Documents, Writings, Signatures, and Notices in International Transportation Conventions: A Challenge in the Age of Global Electronic Commerce, 13 *Nw. J. Int'l. L. & Bus.* 117 (1992); D.J. Greenwood & R.A. Campbell, Electronic Commerce Legislation: From Written on Paper and Signed in Ink to Electronic Records and Online Authentication, 53 *Bus. Law.*, No. 1, 307–309 (1997); J. Clift, Electronic Commerce: the UNCITRAL Model Law and Electronic Equivalents to Traditional Bills of Lading, 27 *International Business Lawyer*, No. 7, 311–316 (July/August 1999); R. Hill & I. Walden, The Draft UNCITRAL Model Law for Electronic Commerce: Issues and Solutions, *The Computer Lawyer* (March 1996), at <http://www.batnet.com/oikoumene/arbunc.html>.

[29] For example, the federal and six of the ten provincial legislatures of Canada are formulating laws on electronic commerce. See L. Guibault, Canada: New Legislation on E-Commerce Underway, *Computer Und Recht International*, No. 1, at 25–26 (2001). In the US, revisions to Article 2 of the Uniform Commercial Code, as well as inclusion of computer information transactions in a new Article 2B were done for this purpose. See further R.T. Nimmer, Article 2B: An Introduction, *16 J. Marshall J. Computer & Info. L.* 211, 227–237 (1997); R.T. Nimmer, Electronic Contracting: Legal Issues, *14 J. Marshall J. Computer & Info. L.* 211–212 (1996); A.H. Boss, Electronic Commerce and the Symbiotic Relationship Between International and Domestic Law Reform, 72 *Tulane L. Rev.* 1931, 1956–1963 (1998). The Draft Code of Conduct for Electronic Commerce proposed by the Electronic Commerce Platform Netherlands (a joint undertaking started by the Dutch business sector and the Ministry of Economic Affairs to foster electronic commerce) offers a non-legal approach to resolving a variety of pressing e-commerce issues. See Draft Code of Conduct For Electronic Commerce, *7 Willamette J. Int'l L. & Dispute Resolution* 173 (2000).

[30] See, for example, Symposium, Doing Deals in Cyberspace: Negotiation, ADR and the Electronic Revolution, 11 *Negotiation J.* 91 (1995); I. MacDuff, Flames on the Wires: Mediating from an Electronic Cottage, 10 *Negotiation J.* 5 (1994).

[31] See R.H. Mnookin, Why Negotiations Fail: An Exploration of Barriers to the Resolution of Conflict, 8 *Ohio St. J. on Disp. Resol.*, No. 2, 235 (1993); see also W.L. Ury, J.M. Brett & S.B. Goldberg, *Getting Disputes Resolved: Designing Systems to Cut the Costs of Conflict*, at xii (Jossey-Bass, Inc., 1988).

if a product or service purchased through the Internet is not received, or gives rise to hidden costs, or is judged by a consumer to be unsatisfactory in some way, the difficulty of obtaining satisfactory redress may render recourse illusory. The distance between the two parties, the different political legal frameworks behind the parties, the possible costs and complexity of legal actions have brought enormous challenges to traditional conceptions. The ensuing disputes are broad in scale, both in quantity and complexity.

Suppose a US merchant sets up a web site with a German server and a Dutch consumer makes a transaction with this merchant through the Internet. During this process, the consumer may have disputes with the merchant. Meanwhile, other disputes could develop: the merchant could have problems with the server concerning the connecting services; the merchant's web site could cause intellectual damage to another company; etc. Ostensibly, this business will occasion a lot of problematic issues, many involving international interests.

How well disputes are resolved shall largely influence the attitudes of Internet merchants and consumers alike. Their attitudes shall in turn determine the fate of electronic commerce. Of course, judging from the present situation, electronic commerce will continue to develop no matter how problematic the business is: so long as there are foreseeable profits, merchants will set up web sites for their businesses; curious consumers eager for convenience will support these businesses. But this is a short-term truth. If disputes pile up and appropriate legal measures to resolve these disputes remain unavailable, the enthusiasm of merchants and consumers, who find their own interests in danger, will no doubt dissipate. Thus, effective dispute resolution measures are needed to guarantee the long-term benefits of electronic commerce.

Dispute resolution is a means of guaranteeing the minimal order and stability necessary for viable social organization.[32] For this end, dispute resolution has been in existence since the emergence of human society. It is not surprising that when looking into historical US files, one discovers a wealth of litigation records, proof that it is as much natural as it is popular for disputing parties to go to court for resolution.

[32] T.E. Carbonneau, *Alternative Dispute Resolution: Melting the Lances and Dismounting the Steeds*, 5 (University of Illinois Press, 1989).

Yet while records provide a good basis for handling dispute resolution in electronic commerce cases, electronic commerce, as a new means of transaction, is different in many aspects from traditional business and therefore requires a new legal approach. Its transnational nature, in particular, has called into question the traditional jurisdictional theory for litigation. Furthermore, the high fees and time required largely deter the disputing parties from bringing electronic commerce cases to court, especially when most consumer transactions are for sum of US$100 or less.

Besides litigation, there exist other means for resolving disputes, which are actually being used rather frequently for the time being. Efficient and low-cost options are most popular. Among them, arbitration is now widely recognized in commercial disputes.

Although it is still possible to use present mechanisms to resolve disputes regarding electronic commerce, doing so should not curtail the possible application of modern technology and thereby limit the meaningfulness of the Internet further. The emergence of electronic commerce requires the development of new dispute resolution tools that will accommodate it. The main problem for the time being is to determine the juncture where the use of the Internet can be well welded to existing dispute resolution mechanisms. While preserving the traditional function of resolving disputes, new technology should be made available to those mechanisms.

It is the primary purpose of this study to explore the rules and principles used in resolving disputes arising out of electronic commerce. The question to be addressed in this study may be formulated as follows: since traditional dispute resolution mechanisms cannot well suit the present situation, what rules and measures should be formulated to procure the peaceful resolution of the disputes therein?

3. *Approach and Scope*

As discussed above, disputes shall arise during the process of electronic commerce. It is not at all a new idea to resolve disputes of this kind with traditional mechanisms. The court has necessarily done so in the absence of other options and, in so doing, modified traditional theories to meet the new demands, for example, setting forth new justifications for its power to hear cases.

But the new characteristics of the new electronic commerce business have called for the further development of the dispute resolution system. While litigation may serve a purpose, alternatives to litigation shall be explored for dealing with electronic commerce. The concept of Alternative Dispute Resolution (ADR) actually includes all other dispute resolution mechanisms except litigation, offering great flexibility to those exploring feasible adaptations of traditional theory to modern practice.

This study does not intend to suggest that ADR should take precedence over traditional litigation or *vice versa*. Rather, it tries to take a complete view of the possible mechanisms for dispute resolution in electronic commerce. While analyzing the problems presented in national litigation, it attempts to formulate alternative ways to fill in the gaps. The author's idea is that litigation shall remain an important mechanism for resolving disputes and, more importantly, as a last valve to secure final justice. However, the use of modern technology has asked for other, more efficient ways to resolve the conflicts. As new technology is widely used in the economy, it should likewise be made use of by mechanisms formulated to supervise this economy; not being used in this way would constitute a waste of extant resources. An examination of how to implement modern technology into the present mechanisms or, more precisely, how to reformulate the mechanism through the use of the Internet itself is required.

The feasibility of the application of Internet technology to dispute resolution is uncertain. Several institutions have been experimenting with making use of the online facilities to deal with disputes in specific areas, but these experiments have not treated electronic commerce in general. In the absence of widespread applications of online mechanisms, the opinions of experts, as well as the existing online practice become more relevant. Since electronic commerce is still a new phenomenon for many people and its potential capability is enormous, the scope of the present study with respect to the possible use of online facilities in dispute resolution is broad and very likely debatable.

4. *Outline*

The present study consists of seven parts. After a brief introduction, Chapter Two gives a general description of the development of electronic commerce, potential disputes related to electronic commerce, and the possible mechanisms for dealing with such disputes. First introduced as a general term for doing business through the Internet, the discussion of electronic commerce shall be further divided into several specific types of electronic commerce, followed by an explanation of the general procedures for doing such business. A general overview of potential contractual and non-contractual disputes as well as present dispute resolution mechanisms shall be offered. Importantly, the shortcomings of the existing mechanisms shall be analyzed and necessary improvements to the present mechanisms will be suggested.

The use of the Internet has fundamentally changed social life and the legal field should follow suit and change through adopting new policies concerning dispute resolution. Several policy issues are singled out for consideration in Chapter Three. Section One examines self-regulation, an ideal way of regulating the Internet, and Section Two treats international cooperation, with all its implications for dispute resolution in electronic commerce across territorial borders. Section Three revisits traditional policies concerning the protection of both consumer and merchant in the wake of what is a new balance of power between transacting parties fueled by the accessibility of information on the internet. Examples are presented to elucidate the process of implementation and the relationship between the three policies.

Bearing the general policies in mind, traditionally mechanized litigation shall be dealt with in Chapter Four. No matter what happens, traditional litigation, representing the power of the States, shall always remain important to dispute resolution. However, developments should be made to accommodate technological improvements, or else outdated theories shall obstruct the further smooth functioning of litigation. For the purpose of this study, two related aspects are singled out for detailed discussion. Section One addresses adjudicative jurisdiction, the assignment of power to hear cases to specific courts, and Section Two deals with the choice of laws in electronic commerce. These are closely related steps in litigation. The courts should justify their position in entertaining a case and further validate their position by applying the right law.

As Chapter Four reveals that litigation is actually not the best choice for dealing with disputes in electronic commerce, Chapter Five goes on to offer several examples of a general trend in formulating a new mechanism. These include the Virtual Magistrate Project, the University of Massachusetts Online Ombuds Office, eBay's Escrow Arrangement, and the World Intellectual Property Organization's (WIPO) treatment of domain name disputes and formulation of Application Service Provider dispute avoidance and resolution practices.

Based on the practices described in Chapter Five but not a simple transplantation of present arbitration, the design of a new general mechanism for electronic commerce is laid out in Chapter Six. The first section sets forth a blueprint for this mechanism, elaborates on its guiding principles and details the particulars of its implementation. Section Two discusses the law for electronic commerce and proposes *lex informatica* for the field in its present state.

Chapter Seven is comprised of a summary of this study's observations and findings as well as closing remarks.

CHAPTER TWO

ELECTRONIC COMMERCE AND DISPUTE RESOLUTION

1. *An Overview of Electronic Commerce*

Electronic commerce is a "buzzword," which has no clear meaning but does have a strong capability to associate itself with a subject area of current interest.[1] Since electronic commerce and its participants are so numerous and their intricate relationships are evolving so rapidly, different parties have a different understanding of what electronic commerce means.[2]

It is not the purpose of this study to give a precise definition of this word, as doing so would be nearly impossible. Rather, the aim is to offer a general description of both the practice and implications of electronic commerce in the modern, Internet-based economy.[3]

Nowadays, electronic commerce most commonly refers to Internet and other network-based commerce. Arguably, this reference is flawed, or at least too narrow.[4] Electronic commerce was not created by or for the emergence of the Internet. The telephone, the fax machine, the television, electronic payment and money transfer systems, and

---

[1] See further M.B. Andersen, *Electronic Commerce: A Challenge to Private Law?*, Centro di Studi e Ricerchedi Diritto Comparato e Straniero, Saggi Conferenze e Seminari 4 Rome, 1998.

[2] For a more elaborate discussion of definitions, see <http://www.oecd.org/dsti/sti/it/ec/act/sacher.html>; see also H.K. Towle, *Electronic Transactions and Contracting*, 520 Prac. L. Inst.: Patents, Copyrights, Trademarks, and Literary Property Course Handbook Series 515, 517 (June 8, 1998); J. Coppel, E-Commerce: Impacts and Policy Challenges, Economics Department Working Papers No. 252, June 2000, OECD, ECO/WKP(2000)25, at 4; Measuring Electronic Commerce, OECD Working Papers Vol. V., No. 97, Paris, at 6, 9.

[3] See for example, S.S. Wu, Incorporation by Reference and Public Key Infrastructures: Moving the Law Beyond the Paper-Based World, 38 *Jurimetrics J.*, No. 3, 317 (1998); D.J. Greenwood & R.A. Campbell, Electronic Commerce Legislation: From Written on Paper and Signed in Ink to Electronic Records and Online Authentication, 53 *Bus. Law* 307–308 (1997); A. Urbaczewski et al., A Manager's Primer in Electronic Commerce, *Bus. Horizons* 5 (September 1, 1998).

[4] See further C. Hsu & S. Pant, *Innovative Planning for Electronic Commerce and Enterprises: A Reference Model*, 7–8 (Kluwer, 2000).

Electronic Data Interchange (EDI) all make it possible to do business in one or more respects electronically.[5] Automated Clearing House (ACH) and electronic fund transfers, for example, are responsible for many international financial transactions and at the heart of the restructuring of consumer banking and payment systems of many countries.

Notwithstanding, it was only after the emergence of the Internet that the notion of electronic commerce became understandable to the public. The reasons are simple. As entire transactions can take place via the Internet, individuals could all of a sudden conduct business without knowing either their client or business associate outside of an electronic reality. Moreover, the Internet is a more convenient tool than the aforementioned instruments, as it offers a more efficient and cheaper way to conduct business, extending benefits to both potential merchants and consumers. While the other instruments offer cheap and efficient services, each exists as a minor modification of traditional business and not as something new—not as what one would like to think of as electronic commerce.

That said, it should be noted that the five instruments are still widely used. In fact, the use of the Internet itself can sometimes be combined with the use of a telephone, a fax machine, or even with traditional non-electronic methods of transaction, like the shipping. However, this only shows that the existence of the Internet offers more choices for consumers. As the Internet is the main instrument for the evolving electronic commerce, it is thus the purpose of the present study to focus on commerce conducted through the Internet.

2. *Business through the Internet*

2.1. *The Internet as a Medium*

The Internet refers to the world of computer-based electronic communication.[6] It is formally defined as the global information system that is logically linked together by a globally unique address space

[5] See further M. Bachetta, P. Low, A. Matto, L. Schuknecht, H. Wager & M. Wedrens, *Electronic Commerce and the Role of the WTO*, 5 (1998).

[6] For a description of the Internet, see N.J. Boddie, II, et al., A Review of Copyright and the Internet, 20 *Campbell Law Review*, 193–206 (1998); see also G. Basque,

based on the Internet Protocol or its subsequent extensions/follow-ons.[7] The Internet acts as a vast web of telecommunication links—a worldwide web—connecting computers all over the world.[8]

The Internet began as a research project by the US Defense Department in the late 1960s,[9] the Advanced Research Project Agency Network (ARPANET), to explore a technology called packet switching, intended to permit robust communications.[10] This technology was first considered for military use as a method for securing safe communication among military units in case of fatal disturbances in communication in times of nuclear war.[11] In 1981, a military communication network linking 300 computers was set up for this purpose.[12] However, this original purpose was later broadened.[13] The

Introduction to the Internet, in E. Mackaay et al. (Eds.), *The Electronic Superhighway*, 7–15 (1995); J. Matthews, A Million Subscribers a Month Can't Be Wrong, Sunday Times, June 26, 1994; L.J. Gibbons, No Regulation, Government Regulation, or Self-Regulation: Social Enforcement or Social Contracting For Governance in Cyberspace, 6 *Cornell J.L. & Pub. Pol'y* 475, 487–489 (1997); C.P. Gaumer, Conflicts, the Constitution, and the Internet, 86 *Ill. B.J.* 502–503 (1998).

[7] Fed. Networking Comm'n, Definition of the Internet (October 24, 1995), at <http://www.fnc.gov/Internet_res.html>.

[8] A. Knoll, Comment, Any Which Way But Loose: Nations Regulate the Internet, *4 Tul. J. Int'l & Comp. L.* 275, 277 (1996); see also G. Bovenzi, Liabilities of System Operators on the Internet, 11 *Berkeley Tech. L.J.*, No. 1, 93, 97 (1996).

[9] L. Lessig, *Code and Other Laws of Cyberspace* 4 (1999); see also K. Cheatham, Negotiating a Domain Name Dispute: Problem Solving v. Competitive Approaches, 7 *Willamette J. Int'l L. & Dispute Resolution* 35, 38 (2000).

[10] D.H. Crocker, An Unaffiliated View of Internet Commerce, in R. Kalakota & A.B. Whinston (Eds.), *Readings in Electronic Commerce*, 4 (1997); see also J.M. Adams, Controlling Cyberspace: Applying the Computer Fraud and Abuse Act to the Internet, 12 *Santa Clara Computer & High Tech. L.J.* 403, 405 (1996). The ARPANET allowed communication between users through the "Network Control Protocol," which converts messages into streams of packets at the source and then reassembled them back into messages at the destination.

[11] See for example G.B. Allison, *The Lawyer's Guide to the Internet*, 31 (1995); J.R. Levine & C. Baroudi, *The Internet for Dummies*, 12 (2nd Ed., 1994); see also *J. Reno, Attorney General of the United States et al. v. American Civil Liberties Union*, Supreme Court No. 96–511, 20 n. 3 (June 26, 1997), at <http://www.ciec.org/SC_appeal/opinion.html>.

[12] K.M. Fitzmaurice & R.N. Mody, International Shoe Meets the World Wide Web: Whither Personal Jurisdiction in Florida in the Age of the Internet?, 71 *Fla. B.J.* 22 (1997).

[13] For thorough description of the Internet's history and origins, see T. Berners-Lee & M. Fischetti, *Weaving the Web: The Original Design and Ultimate Destiny of the World Wide Web by Its Inventor* (1999); A.M. Froomkin, Wrong Turn in Cyberspace: Using ICANN to Route Around the APA and the Constitution, 50 *Duke L.J.* 17 (2000); J. Weinberg, ICANN and the Problem of Legitimacy, 50 *Duke L.J.* 187 (2000); B.M. Leiner et al., *A Brief History of the Internet* (authored by the Director of

Internet would serve as a means to disperse information not exclusively reserved for military purposes, but for other purposes as well.[14]

Since its emergence, the Internet has indeed had the most significant impact on communications in the last century and, in consequence, drastically changed daily life for many.[15] Unlike other media, the Internet allows systematic, large-scale, online, interactive communication between distant parties.[16] Certain tools like E-mail execute specific functions, which are not to be equated with the Internet itself; the Internet is the general name for this new instrument of communication. But the World Wide Web (WWW),[17] invented in Europe, is often equated with the Internet.[18] As the WWW transcends national borders, people all over the world with the necessary facilities, a computer with Internet access, can reach information pasted in relevant web sites at any time.[19]

The Internet has distinct advantages over other communication tools. Regular mail takes a long time, the telephone limits users to oral communication, and the fax machine replaces oral communication. Neither the telephone nor the fax facilitates mass communication and while radio and television are well designed for mass communication, they do not facilitate dialogue between individual

---

the Research Institute for Advanced Computer Science, Senior Vice President of Internet Architecture and Technology at MCI WorldCom, Senior Research Scientist at the MIT Laboratory for Computer Science, President of the Corporation for National Research Initiatives, Professor of Computer Science at UCLA, among others), at <http://www.isoc.org/internet/history/brief.html>.

[14] The network (ARPANET) came to include many university networks. See K. Hafner & M. Lyon, *Where Wizards Stay up Late: the Origins of the Internet*, 249 (1996).

[15] See A.L. Shapiro, *The Control Revolution: How the Internet is Putting Individuals in Charge and Changing the World We Know* (1999).

[16] H.M. White, Jr. & R. Lavria, The Impact of New Communication Technologies on International Telecommunication Law and Policy: Cyberspace and the Restructuring of the International Telecommunication Union, 32 *Cal. W. L. Rev.* 1–2 (1995).

[17] For general description of basic terms and concepts associated with the Internet and the WWW, see *ACLU v. Reno*, 929 F.Supp. 824 (E.D. Penn. 1996); T. Laquey, *The Internet Companion: A Beginner's Guide to Global Networking* (2nd Ed. 1994).

[18] D. Bicknell, Bigger, Better, Faster, More (where the Internet revolution could take us over the next five years), *Computer Weekly*, November 18, 1999, at 44. The Web was begun by T. Berners-Lee while working at the European Laboratory for Parties Physics. He started the WWW project with the purpose of building a distributed hypermedia system. See further Thomas Boutell and Boutell. Com, Inc., World Wide Web FAQ, 1997, at <http://www.boutell.com.faq>. In 1992 Mark Andreessen and others at the University of Illinois pioneered the first graphical WWW browser, Mosaic, from which they spawned the company of Netscape in 1994.

[19] See further L. Tien, Who's Afraid of Anonymous Speech? McIntyre and the Internet, 75 *Or. L. Rev.* 182 (1996).

persons. Only the Internet integrates sounds, text, interpersonal communication and mass advertising.[20]

This transparent communication, according to enthusiastic Internet commentators, will foster tolerance, promote democracy, redistribute wealth, improve writing and reading skills, destroy trade barriers, and bring world peace.[21] It has indeed given rise to innovation among merchants, who make use of the Internet to advertise.[22] Potential consumers can respond to these merchants directly, which makes the exchange of information and goods cheap and efficient.

2.2. *Cyberspace for Electronic Commerce*

The term "cyberspace"[23] came into being with the introduction of the Internet.[24] It refers to the space where all Internet activities take

[20] B. Robin, E. Keeler & R. Miller, *Educator's Guide to the Web* 1–2 (1997).

[21] See for example, F. Cairncross, *The Death of Distance: How the Communications Revolution Will Change Our Lives* 119–120, 155, 209–210, 233–234 (1997); M.L. Dertouzos, *What Will Be: How the New World of Information Will Change Our Lives* 82–85 (1997); E. Dyson, *Release 2.0: A Design for Living in the Digital Age* 83–86, 125 (1997); B. Gates, *The Road Ahead* 135–136, 157–158, 184–185 (1995); N.P. Negroponte, *Being Digital* 55–59 (1995); H. Rheingold, *Why Censoring Cyberspace is Dangerous and Futile*, at <http://www.well.com/user/hlr/tomorrow/tomorrowcensor.html>.

[22] The development of browsers in the 1990s were impetus to the emergence of electronic commerce. Browsers, like Netscape, Internet Explorer, can enable users to search for what they want. See P.L. Spector, The Internet and Intellectual Property: Toward a New Model for the Economics of Content, 4 *Telecommunications and Space Journal* 157–158 (1997).

[23] The term "cyberspace" was first coined by W. Gibson, a science fiction writer and founding author of the "Cyberpunk" literary genre, in his 1984 novel *Neuromancer*. On page 51 he defines cyberspace as "a consensual hallucination experienced daily by billions of legitimate operators, in every nation; a graphic representation of data abstracted from the banks of every computer in the human system; unthinkable complexity." It was used to describe a computer generated "virtual" space that looked and felt like physical space. According to computer scientist D. Gelernter, cyberspace should be viewed as a mirror world, a place where institutions of the physical world are represented in digital form and where we can interact with these digital representations as if we were in the physical space. See generally D.H. Gelernter, *Mirror Worlds, or, the Day Software Puts the Universe in a Shoebox . . . How It Will Happen and What It Will Mean* (1991). See also T.H. Flaming, The Rules of Cyberspace: Informal Law in a New Jurisdiction, 85 *Illinois Bar Journal* 174 (1997). R.T. Muth, Old Doctrines on a New Frontier: Defamation and Jurisdiction in Cyberspace, 68 *Wis. Law.* 11 (September 1995); E.A. Cavazos & G. Morin, *Cyberspace and the Law: Your Rights and Duties in the On-Line World* 1–11 (1994); A.M. Fulton, Cyberspace and the Internet: Who Will be the Privacy Police?, 3 *Commlaw Conspectus* 63 (1995); S.C. Jacques, Comment, *Reno v. ACLU*: Insulating the Internet, the First Amendment, and the Marketplace of Ideas, 46 *Am. U.L. Rev.* 1945, 1948 n. 8 (1997).

[24] Sometimes the Internet is more colorfully referred to as cyberspace or Global

place[25] and differs from real space in that it is invisible and untouchable. The essence of cyberspace today is the search engine: a tool with which one can cross an infinite space to locate and go to the stuff one wants.[26] It is in this space that electronic commerce takes place.

Geographical and time limits faced in real space are not obstacles in cyberspace. While geographical boundaries define our legal jurisdictions in real space, there are no such boundaries in cyberspace, which is everywhere and nowhere in particular.[27] Internet architecture is designed to overcome any possible blockage and avoid the centralization of control on information circulation through the net.[28] It allows large numbers of people around the world to communicate in real time, transmitting information to each other instantaneously and over any distance. Thus, cyberspace creates a virtual community for millions of people in all corners of the world.[29] Sitting in front of screens, people can do almost everything they can do in real life, like exchange ideas and knowledge, engage in intellectual discourse, develop business, play games, or gossip.[30]

Information Infrastructure. See for example, J.C. Ginsburg, Global Use/Territorial Rights: Private International Law Questions of the Global Information Infrastructure, 42 *J. Copyright Society U.S.A.* 318–319 (1995); A.P. Reindl, Choosing Law in Cyberspace: Copyright Conflicts on Global Networks, 19 *Mich. J. Int'l L.* 799–800 (1998); S. Fraser, The Copyright Battle: Emerging International Rules and Roadblocks on the Global Information Infrastructure, 15 *J. Marshall J. Computer & Info. L.* 759, 760 (1997).

[25] See further J. Zanghi, "Community Standards" in Cyberspace, 21 *U. Dayton L. Rev.* 95, 106 (1995).

[26] L. Lessig, Surveying Law and Borders: The Zones of Cyberspace, 48 *Stan. L. Rev.* 1408 (May 1996).

[27] See further R.C. Bordone, Electronic Online Dispute Resolution: A Systems Approach—Potential, Problems, and a Proposal, 3 *Harv. Negotiation L. Rev.* 181 (Spring 1998).

[28] A. Lazzaretti, Internet Regulation and On-Line Gambling: A Brief Study of the US and EU Legal Systems, 31 *Law/Technology*, World Jurist Association, No. 4, 6 (1998).

[29] The Internet is truly global and pervasive in nature. See Vice President A. Gore, Bringing Information to the World: The Global Information Infrastructure, 9 *Harv. J.L. & Tech.* 1 (1996).

[30] See further H. Rheingold, *The Virtual Community: Homesteading on the Electronic Frontier* 3 (1994).

2.3. *Character of Electronic Commerce*

Electronic commerce based on the Internet is novel in most respects. Novel digital technology has been vital to the emergence of electronic commerce in its present form, as nearly all communication during transactions makes use of this technology. Electronic commerce is also not just about putting a catalogue on the web; it fundamentally changes the way a company does business, uses systems, and communicates with its customers, suppliers, and partners. An online business is an entire business, not just a web site! One notable emerging characteristic of electronic commerce is the transitory nature of the relationships between parties, which is largely enabled by the use of web-based facilities.[31]

With the use of the Internet, many business procedures can be omitted or quickened, which largely simplifies commercial processes. For instance, electronic commerce both requires lower recycle times and lower inventory than traditional commerce and can afford more efficient and effective customer service. Such advantages suit the present pace of society and commerce, which are in rapid change and thus require swift responses. The efficiency brought by the Internet is vital to modern commerce.

Electronic commerce also requires low transaction fees, which has afforded various merchants, especially small and medium ones, new commercial opportunities.[32] As several thousand dollars is enough to set up an Internet business, the Internet does not discriminate between merchants. A message posted on an Internet server reaches consumers located all over the globe at the same price and in the same time. Lower overhead, lower purchasing costs, lower sales and marketing costs, new sales opportunities, and a global consumer base can be very attractive.

Consumers are also treated equally. Anyone with the necessary facilities can communicate with merchants instantly and with minimal expense. Large numbers of people who do not and cannot know the physical location of the other party are able to make transactions.

---

[31] A.H. Boss, The Internet and the Law: Searching for Security in the Law of Electronic Commerce, 23 *Nova L. Rev.* 586 (Winter 1999).

[32] Joint EU-US Statement on Electronic Commerce, December 5, 1997, at <http://www.qlinks.net/comdocs/eu-us.htm>; see also The First Annual Report, US Government's Working Group on Electronic Commerce, November 1998, at <http://www.ecommerce.gov/whatsnew.htm>.

2.4. *Preparation and General Procedures for Electronic Commerce*

As indicated above, electronic commerce is doing business through the Internet. While various approaches can be taken towards electronic commerce, there are still threads shared by competing parties. This section shall set out to identify these common threads, or general procedures for electronic commerce.

An important step in facilitating electronic commerce is to set up a web site. But before a merchant pastes his information on a web site, he needs to do some preparatory work.

The primary step in initiating electronic commerce is to set up a telecommunications infrastructure, the basic carrier of information. Telecommunications services are undergoing rapid development. International Telecommunications Union (ITU) has undertaken the supervisory task of coordinating and improving the development of telecommunications in different regions. Since the Uruguay Round negotiations of World Trade Organization (WTO), the economic side of telecommunications services has been protected by General Agreement on Trade in Services (GATS), which ensures full liberalization. This agreement recognizes telecommunications as the basic instrument in electronic commerce and all other areas of services.[33] It gives telecommunication providers access to local facilities, enabling interconnection essential for launching other activities and affording market access to information transferred among computers.

With access guaranteed, the merchant needs an address in the Internet at which he may create a web site to publicize products or services and carry on transactions. Each web site on the Internet has been given one unique numerical address called an Internet Protocol (IP) number, which is comparable to a telephone number.[34] The set of numbers is not special at all and means nothing to users.[35] Domain Names are widely regarded as web addresses in user-friendly form.[36]

---

[33] This achievement lays a solid foundation for global electronic commerce. See S.Y. Choi & A.B. Whinston, The Future of the Digital Economy, in M. Shaw, R. Blanning, T. Strader & A. Whinston (Eds.), *Handbook on Electronic Commerce*, 50 (Springwe-Verlag, 2000).

[34] See F.L. Street, *Law of the Internet*, at xxx (1997); D. Diamond, *Whose Internet Is It Anyway?*, Wired, April 1998, at <http://www.wired.com/wired/archive/6.04/kashpureff.html?topic=internet_law&topic_set=newpolicy>.

[35] This explains the development of the domain name system. See further D.J. Loundy, A Primer on Trademark Law and Internet Addresses, 15 *J. Marshall J. Computer & Info. L.* 465, 468 (1997).

[36] See Interim Report of the WIPO Internet Domain Name Process, December

The domain name system operates in a hierarchical manner.[37] The Top Level Domains (TLDs) are the bases for registration. They provide the least specific component of the address.[38] There are two types: generic and country-code TLDs (gTLDs and ccTLDs). The first type includes seven domain names, each of which is reserved for a different purpose: ".com" is used for commercial entities; ".net" is used for computer sites or networks; ".org" is used for international organizations; etc.[39] Each ccTLD is indicated by a two-letter abbreviation for the country of registration.[40] For example, ".us" represents a TLD under the supervision of the USA. At present, there are around 250 ccTLDs, each representing registration under the name of a specific country. There is not necessarily a close relationship between country and registering party. They are only administratively associated.

After TLDs come the Second Level Domains (SLDs), which identify the registrant of the domain name.[41] A registrant can choose one TLD in one Internet Service Provider (ISP), which is usually a .com, to register his business. The SLD precedes the TLD and only this part has specific meaning. The SLD usually consists of the name of the business or entity seeking registration, and thus often includes a trademark of the business. While trademark law permits use of the same trademark for different types of goods or services, replication is not possible in the domain name system. Thus, it is very important to choose the right name for a web site.

23, 1998, Chapter 1, para. 2(iv), at <http://wipo2.wipo.int/process/eng/rfc3/interim2_ch1.html>; see also D. Davidowicz & P. Vixie, Securing the Domain Name System, *Network Magazine*, January 2000, at 92.

[37] *Panavision Int'l, L.P. v. Toeppen*, 945 F. Supp. 1296, 1299 (C.D. Cal. 1996).

[38] See *Brookfield Communications, Inc. v. West Coast Ent. Corp.*, 174 F.3d 1036, 1044 (9th Cir. 1999).

[39] To be exact, gTLDs can be further divided into two types. Open gTLDs, like .com, .net, .org, impose no restriction on the person or entity that seeks to register a name within one of these domains. Restricted gTLDs allow only certain types of entities to register within the domain. For example, .int, .edu, .gov, .mil are restricted to international organizations, colleges and universities, government agencies and the US military, respectively.

[40] See further O.M. Baratta & D.L. Hanaman, A Global Update on the Domain Name System and the Law: Alternative Dispute Resolution for Increasing Internet Competition—Oh, the Times They Are a-Changin'!, 8 *Tul. J. Int'l & Comp. L.* 332–333 (Spring 2000).

[41] G. Weiswasser, Domain Names, the Internet, and Trademarks: Infringement in Cyberspace, 13 *Santa Clara Computer & High Tech. L.J.* 146 (1997).

With this system, each IP number corresponds to an alphanumeric string that is registered under one of the TLDs.[42] The computer then converts the string to the IP number and transmits the data over the Internet.[43] For example, the domain name *www.amazon.com* locates the web site for Amazon.com, Inc. at IP address 208.216.182.15 and a particular host server named "www". At this stage, information pasted in the web site is freely transmitted in the invisible space.[44]

With the preparatory work accomplished, a merchant can do business in the Internet. He can start by posting an advertisement on his web site for consumers to read or simply look at; three-dimensional pictures of goods offered may be used to give consumers tactual sensations. Consumers can surf through the Internet for particular information using Web browsers (such as Netscape Navigator or Microsoft Explorer) or search engines (such as Google, Alta Vista or Excite). Potential sites satisfying the requests shall be listed for consumers who can then go on and read relevant information. Merchants often attach purchasing facilities to their web sites that take the form of an "accept" or "I agree" button (the so-called adhesion contract), but consumers can also use email or other electronic means to contact the merchants for more information.

Delivering goods or services and securing payments are the next important steps. Goods can be digitized and delivered through the Internet at negligible cost and with negligible difficulty. Consumers can download software from web sites onto their own computers with a simple mouse click.[45] As distribution technology improves, more and more data-intensive goods, like audio-visual files, can be distributed over the Internet. For those products that cannot be digitized, traditional delivery shall still be arranged. Payment can also be made electronically with credit cards.

---

[42] See *Lockheed Martin, Corp. v. Network Solutions, Inc.*, 985 F. Supp. 949, 952 (C.D. Cal. 1997).

[43] R.S. Vermut, File Caching on the Internet: Technical Infringement or Safeguard for Efficient Network Operation, 4 *J. Intell. Prop. L.* 273, 287 (1997); R. Raysman & P. Brown, Dangerous Liasons: The Legal Risks of Linking Web Sites, *N.Y.L.J.* April 8, 1997, at 3.

[44] For further description, see A. Grosso, The National Information Infrastructure, 41 *Fed. B. News & J.* 481 (1994).

[45] See further M.S. Donahey, Dispute Resolution in Cyberspace, *15 Journal of International Arbitration* 4, 129–130 (1998).

The whole transaction is completed without the two parties' meeting. This accounts for reduced transaction time and energy spent making appointments and negotiations. The Internet also reduces transaction costs, which benefits both parties.

2.5. *Types of Electronic Commerce*

As an interested party can use various methods to participate in electronic commerce, electronic commerce could be further classified into different types based on different classifying standards. In practice, it is accepted that there are two types of electronic commerce, namely business-to-business (B2B), and business-to-consumer (B2C). This distinction is based on the nature of the corresponding contracting parties. There is also a third type, business-to-administration, which is important for intra-organizational applications. It enables managers to use the Internet to communicate with employees, distribute relevant documents online to make itself known to public, and realize better coordination of the whole business from production to after-sale services. As it has something to do with regulating transactions but not business in the strict sense of the word, this study shall not treat this type further.

2.5.1. *Business-to-Business*

This type emerged with the help of EDI. Since the emergence of the Internet, Intranet or closed networks have been widely used.[46] With the so-called "Intranet", business information can be exchanged within a closed network between several merchants. EDI has become the typical way of doing business between merchants, facilitating the ordering, shipment, and storage of goods electronically with purchase orders, invoices, shipping notices and remittance advice.[47]

---

[46] A.H. Boss, Electronic Data Interchange Agreements: Private Contracting Toward a Global Environment, 13 *Nw. J. Int'l & Bus.* 31, 38 (1992); see also generally A.H. Boss & J.B. Ritter, *Electronic Data Interchange Agreements: A Guide and Sourcebook* (1993); The Electronic Messaging Services Task Force, The Commercial Use of Electronic Data Interchange—A Report and Model Trading Partner Agreement, 45 *Bus. Law.* 1645 (1990).

[47] J.C. Yates, *Recent Legal Issues in Electronic Commerce and Electronic Data Interchange*, at 271 (PLI/Pat. Copyrights Trademarks & Literary Prop. Course Handbook Series No. 430, 1996); The Commercial Use of Electronic Data Interchange—A Report and Model Trading Partner Agreement, the Electronic Messaging Services Task Force.

One of the most immediate promises of EDI is increased efficiency of procurement and sourcing functions.[48] The Internet streamlines the supply chain, creating an up-to-date trading post. It promises more efficient and direct price and quality comparisons, which makes it possible for the relatively transparent market to rationalize purchasing and selling decisions. This is seen as a fundamental change to traditional business.

Generally speaking, the transacting parties in this type are not the end consumers, but commercial parties linked in a whole chain of transactions. They have known each other in former connections and have basic knowledge about each other. As the so-called "buyer" in B2B is not the actual consumer, but an actual middle man or agent, the value of transactions is usually very large and various systems have been relatively sufficient for this type of transaction.

2.5.2. *Business-to-Consumer (Consumer Transaction)*

The commercial world fundamentally changed only after the introduction of WWW, or open networks. At present, a large part of the profits from electronic commerce goes to B2B. However, consumer transactions are in the process of rapid development and should mean big business in the near future. This business should take several forms, such as electronic shopping, customer support, and product delivery,[49] and the volume of transactions should multiply.

Consumer transaction and not B2B is the actual revolution against traditional commerce. This method involves merchants setting up their own web sites, which introduce goods or services inviting potential consumers, and consumers purchasing goods or services without needing to go outside. The only thing a consumer needs to do is to search the Internet for information and hit relevant buttons. Through this form of electronic commerce, merchants can reach consumers directly.

---

[48] F.P. Philips, *The CPR B2B E-Commerce Initiative, International Conference on Dispute Resolution in Electronic Commerce*, November, 2000, WIPO, ARB/ECOM/00/31.

[49] One form is illustrated by the United Parcel Services (UPS) providing Internet-based interactive services to consumers. Another form is illustrated by the ISPs offering free access to the Internet or the on-line superstore. See further M.S. Raisinghani, Electronic Commerce at the Dawn of the Third Millennium, in S.M. Rahman & M.S. Raisinghani (Eds.), *Electronic Commerce: Opportunity and Challenges*, 6 (IDEA Group Publishing, 2000).

There are two sub-types of consumer transaction. The first is a detached retail relationship, with consumers interactively making purchases online. The second involves the contractual relationships of individual users and specialized online institutions, such as banks facilitating the use of digital cash.[50]

Both ways have overturned the traditional concept of business: the traditional mid-agents or intermediaries can be omitted, which simplifies the chain of transactions. However, new agents come out to accommodate new demand. For example, ISP is there to provide necessary Internet support.

In electronic consumer transactions, many traditional business procedures are abandoned. Consumers do not need to know the merchants; the only impression customers have of the merchants comes from the merchants' web sites. The simple action of button hitting can constitute a commercial acceptance. As is not the case in traditional commerce, there are few mechanisms available to guarantee transactions in cyberspace, and much work needs to be done to safeguard transacting parties, especially from a legal point of view.

3. *Disputes in Electronic Commerce*

Actually, electronic commerce does not change the basic purpose of business transactions, which is to gain profits; the difference lies in the new mode of communication. When it comes to making profits, different parties have divergent objectives, which can easily lead to disputes. Primary commercial considerations existing in traditional business remain constant, though the disputes arising out of electronic commerce can take different appearance than disputes arising out of traditional business. Every dispute arises in a setting or context, and the setting in which it arises may shape the expectations of the parties, the time of settlement, the perceived urgency of resolution, the consequences of and available alternatives to failure, the role of the third party, and even the form of dispute resolution.[51] It

[50] See further E.C. Lide, Note & Comment, ADR and Cyberspace: The Role of Alternative Dispute Resolution in Online Commerce, Intellectual Property and Defamation, 12 *Ohio St. J. on Disp. Resol.* 195 (1996).

[51] E. Katsh, *The Online Ombuds Office: Adapting Dispute Resolution to Cyberspace*, at <http://www.umass.edu/dispute/ncair/katsh.htm>.

is important to assess different types of disputes in electronic commerce before analyzing mechanisms to resolve them.

3.1. *Disputes in the General Sense*

Broadly conceived, disputes represent disagreements between two or more parties in political, economic or cultural arenas. It is the purpose of the present study to focus on economic disputes.

There are different ways of classifying disputes according to different standards. For example, disputes can be classified as interest disputes and rights disputes depending on the existence of norms.[52] Most commonly, disputes are labeled as either contractual or non-contractual disputes. Contractual disputes arise from contractual relationships; non-contractual disputes usually include torts, libels, infringement of intellectual property rights, etc. Insofar as electronic commerce is related to traditional commerce, his traditional classification is relevant to disputes in electronic commerce.

3.2. *Disputes in Electronic Commerce*

While much has been said about electronic commerce and the potential advantages of the digital era, little has been said about disputes arising out of electronic commerce. Potentially, disputes could occur at every stage of electronic commerce, from the initial stage of setting up the necessary infrastructure to the latter stage of consummating business.[53]

Disputes in electronic commerce exhibit no difference in essence from those in traditional business. If a definition for disputes in electronic commerce is needed, then it can be disagreements between or among parties involved in electronic commerce. Electronic commerce provides us with a new marketplace of ideas and also with a

---

[52] Resolution of interest disputes requires the exercise of a rulemaking function by adopting and articulating norms of conduct that have not theretofore existed. Rights disputes involve claims under existing norms and usually require the exercise of adjudicatory power to resolve them. See further H.H. Perritt, Jr., *Electronic Dispute Resolution: An NCAIR Conference*, Washington, DC, May 22, 1996, at <http://mantle.sbs.umass.edu/vmag/PERRITT.HTM>.

[53] However, there have not been any known disputes of any significance concerning EDI. See R. Hill, Electronic Commerce, The World-Wide Web, Minitel, and EDI, *13 The Information Society*, No. 1 (January–March 1997), at <http://www.batnet.com/oikoumene/arbecom.html>.

new marketplace for disputes. Context shall affect not only the persons involved in the disputes, but also the kinds of disputes likely to surface. While containing and reflecting many aspects of the real world, electronic commerce is creating an environment that will confront us with a broad variety of disputing behaviors and attitudes, some of which may be familiar and some of which may not.[54]

As suggested before, it is important to look into the possible disputes arising out of electronic commerce. Notable are classifications based on different standards. For example, classification can be made based on the topic of dispute: there are interconnection disputes, sales disputes, payment disputes, delivery disputes, infringement disputes, disputes concerning the use of trademarks belonging to third parties, etc. One can also differentiate between traditional commercial disputes, like disputes over the quality of goods purchased online, failure to deliver, errors in order taking, and failure to pay; and Internet-specific disputes over problems like posting on the Internet or issues with domain names.[55] The nature and qualifications of the disputing parties constitute another standard of comparison: for example, there are disputes involving consumers, companies, and public authorities. Moreover, one can differentiate between disputes to which can be applied relevant rules and disputes for which new rules must be developed. However, none of these classifications is particularly useful for a discussion of dispute resolution. The contractual and non-contractual classification mentioned earlier, however, is particularly relevant to the present discussion, and will be discussed in more detail below.

3.2.1. *Contractual Disputes*

Contractual relationships take up an important role in regulating mutual performance in Internet business. Most online participants already have some form of contractual relationship with access providers or cyber-domiciliaries.[56] In the first stage of electronic commerce, necessary infrastructure shall be made to undertake future

---

[54] See further M.E. Katsh, Dispute Resolution in Cyberspace, 28 *Conn. L. Rev.* 955 (Summer, 1996).

[55] See further A. Williams, Dispute Resolution and Arbitration for Electronic Commerce, *Deeth Williams Wall*, at <http://www.dww.com/articles/ec_adr.htm>.

[56] See generally M.R. Burnstein, Conflicts on the Net: Choice of Law in Transnational Cyberspace, 29 *Vand. J. Transnat'l L.* 75 (1996).

operations. Thus contracts shall be made firstly between enterprises that operate the infrastructure and those that make use of the infrastructure (generally these refer to ISPs) to offer further business services to consumers. Generally, this type of contract, which lays the foundation for digital business, is called an "interconnection" contract.[57]

"Interconnection" contract disputes are rather sensitive since the telecommunications services have long been under the monopolized supervision of national states. Only after the 1995 WTO Uruguay Round negotiations did they become targets for liberalization with international support. Time shall be needed to realize full liberalization and national states will be highly sensitive to disputes at the present stage, which can be deduced from the cautious attitude towards liberalization shown by the Member States of WTO. Furthermore, this type of contract usually lasts for a long period of time, but the reality is that the contractual context can change rather drastically and might be largely influenced by further contracts. This could cause more disputes concerning interpretation and reasonable application of the relevant provisions of the initial contract, which could occasion technical difficulties.[58] But for the sake of sensitive national interests, national regulatory bodies reserve the power to intervene and dispute resolution mechanisms are provided both at national and international levels.[59] This type of dispute is thus not the target for the present study.

At the second stage, contracts are made between the Internet Service Providers (ISPs) and their customers regarding issues of telecommunications services, more specifically, the services provided by ISPs that grant access to communication networks. Alongside the

[57] Interconnection contracts typically concern use by a new entrant of the last mile infrastructure of the incumbent former monopoly telecommunications operator, and the commercial stakes are more related to voice and other traditional services than to electronic commerce. See R. Hill, The Internet, Electronic Commerce and Dispute Resolution: Comments, 14 *Journal of International Arbitration* 4, 105 (1997).

[58] But according to R. Hill, disputes arising out of the interconnection contracts to date have revolved around a single issue: the price at which the former monopoly should rent its infrastructure to new entrants. Other disputes are speculative. The modification of such contracts does not happen frequently since they are dictated by the incumbent monopoly under the control of national telecommunications regulatory body. See further Hill, *id.*, at 105.

[59] See for example Swiss Telecommunications Act (1998); the ONP Leased Line Directive (Directive 92/44/EEC of 5 June 1992).

growth of their businesses, the ISPs have formed a model contract for negotiations, which sets out the general conditions of contracts.[60] Disputes may arise concerning the price and quality of service and everything from attempts to connect to denial of access and the exclusion of messages can arise.[61] Further disputes could concern the liability of the ISPs versus the responsibilities of the customers for information transmitted. However, such disputes are largely placed under the category of non-contractual disputes.

With the preparatory work accomplished, electronic commerce in the real commercial sense starts and in this phase contracts are concluded between transacting parties. It is at this stage that the special characteristics of electronic commerce and the variety of relationships to which it gives rise become particularly apparent.[62] Contracts at this stage can be further divided into two sub-types of contracts corresponding to the two types of electronic commerce: commercial contracts and consumer contracts.

Commercial contracts have been in existence far longer than the latter. EDI has been the main form for commercial contracts. Transacting parties are likely to have known each other before and continue to maintain good relationships, making use of communication networks to facilitate the ordering, shipment, storage of goods, and electronic payment. No doubt commercial contracts shall continue to exist and further expand.

Meanwhile, consumer contracts are developing in the 21st century and are thought to typify "electronic commerce" in the general sense. In electronic commerce, the end users of goods or services can surf through web advertisements, discriminate between and purchase products. This form of direct transaction brings many structural and conceptional changes to modern commercial theory. With

---

[60] See further J.S. Gale, Note, Service Over the "Net": Principles of Contract Law in Conflict, *49 Case W. Res. L. Rev.* 567 (1999).

[61] This could further involve three sub-types of disputes: disputes between the people not yet on the network and those already on the network who refuse connection; disputes between those asking for the cessation of certain traffic moving on the network and those continuing such traffic; disputes between those on the network who believe that someone else on the network has not lived up to his or her commitments and the defendants. These three subtypes could potentially overlap with each other, as they are based on commitments between the affected parties.

[62] M.E. Schneider & C. Kuner, Dispute Resolution in International Electronic Commerce, 14 *Journal of International Arbitration*, No. 3, at 7 (1997).

a better framework for procuring consumer security and trust, consumer contracts are sure to become the main form of future transactions. As mentioned above, the popularity of these contracts is growing at an explosive rate with online software companies already selling and transmitting their products and online bookstore selling books in far-flung parts of the world.[63]

3.2.2. *Non-contractual Disputes*

Non-contractual disputes have become an important issue since the introduction of the Internet. All disputes not based on contractual relationships can be included in this type, a hodgepodge of many different kinds of disputes in electronic commerce.

Among the most important of non-contractual disputes are infringements on intellectual property. Copyright infringement, trademark infringement, data protection, and defamation disputes are frequent. One notable phenomenon is the emergence of domain name disputes; another is the debate over whether or not ISPs should be held liable for the actions of a third party. These issues have raised problems with the traditional structure of intellectual property protections. Besides issues concerning intellectual property, there are further possible disputes concerning freedom of expression, transmission of materials forbidden in some States, competition law, etc.

The parties involved therein are miscellaneous. Depending on the specific situation, individuals, commercial entities, States, or international organizations can be involved in an electronic commerce non-contractual dispute. Care must be taken to evaluate the position of all relevant parties in a dispute. While disputes involving individuals or commercial entities are not so problematic, disputes involving public authorities may require special consideration and unique solutions. Thus, various levels of mechanisms should be utilized for disputes involving different parties.

4. *Dispute Resolution Mechanisms*

As disputes are unavoidable in daily communications, specific mechanisms have arisen to resolve such disputes. Generally speaking, the process of dispute resolution involves three stages: a problem arises

[63] See for example *Amazon.com*.

between parties; this problem develops into a dispute and the parties seek to resolve the dispute; the dispute is resolved through a certain channel.[64] It is the third stage that we are going to deal with in the present study. Historically, dispute resolution channels have taken various forms, from the extreme and violent feuds and duels of the Middle Ages to the moderator of later times, who was sent to peacefully resolve conflicts between parties. Today, various mechanisms are in play but the very complicated, yet critical search for more efficient mechanisms goes on. An effective means to dispute resolution in electronic commerce is vital to the smooth functioning of such business.

4.1. *Litigation*

Litigation is the orthodox mechanism for resolving disputes. Supported by national power, it is the formal, public process for resolving disputes before national courts. It thus considered indispensable to the whole system of dispute resolution.

However, there is a trend of not employing litigation in the first stage of dispute resolution, often for considerations also applicable to the situation of electronic commerce. First of all, the length of time needed for the whole process of litigation does not suite the present pace of business. For verdicts to have any meaning in the business world, they must come rapidly alongside the development of economic activities.

Secondly, the high cost of litigation is an obstacle. Sometimes the costs of litigation can equal or even exceed the damages sought. The use of litigation for electronic commercial transactions may soon seem ridiculous considering the small amount involved in the disputes: the cost of travel to the Forum State, let alone litigation, could be higher than the value of the transaction in dispute. This shall prevent people from applying litigation to protect their own rights. If a cheaper mechanism were available, why would anyone litigate?

Thirdly, the issues of jurisdiction and choice of laws become particularly complicated at an international level. A problem specific to

[64] See further F. Schwank, Before the Battle Commences, in D. Campbell & P. Summerfield (Eds.) *Effective Dispute Resolution for the International Commercial Lawyer*, 9 (1989).

electronic commerce is lack of information about the transacting parties. When an injured party wants to raise a suit, he has to know location of the other party, but in cyberspace, everyone is everywhere and nowhere. Traditional theories for deciding jurisdiction and appropriate laws must be reevaluated in the wake of a digital world.

Fourthly, the atmosphere of litigation could be destructive to the future relationship of transacting parties and, in consequence, adversely effect further transactions between such parties. With that in mind, the winning party in court may not get what he wants or needs out of electronic commerce in the long run.

Besides the shortcomings mentioned above, there are other drawbacks to litigation. For instance, the congested court system is often an unsatisfactory avenue for dispute resolution.[65] Congestion lengthens the whole court procedure and imposes unnecessary expenses upon litigants and taxpayers alike.[66] There is also the matter of recognizing and reinforcing judgements once passed at an international level.

Thus, litigation has been challenged as a means of dispute resolution.[67] An efficient and affordable alternative is needed in order to address current disputes in electronic commerce as well as to plan for the future as the cyber community[68] continues to grow. Litigation can never be abandoned entirely, but it can be modified to suit its role as part of a whole system of dispute resolution. The efforts of the international community bear testament to this fact.

---

[65] See further C.L. Mudd, Jr., *Cybercourt: A Virtual Resolution of Differences or An Alternative Proposal for Law and Order in Cyberspace*, at <http://www.mudd.org/professional/articlesclm/cybercourt.htm>.

[66] J.O. Newman, "Rethinking Fairness": Perspectives on the Litigation Process, 94 *Yale L.J.*, 1643–1644 (1985).

[67] T.D. Rowe, Jr., American Law Institute Study on Paths to a "Better way": Litigation, Alternatives, and Accommodations: Background Paper, 38 *Duke L.J.*, 824 (1989).

[68] In this research, cyber community, Internet society, etc. are used interchangeably and are all defined as social aggregations of a critical mass of people on the Internet who engage in public discussions, interactions in chat rooms, and information exchanges with sufficient human feeling on matters of common interest to form webs of personal relationships. See P.K. Kannan, A.M. Chang & A.B. Whinston, The Internet Information Market: The Emerging Role of Intermediaries, in M. Shaw et al. (Eds.), *Handbook on Electronic Commerce*, 583–584 (Springer-Verlag, 2000).

4.2. *Alternative Dispute Resolution (ADR) Mechanisms*

Considering the limitations of litigation, alternative means have been suggested and formulated to complement the dispute resolution system.[69] ADR is a general term to distinguish between litigation in courts and other methods designed to assist parties in resolving differences. Though there is no consensus in the academic or business fields on the exact meaning of ADR, most experts view ADR as a range of approaches that fits within the broader spectrum of dispute resolution, which includes corporate consumer complaint services, ADR, and litigation.[70] These methods are not intended to supplant litigation, but rather to supplement it.

ADR encompasses a wide range of mechanisms for resolving disputes between two or more parties outside formal court procedures. Its emergence can be dated to the intellectually appealing 'multi-door courthouse' advanced by Professor Frank Sander in the late 1970s.[71] ADR does not, for most part, involve the endless motions, voluminous proceedings, procedural wrangling, and years of arguing and waiting for a judgment that characterize the "old" litigation system for most modern business people and consumers.[72] Thus, it is rather welcomed by the commercial society.

4.2.1. *Advantages of ADR Mechanisms*

In view of the disadvantages entailed in litigation, ADR has indeed made many improvements. First of all, the ADR process can help disputing parties to reach a speedy and cost-effective resolution. As

[69] E.U. Petersmann & G. Jaenike, *Adjudication of International Trade Disputes in International and National Economic Law*, 3 (University Press Fribourg, Switzerland, 1992).

[70] Building Trust in the Online Environment: Business to Consumer Dispute Resolution, Joint Conference of the OECD, HCOPIL, ICC, The Hague, 11–12 December 2000, Orientation Document, DSTI/ICCP/REG/CP(2000)1–UPDATED as of 7 December 2000, at 4.

[71] See further R. Smith, Access to Justice: Innovation in North America, in R. Smith (Ed.), *Achieving Civil Justice: Appropriate Dispute Resolution for the 1990s*, 42 (1996). Professor Sander expected that by the year 2000, the courthouse would be not simply a courthouse, but a Dispute Resolution Center, where the dispute would first be channeled through a screening clerk who would then direct the disputing party to the process (or sequence of processes) most appropriate to the type of case. The room directory of such a center was suggested as follows: screening clerk—room 1; mediation—room 2; arbitration—room 3; fact-finding—room 4; malpractice screening panel—room 5; superior court—room 6; and ombudsman—room 7.

[72] Williams, *supra* note 55.

disputes over commercial matters may involve technical issues difficult for laymen to comprehend, experts may be asked to step in and cooperate with legal members to deal with those issues and reach objective decisions regarding the disputing parties. ADR mechanisms also require cooperation between disputing parties, who affect the formulation and implementation of final decisions. Ideally, early resolution in an easy-going atmosphere helps to preserve business relationships.

Secondly, issues regarding jurisdiction shall be resolved once for all by ADR mechanisms. With more and more transnational cases involved in disputes, the annoying issues of determining adjudicative forum and applicable law have been under severe scrutiny. Even with the updated theory of conflict of laws, no satisfactory resolution to jurisdictional issues can be found. As a private process based on party agreement, ADR eliminates the need for a claiming party to prosecute its claims in a potential multitude of jurisdictions implicated by the underlying commercial relationship giving rise to the dispute. This benefit cuts down the time and cost needed for the dispute resolution.

Thirdly, ADR can lead to creative business-driven solutions. Avoiding litigation is important to disputing parties in a mature and mutually beneficial supply chain relationship not only to save costs but also to reduce commercial uncertainty and preserve valuable long-term relationships that might be jeopardized by short-term hostilities and belligerence. The amicable resolution atmosphere should work as a catalyst for more participation in electronic commerce. Cooperative parties may ultimately find a win-win solution to their problem and thus renew their faith in legal guarantees. Additionally, resolution attained via an expert in the area instead of a judge or a lawyer could not only be time effective, but it could also help parties look beyond the particular dispute to broader concerns. This looking ahead should aid in the improvement of future business practices.

As a private procedure, ADR also helps to protect privacy and confidentiality. In most businesses, it might be of vital importance that the dispute between the parties remains private so as not to occasion adverse effects on future commercial activities. This is particularly important in electronic commerce when the disputes arise out of a failure of major security systems to function or as a result of a technical problem with a major system. Involved corporations would not wish to risk bad publicity damaging their reputations.

ADR is also flexible in terms of both procedures and substance. The involved parties are free to choose any procedure or set of rules they like, or they can agree to make a relevant modification of prescribed rules to fit their case. Furthermore, they can agree in advance to the substantive part of the case. For example, they can define the factual and legal issues at hand. In a binding adjudicative process such as arbitration, the parties agree to waive their right to litigation. In other circumstances, they can still go to litigation if they like. Even after a binding process, they can still go to court for the purpose of obtaining interim relief or aid in the arbitration process. There are even cases when the court can declare arbitration decisions void.

Actually, there are still further features to ADR, all of which share the aim of resolving disputes in a speedy and cost-efficient way. It is not surprising then that ADR is generally considered the best succedaneum for formal litigation, especially in the area of electronic commerce. It is a tailor-made solution that is better adapted to the particulars of the network than traditional procedures.[73]

4.2.2. *Commonly Used ADR Mechanisms*

Various processes have been employed in formulating proper ADR mechanisms. From the most formal to the least formal, nine types can be listed as follows: arbitration, dispute review board, ombudsman, neutral fact-finding expert, early neutral evaluation, mini-trial, mediation, settlement counsel, and negotiation.

To a certain extent, the processes commingle. For example, when arbitration is used, fact-finding expert or other techniques might also be needed to make a reasonable decision. Meanwhile, with a view towards integration, only arbitration or mediation represents the best candidate for resolving disputes, as each provides a complete set of methods for resolving disputes. All other techniques only touch on a small area of disputes, like clarifying disputing facts or providing objective opinions. They can help dispute resolution in certain detailed aspects, but they cannot be a dispute resolution "mechanism" in the strict legal sense. The much too informal, unbinding character of

---

[73] See further A. Salaun, E-Commerce: Consumer Protection—Proposals for Improving the Protection of Online Consumers, 15 *Computer Law & Security Report* 3, 165 (1999).

some techniques has further limited their validity and applicability. In this study, arbitration and mediation are most important.

Mediation is a private, voluntary, informal, non-binding, confidential, and flexible procedure in which a neutral intermediary endeavors at the request of the parties in a dispute to assist them in reaching a mutually satisfactory settlement. Or if requested, he provides a neutral evaluation of the parties' respective positions and the final outcome. Though the procedure is thought to be singular in form, there are in fact often many different models and applications of this form of dispute resolution.[74] This mechanism, as an adjunct to negotiation, is only an intermediate step towards final resolution. A mediator has no power to decide, but only power to assist the disputing parties to negotiate a resolution.[75] The only compulsory feature of mediation is the mutually negotiated settlement agreement that usually results in. The provision of an evaluation of the final outcome also has great influence on the ultimate results.

Arbitration is a private, voluntary, and confidential procedure involving the adjudication of rights in accordance with the applicable law by a tribunal of one or more arbitrators that has the power to render a decision that is final and binding on the parties. Arbitration can also be non-binding in limited situations. Arbitration is the most widely used ADR mechanism for resolving disputes in commercial matters.[76] The advantages entailed in arbitration are obvious. Besides the advantages discussed above, arbitration is more or less legal-oriented. Arbitration proceeds according to relevant legal rules, though it needs not stubbornly stick to them; the final decision has legal power and the corresponding mechanism for enforcement is provided. The flexibility of arbitration under the legal framework has won much interest from business and legal practitioners. While electronic commerce develops with the basic character of business, it is expected that arbitration shall continue to occupy a vital position in dispute resolution.

---

[74] See J. Conley & W. O'Barr, *Just Words: Law, Language, and Power*, 40 (1998).

[75] See generally S. Cobb & J. Rifkin, Practice and Paradox: Deconstructing Neutrality in Mediation, 16 *Law & Social Inquiry*, No. 1, 35 (1991).

[76] S.L. Hayford, Commercial Arbitration in the Supreme Court 1983–1995: A Sea Change, *31 Wake Forest L. Rev.*, 1 (1996).

4.3. *The Necessity of a New Mechanism for Electronic Commerce*

Various mechanisms applying the ADR techniques have been constructed to resolve disputes and have been working fairly well up to the present. But as electronic commerce disputes enter the arena, doubt arises concerning whether the present mechanisms are sufficient to resolve them. What are the implications of a global economy driven by new technologies for dispute resolution processes?

Electronic commerce differs drastically from other means of transactions. Different contexts are important in determining approaches to dispute resolution. Which approach shall be most appropriate for resolving disputes in a new context? What is the nature of the relationship between the two parties in the new context? Is there a need for a public standard setting, or would private resolution be desirable?[77] The answers to these questions should elicit policy changes for dispute resolution.

Ostensibly, the application of modern technology to dispute resolution mechanisms has been made urgent by the introduction of the Internet and the development of electronic commerce. Traditional mechanisms are lagging behind technologically. Indeed, important economic and business interests are at stake.

It has been generally recognized that consumers should have access to fair, timely, effective and affordable means for resolving problems with any transaction.[78] While litigation occupies an important part in dispute resolution, new principles should be found to meet the demands of electronic commerce. ADR offers a way to rapidly, cheaply, and efficiently resolve disputes, which is seen to complement judicial procedures.[79] As a mechanism to solve disputes arising on

---

[77] See further Katsh, *supra* note 54, 963.

[78] See for example, Principles of Consumer Protection for Electronic Commerce: A Canadian Framework, Working Group on Electronic Commerce and Consumers, <http://strategis.ic.gc.ca/oca>. Principle 5 reads: Vendors should provide adequate resources to handle consumer complaints efficiently and effectively. When internal mechanisms have failed to resolve a dispute, vendors should make use of accessible, available, affordable and impartial third-party processes for resolving disputes with consumers. However, vendors should not require consumers to submit to such processes. Governments, businesses and consumer groups should work together to develop appropriate standards for dispute resolution mechanisms. So that consumers are not disadvantaged, governments should cooperate in the development of clear rules regarding applicable law and forum, as well as in the mutual enforcement of judgements in the event of cross-border disputes.

[79] However, there are situations when ADR is forbidden in consumer contracts, for example, French legislation forbids clause compromissoire in consumer contracts.

the network, it satisfies consumers' expectations[80] and thus fosters consumer confidence in online purchasing and other services, which has enormous benefits for merchants. The application of ADR should also benefit governments by mitigating the need to involve more formal systems of adjudication. Some scholars have suggested that electronic commerce is particularly likely to adopt non-court methods of dispute resolution.[81]

The present legal remedies in the context of online transactions are not the most effective means of redress because of the nature of long-distance transactions and jurisdiction problems. Moreover, as consumer transactions generally involve a small amount of money, it is unrealistic to oblige disputing parties to submit large filing fees for arbitration.[82] With the present mechanisms, a case could be prolonged for a year or longer, a ridiculous stretch of time for a dispute over several dollars. Thus, only when it is demonstrated that disputes can be heard more quickly and disposed of more effectively with the use of the Internet that the net effect will achieve consumer trust in real consumer protection.[83]

Without other choices at hand, disputing parties today must rely on mechanisms for resolution that emerged long before the Internet age. So long as no mechanism targeting disputes concerning elec-

[80] See further Salaun, *supra* note 73, at 165.

[81] See for example, M.C. Karamon, Note, ADR on the Internet, 11 *Ohio St. J. on Disp. Resol.* 537 (1996); M.E. Katsh, The New Frontier: Online ADR Becoming a Global Priority, *Disp. Resol. Mag.*, 6, 8 (Winter 2000); Lide, *supra* note 50, at 193, 216–222.

[82] For example, the present filing fee for an ICC Arbitration is US$2500.

[83] See for example, Consumer Protection Principles in Electronic Commerce, at <http://www.accc.gov.au/acomm/principles.htm>. The Part entitled Consumer Complaints and Dispute Resolution reads as follows: fair and effective policies and internal mechanisms shall be in place to address and respond to consumer complaints and difficulties within a reasonable time, in a reasonable manner, without undue cost of burden to the consumer, and without prejudice to judicial redress; Such procedures might include, but need not be limited to: providing online information about the existence of consumer complaints services and relevant dispute resolution mechanisms; the timely receipt, acknowledgement, and handling of consumer complaints; dealing with complaints fairly, thoroughly and in manner which would assist any further examination which may be necessary such as referral to a dispute resolution mechanism; and providing a notice to consumers regarding any third party dispute resolution mechanisms available through the business; and promptly informing the consumer of the outcome.

tronic commerce is in play, the interests of those involved in Internet-based business cannot be fully realized or protected. Reserving their confidence, consumers will waver at the gate of cyberspace, looking ahead for the green light: a specialized mechanism for dispute resolution in electronic commerce.

CHAPTER THREE

POLICY CHOICE

The Internet has fundamentally changed the commercial world. This "information revolution" has altered basic principles of how people interact with each other.[1] It has created complex economic, cultural, social, and educational challenges which governments, in even the most industrially advanced nations, are only beginning to understand.[2] These socio-economic changes should directly impact conceptions of how to deal with disputes in electronic commerce.

Traditional regulations are too static and cannot effectively govern the inconstant and infinite cyberspace.[3] As no media other than the Internet has ever been so efficient in transmitting information across borders, there is no appropriate framework for regulating Internet activities. Without identifying anyone to undertake the task of regulation, the old regulatory structure is applied as an expedient measure and also as a last resort. Yet with more and more commercial activities taking place through the Internet on a daily basis, seeds for a more harmonious and feasible regulatory framework are now being planted to deal with electronic commerce as a whole, and these can certainly be applied to dispute resolution. In broad scope, socio-economic, legal and technological elements shall be taken into account to offer guidance on formulating a fair and effective ADR for electronic commerce and fostering its future implementation.

---

[1] See N. Mandela, Address at the Telecom 95, October 3, 1995, quoted in V. Montviloff, *Some Legal and Ethical Issues of the Access to Electronic Information*, John F. Kennedy School of Government Symposium on Information, National Policies, and International Infrastructure (Jan. 28, 1996), at 1, <http://ksgwww.harvard.edu/iip/montpap.html>.

[2] *Id.*

[3] Cyberspace blurs the boundaries between once distinct types of media and thus demands evolutionary and even revolutionary approaches in formulating new legal doctrine. Lawmakers should recognize, empower, and learn from the multitude of self-regulating structures that have already been developed by the users and administrators of cyberspace. See M. Johns, Comment, the First Amendment and Cyberspace: Trying to Teach Old Doctrines New Tricks, 64 *U. Cin. L. Rev.*, 1437 (1996); see also A.M. Fulton, Comment, Cyberspace and the Internet: Who Will be the Privacy Police?, *3 COMMLAW Conspectus* 64 (1995).

1. *Self-Regulation*

Originally a governmental project, the Internet's purpose was diverted to suit the commercial world. This fact may suggest the government's attempt to regulate any aspect of the Internet might be unwarranted. From its application in electronic commerce, the Internet has been regulating itself in a much more productive way than any broad attempts the legislature may take.[4] Against this background, the policy of self-regulation is featured.

1.1. *Basic Understanding of Self-Regulation*

Self-regulation is not a new phenomenon in the commercial world. It can be dated back to medieval times when guilds maintained standards among those in the trade of a particular geographic location and protected their interests against outside competitors.[5] In its later development, self-regulation has become more diverse and multi-leveled.

Self-regulation has different meanings for different groups of people. Generally speaking, self-regulation involves businesses agreeing to regulate their own behavior, adopting principles, either individually or collectively, which bind them in their daily commercial dealings.[6] In other words, self-regulation means that a regulatory body, distinct from a technical body, undertakes the task of regulating the activities carried out by a group to which it belongs. This group can be large enough to include an industry as a whole; it can also be as small as a single company.

Assistant Secretary of Commerce Larry Irving said, "the term 'self-regulation' itself has a range of definitions. At one end of the spectrum, the term is used quite narrowly, to refer only to those instances

[4] See further E.A. Cavazos & G. Morin, *Cyberspace and the Law: Your Rights and Duties in the Online World*, xiii (1994); see also *ACLU v Reno*, 929 F. Supp 824, 858–859 (E.D. Pa. 1996).

[5] D.I. Baker & W.T. Miller, Privacy, Antitrust and the National Information Infrastructure: Is Self-regulation of Telecommunications-related Personal Information a Workable Tool? in *Privacy and Self-Regulation in the Information Age*, U.S. Department of Commerce, NTIA 1997, <http://www.ntia.doc.gov/reports/privacy/privacy_rpt.htm>.

[6] See further An Analysis of the Bertelsmann Foundation Memorandum on Self-Regulation of Internet Content: Concerns from a User Empowerment Perspective, October 1999, <http://www.cdt.org/speech/991021bertelsmannmemo.shtml>.

where the government has formally delegated the power to regulate, as in the delegation of securities industry, oversight to the stock exchanges. At the other end of the spectrum, the term is used when the private sector perceives the need to regulate itself for whatever reason—to respond to consumer demand, to carry out its ethical beliefs, to enhance industry reputation, or to level the market playing field—and does so."[7]

Regulators can be understood to perform three tasks: legislation—the self-regulator formulates standards or rules to be implemented in daily activities; enforcement—the self-regulator acts to help realize the purpose and aims of relevant rules or regulations; and adjudication—the self-regulator decides upon the violation of its own members and imposes relevant sanction to procure the justified interests.[8] This forms the complete list of tasks for self-regulation.[9] However, in normal performance, self-regulation may be undertaken to perform only one or two tasks.[10]

The job of regulation can be undertaken by various actors: industry,[11] as a whole; the private commercial actors, which are components of the industry; social bodies; etc. Thus, it is necessary to examine the meaning of "self."

1.1.1. *The Meaning of "Self"*

"Self" can refer to an industry, or a group of companies acting collectively in the form of a trade association or other organizations representing the interest of the industry, just like medieval guilds. The Internet has given rise to numerous regulatory organizations: Internet Watch Foundation, Internet Local Advertising and Commerce

---

[7] L. Irving, Introduction to Privacy and Self-regulation in the Information Age, *in Privacy and Self-regulation in the Information Age, supra* note 5.

[8] See further P.P. Swire, Markets, Self-Regulation, and Government Enforcement in the Protection of Personal Information, in *Privacy and Self-Regulation in the Information Age, supra* note 5, at 9.

[9] Some scholars define self-regulatory activities more broadly. See for example, E.E. Dennis, Internal Examination: Self-Regulation and the American Media, 13 *Cardozo Arts & Entertainment Law Journal*, 697 (1995).

[10] See further F. Kuitenbrouwer, Self-regulation: Some Dutch Experiences, in *Privacy and Self-Regulation in the Information Age*, supra note 5, at 113.

[11] "Industry" can have a broad as well as a narrow meaning. Narrowly understood, industry refers to groups of companies directly involved in producing, functioning, and processing certain goods or services; broadly understood, it could refer to those involved in or influenced by certain goods or services. For the present paper, the narrow meaning is taken.

Association, Internet Services Association, Better Business Bureau, Consumer Bankers Association, Direct Marketing Association, the Internet Privacy Working Group (IPWG),[12] TRUSTe's,[13] etc. Each treats a different aspect of electronic commerce and strives to provide a basis for protecting and balancing the interests of the parties they represent.

"Self" can also be a single company. Companies can set up a special department which specifically takes up the task of regulating their own operations. If a company is strong enough, its own methods of regulation can be extended to or accepted by other companies.

"Self" can also refer to social bodies. They are not the directors of industry, but they are important applicants and customers of industry. Their actions can have vital effects on the future industry.

The three types of "self" are all important to regulation. A lone self might carry out the task of self-regulation, but on most occasions, different groups of selves operate together in order to realize maximum benefits. Each has its own interests, but none can act without taking into account the interests of the others and the industry as a whole. As they represent the different aspects of electronic commerce, missing one self may lead to a failure in appropriate regulation.

For the present discussion, a distinction should be drawn between user empowerment and self-regulation. User empowerment emphasizes the user's capability to exercise control over relevant activities—in the case of the Internet, those activities enabled by the technologies developed and made available by the private sector.[14] Self-regulation arises out of the industry or profession's own initiative, not from user empowerment. The users' opinions might be considered in self-regulation, but the regulation itself does not depend on the user empowerment. Empowerment is not the same as mandate. There are indeed situations when government mandates that an industry adopt and enforce a code of self-regulation.[15] Self-regulators can regulate based on the suggestions or mandates, but they do so of their own accord.

---

[12] IPWG's work is one component of the World Wide Web Consortium's Platform for Privacy Preferences, which will enable consumers to exercise control over the flow of personal information by giving them notice of the information. See further <http://www.cdt.org/privacy/ipwg>.

[13] TRUSTe, the leading privacy seal program, is an independent non-profit organization dedicated to building consumer trust and confidence in the Internet. See further <http://www.truste.org>.

[14] See An Analysis of the Bertelsmann Foundation Memorandum, *supra* note 6.

[15] According to Australian Broadcasting Services Act (1992) 123, broadcasting

1.1.2. *Evaluation of Self-Regulation*

For many scholars and practitioners, the advantages of self-regulation are obvious. Self-regulators are generally experts in the industry capable of producing appropriate, objective decisions.[16] Experts are particularly valuable when technical knowledge is needed to develop appropriate rules and determine whether they have been violated.[17] Respectful followers ensure compliance in the enforcement of said decisions.[18] This willingness to follow rules made by the experts rather than those passed by administrators[19] could directly affect the expense of governmental regulation. The cost of regulation is shifted to the industry and less enforcement is required.

The private nature of self-regulation also makes industry policy more flexible.[20] Technology is developing rapidly and the situations based on modern technology are following suit. The rules made today could become outdated with the development of a new situation. Self-regulation allows the regulators to follow the situation closely and make timely adjustments.[21] Furthermore, once practice proves a decision faulty the regulators can immediately obtain resources and take measures to avoid further damage.

Self-regulation also serves as a testing bed for official government regulations.[22] The measures taken can act as a forerunner to government regulation. The period between the implementation of the

---

industry groups should develop codes of practice, in consultation with the regulatory authority, concerning such topics as preventing the broadcast of unsuitable programs, promoting accuracy and fairness in news and current affairs, and protecting children from harmful program materials. See further I. Ayres & J. Braithwaite, *Responsive Regulation: Transcending the Deregulation Debate* 103 (1992).

[16] See further D.C. Michael, Federal Agency Use of Audited Self-Regulation as a Regulatory Technique, 47 *Administrative Law Review*, 171, 181–182 (1995).

[17] A.J. Campbell, Self-Regulation and the Media, 51 *Federal Communications Law Journal*, 715–716 (1999).

[18] The basic position is that they know their own best interests and that respect for preferences, as expressed in market transactions, is the best way to promote aggregate social welfare. See further M.A. Utton, *The Economics of Regulating Industry*, 1 (1986); C.R. Sunstein, Disrupting Voluntary Transactions, in J.W. Chapman & J.P. Pennock (Eds.), *Markets and Justice*, 279, 281 (1989).

[19] See further Michael, *supra* note 16, at 181, 183–184; Ayres, *supra* note 15, at 115–116; Swire, *supra* note 8, at 4.

[20] See further Michael, *supra* note 16, at 181–182; Ayres, *supra* note 15, at 110–112.

[21] This is one advantage over governmental regulation. Governmental agencies have to follow formal procedures provided in the national legislation, which prolongs the period for adoption of new rules. They must also do a lot of work to obtain the political support and consensus needed to act.

[22] It is claimed that self-regulatory measures can avoid constitutional issues. See further D.A. MacDonald, Privacy, Self-Regulation, and the Contractual Model: A

two types of regulatory mechanisms can serve as both a feedback stage and a transitional period. This arrangement shall on the one hand help a smooth adjustment of commercial strategy and, on the other hand, strengthen the validity of governmental rules.

Nevertheless, self-regulation faces some criticism. For one, self-regulators may confuse self-regulation with self-service.[23] There are also concerns over anti-competitiveness.[24] Competing parties may, while carrying out a regulatory job together, agree on certain issues, which could raise antitrust problems. Additionally, the private nature of self-regulation may fail to give adequate attention to the needs of the public or the views of affected parties outside the industry.[25] In part because of its private nature, the issue of enforcement may be a problem. Voluntary compliance cannot always be taken for granted.[26] Moreover, when enforcement actions are taken, concerns are raised about the exercise of unreviewable discretion.[27] Without a strong commitment to ensuring adherence to policies, self-regulation is doomed to squelch needed regulatory activities.[28] Determining how to ensure the enforcement of the regulation is a severe challenge to private self-regulation.[29]

While there is criticism, self-regulation is well accepted in the commercial world. The problem lies not in the mechanism itself, but in its implementation. Structuring self-regulation to best realize its benefits is the task at hand.

Report from Citicorp Credit Services, Inc., in *Privacy and Self-Regulation in the Information Age, supra* note 5, at 133–134.

[23] See further Baker, *supra* note 5, at 93–94.

[24] See further J. Kattan & C. Shapiro, Privacy, Self-Regulation, and Antitrust, *in Privacy and Self-Regulation in the Information Age, supra* note 5, at 99.

[25] Campbell, *supra* note 17, at 718.

[26] See further S. Balkam, Content Ratings for the Internet and Recreational Software, in *Privacy and Self-Regulation in the Information Age, supra* note 5, at 145.

[27] Michael, *supra* note 16, at 190; Ayres, *supra* note 15, at 124–125.

[28] D.K. Mulligan, & J. Goldman, The Limits and the Necessity of Self-Regulation: The Case for Both, in *Privacy and Self-Regulation in the Information Age, supra* note 5, at 67–68.

[29] There are several enforcement measures. For example, a trade association may punish non-compliance with expulsion or denial of the right to display a seal. However, the effectiveness of those sanctions shall depend on whether the benefits are important. Thus, the validity of those sanctions shall still depend on whether a company can make greater profits by ignoring self-regulation than it can by complying. See further H.H. Perritt, Jr., Regulatory Models for Protecting Privacy in the Internet, *in Privacy and Self-Regulation in the Information Age, supra* note 5, at 110.

1.1.3. *Best Practice of Self-Regulation*

For self-regulation to run smoothly, several things must be ensured. First of all, the quality of self-regulators is vital to the actual performance of self-regulation. They must be experts in the regulated industry. They should have a broad understanding of the industry and its relationships with other relevant industries. The self-regulators should be objective. They should work quite independently of normal operational departments. Furthermore, they should be motivated to regulate and creative in dealing with complicated situations in the industry.

The regulators involved in regulation determine the success of the process. There are several types of self-regulators, who may be arranged to handle different aspects of regulation and to check and balance each other. An institution within which different sectors exist to undertake different but related tasks could be established to standardize self-regulation.

Although some scholars have argued that government can be left out of the process of regulation,[30] actually, this is not feasible. Some have suggested audited self-regulation.[31] While delegating the power of regulation to a non-governmental entity, the government should verify the soundness of rules, check compliance, and spot-check the

[30] See further J.P. Barlow, *A Declaration of the Independence of Cyberspace*, <http: //www.eff.org/pub/Publications/John_Perry_Barlow/barlow_0296.declaration>; see also J. Kay, Sexuality, Live Without a Net: Regulating Obscenity and Indecency On the Global Network, *4 S. Cal. Interdisciplinary L.J.* 355, 387 (1995); K.J. Epstein & B. Tancer, Enforcement of Use Limitations By Internet Services Providers: "How to Stop that Hacker, Cracker, Spammer, Spoofer, Flamer, Bomber", 9 *Hastings Comm/Ent. L.J.*, 661, 664 (1997); R. Corn-Revere, Self-Regulation and the Public Interest, in C.M. Firestone & A.K. Garmer (Eds.), *Digital Broadcasting and the Public Interest: Reports and Papers of the Aspen Institute Communications and Society program* 63 (1998), at <http://www.aspeninst.org/dir/polpro/CSP/DBPI/dbpi14.html>. Corn-Revere argued that self-regulation is best promoted by ending all direct and indirect government content control and that efforts to promote government policies by means of threat, indirect pressure, or suggested industry codes are not true self-regulation.

[31] See, for example, Michael, *supra* note 16, at 171, 181–182, 192. He assumes audited self-regulation will work best if these conditions are met: firstly, the private entity to which self-regulatory authority is granted has both the expertise and motivation to perform the delegated task; secondly, the agency staff possesses the expertise to audit the self-regulatory activity, which includes independent plenary authority to enforce rules or to review decisions of the delegated authority; thirdly, the statute consists of relatively narrow rules related to output-based standards; and finally, the agency's and delegated authority's decision observes the rules for notice, hearing, impartiality, and written records of proceedings and decisions.

accuracy of information supplied to it.[32] The government must serve a function in ensuring that violations do not occur.[33]

Self-regulation cannot be single-handed self-regulated.[34] Successful instances of self-regulation involve governmental regulation.[35] It has to be complemented and backed up by governmental law and enforcement, a hybrid framework combining industry and state authority.[36] The government strengthens the credibility of self-regulation and promotes compliance. When self-regulation is not complied with, relief can be sought in government. To have at once freedom and accountability, self-regulation must adopt certain constraints.[37]

Furthermore, there should arise some channels through which feedback on self-regulation can be dealt with. Self-regulation should engage in its rulemaking on the record, with notice and opportunity for comments or feedback given to all affected groups to the extent possible, with particular emphasis on notice to nonmembers who might be adversely affected by proposed rules, and responses to all significant comments logged in the rulemaking record.[38] Without feedback, self-regulation functions blindly and possibly strays from industry demands.

---

[32] Campbell, *supra* note 17, at 719.

[33] J.E. Gaylord, State Regulatory Jurisdiction and the Internet: Letting the Dormant Commerce Clause Lie, 52 *Vand. L. Rev.* 1103 (May 1999).

[34] To a certain extent, self-regulation is involuntary. It usually occurs only under the threat of state regulation, and it can therefore be considered a variant of direct regulation. See E.M. Noam, Privacy and Self-Regulation: Markets for Electronic Privacy, in *Privacy and Self-Regulation in the Information Age*, *supra* note 5, at 21, 25.

[35] For further discussion of government regulation in protecting consumers, see P. Asch & R. Seneca, *Government and the Marketplace* 397–420 (1985); C.R. Sunstein, Legal Interference with Private Preferences, 53 *U. Chi. L. Rev.* 1129, 1132 (1986).

[36] See An Analysis of the Bertelsmann Foundation Memorandum, *supra* note 6; see also E. Harrington, *Consumer Protection in Cyberspace: Combating Fraud on the Internet* (June 25, 1998) (Federal Trade Commission Report to the Telecommunications, Trade, and Consumer Protection Subcommittee of the House (Committee on Commerce)).

[37] See further Dennis, *supra* note 9, at 703–704. In America, self-regulation always lies somewhere between market forces on the one hand and government regulation on the other.

[38] See further Campbell, *supra* note 17, at 761.

1.2. *Self-Regulation of Dispute Resolution in Electronic Commerce*

1.2.1. *General Remarks*

The current mantra is that the Internet should not be regulated by the government,[39] and should be self-regulated instead.[40] Ideological hostility to government intervention shared by early Internet enthusiasts has now been bolstered by the free market vision of the commercial users.[41] Privatization is all the rage[42] in commercial law and it is perhaps nowhere as popular as on the Internet.[43]

This attitude is held not only by the Internet society, but also by the governments.[44] Self-regulation has been called for in the US to address various features of the Internet.[45] On July 1, 1997, President

---

[39] The Internet should remain a "regulation-free" zone. See further D.R. Johnson & D.G. Post, And How Shall the Net Be Governed?: A Mediation on the Relative Virtues of Decentralized, Emergent Law, in B. Kahin & J.H. Keller (Eds.), Coordinating the Internet 62–91 (1997); D.G. Post, Governing Cyberspace, *43 Wayne L. Rev.*, 155, 157 (1996); R.E. Litan & W. Niskanen, *Going Digital!* 67–81 (1998).

[40] M.J. McCloskey, *Bibliography of Internet Self-Regulation*, <http://www.ilpf.org/selfreg/bis4_15.htm>.

[41] E.G. Thornburg, Going Private: Technology, Due Process, and Internet Dispute Resolution, 34 *U.C. Davis L. Rev.* 156 (Fall 2000).

[42] S.J. Ware, Default Rules from Mandatory Rules: Privatizing Law Through Arbitration, *83 Minn. L. Rev.* 703–704 (1999); L.S. Mullenix, Resolving Aggregate Mass Tort Litigation: The New Private Law Dispute Resolution Paradigm, 33 *Val. U. L. Rev.* 413 (1999).

[43] M.A. Lemley, The Law & Economics of Internet Norms, 73 *Chi.-Kent L. Rev.* 1257 (1998).

[44] J.H. Birnbaum, Getting to Know the Hill, *Time*, August 14, 2000, at B12, B15, at <http://www.time.com/time/magazine/articles/0,3266,52104,00.html>. Some scholars still think that the large and diverse nature of the Internet community makes self-regulation extremely unlikely. See, for example, J.I. Edelstein, Anonymity and International Law Enforcement in Cyberspace, 7 *Fordham Intell. Prop. Media & Ent. L.J.* 231, 284–286 (1996).

[45] President Clinton's call for industry self-regulation to address consumer privacy concerns on the Internet has been echoed by the Department of Commerce's National Telecommunications and Information Administration (NTIA) and the Federal Trade Commission (FTC). See Elements of Effective Self-Regulation for the Protection of Privacy and Questions Related to Online Privacy, Notice and Request for Public Comment, 63 *Federal Register* 30, 729 (NTIA 1998); FTC, Privacy Online: A Report to Congress i–ii (1998). On September 10, 1999, the Bertelsmann Foundation released a Memorandum entitled Self-regulation of Internet Content at its Internet Content Summit in Munich, Germany, which endorses a vision of self-regulation widely shared by the US government, industry, and civil libertarians. In the US, advocacy organizations and the Internet industry have supported self-regulation as an alternative to government or Internet Service Provider (ISP) limits on content. See An Analysis of the Bertelsmann Foundation Memorandum, *supra* note 6.

Clinton issued a report entitled A Framework for Global Electronic Commerce, more commonly called the "Magaziner Report," which explicitly calls for self-regulation in the Internet.[46] Five principles are presented intending to guide the development of the new digital economy.[47] Its tenets are these: the private sector should lead; governments should avoid undue restrictions on electronic commerce; where government involvement is needed, its aim should be to support and enforce a predictable, minimalist, consistent, and simple legal environment for commerce; governments should recognize the unique qualities of the Internet; electronic commerce over the Internet should be facilitated on a global basis.[48]

Since it first addressed Internet issues in 1991, the EU has changed its Internet regulation policy to support self-regulation.[49] In September 1997, the European Internet Services Providers Association (EuroISPA)

[46] See further W.J. Clinton & A. Gore, Jr., *A Framework for Global Electronic Commerce*, <http://www.iitf.nist.gov/eleccomm/ecomm.html>; see also N.W. Allard & D.A. Kass, Law and Order in Cyberspace: Washington Report, 19 *Hastings Comm. & Ent. L.J.* 563, 596–601 (1997); L. Kehoe, Clinton Takes Hands-Off Over Internet, *Financial Times*, July 2, 1997. The report states: "[T]hough government played a role in financing the initial development of the Internet, its expansion has been driven primarily by the private sector. For electronic commerce to flourish, the private sector must continue to lead. Innovation, expanded services, broader participation, and lower prices will arise in a market-driven arena, not in an environment that operates as a regulated industry. Accordingly, governments should encourage industry self-regulation wherever appropriate and support the efforts of private sector organizations to develop mechanisms to facilitate the successful operation of the Internet. Even where collective agreements or standards are necessary, private entities should, where possible, take the lead in organizing them. Where government action or intergovernmental agreements are necessary, on taxation for example, private sector participation should be a formal part of the policy making process." For analysis, see also W. Kleinwaechter, ICANN Governance: From Self-Governance to Public-Private Partnership: The Changing Role of Governments in the Management of the Internet's Core Resources, 36 *Loyola of Los Angeles Law Review* 1109–1111 (Spring 2003).

[47] K. Lui-Kwan & K. Opsahl, The Legal and Policy Framework for Global Electronic Commerce: A Progress Report, 14 *Berkeley Tech. L.J.* 504 (Spring 1999).

[48] See Clinton, *supra* note 46.

[49] See further M.J. Feeley, EU Internet Regulation Policy: The Rise of Self-Regulation, 22 *Boston College International and Comparative Law Review*, 161, 164–169 (1999). The document entitled Europe's Way to the Information Society: An Action Plan issued by the European Commission on July 19, 1994 proposes a broad regulatory framework package. The Opinion issued by the Economic and Social Committee advocates a high level of regulation. The resolution issued by the European Parliament in 1996 calls for a strong regulatory framework. But none of the above mentioned self-regulation. From 1991 till 1997, the EU focused on a high level of broad governmental regulation.

was established, thus marking transformation in EU policy.[50] The EU provided funding to this Association and encouraged industry self-regulation of the Internet.[51] This transformation can be viewed as a reaction to the US stance,[52] which recognizes the need to facilitate and expedite European commercial entry and positioning in the Internet market.[53]

Self-regulation appears to be a viable option for regulating the Internet and Internet-based commerce.[54] Some commentators have suggested that self-regulation is the key to success for electronic commerce.[55] The existing governmental regulation on the Internet has faced various criticisms.[56] It is incumbent upon the Internet community to create its own commercially reasonable code of behavior by which electronic commerce will be formed and executed.

---

[50] See European Internet Services Providers Association: EuroISPA established in Brussels, M@PRESSWIRE, September 15, 1997.

[51] The EU made up to seven million ECU available to EuroISPA as part of a European Action Plan for Information Society initiatives. See *id.*

[52] On July 9, 1997, subsequent to the release of the Report, US and EU officials met in Brussels to discuss the Internet with the aim of fostering industry self-regulation of the Internet. See further Press Release Re EU-US Meeting to Discuss Internet, SPICERS CENTER FOR EUROPE, July 8, 1997; see also Press Release: European Union and United States Meet to Discuss Internet, RAPID, July 8, 1997.

[53] See further Feeley, *supra* note 49, at 170–172.

[54] See further J.T. Delacourt, The International Impact of Internet Regulation, *38 Harvard International Law Journal,* 235 (1997). See for example, K.L. Macintosh, The New Money, 14 *Berkeley Tech. L.J.* 665 (1999); M. Lemley, Standardizing Government Standard-Setting Policy for Electronic Commerce, 14 *Berkeley Tech. L.J.* 748 (1999); L. Lessig, The Limits in Open Code: Regulatory Standards and the Future of the Net, 14 *Berkeley Tech. L.J.* 761 (1999); V. Mayer-Schonberger, The Shape of Governance: Analysing the World of Internet Regulation, 43 *Va.J.Int'l L.* 620–626 (Spring 2003).

[55] See further D. Spar & J. Bussgang, Ruling Commerce in the Network, 2 *Journal of Computer-Mediated Communication,* No. 1, <http://www.usc.edu/dept/annenberg/vol2/issue1/commerce.html>. The author writes that "before commerce can flourish online some trusted intermediary must create the basic rules of the game. If governments are not well-positioned to make and enforce these rules, then business entities are likely to fill the vacuum. In this process, they will shift the delicate balance between business and government and also stand to reap tremendous profits, which lies squarely with the rules, or standards, of electronic commerce. Accordingly, the generation of profit will occur largely in the cybercommunities that establish and support these rules." See also D.G. Post & D.R. Johnson, "Chaos Prevailing on Every Continent": Towards A New Theory of Decentralized Decision-Making in Complex Systems, 73 *Chi.-Kent. L. Rev.* 1055 (1998); J.R. Reidenberg, Governing Networks and Rule-Making in Cyberspace, 45 *Emory L.J.* 911–913 (1996); L.J. Gibbons, No Regulation, Government Regulation, or Self-Regulation: Social Enforcement or Social Contracting for Governance in Cyberspace, 6 *Cornell J.L. & Pub. Pol'y* 475 (1997).

[56] For example, complaints have been made about the adverse consequences

Regulatory mechanisms for the Internet are in the testing stage. Noted for its fluidity and ambiguity,[57] the Internet demands flexible self-regulation to pave the way for more formal regulation. A period of self-regulation on the Internet can at once afford the government time to familiarize itself with the new issue and also fill in the gap left where the government's capacity to regulate falls short. Only after the government learns from mechanisms of self-regulation can it develop a credible regulatory system. Trying to transplant a non-virtual world system of law that is fundamentally grounded in physical space and geography in a virtual world that transcends time, space, and borders will prove difficult, if not impossible.[58] Just as the EU Internal Market Commissioner, Mario Monti, stated in April 1997, "We definitely want to avoid, like in other sectors, having too much legislation too early".[59] This statement justified the need to use creative and flexible regulatory regimes in the face of the novel situation.

Any individual governmental regulation will have difficulties controlling cross-border digital transactions[60] and its implementation will have spillover effects on other nations. Efforts to rigorously control the flow of electronic information across physical borders are likely

caused by the European Directive on Data Protection (Council Directive 95/46 of October 24 1995 on the Protection of Individuals with regard to the Processing of Personal Data and on the Free Movement of Such Data, 1995 O.J. (L281) 31.) The Federal Communications Decency Act of 1006 (CDA) was declared unconstitutional by the court because its vagueness and sweeping breadth shall impermissibly chill protected speech. See further *Reno v. ACLU*, 117 S. Ct. 2350 (1997).

[57] See, for example, J. Mnookin, Virtual Law; The Emergence of Law in LambdaMOO, in Symposium, Law on the Electronic Frontier, 2 *Journal of Computer-Mediated Communication*, 1 (1996), <http://www.usc.edu/dept/annenberg/vol2/issue1>.

[58] See J. Goldring, Netting the Cybershark: Consumer Protection, Cyberspace, the Nation-State, and Democracy, in B. Kahin & C. Nesson (Eds.), *Borders in Cyberspace: Information Policy and Global Information Infrastructure*, 321, 345 (the MIT Press 1997).

[59] S. Perry, EU to Propose Electronic Commerce Regulation, *THR REUTER EUR. COMMUNITY REP.*, April 16, 1997.

[60] Controlling flowing digital transactions shall be costly; however, there is possibility of such extraordinary control. See further D.L. Burk, Virtual Exit in the Global Information Economy, *73 Chi.-Kent L. Rev.* 960–961, 992–993 (1998); T.S. Wu, Cyberspace Sovereignty?—The Internet and the International System, 10 *Harv. J.L. & Tech.* 647, 651 (1997); M. Stefik, Shifting the Possible: How Trusted Systems and Digital Property Rights Challenge Us to Rethink Digital Publishing, *12 Berkeley Tech. L.J.*, No. 1, 137, 139–144 (1997); S.D. Krasner, Global Communications and National Power: Life on the Pareto Frontier, 43 *World Politics*, No. 3, 336, 344–349 (April, 1991); J. Boyle, Foucault in Cyberspace: Surveillance, Sovereignty, and Hard-wired Censors, 66 *U. Cin. L. Rev.* 177, 202–204 (1997); L. Lessig, Reading the Constitution in Cyberspace, 45 *Emory L.J.* 869, 893–895 (1996).

to prove futile.[61] Thus, regulation shall require a coordinated policy among nations with differing political, economic, religious, and cultural ideas and values. To achieve such a harmony on the governmental level shall require time and effort. Unlike governmental regulation, self-regulation facilitates the speedy coordination of policies needed in the quickly developing Internet world. With experts at hand and in the absence of excessive bureaucracy, the quick adaptation of coordinated regulatory rules, flexible enforcement procedures, and internalized costs are possible.[62]

We can do away with neither self-regulation nor governmental regulation.[63] Of course, we can imagine that even when the government has set rules for regulation, self-regulation shall be needed to make immediate adjustments as the Internet situation requires.[64] The Internet is a rapidly changing marketplace. The flexibility of self-regulation allows industry to respond quickly to technological changes and employ new technologies to deal with digital issues.

The appropriate regulatory mechanism for dispute resolution should be a mixture of self and governmental regulation, with self-regulation playing a major role.[65] In the long-term, market-based responses to disputes should dominate political ones and either render a policy reaction unnecessary or induce the policy to move in a particular direction.[66] The 1997 White Paper on Internet policy rightly argues that the private sector shall take the lead on Internet issues, though some modest role for government is still envisioned (primarily to help close the so-called "digital divide").[67]

[61] See further D.R. Johnson & D.G. Post, Law and Borders: The Rise of Law in Cyberspace, 48 *Stanford Law Review*, 1367 (1996).

[62] See further G. Majone, Regulating Europe, in J. Richardson (Ed.), European Union Power and Policy-Making 23–26 (London and New York, Routledge, 1996).

[63] See further Boyle, *supra* note 60, at 177.

[64] Cyberspace is partly a model and partly a metaphor for a fundamental restructuring of our political institutions. See further N.W. Netanel, Cyberspace Self-Governance: A Skeptical View from Liberal Democratic Theory, 88 *Cal. L. Rev.* 395, 401 (2000).

[65] See, for example, M.A. O'Rourke, Progressing Towards a Uniform Commercial Code for Electronic Commerce or Racing Towards Nonuniformity?, 14 *Berkeley Tech. L.J.* 635 (1999); K. Werbach, *Digital Tornado: The Internet and Telecommunications Policy* (FCC, Office of Plans and Policy, Working Paper No. 29, 1997), at <http://www.fcc.gov/opp/workingp.html>.

[66] R.E. Litan, Law and Policy in the Age of the Internet, 50 *Duke L.J.*, 1057 (February, 2001).

[67] Management of Internet Names and Addresses, 63 *Fed. Reg.* 31, 741 (1998),

Dispute resolution is important to electronic commerce and should be subject to self-regulation, whose work involves adjudication;[68] this has been recognized by most practitioners.[69] Any self-regulatory mechanism that is accepted by the Internet community will promote dispute resolution; or rather, dispute resolution principles will drive the effort to self-regulate, obviating the need for governments to intervene and legislate along geopolitical lines.[70]

Indeed, self-regulation has been widely implemented in dispute resolution in electronic commerce, and the position of governments is to provide minimum acceptable standards.[71] Case examples include the Virtual Magistrate Project, the University of Massachusetts Online Ombuds Office, and eBay's Escrow and Insurance Arrangement.[72] The position of litigation in dispute resolution has been limited with the continuation of such projects. Cybersettle.com, Inc., the world's first Internet-based dispute resolution company, has successfully settled claims of over 20 million dollars online.[73] This example could serve well as the basis for wider applications in the future. Chapter Five shall examine these projects and make further analysis.

---

at <http://www.ntia.doc.gov/ntiahome/domainname/6_5_98dns.htm>. When governmental involvement is needed, its aim should be to support and enforce a predictable, minimalist, consistent, and simple legal environment for electronic commerce. And this legal environment should be based on a decentralized, contractual model of law rather than one based on top-down regulation.

[68] A Global Action Plan for Electronic Commerce, Prepared by business with Recommendations for Governments, at <http://www.uscib.org/policy/actplan.htm>.

[69] See further Internet Self-Regulation: Comments on How the Internet can Arrange Its Own Regulation, <http://www.endispute.co.uk/isr/cirb.htm>. One reason is that the Internet knows no boundaries and a state court system may be easily evaded by moving off-shore. See also A Global Action Plan for Electronic Commerce, Prepared by Business with Recommendations for Governments, 2nd Edition, October 1999, at 33.

[70] A.E. Almaguer & R.W. Baggott III, Shaping New Legal Frontiers: Dispute Resolution for the Internet, 13 *Ohio State Journal on Dispute Resolution*, 714 (1998).

[71] L.J. Gibbons, Rusticum Judicium? Private "Courts" Enforcing Private Law and Rights: Regulating Virtual Arbitration in Cyberspace, 24 *Ohio N.U. L. Rev.* 775 (1998); C. Menkel-Meadow, Do the "Haves" Come Out Ahead in Alternative Judicial Systems?: Repeat Players in ADR, *15 Ohio St. J. on Disp. Resol.* 60 (1999); M.J. Radin & R.P. Wagner, The Myth of Private Ordering: Rediscovering Legal Realism in Cyberspace, 73 *Chi.-Kent L. Rev.* 13,17 (1998).

[72] Some other existing initiatives and projects could be mentioned here: e-Resolution (Canada), BBB-Online (USA and Canada), IRIS mediation (France), Eurochambres (Association of European Chambers of Commerce), FEDMA (Federation of European Direct Marketing Associations) and EASA (European Advertising Standards Alliance), Visa International, Barclays Bank PLC, WebTrader (EU), etc.

[73] Over 20,000,000 Dollars in Claims Settled Online: Insurance Companies,

1.2.2. *Evaluation*

Self-policing and regulation is now standard for Internet practices.[74] Insofar as objectives like avoiding intrusive government regulation or restricting competition have been met, self-regulation has been successful.[75]

Different forms of voluntary self-regulation have emerged, some from comparative research and long theoretical considerations. For example, a variety of contracts provide a type of advisory board or management committee to settle disputes.[76] The Virtual Magistrate Project came out with the assistance of American Arbitration Association (AAA), a private organization. Some procedural rules of the AAA have been adopted and well applied in real dispute resolution. Some others, like market research-oriented credibility and public attitude studies, are associated with profit motives, the bottom line, and corporate public relations.[77] This has been best represented by the eBay's practice and the activities of Cybersettle.com, which acts out of consideration of its own commercial interests. As so-called experiments, these project examples have developed a protective shield against the kind of legal and quasi-legal accountability commonly imposed.[78]

Lawyers Go Online to Settle Disputes, <http://www.udiweb.com/udi1020b.htm>. Cybersettle.com offers confidential claims settlement by matching offers and demands via a patent-pending, secure web site. Insurance companies, corporations, government agencies, attorneys and claimants can resolve disputes instantly, 24-hours a day, 7-days a week using the Cybersettle system.

[74] J. Krasovec, Comment: Cyberspace: the Final Frontier, for Regulation?, 31 *Akron Law Review*, 143 (1997). Recent legislative attempts at regulating some aspects of the Internet have so far proven to be ineffective and undesirable. A good example is the Communications and Decency Act (CDA) of 1996, which restricted certain indecent communication over computer networks. The CDA was struck down by the Supreme Court in *Reno v. ACLU*, 117 S. Ct 2329, 2331–2332 (1992). The court held that, as key provisions of the CDA were overbroad and vague, the statute would effectively keep indecent material from adults who have a right to see such materials.

[75] See further Campell, *supra* note 17, at 757.

[76] Such arrangements usually exist in business-to-business electronic commerce when both parties would like to maintain good relations. For example, British Data Interchange on Shipping (DISH) program and its Pilot Project Interchange Agreement provided for a preliminary procedure before the DISH Management Committee.

[77] See Dennnis, *supra* note 9, at 704.

[78] For example, the Virtual Magistrate Project requires parties agree to exempt the magistrate, project administrators, and other relevant parties from possible liability arising out of the activities associated with the project.

At this stage, the main function of those examples is to prove that it is technically possible to resolve disputes in electronic commerce.[79] Meanwhile, they provide a nice testing laboratory for developing online systems for non-cyberspatial disputes. This self-regulatory framework shall definitely give way to online courtrooms for future disputes, whether arising out of online or non-online activities. As this occurs, we may see processes of dispute resolution that are not only attuned to the online environment but may also encourage change in how we work out problems in the physical world.[80]

2. *International Orientation*

The whole world has become smaller with the help of the Internet, which allows people around the world to instantaneously interact with each other. National borders are just speedbumps on the information superhighway.[81] New strategies are required to accommodate new phenomena. A global problem requires an international solution. In September 1996, the European Parliament issued a resolution[82] indicating that the European Parliament was interested in effectuating broad legislation in order to produce a structured and equitable environment.[83] This document, while never mentioning industry self-regulation, stressed the need for an international regulatory regime.[84]

---

[79] See further Cyberspace Law Institute, the Virtual Magistrate Pilot Project, at <http://www.11.georgetown.edu/lc/cli.html#VM TOP>.

[80] Online Dispute Resolution, Cyberspace Law for Non-Lawyers, <http://www.ssrn.com/update/isn/cyberspace/lessons/disput04.html>.

[81] See further H.M. White, Jr. & R. Lavria, The Impact of New Communication Technologies on International Telecommunication Law and Policy: Cyberspace and the Restructuring of the International Telecommunication Union, 32 *Cal. W.L. Rev.*, 1–2 (1995).

[82] European Parliament Comm. Econ. and Monetary Affairs and Industrial Policy Report on Resolution on "Europe and the Global Information Society-Recommendations to the European Council" and on a communication from the Commission of the European communities: "Europe's Way to the Information Society: An Action Plan" 1996 O.J.C 320.

[83] *Id.*, paragraph 1.

[84] *Id.*, paragraph 32. The resolution emphasises the need for an appropriate and well-timed regulatory and legal framework to provide a simultaneous accompaniment to the prospect of an information society, which if it is to have a positive impact, also needs to be guided and governed at a supranational level.

2.1. *An International Policy*

2.1.1. *Justification for the Policy*

Regulating the Internet has become a priority for various reasons, among which commercial potentiality has been one of the most important. Many nations have spontaneously adapted old rules to regulate the new issues as a temporary measure. Self-regulation has been identified as the best policy in regulating Internet issues. However, earlier than the official declaration of this policy, an international policy had been adopted and widely recognized.

This policy came into the arena free from suspicion. The nature of the Internet and the globalization of the world economy have meant that regulation of electronic commerce should be addressed on an international level. Physical frontiers have lost their meaning which, with the speed and efficiency brought by the Internet, has presented a severe challenge to Internet regulation.

Theoretically speaking, each nation shall have no problem in legislating and enforcing certain rules within national borders to govern the activities of the Internet. According to national sovereignty, one state should have the exclusive power to apply its laws to the local effects of a transborder transaction.[85] However, it does not follow that every nation where an Internet information flow appears can regulate that information flow.[86] In modern society, a nation cannot use arbitrary measures to prohibit information flow. There is no big "off" switch for the Internet. While a country may gain control over computers within its borders, one has no leverage against the whole system.[87] Moreover, electronic commerce may be stifled by conflicting national rules, with the potential for overlapping and contradictory approaches likely to increase as electronic commerce takes hold.[88]

---

[85] M.N. Shaw, *International Law* 277–314 (3rd Ed. 1991); see also L. Brilmayer, Consent, Contract, and Territory, 74 *Minn. L. Rev.* 1, 11–12 (1989).

[86] See further J. Goldsmith, Unilateral Regulation of the Internet: A Modest Defense, 11 *EJIL*, No. 1, 139 (2000).

[87] S. Selin, Governing Cyberspace: The Need for an International Solution, 32 *Gonz. L. Rev.* 368–369 (1996/1997).

[88] A broad principle of co-operation among nations, requiring each nation to account for the constraints it would impose on the citizens of other nations, would entail a breathtaking degree of co-operation and consideration among nations. CUT See Y. Benkler, Internet Regulation: A Case Study in the Problem of Unilateralism, 11 *EJIL*, No. 1, 171 (2000).

Furthermore, national regulation cannot always limit the Internet's effects. It is almost impossible for a state to regulate the Internet without causing a rippling effect in other states.[89] Consider the case of *New York v. Vacco*. Golden Chips Casino, a subsidiary of a New York corporation, is an Antiguan corporation licensed to operate gambling facilities in Antigua. Golden Chips operated web sites from Antigua, which were accessible to Internet users in New York. The New York Supreme Court ruled that Golden Chips violated New York's anti-gambling laws.[90] This ruling was able to be enforced successfully as Golden Chips' directors and employees were in the US. Also, this ruling further prohibits Golden Chips from operating Internet gambling on a worldwide scale.

In another example, one of the EU regulations, the European Data Protection Directive, prohibits transfer of personal information from the EU to countries lacking adequate privacy protection.[91] This directive could be enforced against non-European companies with a presence in the EU. However, this shall constitute impermissible extraterritorial regulation to those with less restrictive privacy laws since it threatens to cut off their computers from European data.[92]

From the examples above, we can see that individual Internet regulation shall cause conflicts across borders. A lack of a coherent international system has forced countries to enact inconsistent regulatory schemes that focus on different parties in Internet transactions,[93] thus creating a potentially hazardous business environment[94] and spillover effects that adversely affect freedom of expression.[95] Successful implementation of policy requires the cooperation of divergent international players.[96]

[89] J.S. Bauchner, State Sovereignty and the Globalization Effects of the Internet: A Case Study of the Privacy Debate, 26 *Brooklyn J. Int'l L.* 695–696 (2000).

[90] *New York v. Vacco*, No. 404428/98, Supreme Court, 22 July 1999.

[91] Directive 95/46/EC of the European Parliament and the Council, 24 October 1995.

[92] See further P. Swire & R. Litan, *None of Your Business: World Data Flows, Electronic Commerce, and the European Privacy Directive*, 3–4 (1998).

[93] I. Brownlie, *Principles of Public International Law* 314 (5th Ed. 1998).

[94] C. Gregoire, Law Enforcement Challenges in Cyberspace, 34 *Prosecutor* 29 (September–October 2000)

[95] See A Proposal for Removing Road Blocks from the Information Superhighway by Using an Integrated International Approach to Internet Jurisdiction, 10 *Minn. J. Global Trade* 397 (Summer, 2001); J.L. Goldsmith, The Internet and the Abiding Significance of Territorial Sovereignty, *5 Ind. J. Global Legal Stud.* 488–489 (1998).

[96] S.M. Hanley, International Internet Regulation: A Multinational Approach, *16*

2.1.2. *An International Policy and Self-Regulation*

For its appropriateness for Internet regulation and also for its novel application, self-regulation holds the most popular position on the stage of dispute resolution. On the other hand, the simple international policy lacks the attention of the academic and practical world, even though people are actually applying it in one way or another. These two policies are different in many aspects, but in the end, they are closely related.

Compared with the policy of self-regulation, international policy requires much more preparatory work and thus more difficulties exist in its application. International cooperation and coordination involve a lot of pre-regulation activities, which give way to complicated considerations. In contrast, self-regulation is initiated by a private party with relatively clear objectives. Nevertheless, these two policies are generally carried out in unison. Emphasizing an international policy, regulatory efforts can be made by industry at a global scale; the same industry in different nations could get together to discuss possible regulation for the whole industry. In most situations, self-regulation in the Internet shall naturally be carried out before an international background. National regulatory mechanisms could be sufficient in some cases, but most Internet regulations shall have spillover effects. Importantly, an international policy could be carried out in different levels, not only by the industry, but also by the governments, governmental organizations, etc., which adds authority to enforcement. Furthermore, for those advocating governmental regulation on electronic commerce, an increasing degree of centralization of control can be achieved by means of increasing international coordination among existing sovereigns, through multi-lateral treaties and/or the creation of new international governing bodies.[97]

Working in unison and in their own arenas, both policies are fundamental to the regulation of electronic commerce. While placing

---

Journal of Computer & Information Law 1011 (1998); S.K. Thomas, The Protection and Promotion of E-Commerce: Should There be a Global Regulatory Scheme For Digital Signatures?, 22 *Fordham Int'l L.J.* 1063 (March 1999); S. Tavakol, Digital Value Units, Electronic Commerce and International Trade: An Obituary for State Sovereignty over National Markets, 17 *Journal of Computer & Information Law* 1229–1232 (1999).

[97] See generally G.S. Wood, *The Radicalism of the American Revolution* 262 (1992); G. Stourzh, *Alexander Hamilton and the Idea of Republican Government* (1970); C. McManis, Taking TRIPs on the Information Superhighway: International Intellectual Property Protection and Emerging Computer Technology, 41 *Vill. L. Rev.* 207 (1996).

importance on allowing the private sector to take the lead in the economic and commercial development and implementation of Global Information Infrastructure, Global Information Society (GII-GIS), there is need for all social partners to become involved.[98]

2.1.3. *Means to Implement an International Policy*

There are two basic ways of enforcing international cooperation in electronic commerce. Either there should exist a series of treaties between international players, or they should create a supranational body like WTO to deal with the electronic commerce. Governments could enter into bilateral and multilateral cooperation agreements on specific areas like recognition of foreign decisions and cross-border investigations.[99] Creating treaties on the Internet could help unify the international practice and cut down the conflicts arising out of different national provisions. Many scholars have discussed on the possibility of law for the Internet aimed at avoiding disputes and also facilitating dispute resolution. UNCITRAL has taken the initiative to formulate a model law for electronic commerce. A complete international law for the Internet shall basically resolve the question of applicable law in dispute resolution processes. This law shall be discussed further later in this work.

It is the limited purpose of this section to discuss the second means of enforcing international cooperation: the creation or empowerment of an international body to regulate electronic commerce and undertake the resolution of disputes. Indeed, several international organizations have already launched efforts to pursue appropriate means to resolve disputes in electronic commerce. Such steps to promote an international environment are conducive to the growth of electronic commerce. Universal acceptance of common principles and policies to underpin national and international actions is warranted.

---

[98] See further OECD (1997b), Global Information Infrastructure—Global Information Society, working paper 81.

[99] For example, countries can share confidential information relating to the enforcement of competition laws. See further N. Hachigian, Essential Mutual Assistance in International Antitrust Enforcement, 29 *Int'l Law.*, 117 (1995).

2.2. *International Attempts*

2.2.1. *General Remarks*

Several international organizations have already launched efforts to regulate electronic commerce within their jurisdiction. Some have experimented with more formal dispute resolution procedures, which serve as models for future practices. But as a result of their influence on international society, their activities have achieved much more publicity than self-regulation.

2.2.2. *European Union (EU)*

The EU is unique amongst international organizations in that it is able to create norms that are legally binding on its members or which confer rights and obligations directly onto its citizens. It has long recognized the need to address the Internet questions and to develop and implement a sound solution.[100] Various EU regulations have related to technological aspects of Europe's economic integration.[101] The first attempts to regulate computers occurred in 1991.[102] On July 19, 1994, the European Commission presented a document entitled Europe's Way to the Information Society: An Action Plan, which advocates a regulatory role for the EU.[103] In April 1997, the European Commission issued "A European Initiative in Electronic Commerce," which aims at encouraging the vigorous growth of e-commerce in Europe by providing a coherent policy framework for future community action and establishing a common European position to achieve global consensus through international negotiations.[104]

---

[100] S. Murray & R.L. Hudson, A Fair Deal and Real Choice, *Wall St. J. Eur.*, March 14, 1996.

[101] F.C. Mayer, Europe and the Internet: The Old World and the New Medium, 11 *EJIL*, No. 1, 156 (2000); J. Dickie, *Internet and Electronic Commerce Law in the European Union* 3 (1999). Besides measures within the organization, the EU has reached a Joint Statement with the US. See Joint E.U.—U.S. Statement on Electronic Commerce, 5 December 1997, at <http://www.qlinks.net/comdocs/eu-us.htm>.

[102] See J. Rosener, *Cyberlaw: The Law of the Internet*, 271 (1997). The EU issued the Privacy Directive, which was later formally adopted by the European Council of Ministers in 1995 as the Directive on the Protection of Personal Data.

[103] See further Commission of the European Communities, Europe's Way to the Information Society: An Action Plan, (COM (94) 347 final, at Intro.), <http://www.echo.lu/eudocs/en/com-asc.html>.

[104] See further Commission Communication "A European Initiative in Electronic Commerce", COM (97) 157 of April 15, 1997, at 12–14, <http://www.ispo.cec.be/ecommerce/answers/what.html>.

The EU has done much to implement online dispute resolution. In end of 1999, the European Commission launched a new initiative entitled "eEurope-An Information Society for All", which establishes goals for bringing the benefits of the Information Society within the reach of all Europeans.[105] One such goal is to encourage "online dispute settlement" and alternative consumer redress procedures. This goal was reformulated in the Directive on Electronic Commerce issued in 2000,[106] which set forth several key principles for determining an appropriate dispute resolution mechanism for electronic commerce. The directive encourages *inter alia,* the drawing-up of codes of conduct at community level by trade, professional, and consumer associations and requires member states to provide in their legislation for possibilities such as (electronic) out-of-court dispute resolutions.[107] Additionally, the directive requires member states to ensure that appropriate court actions are available and examine the need to provide access to judicial procedures by appropriate electronic means.[108]

2.2.3. *World Trade Organization (WTO)*

It was as late as 1998 that the WTO became involved with issues of electronic commerce.[109] On September 25, 1998, ministers adopted the WTO Declaration on Global Electronic Commerce, which urges the general council to establish a comprehensive work program to examine all trade-related issues pertaining to global electronic commerce. While the electronic world poses certain challenges to the present trade policy framework, traditional WTO principles of nondiscrimination, transparency, and market openness remain valid for

---

[105] See the European Commission's Communications of December 8, 1999, eEurope—An Information Society for All, (p. 9), European Commission Press Release of December 8, 1999, IP/99/953, <http://europa.eu.int/comm/information_society/eeurope/index_en.htm>.

[106] See further Directive 2000/31/EC of the European Parliament and of the Council of 8 June 2000 on certain legal aspects of information society services, in particular electronic commerce, in the internal market, Official journal of the European Communities, 17 July 2000, L 178/1.

[107] See further Article 16 and 17 of the Directive on Electronic Commerce.

[108] See further Article 18 of the Directive on Electronic Commerce.

[109] See generally C.L. Mann & S.C. Knight, Electronic Commerce in the World Trade Organization, in J. Schott (Ed.), *The WTO after Seattle* (Institute for International Economics, July 2000); E-Commerce in the World Trade Organization: The Need for a Horizontal Approach, International Communications Round Table, 12 July 2000.

electronic commerce. The present framework only roughly provides for those forms of electronic commerce changing the global economy.[110] Much effort has been dedicated to involve them into the next round of trade negotiations.[111]

As far as dispute resolution is concerned, WTO has a new mechanism for resolving disputes.[112] Generally considered to be a major improvement on the former WTO mechanism, this mechanism came into being after the Uruguay Round of negotiations and has been welcomed by most member states. Importantly, all trade disputes arising out of the WTO framework shall be submitted to this mechanism for resolution.[113] The WTO Dispute Settlement Understanding establishes an integrated dispute settlement system for all multilateral and plurilateral agreements under the WTO umbrella.

The problem with this mechanism for electronic commerce is its exclusive availability to member states. This mechanism is not the one to resolve a private dispute unless, of course, that dispute was supported by a member state.

2.2.4. *International Chamber of Commerce (ICC)*

ICC is another organization dealing with international business. It offers dispute resolution services through the ICC International Court of Arbitration (the ICC Court) located in Paris, France. Demand for arbitration under ICC rules continues to rise after their first revision in 20 years came into force at the beginning of 1998. The updated

---

[110] For a detailed discussion of the present WTO framework for electronic commerce, see H. Hauser & S. Wunsch-Vincent, A Call for a WTO E-Commerce Initiative, 6 *Int'l J. Comm. L. & Pol'y* 1–30 (Winter, 2000/2001).

[111] According to suggestions by the EU, the future WTO work program on electronic commerce should be subjected to the General Council rather than fragmented throughout the WTO, or put under the Services Council.

[112] For discussion on the WTO mechanism, see L. Wang, Some Observations on the Dispute Settlement System in the World Trade Organization, 29 *JWT*, No. 2, 173–178 (1995); G. Horlick, Dispute Resolution Mechanism: Will the United States Play by the Rules?, 29 *JWT*, No. 2, 163–171 (1995); E. Vermulst & B. Drissen, An Overview of the WTO Dispute Settlement System and its Relationship with the Uruguay Round Agreements: Nice on Paper but Too Much Stress for the System?, 29 *JWT*, No. 2, 131–161 (1995); N. Komuro, The WTO Dispute Settlement Mechanism: Coverage and Procedures of the WTO Understanding, 29 *JWT*, No. 4, 5–95 (1995); P.T.B. Kohona, Dispute Resolution under the World Trade Organization: An Overview, 28 *JWT*, No. 2, 23–47 (1994).

[113] EU Committee Position Paper on the Millennium Round, September 1999, at <http://www.eucommittee.be/pop/pop1999/Tra/trade%2023.htm>.

rules make the system more flexible and user-friendly.[114] Based on its traditionally commercial nature, this center is one of the most welcomed participants in the commercial world. While most arbitration institutions are regional or national in scope, the ICC Court is truly international. Composed of members from some 60 countries and every continent, the ICC Court is the world's most widely represented dispute resolution institution.[115]

In the era of electronic commerce, ICC initiatives include policy making, e-commerce projects, instruments, and services.[116] The ICC Information Security Working Party drafted General Usage for International Digitally Ensured Commerce (GUIDEC) under the auspices of the ICC Electronic Commerce Project.[117] This document intends to draw together the key elements involved in electronic commerce and provide an indicator of terms and an exposition of the general background of the issue. Though it has no direct relationship with dispute resolution, it suggests a so-called digital signature or authentication, which does provide a solid basis for carrying out online business and facilitating dispute resolution.

The ICC also led the way in drawing up a Global Business Action Plan for Electronic Commerce that has been submitted to OECD ministers. This plan advocates the development of a tailor-made, speedy, and expert-oriented mechanism for resolving disputes in electronic commerce. In the meantime, it suggests governments to encourage the use of self-regulatory dispute resolution mechanisms as an effective way of resolving disputes; courts, in particular, should develop electronic expertise.[118] As regards jurisdiction, the plan recognizes the validity of alternative dispute resolution mechanisms, which are being developed by existing dispute resolution institutions and require cooperative efforts by the legal profession at an international level.

---

114 Business Consultancy—Overseas and Local, <http://www.firmholdings.com.au/bus-consultancy.html>.

115 The ICC International Court of Arbitration: Introduction to Arbitration, <http://www.iccwbo.org/court/english/arbitration/introduction.asp>.

116 Dawn C. Valdivia, Panel Report: Panel I: Report on the E-Commerce Activities of the OAS, ICC, ABA, and Unicitral, 17 *Ariz. J. Int'l & Comp. Law* 113 (Winter 2000).

117 General Usage for International Digitally Ensured Commerce, <http://www.iccwbo.org/home/guidec.asp>.

118 A Global Action Plan for Electronic Commerce, *supra* note 68.

2.2.5. *Organization for Economic Cooperation and Development (OECD)*
The OECD has been rather active in the field of electronic commerce. It provides a forum for public-private dialogue and analysis to deal with the technological realities of the global economy. In the autumn of 1998, Consumer International (CI) called for the implementation of guidelines drafted in Guidelines for Consumer Protection in the Context of Electronic Commerce, which include consumer redress measures. Although not binding, they help direct governments to provide consumers with basic protection, educate consumers and businesses of their rights and responsibilities, and facilitate ADR mechanisms.[119] They acknowledge a need for mechanisms to resolve international disputes and suggest that existing international commercial bodies should be encouraged to take on this role.[120]

2.2.6. *World Intellectual Property Organization (WIPO)*
WIPO deals with the issue of intellectual property. Its connection to electronic commerce results from the fact that many disputes arising out of electronic commerce have been closely related to the protection of intellectual property. Furthermore, the WIPO Mediation and Arbitration Center (the WIPO Center) have already been successful in carrying out dispute resolution services. Based in Geneva, Switzerland, the WIPO Center was established in 1994 to offer arbitration and mediation services for the resolution of international commercial disputes between private parties. The center has since focused significant resources on establishing an operational and legal framework for the administration of disputes relating to the Internet and electronic commerce.

Accommodating the trend of liberalization in the Internet sphere, a not-for-profit corporation entitled the Internet Corporation for Assigned Names and Numbers (ICANN) was developed in the US

[119] C.L. Mann, S.E. Eckert & S.C. Knight, A Policy Primer: Global Electronic Commerce, 136 (Institute for International Economics, 2000); see also K. Alboukrek, Adapting to a New World of E-commerce: The Need for Uniform Consumer Protection in the International Electronic Marketplace, 35 *George Washington International Law Review* 444–446 (2003).

[120] See Cryptography Policy Guidelines and the Report on Background Issues of Cryptography Policy, OECD Privacy Guidelines in the Electronic Environment: Focus on the Internet, 1997, at <http://oecd.org/dsti/sti/it/secur/pro/GD97–204.htm>. See also C. Swindells & K. Henderson, Legal Regulation of Electronic Commerce, 3 *The Journal of Information, Law and Technology (JILT)*, (1998), at <http://elj.warwick.ac.uk/jilt/98–3/swindells.html>.

to take over the management of the domain name system (DNS).[121] The WIPO was the designated dispute resolution provider for disputes involving this system. The mechanisms it has employed in dealing with such cases will be addressed in Chapter Five.

Its role in assisting the Application Service Provider Industry Consortium to develop a set of guidelines and best practices for cross-border dispute avoidance and settlement has further strengthened WIPO's pioneering position in the pursuit of a best practice for dispute resolution in electronic commerce. Based in Wakefield, Massachusetts, the consortium is an international advocacy group consisting of more than 650 companies. It was formed in May 1999 to promote the application service provider industry by sponsoring research, promoting best practices, and articulating the measurable benefits of this evolving delivery model. With demands for ASP market growing and the number of disputes rising as a result of the failure of providers to meet service-level commitments to end-user satisfaction, the consortium requested the WIPO to do research on dispute avoidance and settlement for the Industry. A white paper entitled ASPresolve: Dispute Avoidance and Resolution Best Practices for the ASP Supply Chain contains a summary of the recommendations and guidelines WIPO offered.

The white paper identifies characteristics of ASP supply chain disputes: one-to-many, multi-jurisdictional, problem-sourcing complexities, cutting-edge legal and business issues, symbiotic relationships, unique characteristics of the parties and wide value range.[122] Unfortunately, their complex nature suggests that even with the most comprehensive and well-conceived risk management and dispute avoidance measures in place, there will be always situations when disputes arise to the level where settlement is required. Litigation is not done away

[121] The formation of a not-for-profit corporation presents a unique challenge and opportunity for the Internet community. For information on the development of the ICANN, see further Domain Name Resolutions: CPSR Proposals for the New Corporation, <http://www.cpsr.vacia.is.tohoku.ac.jp>. For analysis of the ICANN, see K. Perine, Throwing Rocks at ICANN, <http://www.thestandard.net/article/display>, viewed on 27 March 2000.

[122] For further description of the characteristics, see A.H. Ali & N. Shah, Executive Summary: Dispute Avoidance and Resolution Best Practices, Dispute Avoidance and Resolution Team (DART), Best Practice Committee, International Conference on Dispute Resolution in Electronic Commerce, WIPO, November, 2000, ARB/ECOM/00/25a.

with. Alternative dispute resolution mechanisms are merely being experimented with and recommended for resolving disputes between ASPs and their vendors, partners, and customers.

The white paper lists ADR techniques in order of their formality. The least formal technique is negotiation, the most formal one is litigation, and in-between from least formal to most formal are settlement counsel, mediation, mini-trial, early neutral evaluation, neutral fact-finding expert, ombudsperson, dispute review board and arbitration. The following important features of these techniques are identified to assist disputing parties in choosing an appropriate model for their case: the underlying business model, the contractual relationship, the amount in controversy, and the identity of the parties involved.

The white paper further advises a dispute resolution clause be included in their initial commercial agreement, which could provide both parties with a degree of certainty regarding dispute resolution. Model clauses are based on a DART review of numerous clauses provided by the ASP Industry Consortium members, a wide range of resources at the WIPO Center and views expressed by a group of leading experts in the field of dispute resolution. Dispute resolution can be conducted *ad hoc* depending on the particular arrangements of the parties, or processed according to set of rules made available by an institutional dispute resolution service provider.

2.2.7. *Analysis*

The nature of the Internet has required international efforts in resolving disputes arising out of its application. In the quest for appropriate dispute resolution mechanisms, international organizations are apparently the right bodies to represent the international community as a whole.

The WTO's dispute resolution mechanism cannot access private parties. However, the ICC International Court of Arbitration has no problem in dealing with disputes in electronic commerce. Though its arbitration rules are not tailor-made for disputes arising out of the Internet, the ICC has been actively involved in electronic commerce.

The success of the WIPO in conjunction with ICANN in facilitating arbitration domain name disputes reveals possibilities for international organizations. Not only is international cooperation useful, but it is requisite. Only through international cooperation can the heavy demands of the digital society be satisfied.

3. *The Policy of Consumer Protection*

Recent heated discussion regarding consumer protection has led to advances in legislation.[123] Generally speaking, there are two categories of guarantees for consumers: legal guarantees, which create remedies for consumer goods or services that do not conform to the contract; and commercial guarantees, which create remedies for consumer goods or services that do not conform to the seller's express promises about the transaction.[124] A popular catch-phrase in media and politics nowadays, consumer protection proposes protection for the real bearer of goods or services, which includes laws that mandate an increase in the amount of information available to them and laws that may expose commercial actors to increased liability.

Considering the important role the consumers maintain, together with the reality that consumers are usually individuals and thus in a weak position, it is more than necessary to provide them with adequate protection. This standpoint is acceptable to merchants as well as consumers, as without consumers, their original purpose for transacting is moot. Consumer protection policies will urge consumer confidence and thus further their participation in transactions and improve business.

Are consumers equally protected when transacting on the Internet and when transacting in a traditional environment, and is their protection always adequate? Consumers would expect to see their interests being protected on the Internet, but the increasing cross-border nature of electronic commerce makes it difficult to protect consumers from fraud and other damaging activities.[125] Attempts by consumers to enforce their rights through private law suits naming foreign defendants are subject to all of the difficulties experienced by government agencies attempting to enforce law across borders. The costs of main-

---

[123] For a general background of consumer protection law, see J.A. Spanogle et al., *Consumer Law* (1991); D.J. Whaley, *Problems and Materials on Consumer Law* (1991).

[124] This is shown in Article 2 and 3 of the Amended Proposal for a Directive of the European Parliament and of the Council on the Sale of Consumer Goods and Associated Guarantees in April 1998. For further analysis, see G.T. Brady, Consumer Protection in the European Community: Hope for the Consumer or Unfulfilled Promises?, 23 *North Carolina Journal of International Law & Commercial Regulation*, 166–172 (Fall, 1997).

[125] J. Rothchild, Protecting the Digital Consumer: The Limits of Cyberspace Utopianism, *74 Indiana Law Journal*, 925 (Summer 1999).

taining an action against a defendant located outside national jurisdiction are likely to deter all but the most seriously injured consumers from pursuing this option.[126] Traditional consumer protection policies are unsuitable for the Internet age and require timely adjustment.

3.1. *General Understanding of Consumer Protection in Electronic Commerce*

As early as 1998, OECD recommended that the "same level of protection provided by the laws and practices that apply to other forms of commerce should be afforded to consumers participating in commercial activities through the use of global networks".[127] Consumer protection is not only important to parties in normal transactions, but is also vital to electronic commerce.

Consumer protection faces a severe challenge from the revolution brought by the Internet with regard, *inter alia*, to commercial communications and contracts concluded at a distance. The applicability and effectiveness of traditional rules of consumer protection in the online environment is limited. Traditionally, consumers were those within the national borders over which the state and its policy were sovereign. Traditional policy is not easily applied to everyday consumers who are players on the global market, even when that market exists in the real world.[128] With the development of an invisible world, in which consumers from all corners of the globe do business, difficulties in implementing traditional law are exacerbated.

---

[126] See G. Rosenberg, Legal Uncertainty Clouds Status of Contracts on Internet, *N.Y. Times*, July 7, 1997, at D3.

[127] OECD, DSTI/CP(98)4, April 1998, Section 27. This draft has been revised twice: DSTI/CP(98)4/REV1; DSTI/CP(98)4/REV2. This statement could be seen as a minimum basis since better protection could be provided answering the specific needs of consumers participating in electronic commerce.

[128] International transactions are problematic for the consumers due to issues concerning the applicable law, differences between national laws, and difficulties involved in actually invoking the commercial guarantee. The impact of these problems is significant since consumers who have had trouble with cross-border transactions will be reluctant to repeat the experience. It is thus necessary for guarantees concerning products purchased by consumers in another country to be honoured without discrimination in the consumers' country of residence. See for example, Commission Proposal for a European Parliament and Council Directive on the Sale of Consumer Goods and Associated Guarantees, COM (95) 520 final at 3–4; Commission Green Paper on Guarantees for Consumer Goods and After-Sales Services, COM (93) 509 final at 8–9; see also T.C. Hartley, *The Foundations of European Community Law* 11 (1994).

The current legal system protects consumers in a variety of ways. Specific legislation has been passed and institutions have been created to implement policy.[129] But these measures cannot sufficiently provide one-for-all protection to consumers. Consumers today still face lots of difficulties or unfair treatment in transactions. They are pressured by strongly organized production and distribution groups,[130] who exert more control than consumers do over market conditions.[131]

For better or worse, electronic commerce is modifying the way consumers transact. With the help of the Internet, business is piercing borders and offering consumers greater access to goods and services at lower prices. Online companies are trying their best to attract and retain consumers.[132] Consumers are in a comparatively better position than companies.[133] According to the media, stiff merchant competition has offered consumers the upper hand in on-line transactions, especially in the area of sales and services.[134] They are certainly being provided with more opportunities to participate in economic decision-making and implementation through which they can protect themselves. Some suggest consumer self-help as an avenue for consumer protection.[135] This is understandable since Internet users

---

[129] See further Interim Report on New Approaches to Consumer Law in Canada, Industry Canada, October 1996.

[130] See further the Council Resolution on a Preliminary Program of the European Economic Community for a Consumer Protection and Information Policy, 1975 O. J. (C 92), at 3, paragraph 6.

[131] See further F.E. Zollers, S.N. Hurd & P. Shears, Consumer Protection in the European Union: An Analysis of the Directive on the Sale of Consumer Goods and Associated Guarantees, *20 U. Pa. J. Int'l Econ. L.*, 99 (Spring 1999).

[132] The online companies take various measures, which include giving away frequent flyer miles and points towards product purchases, increasing site speed, improving customer services, and even giving away cash. See further S.C. Miller, Anybody in There? Sites Strain to Build in Customer Service, *N.Y. Times*, September 22, 1999, at D51.

[133] See further D.T. Rice, Jurisdiction in Cyberspace: Which Law and Forum Apply to Securities Transactions on the Internet? Appendix, 21 *U. Pa. J. Int'l Econ. L.*, 589 (Fall 2000).

[134] See further S. Hansell, A Feeding Frenzy Made for Consumers, *N.Y. Times*, September 22, 1999, at D1; E. Goode, The Online Consumer? Tough, Impatient and Gone in a Blink, *N.Y. Times*, September 22, 1999, at D22; T. Golsberg, Online Shopping Gets Sticky, October 18, 1999, at <http://www.msnbc.com/news/302106.asp>; B. Sullivan, Surfing—and Recruiting—for Cash, October 6, 1999, at <http://www.msnbc.com/news/319148.asp>.

[135] See further D. Pridgen, Wyoming Division: Speech: How Will Consumers be Protected on the Information Superhighway?, 32 *Land & Water Law Review*, 253–255 (1997); R. Frieden, Does a Hierarchical Internet Necessitate Multilateral Intervention?, 26 *N.C.J. Int'l Law & Com. Reg.* 400 (Spring 2001).

label themselves as "netizens" or citizens of the Internet world and agree to abide by their own self-imposed rules of "netiquette".[136]

Is it necessary to emphasize consumer protection in electronic commerce since consumers are better protected now? The answer is yes.[137] Consumer protection policy is needed in the world of electronic commerce for main reasons: to facilitate consumer transactions;[138] to respond to the increased ambiguity and risk in online transactions;[139] to deal with market failure; to protect consumer interests in the formulation of legislation regarding Internet transactions.[140, 141]

---

[136] M.A. O'Rourke, Fencing in Cyberspace: Drawing Borders in a Virtual World, 82 *Minn. L. Rev.* 609, 641 (1998).

[137] The EU tries to utilize consumer protection laws to address the imbalance of economic power between e-business and consumers. On the other hand, the US feels that the Internet's rapid changing technology would quickly outstrip and outdate any consumer protection laws and that government can do little to effect consumer protection except when fighting cybercrime. See further G. Miller, Clinton Pushes Initiatives for Electronic Commerce, *L.A. Times*, December 1, 1998, at C3, P10.

[138] The lack of regulation shall hinder sales and cause consumers anxiety. See further J. Covitz, A Framework for Global Electronic Commerce, 1075 PLI/Corp. 11 at 22, 25; C.E. Dubuc, Cyberspace: The Advertising Super Highway—Some Bumps Need Repair, 790 PLI/Comm 165 (April 1999); A. Boss, The Internet and the Law: Searching for Security in the Law of Electronic Commerce, *23 NOVA Law Review*, 583, 590–596 (Winter 1999); J.K. Winn, Open Systems, Free Markets, and Regulation of Internet Commerce, 72 *Tulane Law Review*, 1177, 1190 (March 1998).

[139] The lack of physical communication between contracting parties can cause each to become sceptical about the others. See B. Wright & J.K. Winn, *The Law of Electronic Commerce* (1999), at 13.03, 14.02; A. Boss & J.K. Winn, The Emerging Law of Electronic Commerce, 52 *Bus. Law.* 1469 (August 1997); R. Nimmer, Selling Products Online: Issues in Electronic Commerce, 467 PLI/Pat 823 (January 1997).

[140] See, for example, Uniform Computer Information Transactions Act (UCITA); Uniform Electronic Transactions Act (UETA), both available at <http://www.law/upenn.edu/bll/ulc_frame.htm>; United Nations Commission on International Trade Law (UNCITRAL) Model Law on Electronic Commerce, at <http://www.uncitral.org/english/texts/electcom/ml-ec.htm>; Proposal for a European Parliament and Council Directive on Certain Legal Aspects of Electronic Commerce in the Internal Market, COM (1998) 586 final-98/0325 (COD); Directive 97/7/EC of the European Parliament and of the Council of 20 May 1997 on the Protection of Consumers in respect of Distance Contracts, 1997 O.J. L 144, at <http://europa.eu.int/eur-lex/en/lif/1997/en_397L0007.html>; Canada's Personal Information Protection and Electronic Documents Act (Bill C-6), at <http://www.parl.gc.ca/36/2/parlbus/chambus/house/bills/government/C-6/C-6_3/C-6_cover-E.html>; International Chamber of Commerce General Usage for International Digitally Ensured Commerce (GUIDEC), at <http://www.iccwbo.org/home/guidec/guide.asp>; OECD Guidelines for the Security of Information Systems (1992), at <http://www.oecd.org//dsti/sti/it/secur/prod/e_secur.htm>.

[141] For a detailed explanation, see further S. Zain, Regulation of E-Commerce by Contract: Is It fair to Consumers?, 31 *University of West Los Angeles Law Review*, 166–170 (2000).

Acknowledging the important role electronic commerce shall play in the coming economic world and the necessity of consumer protection in electronic commerce, many countries have set up commissions to study possible ways of realizing such policy. On December 14, 1998, the Federal Trade Commission (FTC) announced that it would organize a workshop on consumer protection in the global electronic marketplace.[142] Its work in protecting consumers online was highlighted in the First Annual Report of the US Government Working Group on Electronic Commerce.[143] The European Commission has also attempted to harmonize EU mechanisms for dealing with consumer protection in the field of electronic commerce. The newly drafted Directive on Electronic Commerce, for instance, contains a kind of emergency brake for the protection of consumers and investors.[144]

Nevertheless, the inherently international nature of digital networks and computer technologies that comprise the electronic marketplace necessitates a global approach to consumer protection. Policies for consumer protection should be developed as part of a transparent and predictable legal and self-regulatory framework for electronic commerce.[145] OECD has rightly undertaken this initiative. In April 1998, the OECD Committee on Consumer Policy began to develop a set of general guidelines to protect consumers participating in electronic commerce without erecting barriers to trade. These guidelines are likewise important to harmonizing standards of consumer protection among various countries.

Such guidelines address consumer protection in electronic commerce as a whole, not specifically in dispute resolution. Determining how to realize consumer protection in resolving disputes related to the Internet is another matter.

---

[142] FTC to Study Consumer Protection in International Electronic Commerce, *Tech Law Journal*, <http://www.techlawjournal.com/internet/81215.htm>. The workshop explores various issues that consumers confront as they buy goods or services from foreign businesses; these issues concern questions of what laws apply to direct, international business-to-consumer transactions, where disputes are heard, and which governments have authority to protect consumers.

[143] FTC to explore International Consumer Protection Concerns in the Electronic Marketplace: Spring Workshop to Examine How to Protect Online Consumers When They Do Business with Foreign Firms, <http://www.techlawjournal.com/internet/81215.htm>.

[144] See further Article 3 (4) (a) of the Directive on Electronic Commerce.

[145] Recommendation of the OECD Council Concerning Guidelines for Consumer Protection in the Context of Electronic Commerce, <http://www.ftc.gov/opa/1999/9912/oecdguide.htm>.

3.2. *Consumer Protection in Dispute Resolution with the Internet as a Medium*

There are various legal systems in place to protect consumers.[146] However, consumers still face a variety of problems. For example, they do not have enough choices in the markets and often have difficulties in understanding contract terms. More importantly, consumers still do not always have effective methods for asserting their rights and resolving disputes.[147]

Businesses have long acknowledged that information distribution is very important to their survival because without relevant knowledge at hand, consumers may choose not to spend money on particular products or services. In consequence, they struggle to make themselves and their products known to consumers using all available forms of communication: radio, television, newspapers, magazines and billboards.

However, the relatively high cost of advertising through the media mentioned above has largely limited the scope of information presented. Most of the time, only a small amount of information can be conveyed. This issue is less important for those researching simple products or products about which consumers generally have a fair amount of knowledge. But when it comes to more complicated products or services, the lack of information available has adverse effects on consumer confidence. With doubts in mind, customers may fail to make a transaction. Or worse, they do purchase some dubious product over which disputes then immediately arise.

Often when important or expensive products are exchanged, a formal contract stipulates the rights and duties of each party. The general practice is that a standard contract shall be deemed to have been agreed upon by both parties once consumers accept the product. As a consumer, you rarely need to negotiate the detailed provisions in the final contract because most of such contacts are pre-prepared, even put in the boxes containing products you purchase. Reviewing contract details after receiving a purchase may seem counterintuitive, but there is no better realistic alternative.[148]

---

[146] For example, the common law of contracts and the Uniform Commercial Code afford traditional safeguards to consumers.

[147] See further G.E. Maggs, Internet Solutions to Consumer Protection Problems, *49 South Carolina Law Review*, 889 (Summer 1998).

[148] See, for example, *Hill v. Gateway 2000, Inc.*, 105 F.3d, 1147–1151 (7th Cir. 1997).

Various scholars debate the appropriateness of standard contracts,[149] but the fact is that these contracts are widely used in modern commerce and the burden of risk is undertaken by consumers no matter how unfair doing so may appear. When disputes arise, courts give preference to businesses concerning such contracts.

Apparently, how well consumers are protected before disputes and during dispute resolution shall to a certain extent depend on early disclosure of contract provisions. Yet when provisions are available to consumers, the diction of these provisions may pose a problem. Their legal wording, for instance, is difficult for laymen to understand.[150] In resolving this dilemma, general legal practice has again nudged consumers between a rock and a hard place. Consumers are expected to thoroughly read and live up to contractual provisions, except in exceptional cases when the wording of the provision is regarded as incomprehensible. In such cases, it can be argued that businesses could take a more active role in communicating contract information, whether by phone, fax, or verbal communication. But the cost of doing so may then add to transaction costs, which are always shifted back to the consumer.

The Internet can provide technological solutions to such problems. Accessible to people all over the world, the Internet can transfer detailed information to innumerable consumers both cheaply and efficiently.[151] Businesses can post basic contract information as well as explanatory information, including audio resources, for their consumers in cyberspace. In this way, businesses save on advertising costs and consumers have full and transparent access to their contracts.

The Internet also offers an alternative to the courtroom. Historically, informal consumer complaints have been of no consequence. Consumers have had to rely on bodies of law to persuade businesses

[149] See M.I. Meyerson, Efficient Consumer Form Contracts: Law and Economics Meet the Real World, 24 *Ga. L. Rev.* 597–600 (1990); T. Rakoff, Contracts of Adhesion: An Essay in Reconstruction, 96 *Harv. L. Rev.* 1173, 1226 (1983).

[150] The attendant cost of attempting to understand such legal wording would outweigh the perceived benefits as far as time, effort, and money were concerned. See further R. Barnett, The Sounds of Silence: Default Rules and Contractual Consent, 78 *Va. L. Rev.* 821, 886 (1992).

[151] A potential user only has to pay an Internet hosting provider a small monthly fee for space on a computer accessible through the Internet. Many of the providers allow a user to obtain space online in a matter of hours simply by transmitting credit card information. A list of Internet hosting providers can be found at <http://www.nerdworld.com/nw500.html>.

to cooperate once disputes arise. But the cyber-world gives weight to consumer commentary. The Internet provides consumers with a forum in which to complain to businesses as well other potential consumers.[152] Many businesses monitor consumer opinions web sites carefully to ensure that no public relations problems emerge.[153] In fear of losing business, merchants eagerly and quickly work to resolve disputes.

Obviously, the Internet can impact both consumers and businesses alike in terms of dispute resolution. But the evidence presented thus far leaves aside important legal issues for which this document must account.

3.3. *Consumer Protection in Electronic Commerce Dispute Resolution*

The most effective way of protecting consumers in dispute resolution is to provide them with access to redress.[154] And presumably, with the rise in the use of the Internet for exchanging ideas and complaints, consumer protection can be improved. But this is not consumer protection in the legal sense. In former legal regimes, many national consumer protection laws even prohibited arbitration in disputes arising out of consumer transactions.[155] Whether or not such law is still applicable is the issue at hand, and can be best dealt with by examining the representative legal efforts of two regions, the US and the EU.

3.3.1. *The US Practice*

The US has relatively few consumer protection laws.[156] However, an agency called the FTC[157] has been protecting consumers online since

---

[152] Consumers have already established more than one hundred web sites to air their complaints about major businesses. See, for example, the web site of Wal-Mart Sucks, <http://www.walmartsucks.com>.

[153] See J. Tanaka, Foiling the Rogues: "Anti" Web Sites are Great for Angry Customers, but Now Companies Are Trying to Fight Back, *Newsweek*, October 27, 1997, at 80.

[154] As Professor T. Fukuhara says, the application of damage recovery is an important aspect of consumer protection. OECD Proceedings: Gateways to the Global Market: Consumers and Electronic Commerce, 119 (1998).

[155] For example, Article 1d of Chapter 11 of the Finnish Consumer Protection Act of 1978 (January 20, 1978/38) provides disputes in consumer transactions are non-arbitrable.

[156] Maggs, *supra* note 147, at 887–889.

[157] The FTC is the only US agency at the national level with a broad consumer

1995.[158] One of its core missions has been to promote the efficient functioning of the marketplace by protecting consumers from unfair or deceptive acts or practices and increasing consumer choice by promoting vigorous competition.[159] As stated in the FTC Act section 5, this mission does not distinguish between online and offline commerce.[160] Other rules and statutes enforced by the FTC do specifically concern online commerce.[161] It is aggressive with its approach to the Internet world, and it needs to be, lest the Internet deteriorate into "the Wild West".[162]

The FTC has proposed a 4-part strategy for consumer protection. Firstly, it emphasizes the importance of consumer and business education. Realizing that educating those who are new to the Internet or unfamiliar with the general requirements of advertisement, the FTC's Office of Consumer and Business Education, sometimes in cooperation with private businesses or consumer organizations, produces publications targeted at particular consumer problems and compliance requirements.[163] Making use of its own home page and other cooperative web sites,[164] it alerts consumers to the latest scams and offers channels for reporting possible violations. It distributes

---

protection law enforcement mandate. It also enforces a variety of antitrust laws as part of its mission to maintain competition.

[158] See further FTC, Anticipating the 21st Century: Consumer Protection Policy in the New High-Tech, Global Marketplace, Volume II (last modified November 6, 1996), <http://www.ftc.gov/opp/global/report/global2.htm>.

[159] FTC Act 5(a), 15 U.S.C. 45 (a) (1994).

[160] See further R.B. Starek, III & L.M. Rozell, A Cyberspace Perspective: The Federal Trade Commission's Commitment to On-Line Consumer Protection, 15 *J. Marshall J. of Computer & Info. L.* 683–684 (Summer, 1997).

[161] For example, the Mail or Telephone Order Merchandise Rule, 16 C.F.R. 435 (1997) applies not only to goods ordered by mail or telephone but also to goods ordered by fax or computer. Note the Fair Credit Billing Act, 15 U.S.C 1666–1666j (1994); the Electronic Fund Transfer Act, 15 U.S.C. 1693–1693r (1994) and its implementing regulation E, 12 C.F.R. 205 (1997).

[162] The FTC has entered into consent agreements with nine online advertisers who allegedly engaged in unfair and deceptive trade practices as early as 14 March 1996. See further FTC Tackles Fraud on the Information Superhighway, Charges Nine On-Line Scammers, at <http://www.ftc.gov/opa/9603/netsc.htm>; Internet Advertisers are Targets in Nine FTC Cases; Eight Firms Settle, 70 *Antitrust & Trade Reg. Rep.* (BNA) 320 (21 March 1996).

[163] Most of the publications are available at the FTC Home Page, <http://www.ftc.gov>.

[164] This could include the web site of the Council of Better Business Bureau <http://www.bbb.org> and the National Fraud Information Center <http://www.fraud.org> of the National Consumer League.

informative brochures[165] and organizes various workshops to advance study on legitimate practice.[166]

Secondly, the FTC supports law enforcement as an effective means to protect consumer interests. It often attempts to prevent future damage to consumers through the issuance of court or commission orders prohibiting misleading practices[167] and seeks redress or disgorgement of illicitly obtained funds.[168] Section 5 of the FTC Act primarily addresses the prohibition of fraudulent online marketing.[169] A highly publicized technique called Sweep has been developed to attack similar law violations, such as fraudulent prize promotions or advance fee loan scams.[170] Complaints can be sent through FTC's web complaint form. Moreover, Implementing Regulation E of the Electronic Fund Act[171] provides methods for collecting errors and resolving disputes.[172]

Thirdly, the FTC encourages self-regulation by the industry.

Fourthly, the FTC upholds an inclusive approach to policy making.

The FTC takes seriously the issue of consumer protection in the global electronic marketplace.[173] It has made policy recommendations to realize consumer protection in dispute resolution.[174]

---

[165] The FTC has already published a consumer bulletin entitled Online Scams: Road Hazards on the Information Superhighway, at <http://www.ftc.gov/bcp/scamso1.htm>.

[166] For example, the June 1999 workshop on global issues and later ADR workshop, etc.

[167] See 15 U.S.C. 53 (b) (1994).

[168] See 15 U.S.C. 57 (b) (1994).

[169] See further Starek, *supra* note 160, at 686–694. So far, these have targeted credit repair schemes, business opportunities, pyramid scams and deceptive billing practices.

[170] See further Starek, supra note 160, at 687. This technique makes efficient use of information that is shared among different law enforcement authorities and results in greater publicity for law enforcement actions that, in turn, increases consumer awareness of fraud and deters fraudulent marketers.

[171] Electronic Fund Transfer Act, 15 U.S.C. 1693–1693r (1994); Electronic Fund Transfers (Regulation E), 12 C.F.R. 205 (1997).

[172] 15 U.S.C. 1693f; 12 C.F.R. 205.11.

[173] See, for example, FTC to Study Consumer Protection in International Electronic Commerce, Tech Law Journal, <http://www.techlawjournal.com/internet/81215.htm>. When considering the industry's difficulty in adopting self-regulatory techniques, quick enforcement of self-regulatory policies seems less than realistic. For the time being, US policies leave consumers with little recourse for electronic commerce disputes.

[174] The following discussion is based on the Public Workshop, June 6–7, 2000 by Department of Commerce of FTC, a summary of which can be found at <http://www.ftc.gov/bcp/altdisresolution/summary.htm>.

Firstly, a workable framework for jurisdiction shall be developed. Litigation has been traditionally regarded as the one main way of realizing legal justice. In the field of electronic commerce, some scholars have advocated the doctrine of country of origin. The FTC, however, does not support this suggestion. There are multiple disadvantages to the application of a doctrine so biased to a seller that it allows him to choose possible forums and applicable law. It not only obligates consumers to understand the laws of other countries but also, in most cases, deprives them of redress; the complexities entailed by redress are too intense. Additionally, it deprives governments of their ability to protect their consumers. The strict use of such a doctrine could be detrimental to the further development of electronic commerce. An alternative, sustainable framework of jurisdiction, will be discussed later.

Secondly, legal convergence shall be pursued. Appropriately converged consumer protection laws should provide a basic structure for protecting consumers no matter which country they reside in. They shall in turn make less burdensome the fabrication of jurisdictional structure.

Thirdly, the FTC encourages private sector initiatives. As we discussed, self-regulation shall be an appropriate choice for dispute resolution in electronic commerce.[175] Private sector initiatives shall better inform consumers and prevent disputes.

Fourthly, cross-border consumer redress and enforcement are emphasized. The FTC insists possible ways for realizing justice should be made available to international consumers. Moreover, it believes coordinating the legal activities among different countries and supporting their valuable judgements to be important to both legal and commercial aspects of the new electronic world.

The aforementioned recommendations support the use of the cheap and efficient ADR for dispute resolution. Litigation and the enforcement of judgments are expensive and require the additional investment of time. Formal procedures are particularly expensive for parties disputing over small amounts.

---

[175] W.J. Clinton, Memorandum for the Heads of Executive Departments and Agencies, at PP 10, 12 (1) (July 1, 1997), at <http://www.ecommerce.gov/presiden.htm>; Info. Society: Common Launches Debate on Virtual World, *European Report*, February 4, 1998, at No. 2288, at P3; Miller, *supra* note 137, at C3, at PP 1–5; W.M. Daley, U.S. Secretary of Commerce, The Administration's Position on Electronic Commerce: Let Markets, Not Regulations, Define How Electronic Commerce Matures, at <http://www.ecommerce.gov/16.htm>.

To realize an appropriate framework for the use of ADR in electronic commerce, international cooperation is needed. Globally compatible dispute resolution systems for electronic commerce require cooperation among governments.[176]

Technological innovation should also positively effect the use of ADR in electronic commerce. Information technology can help consumers protect themselves by encouraging compliance on the part of businesses. Potential advances in technology used for transferring relevant documents and downloading evidence and improvements in audio or video communication could additionally help to facilitate dispute resolution by reducing outside interference and procuring objectivity.

Within the new ADR framework, law enforcement is needed. At the moment, the FTC still has law enforcement power over fraudulent and deceptive ADR practices. Discussions are also underway with companies involving complaint procedures. It is particularly important to preserving consumer confidence that impartial dispute resolution practices are developed. They should be free or of low cost to consumers, easily accessible, and speedy. Additionally, consumers should have enough information to make informed decisions.

The new ADR shall involve the cooperation of domestic and international stakeholders in consumer and business education, guideline development, and a combination of public and private law enforcement. One size does not fit all. Rules concerning procedures and disclosure requirements could be different in different states as well as nations.

The transparency of results, rules of decision, and the validity of final decisions (binding or non-binding compared with the judgment) may present further problems for policy makers, who need to balance the interests of different stakeholders.

Consumer and business education is vital. Stakeholders should work together to promote education about seal programs, codes of conduct, and ADR.[177] The FTC has carried out various activities to familiarize consumers with new proposals.[178] It has found publicity

---

[176] See further H.K. Towle, On-Line: Selected Issues in Contracts, 557 PLI/Pat 242–245 (April 29–30, 1999).

[177] Summary of Public Workshop, June 6–7, 2000, Federal Trade Commission, Department of Commerce, November 2000, <http://www.ftc.gov/bcp/altdisresolution/summary.htm>.

[178] The FTC has hosted several conferences and participated in several federal

to be the best way of realizing the goal of educating the largest group of people, but it has also attempted to educate through various workshops and the publication of various materials both off and online; many publications are available on the FTC's home page. Both the ease with which government and consumer protection groups can post educational materials on the Internet and the ease with which consumers can access those materials make consumer and business education on the Internet particularly efficient and effective. Brochures containing key information sources are also distributed to various persons and groups across the US, including state and local government offices, national consumers and business organizations, Better Business Bureaus (BBBs),[179] and universities.[180] Such materials have helped many consumers to understand how they can better protect themselves.

3.3.2. *The EU Practice*

EU policies value consumer protection.[181] It is an important concern of the European Economic Community (EEC),[182] which enacted the first consumer program in 1975.[183] This policy was further boosted by the introduction of the 1986 Council Resolution recognizing the difficulties encountered by consumers invoking guarantees on products

government agency working groups treating topics such as electronic money and privacy, etc. Perhaps the most notable was the public workshop held on June 8–9, 1999 concerning Consumer Protection in the Global Electronic Marketplace, Bureau of Consumer Protection of FTC, a summary of which can be found at <http://www.ftc.gov/bcp/icpw/lookingahead/electroniicmkpl.pdf>. Other workshop documents can be found at the FTC web site, <http://www.ftc.gov>.

[179] The Better Business Bureau Web Server for the US and Canada can be found at <http://www.bbb.org>.

[180] Starek, *supra* note 160, at 695.

[181] In the early years after the establishment of the EEC, consumer protection was not seen as vital. Information about consumer rights was often non-existent and applicable national laws were complex. But the situation has changed since then. See for example, R. Evans, Time for Action: EU Consumer Policy, 4 *Consumer Policy Review*, 18 (1994); H.W. Micklitz & S. Weatherill, Consumer Policy in the European Community, 16 *Journal of Consumer Policy*, 285–292 (1993).

[182] See further the Council Resolution on a Preliminary Program of the European Economic Community for a Consumer Protection and Information Policy, 1975 O.J. (C 92), at 12, 13. This resolution includes a compilation of actions of interest to consumers prepared by the Community and Council Directives of Interest to Consumers.

[183] See Three Year Action Plan of Consumer Policy in the EEC (1990–1992), COM (90) 98 final 1, 1.

purchased in other member states[184] and the Single European Act of the mid-1980s, which proposed significant legislative procedures that have paved the way for improved consumer protection.[185]

At the moment, numerous consumer protection laws exist in the EU. On the one hand, all member states have their own set of rules related to consumer protection.[186] For example, Germany has some 120 laws concerning consumer protection on the federal level alone. Of course, laws in the EU may differ considerably at the national level.[187] On the other hand, the EU itself has some 80 laws and by-laws concerning consumer protection.[188] There are not enough laws in place, nor are the laws in place sufficiently broad in scope to assist consumers during disputes.[189] Arguably, consumers are more frustrated than they are helped by this puzzling, multi-layered abundance of laws. The dilution of the protections offered by even the most protective national regulatory regimes may be unfavorably received by residents of such jurisdictions.[190]

Combating complexity, the principle of subsidiarity is generally applied to harmonize relevant provisions within the EU.[191] That is, the EU chooses partial harmonization.[192] Member states' laws control

---

[184] Council Resolution Concerning the Future Orientation of the Policy of the European Economic Community for the Protection and Promotion of Consumer Interest, 1986 O.J. (C 167) 1.

[185] Article 100A of the Single European Act declares that future measures would only require the approval of the majority of member states, rather than a unanimous approval, in order to be adopted. This provision was seen as necessary to ensure the adoption of the controversial legislation needed to remove internal borders. See further Micklitz, *supra* note 181, at 295.

[186] See further Opinion on Consumer Protection and Completion of the Internal Market, 1991 O.J. (C 339); see also Three Year Action Plan of Consumer Policy in the EEC (1990–1992), COM (90) 98 final 1.

[187] See further A.R. Young, Towards a More Vigorous European Consumer Policy?, 7 *European Business Journal*, No. 4, 34 (1995).

[188] Out-of-Court Dispute Settlement Trans-Border Electronic Commerce, Joint Research Center, European Commission, <http://dsa-isis.jrc.it/ADR/consumer.htm>.

[189] See further Commission Green Paper on Guarantees for Consumer Goods and After-Sales Services, COM (93) 509 final at 53.

[190] See Consumer Protection: An Essential Priority for Cross-Border Commercial Communications, Com. Comm., June 1997, at 6.

[191] For a further description of subsidiarity, see G.A. Bermann, Taking Subsidiarity Seriously: Federalism in the European Community and the United States, 94 *Columbia Law Review*, 403 (1994).

[192] Harmonization is a technical term of European Community law that refers to formal attempts to increase the similarity of legal measures in member states. See further P.M. Schwartz, European Data Protection Law and Restrictions on

distinct areas; the EU is restrained from resolving issues that appear to be appropriately in the hands of a member state.[193] The EU shall take action in areas falling outside the exclusive competence only if and insofar as the objectives of the proposed action cannot be sufficiently achieved by member states.

But this principle is not appropriate for consumer protection legislation.[194] It gives rise to the situation wherein all powers other than that of exclusive competence remain vested in the member states while the community can exercise these powers only in limited situations.[195] In view of this problem, the commission has proposed directives calling for minimal harmonization of existing national laws.[196]

Bearing this background in mind, we come back to electronic commerce. Supposing member states were to be in the awkward situation of trying to deal with a business that rejects national borders and protect consuming residents of their state, and keeping in mind that different states have different laws, the EU must step in to regulate. The application of a unitary set of rules concerning consumer protection in electronic commerce would be desirable. The EU may also establish a set of rules containing basic principles of consumer protection laws applicable within all member states. To minimize dissenting opinions, it should first formulate those laws member states consider mandatory for the protection of their consumers. The basic EU policy protects consumers[197] from overzealous electronic commerce that by way of cutting a few legal contractual corners to gain advantages over competitors unintentionally harm consumers.[198]

EU measures address the consumer's need for easily accessible legal remedies by adopting a high level of consumer protection and

International Data Flows, 80 *Iowa L. Rev.* 481 (1995); G.A. Bermann et al., *Cases and Materials on European Community Law* 430 (1993).

[193] H. McGregor, Law on a Boundless Frontier: The Internet and International Law, 88 *Ky. L.J.* 980 (Summer, 1999/Summer, 2000).

[194] It is regarded as a thorn in the side of attempts at consumer policy legislation. See further Evans, *supra* note 181, at 19.

[195] A.G. Toth, The Principle of Subsidiarity in the Maastricht Treaty, 29 *Common Market Law Review*, 1079, 1103 (1992).

[196] See further S. Prechal, *Directives in European Community Law* 3 (1995).

[197] European Council Resolution of 28 June 1999 on Community Consumer Policy 1999 to 2001, 1999 O.J. (C 206) at 1, section II (4).

[198] See further J.R. Aguilar, Over the Rainbow European and American Consumer Protection Policy and Remedy Conflicts on the Internet and a Possible Solution, 4 *International Journal of Communications Law and Policy*, 15–16 (Winter, 1999/2000).

incorporating pro-consumer minimal directives within EU policy.[199] Two notable conventions have focused on the issue of dispute resolution at the EU level: the 1980 Rome Convention on the Law Applicable to Contractual Obligations (Rome Convention) and the 1968 Brussels Convention on Jurisdiction and the Enforcement of Judgments in Civil and Commercial Matters (Brussels Convention). The next chapter shall address how these conventions suggest confronting dispute issues arising out of electronic commerce.

Most regulations have singled out consumer issues. The directive on the protection of consumers in respect to distance contracts covers all consumer contracts concerning goods or services, which could include electronic commerce.[200] The newly passed Directive on Electronic Commerce advocates this state-of-origin principle: an information society shall comply with the national provisions applicable in the member state where it is established.[201] But according to the Annex to the Directive, this provision is not applicable to consumer contracts. This exemption of consumer contracts from the applicability of the state-of-origin principle returns consumers to the law of the state wherein he resides. This may sound ridiculous,[202] but if the state-of-origin principle were to be used in such cases, consumers could have difficulties assessing their rights according to the law of the state where the service is received. Neither principle is problem-free.

---

[199] Opinion of the Economic and Social Comm. On the 'Communication from the Comm'n to the Council, the European Parliament, the Economic and Social Comm. and the Comm. of the Regions: A European Initiative in Electronic Commerce, 1998 O.J. (c 019) at 72, P21.4(1); the Fed. Republic of Germany and the Eur. Comm'n Have jointly Organized the Eur. Ministerial Conference Entitled "Global Info. Networks: Realizing the Potential", Bonn, 6–8 July 1997, at P22, at <http://www2.echo.lu/bonn/final.html>; Opinion of the Economic and Social Comm. on the 'Single Market and Consumer Protection: Opportunities and Obstacles, 1995 O.J. (C 039) at 55, section 2.2.2.2.

[200] For further discussion, see P. Stoll & B. Goller, Electronic Commerce and the Internet, 41 *German Yearbook of International Law* 163 (1998).

[201] See Article 3(1) of the directive. This principle is supported by Article 3(3) in conjunction with the appendix for this directive for copyrights, related rights, topography and database protection, in particular, and for all other industrial property rights, e.g., trademarks, to the extent that the traditional principle of territoriality applies to these rights. See also the Berne Convention and Trade Related Aspects of Intellectual Property (TRIPs) as well as the WIPO Copyright Treaty.

[202] See further M. Lehmann, Electronic Commerce and Consumer Protection in Europe, *17 Santa Clara Computer & High Technology Law Journal*, 106–107 (December, 2000).

Nevertheless, the directive provides assurance for court actions, which is important to the protection of consumers.[203] Member states should ensure that appropriate court actions are available and examine the need to provide access to judicial procedures by appropriate electronic means.

In light of the problems existing in dispute resolution for electronic commerce, the EU has also recommended out-of-court dispute settlement mechanisms. Opening the door to ADR mechanisms, this suggestion is made in the directive on electronic commerce. According to Article 17, each member state shall be required to amend legislation liable to hamper the use of schemes for the out-of-court settlement of disputes through electronic channels.[204] The amendment promises to ensure that the out-of-court scheme shall function genuinely and effectively in law and in practice, even across borders.[205]

3.3.3. *Analysis*

New threats to consumer protection call for new protective rules and measures. We should recognize the fact that better consumer protection in online environments shall have a positive impact on the further development of electronic commerce and thereby on merchants. Generally speaking, if electronic commerce is to thrive, consumers must be provided with at least the same guarantees they would be provided with in the more traditional marketplace.[206]

The US and the EU have affirmed the importance of protecting a new breed of consumers. With the rise of electronic commerce, the role of consumers has changed dramatically. While consumers were formerly an inactive body, today they have power in transactions.[207]

---

[203] Article 18(1) of the directive suggests member states ensure that effective court actions can be brought against information society services by allowing the rapid adoption of interim measures designed to remedy any alleged infringement and to prevent any further impairment of the interests involved.

[204] See further Article 17 of the directive, which provides for the possible use of out-of-court dispute settlement and the relevant applicant principles for settling disputes: community law, the principle of independence and transparency, adversarial techniques, procedural efficacy, legality of the decision and freedom of the parties and of representation.

[205] Legislative Acts and Other Instruments, Council of the European Union, 14263/1/99 REV1, Brussels, 28 February 2000 (OR.en).

[206] See S. Baker & M. France, Taming the Wild, Wild Web: With-out Strong Laws, the Net's Growth Will be Stunted, *Bus. Wk.*, October 4, 1999, at 154.

[207] The consumer is king, commanding in virtue of the way he uses his money.

Sellers are now in a relatively passive position. Their job is to simply to paste that product information it becomes the responsibility of consumers to evaluate and make active decisions upon.

Where the specific field of dispute resolution is concerned, both the US and the EU realize the best way to protect consumers could be to provide them with appropriate measures for redress. Consumer protection groups have created forums where consumers can both submit e-mail-based complaints when dissatisfied with advertisements, goods or services, and accuse violators of self-regulatory codes of ethics.[208]

While consumer protection can take on different forms, dispute resolution mechanisms are its final insurance. Standards for dispute management are ultimately more attractive to regulators than less formal voluntary arrangements since they can encourage more consistent treatment of consumer interests.[209] In light of government experience, protection offered by state power is trusted. Some consumers even seek sanctuary in the court. In order to accommodate the special character of modern business without straying too far from tradition, ADR mechanisms for dispute resolution very wisely entail state enforcement support.[210]

Policy for consumer protection in electronic commerce dispute resolution must extend beyond national limits. Individual states lack the ability and initiative to adequately address issues related to consumer protection in the context of electronic commerce. Many of the issues that arise from cross-border disputes are exacerbated by the fact that deceptive marketing practice laws vary from one jurisdiction to another. Possible baseline electronic consumer policies should be

---

See further P. Smith & D. Swann, *Protecting the Consumer* 8 (1979); see also G.P. Penz, *Consumer Sovereignty and Human Interests* (1986).

[208] For example, web portals such as Yahoo! and new technology by a California-based software producer provide a space for consumer complaints. See further A. Endeshaw, The Law Vis-á-Vis Electronic Commerce, in S.M. Rahman & M.S. Raisinghani (Eds.), *Electronic Commerce: Opportunity and Challenge*, 371 (IDEA Group Publishing, 2000). For description of the new software, see Start-Up is Unveiling Software to Let Users Annotate Web Sites, *The Wall Street Journal* April 17, 1999, B13.

[209] A. McChesney, Feasibility Studies for New Standards Relating to Consumers and Electronic Commerce, 14 February, 2000, <http://strategis.ic.gc.ca/SSG/ca01275e.html>.

[210] The ISA believes that the most effective solution will ultimately be found through technology and organisation, and its members are committed to help in finding such a solution. See further Internet Alliance, ISA Addresses Unsolicited Bulk E-Mail, June 24, 1997, <http://www.isa.net/news/970624.html>.

applicable to cross-border transactions to which all or most countries can subscribe.[211]

OECD Member States have recognized the necessity of an international coordinated approach to deal with the issue of dispute resolution in electronic commerce. In one important document formulated by the OECD, Guidelines for Consumer Protection in the Context of Electronic Commerce, guidelines for consumer protection in dispute resolution and redress aim to protect consumers participating in electronic commerce without erecting barriers to trade.

The guidelines serve as a recommendation to governments, businesses, consumers, and their representatives of the characteristics of effective consumer protection for electronic commerce.[212] The thinking behind them is similar to that of the US and EU. Firstly, applicable law and jurisdiction are singled out for possible modification. No detailed formulation of the new applicable law or principle of jurisdiction is pointed out, but the guidelines do describe features of appropriate modifications. Fairness, they suggest, is one of the most important factors in realizing consumer protection. The purpose of the fairness is to offer consumers a level of protection not less than that afforded in other forms of commerce and to provide consumers with meaningful access to fair and timely dispute resolution and redress without undue cost or burden.[213] To accomplish fairness, one must provide a framework for rectifying unfairness.

As said in the guidelines, businesses, consumer representatives, and governments should work together to continue to use and develop fair, effective, and transparent self-regulatory and other procedures, which provide consumers with the option of mechanisms to resolve their disputes arising out of consumer transactions.[214] Moreover, these efforts should be pursued at an international level. To achieve the maximum benefits of the new arrangements, modern technology

---

[211] Rothchild, *supra* note 125, at 972.

[212] Recommendation of the OECD Council Concerning Guidelines for Consumer Protection in the Context of Electronic Commerce, <http://www.ftc.gov/opa/1999/9912/oecdguide.htm>. Nothing contained shall restrict any party from exceeding these guidelines nor preclude member states from retaining or adopting more stringent provisions to protect consumers online.

[213] Recommendation of the OECD Council Concerning Guidelines for Consumer Protection in the Context of Electronic Commerce, Annex, Part Two (VI) (A), paragraph 3, <http://www.ftc.gov/opa/1999/9912/oecdguide.htm>.

[214] See further *id.*, Part Two (VI) (B).

should be used to enhance consumer awareness and freedom of choice.

From the analysis above, we can conclude that the international community has reached a consensus on the general attitude toward consumer protection. While making improvements on court procedures and the application of principles, new means should be found out to accommodate the new needs of electronic commerce. The means should enable the development of new shops operating in a responsible manner and resolving disputes conveniently online and, along with them, greater choices and more competition.[215] With new facilities in place, consumers shall certainly be protected from unnecessary costs of compliance with duplicative or inconsistent regulations.

4. *Conclusion*

Approaching the end of the twentieth century, people witnessed the rapid development of a digital economy, which overturned normal commercial transactions. To fully appreciate the legal complexities of regulating this economy, one must first understand the magnitude and nature of the Internet, which justify the policy of self-regulation and international orientation.[216] These two policies are closely related and can never be separately discussed. They can, on the other hand, be easily distinguished from the policy of consumer protection. The first two policies define the procedural aspects of the new mechanism; the latter one concerns the substantial side.

Consumer protection policy is indispensable in building consumer confidence and establishing a balanced relationship between businesses and consumer in transactions.[217] Electronic commerce, still at a fledging stage, urgently needs consumer participation. The first step

---

[215] The Electronic Commerce and Consumer Protection Group, a coalition of leading companies in the Internet, online, and electronic commerce industries, developed the guidelines for business-to-consumer transactions as a first step toward establishing a global jurisdictional framework for electronic commerce. See <http://www.ecommercegroup.org/statement.htm>.

[216] G. Anthes, The History of the Future: As the ARPNET Turns 25, Its Founders Reunite to Talk About the Network That Became the Internet, *Computer World*, October 3, 1994, at 101.

[217] Responsible businesses often find it advantageous to take steps both to build consumer confidence in their industries and to protect consumers from being lured away by deceptive practices. See further Starek, *supra* note 160, at 697, 695.

to activate consumers shall be to provide a complete, trustable structure for transacting procedures. As the OECD says, the same level of protection provided by the laws and practices that apply to other forms of commerce should be afforded to consumers participating in commercial activities through the use of global networks.[218]

By way of information transfer, the Internet has advanced consumer protection in modern business. However, complete consumer protection shall need measures from structural and substantial side as well. Acknowledging the importance of consumer protection in electronic commerce, various countries and international organisations have while making wide use of the Internet simultaneously established projects to deal with providing protection to consumers.

How can we ensure consumer protection in dispute resolution? How, in other words, can we protect consumers as well as the possibility of their procuring benefits? It is this important question that links the main three policies. The value of the present remedies for electronic commerce has been largely limited by difficulties faced in enforcing redress mechanisms. Only when these three policies are upheld shall we achieve success in dispute resolution cases and observe the most impressive developments of electronic commerce.

---

[218] OECD Recommendation Consumer Protection, *supra* note 213, DSTI/CP (98) 4, point 27. This statement should be seen as the minimum basis for offering protection to consumers.

CHAPTER FOUR

DEVELOPMENT OF LITIGATION FOR ELECTRONIC COMMERCE

1. *Introduction*

Computer technology has changed the administration of litigation. It has sped up the writing of court records, notes of proceedings and judgments, and alongside presenting new means for disseminating and recording evidence it has offered new forms of evidence like videoconferences and emails. Using the Internet, judges can also more efficiently retrieve necessary documents and consult experts. That said, the impact of the Internet on litigation goes beyond such methodological improvements.[1] Legal principles are also affected. Developments in electronic commerce require a new perspective on contract law and the law of evidence, for example, the validity of electronic signature; meanwhile, new dimensions shall arise requiring the courts to protect participants' rights as regards technological inventions. In view of all those changes, litigation should still be able to make decisions yielding maximum fairness to all involved parties and also society at large.

The Internet poses certain challenges to legislation. The trans-jurisdictional, or more exactly a-jurisdictional character of the Internet has become the focal point for most legal issues. Legal applications based on geographical locations are under threat. The emergence of business-to-consumer commerce, in particular, has necessitated altering not only the traditional conception of consumers, which is that they are weak parties in transactions, but also the conception of international transactions in general. Because of the general ambiguity of legal structures to deal with electronic commerce, it has been proven to be especially difficult to justify mechanisms for dispute resolution in such cases.

---

[1] P.D. Carrington, Virtual Civil Litigation: A Visit to John Bunyan's Celestial City, 98 *Colum. L. Rev.* 1516 (1998).

The last few years have seen the beginnings of cyberspace litigation with disputes involving copyright,[2] obscenity,[3] libel,[4] and free expression[5] resulting in judicial decisions. Though other forms of resolution should be developed to complement litigation, litigation will remain the guarantor of final justice. Access to a judge (*juge d'appui*)[6] in the course of the ADR, for example, may be helpful to solve an unexpected problem[7] and facilitate a smooth and successful process. It is very important in the first place to provide a complete structure for litigation in light of which other mechanisms will be successfully devised.

It is vital to establish a waterproof framework for jurisdiction in litigation. There are three issues at hand: adjudicative jurisdiction, choice of law, and jurisdiction of enforcement.[8] Though separate and unique, these are also interdependent and often involve similar considerations.

When litigation is called upon, the decision regarding which court shall have the jurisdiction to make judgment is the first important problem encountered. If the wrong court makes a judgment, procedural injustice will be cited as a reason for refusing enforcement.

Once adjudicative jurisdiction is confirmed, the next important decision regards the choosing applicable law.[9] Appropriate judgments are made according to the facts and rules selected.[10]

---

[2] For example, *Religious Tech. Ctr. V. Netcom On-line Com. Serv.*, 907 F.Supp. 1361 (N.D. Cal. 1995).

[3] For example, *United States v. Thomas*, 74 F. 3d 701 (6th Cir. 1996).

[4] For example, *Stratton Oakmont, Inc. v. Prodigy Serv. Co.*, No. 31063/94, 1995 N.Y. Misc. LEXIS 229 (N.Y. Sup. Ct. May 24, 1995).

[5] For example, *ACLU v. Reno*, 929 F.Supp. 824 (1996).

[6] While facing difficulties in organizing, implementing, and enforcing the arbitration procedure, the parties or the court of arbitration can refer to a *juge d'appui*, who is complementary to and co-operates in the arbitration procedure. He may be asked to intervene in the constitution of the court of arbitration (either *ab initio* or during the course of arbitration, if the tribunal is truncated and the remaining parties or arbitrators cannot reach agreement to rectify the situation). He can also be called upon in cases of urgency, (although all national laws do not provide for this role), in cases of difficulty in obtaining proof (more rarely), and to compel the enforcement of measures ordered by the court of arbitration. His exact role depends on the law applicable to the arbitration, which is different to that applicable to the root of the dispute, and to that applicable to the arbitration procedure itself.

[7] For example, the service provider disappears during the arbitration procedure, or there is a serious violation of the principles of independence and impartiality.

[8] See L. Henkin et al., *International Law* 1046 (3rd Eds. 1993).

[9] See for example M.S. Yeo & M. Berliri, Conflict Looms Over Choice of Law in Internet Transactions, 4 *Electronic Commerce & Law Report*, 85 (1998).

[10] Restatement (3rd) of Foreign Relations Law of the United States, section 401 (1987).

Electronic commerce poses challenges for the first two issues. The existing rules and agreements concerning enforcement of judgments shall still to a large extent apply in the case of electronic commerce. Thus, it is the purpose of this chapter to treat the first two major problems with a view to possibilities for the use of technology in litigation.

2. *Adjudicative Jurisdiction*

2.1. *Basic Understanding of Jurisdiction in the Era of Technology*

Adjudicative jurisdiction is defined as a state's authority to subject persons or things to the process of its courts or administrative tribunals.[11] The process generally involves one's selecting one court out of many before bringing a case to court and courts using discretionary power to decide whether they can handle the case before taking it. It is sometimes considered to be the gateway to the success of litigation.

The Internet is not a physical entity, and yet the existing legal precedent for adjudicative jurisdiction is limited by a complex system of physical borders on the local, state, national, and international level.[12] Adjudicative jurisdiction has traditionally been based on territorial connection, with courts being allocated indisputable power over acts within their administrative territory. In traditional international trade, territorial connections are identifiable because the players exist in the visible world. But this is not the case for electronic commerce, which happens in virtual space and whose players, indifferent to geographic location, are everywhere and nowhere.[13] There is no framework for the objective allocation of adjudicative jurisdiction.[14]

Considering the new face of commerce, some lawyers have called

---

[11] See Restatement (3rd) of Foreign Relations 402 (1986).

[12] C.N. Davis, Personal Jurisdiction in Online Expression Cases: Rejecting Minimum Contacts in Favor of Affirmative Acts, 14 *International Review of Law, Computer & Technology*, 44 (2000).

[13] The trouble with cyberspace is that there is no "there" there. See further R. Resnick, Cybertort: The New Era, *National Law Journal*, July 18, 1994, at A1.

[14] V. Heiskanen, Dispute Resolution in International Electronic Commerce, 16 (3) *Journal of International Arbitration*, 36 (1999).

for a new jurisdictional system to accommodate electronic commerce.[15] As territorial connecting factors have been made indeterminate, they suggest the invention of a new connecting factor. However, this idea has not received much support.

In principle, electronic commerce still belongs to the known world of international trade. For one, basic international commercial interests remain constant. Moreover, although electronic commerce can accomplish entire transactions online, many Internet-based businesses use additional, traditional communicative means. Systems of communication always change, but they should not entail the development of specific laws. Based on traditional commercial theory, electronic commerce does not require an individual system of law to deal with the problems occasioned by the Internet.[16]

Furthermore, the mere possibility that individuals might be able to escape the jurisdiction of one nation by relocating computer-mediated information and services to another nation is an insufficient reason to formally create a separate jurisdiction for electronic commerce.[17] It is more advisable to explore resolution based on present jurisdictional theory.[18] New features to suit the special character of electronic commerce can be imposed on existing law.

The US and the EU have been at the forefront of dealings with electronic commerce, and it is thus useful to examine their practices here.

2.2. *US Case Law in Adjudicative Jurisdiction*

2.2.1. *Basic Theory in Adjudicative Jurisdiction*

Generally, the jurisdiction of the courts of a state to adjudicate a person or thing is based on some link between the forum and the person or thing over which jurisdiction is to be exercised.[19] The US

[15] D.R. Johnson & D. Post, Law and Borders—The Rise of Law in Cyberspace, 48 *Stanford Law Review*, 1357, 1367 (1996).

[16] Just as E.M. Katsh mentioned in Cybertime, Cyberspace and Cyberlaw, *Journal of Online Law* (1995), article 1, paragraph 36, when the law changes with every new event, then there is no law. See also L. Fuller, *The Morality of Law* 37 (1964).

[17] J.M. Oberding & T. Norderhaug, *A Separate Jurisdiction for Cyberspace?* <http://www.ascusc.org/jcmc/vol1/issue1/juris.html>.

[18] Whether or not there should be separate jurisdiction for the Internet is under discussion. Most believe that forming appropriate jurisdictional principles for the Internet will require mixing existing concepts with innovative, new technological solutions and industry self-regulatory initiatives.

[19] Prospectus: Transnational Issues in Cyberspace: A Project on the Law Relating to Jurisdiction, <http://www.abanet.org/buslaw/cyber/initiatives/prospect.html>.

has developed two types of adjudicative jurisdiction: personal jurisdiction and *in rem* jurisdiction (and a third type, *quasi in rem* jurisdiction).[20] The former concerns personal contact: when a person has connections with a certain state, the state shall have the jurisdiction. The relationship of a person to a state determines the existence of jurisdiction.[21] Where the person resides is determined on the basis of criteria regarding assets such as their physical presence.[22]

Jurisdiction has historically depended upon control held over a certain person or object. Late in the 19th century, for example, an American citizen or company was only subject to the jurisdiction of the courts that presided over fora in which the citizen or company had a physical presence.[23] But principles concerning jurisdiction must always be developed to meet new demands. With the rapid increase of international trade in the second part of 20th century, in large part a reaction to developments in communication, new and necessary principles developed.

Today, with improved communication and Internet-based business, it is difficult to determine the location of relevant property and to establish a relevant connection between transactions and the forum states. The real challenge for courts is to establish this connection.[24]

2.2.2. In Rem *Jurisdiction*

An *in rem* proceeding involves the exercise of control over property found within the forum state.[25] Two types of *in rem* jurisdiction can be identified: true *in rem* proceedings and *quasi in rem* proceedings.

---

[20] This was established in the landmark *Pennoyer v. Neff* decision, 95 U.S. (1877).

[21] Such a relationship test is the starting point of any personal jurisdiction analysis according to most US international civil procedure laws. See further S. Wilske & T. Schiller, International Jurisdiction in Cyberspace: Which States may Regulate the Internet?, 50 *Fed. Comm. L.J.* 117, 146 (1997).

[22] See Restatement (Second) Conflicts of Laws, Chapter 3, Introductory Note (1971); and *Shaffer v. Heitner*, 433 U.S. 186, 199 (1977). If a court's jurisdiction is based on its authority over the defendant's person, the action and judgment are denominated '*in personam*.' If jurisdiction is based on the court's power over property within its territory, the action is called '*in rem*' or '*quasi in rem*'. See also *Black's Law Dictionary* 854 (6th Ed. 1990).

[23] See *Pennoyer v. Neff*, 95 U.S. (5 Otto) 714 (1877).

[24] Courts face multiple procedural as well as substantive problems in dealing with Internet suits. See further S.R. Salbu, Who Should Govern the Internet? Monitoring and Supporting a New Frontier, 11 *Harv. J.L. & Tech.* 429, 435 (1998).

[25] For a detailed description of *in rem* jurisdiction, see T.R. Lee, *In Rem* Jurisdiction in Cyberspace, 75 *Washington Law Review*, 111–112 (2000).

A true *in rem* proceeding is one in which the plaintiff asks the court to determine the identity of those who have title to the property or thing in question, whether they are named in the action or not.[26] There are two types of *quasi in rem* jurisdiction. The first type differs from true *in rem* jurisdiction in that the plaintiff asserts an interest in the property as against specifically identified individuals and the judgment affects the rights of those individuals.[27] The second type seeks to establish an interest in the defendant's property as a basis for exercising jurisdiction over the defendant when personal jurisdiction is not available.[28]

In rem jurisdiction is based on the location of certain property. Thus, it is important to tackle the difficult tasks of first determining what should be regarded as property in electronic commerce and then locating that property. In normal situations, goods or real estate would easily be identified. But as participants in electronic commerce are unknown in consumer transactions, it is impossible, or takes efforts to ascertain the location of relevant property.

Steps can be taken to resolve these issues. It has been suggested that in the case of domain disputes, for example, the address of domain can serve as property and the location of the related server can be regarded as the relevant environment for *in rem* jurisdiction.[29] Pursuant to the Anticybersquatting Consumer Protection Act,[30] *in rem* jurisdiction may exist in disputes regarding forfeiture and cancellation of domain names or in cases that involve transferring a name to its rightful owner.[31] Occasionally domain name registrants misrepresent themselves, trafficking in, or using names in bad faith with intentions to profit.

In *Porsche Cars N. Am., Inc. v. PORSCH.COM*, the court refused assertion of *in rem* jurisdiction on account of the possibility of its being inconsistent with the language of the Lanham Act, its possibly violating due process, and the technical problem of location.[32]

---

[26] Restatement (second) of Judgments, section 6 cmt. a (1982).

[27] 16 J.Wm. Moore et al., *Moore's Federal Practice*, 108.70 [1] (3rd Ed. 1999).

[28] Restatement (Second) of Conflict of Laws, section 66 cmt. a (1971); Restatement (Second) of Judgments, section 6 cmt. a (1982).

[29] Another view is that personal jurisdiction over property, asserted by attachment, is a form of *in rem* jurisdiction. See further H.H. Perritt, Jr., *Note on Personal Jurisdiction*, <http://mantle.sbs.umass.edu/vmag/PJ2.HTM>.

[30] This Act took effect on November 29, 1999.

[31] See 15 U.S.C. section 1125 (d)(2)(D)(I).

[32] 51 F.Supp. 2d 707, 711–712 (E.D. Va. 1999).

This did not constitute obstruction[33] because the issue of located relevant property was out of the court's hands. For purposes of an *in rem* action, the domain name must be deemed to be situated in the judicial district where the domain name register, registry, or other domain name authority that registered or assigned the domain name is located or where "documents sufficient to establish control and authority regarding the disposition of the registration and use of the domain name are deposited with the court."[34]

Notably, it is now only theoretically possible to sue a domain name itself (*in rem*) rather than suing a person or corporation (*in personam* jurisdiction) and the reality is that *in rem* proceedings are adjusted under the *International Shoe* standard, which will be examined later. Presently, it makes no difference for purposes of domain name analysis whether the suit is *in personam* or *in rem*.[35]

Domain name disputes are only a small area of *in rem* jurisdiction. Further analysis is needed to determine *in rem* jurisdiction in a broader sense.

2.2.3. *Personal Jurisdiction*

Personal jurisdiction or so-called *in personam* jurisdiction refers to the power of a court or similar tribunal over an individual or property.[36] Since plaintiffs choose a court in which to file a lawsuit, the personal jurisdiction doctrine acts as a constitutional standard that limits a court's power by protecting an individual's interest in not being subject to the binding judgments of a forum with which he has established no meaningful contacts, ties, or relations.[37]

In cases where the defendant is frequently outside the jurisdiction of the state where the damage occurred and thus is the one commonly asserted in the case of electronic commerce, the applicability

---

[33] This has been elaborated by T.R. Lee, *supra* note 25.

[34] 15 U.S.C. section 1125 (d)(2)(C).

[35] See further *Shaffer v. Heitner*, 433 U.S. 212 (1977).

[36] Perritt, *supra* note 29.

[37] *International Shoe Co. v. Washington*, 326 U.S. 310, 319 (1945). International Shoe Co. (defendant), a Delaware Corporation headquartered in Missouri, has places of business in several states, but not the State of Washington, where the corporation manufactures and distributes its products. But 12 agents were employed in Washington to display merchandise and accept orders. A suit was brought against the corporation in a Washington court. The court ruled that defendant's business activities in Washington rendered it amenable to suit in that state.

of personal jurisdiction becomes especially important. The *Pennoyer*[38] and *International Shoe* Courts have faced difficulties similar to those concerning the applicability of personal jurisdiction in electronic commerce today.[39] As the US hosts the largest number of Internet users in the world and has the most complete network for electronic commerce, it is not surprising that lots of cases have been brought to court for resolution there, and the American court proved to be rather creative in dealing with the jurisdictional issue.[40] It recognized two types of personal jurisdiction: general and specific jurisdiction.

2.2.3.1. General Jurisdiction

General jurisdiction is based on continuous and systematic or substantial connections between the person and the court.[41] Once general jurisdiction is obtained over a defendant, the court shall have jurisdiction in any lawsuit, even one which has no relation to the forum state. Generally, if an office is established carrying out business in a forum state, general jurisdiction can be inferred. The quality and quantity of the business' commercial interactions with residents shall determine whether it qualifies as continuous and systematic, subjecting the participants in electronic commerce to the state's general jurisdiction.[42]

---

[38] *Pennoyer v. Neff*, 95 U.S. 714 (1877). Mitchell, an Oregon resident, sued Neff for unpaid legal fees. At the time, Neff was a non-resident who was not personally served with process, and did not appear. Default was entered after constructive notice by publication. Neff had acquired 300 acres of land and Michell had the sheriff seize and sell theland. Pennoyer bought the land and Neff brought an action forward to recover possession of the land. The US Supreme Court affirmed the Circuit Court judgment by finding the Oregon state court judgment was invalid because (1) Neff was never personally served the summons and (2) the court did not have jurisdiction over his real property at the time the judgment was entered.

[39] I.S. Nathenson, Showdown at the Domain Name Corral: Property Rights and Personal Jurisdiction Over Squatters, Poachers and Other Parasites, 58 *U. Pitts. L. Rev.*, 991 (1997), <http://www.pitt.edu/~lawrev/58-4/articles/domain.htm>; see also M.N. Breen, Personal Jurisdiction and the Internet: "Shoehorning" Cyberspace into International Shoe, 8 *Seton Hall Const. L.J.* 779 (1998).

[40] For a complete description of the cases concerning personal jurisdiction and the Internet, see further M. D'Amico, *A Survey of the Current Cases of Personal Jurisdiction and the Internet*, <http://www.madcapps.com/~Writings/asurvey.htm>; see also D. Bender, *Emerging Personal Jurisdictional Issues on the Internet, in PLI's Second Annual Institute for Intellectual Property Law*, at 7, 10 (PLI Pat., Trademarks, and Literary Prop. Course Handbook Series No. 453, 1996); R.S. Zembek, Comment, Jurisdiction and the Internet: Fundamental Fairness in the Networked World of Cyberspace, 6 *Alb. L.J. Sci. & Tech.* 339, 367 (1996).

[41] See further J.W. Glannon, *Civil Procedure Examples and Explanation* 5 (2nd Ed. 1992); see also *Helicopteros Nacionales de Colombia v. Hall*, 466 U.S. 408, 414 (1984).

[42] T.P. Vartanian, The Confluence of International, Federal, and State Jurisdiction

Considering the nature of electronic commerce, the assertion of general jurisdiction is not popular.[43] There are not many model cases,[44] and more importantly, no general jurisdiction has thus far been asserted purely based on contacts through the Internet in the case of electronic commerce.

In *California Software, Inc. v. Reliability Research, Inc.*, the court held that the use of nationally-disseminated, computer-based information services and regular communications with forum residents through that service did not establish the minimum contacts necessary to support general jurisdiction.[45] And in one other recent case, *McDonough v. Fallon McElligott, Inc.*, the court held that the use of the agency's web site by the residents of the forum state could not by itself establish jurisdiction and the purchase of advertisements, which was unrelated to the cause of the action, was insufficient to support an assertion of general jurisdiction. Examination revealed that no residents of the forum state actually purchased this agency's products.[46] Perhaps if sufficient contact is established with the residents of the forum state and this agency, general jurisdiction will stand a chance.

General jurisdiction may be asserted based on a combination of non-Internet and Internet contacts. In *Mieczkowski v. Masco Corp.*,[47] the court held that the Internet connections alone were insufficient for the assertion of general jurisdiction. Though customers could shop, place orders, pay, track orders, and even communicate with personnel electronically on the defendant's web site, such were all deemed passive acts and not determinative of significant contact. But when combined with its non-Internet interactions, including mail order transactions between suppliers and customers, these Internet connections earned the defendant's general jurisdiction.[48] Whether

over E-commerce (Part II), *Journal of Internet Law*, <http://www.gcwf.com/articles/journal/jil_dec98_2.html>.

[43] As the developing standard for general jurisdiction is very high, it will likely only be applicable to large corporations that carry on significant, continuous business in a visible manner. See *Helicopteros Nacionales de Colombia, S.A. v. Hall*, 466 U.S. 408, 414–416, n. 9 (1984).

[44] Three other cases could also be noted here: *Millennium Enterprises, Inc. v. Millennium Music*, LP, No. 98-1058, 1999 WL 27060 (D. Or. January 4, 1999); *Grutkowski v. Steamboat Lake Guides & Outfitters, Inc.*, 1998 WL 962042 (E.D. Pa. December 28, 1998); *ESAB Group, Inc. v. Centricut, LLC*, 1999 WL 27514 (D.S.C. Jan. 15, 1999).

[45] 631 F.Supp. 1356 (C.D. Cal. 1986).

[46] No. 95-4037, 1996 U.S. Dist. LEXIS 15139 (S.D. Cal. Aug. 5, 1996).

[47] 997 F. Supp. 782 (E.D. Texas 1998).

[48] See further J.L. Gedid, *U.S. Judicial Decisions on E Commerce Jurisdiction*, <http://www.ilpf.org/confer/present99/gedidpr.htm>.

or not Internet contacts are enough to support general jurisdiction is still to be seen.

2.2.3.2. Specific Jurisdiction

Specific jurisdiction is based on the relationship of a specific action and the forum state. When business occurred in certain areas such jurisdiction was easy to determine, as each state possesses exclusive jurisdiction within its territory. However, as interstate business and travel increased during the Industrial Revolution, territorialism proved insufficient for asserting jurisdiction. Thus, the court made developments for persons outside certain territory, as evidenced in *International Shoe v. Washington*,[49] which laid the foundation for the modern theory of personal jurisdiction.

To assert specific jurisdiction, long-arm statute[50] and due process requirement conditions, which heighten scrutiny of assertions of judicial jurisdiction over foreign entities,[51] must be met. The long-arm statute concerns going out-of-state and bringing a nonresident defendant into the state to defend a lawsuit.[52] The court must initially determine whether the forum state's long-arm statute applies to the defendant.[53] When this purpose is met, then due process requirements under the constitution must be satisfied.[54]

[49] 326 U.S. 310 (1945).

[50] Long-arm statutes are state legislative acts which provide for personal jurisdiction, via substituted service of process, over persons or corporations which are non-residents of the state, and which voluntarily go into the state, directly or by agent, or communicate with persons in the state, for limited purposes, in actions which concern claims relating to the performance or execution of those purposes. See *Black's Law Dictionary* 942 (West, 6th Ed. 1990).

[51] See further G.B. Born, Reflections on Judicial Jurisdiction in International Cases, 17 *Ga. J. Int'l & Comp. L.* 1, 33 (1987).

[52] Glannon, *supra* note 41, at 26. See for example, N.Y.C.P.L.R., section 302 (a): New York Long-arm Statute; Calif. Code Civ. Pro., section 410.10: California Long-arm Statute; Conn. Gen. Stat. Ann., section 33–411 (c) (West 1997): Connecticut Long-arm Statute; Mass. Gen. Laws Ann., ch. 223A, 3 (West 1985): Massachusetts Long-arm Statute; Mo. Ann. Stat., 506.500 (West 1986): Missouri Long-arm Statute; Ohio Rev. Code Ann., 2307.382 (A) (Anderson 1995): Ohio Long-arm Statute.

[53] S.D. Jones, *Internet Use and Personal Jurisdiction: Have Mouse, Will Travel?* <http://www.ralaw.com/frame8118.html>.

[54] *Reynolds v International Amateur Athletic Federation*, 23 F. 3d, 1115 (6th Cir. 1994). The Due Process Clause demands that no State shall make or enforce any law which shall abridge the privileges or immunities of citizens of the United States; nor shall any State deprive any person of life, liberty, or property, without due process of law; nor deny to any person within its jurisdiction the equal protection of the law. See further U.S. Constitution Amend. XIV.

Due process requires that the defendant has only limited contacts within the forum state,[55] so as to preserve the sovereignty of the states in the federal system and to grant the right to a defendant to affiliate himself with one or another of those sovereigns.[56] The appropriate level of contact between defendant and forum state is judged as follows. Firstly, the defendant must have purposefully availed himself to the forum state.[57] In other words, the defendant must have purposefully directed action towards the forum state and revealed a substantial connection to the forum state.[58] In *Bensusan Restaurant Corp. v. King* case, the court ruled that the defendant's simple creation of a web site, that was available to any user who could find it on the Internet, was not an act of purposeful support.[59] Secondly, the contact of the defendant with the forum state must be sufficient to confer jurisdiction based on the relatedness of the contact to the cause of action.[60] It is important that the claim arises out of the defendant's contacts. Thirdly, the exercise of jurisdiction must be reasonable.[61] The defendant should reasonably expect to be brought to court,[62] particularly if most of the records of transaction exist within the state.

Due process further requires that maintenance of the suit in the forum state not offend traditional notions of fair play and substantial justice.[63] The court shall look into the extent of pre-litigation connections of the defendant with the forum state and then evaluate the fairness of asserting jurisdiction.[64] The Supreme Court has

---

[55] M.J. Raisch & R.I. Shaffer, *Introduction to Transnational Legal Transactions* 42 (New York 1995).

[56] See D.L. Burk, Jurisdiction in a World Without Borders, 1 *Va. J.L. & Tech.* 3, 26 (1997).

[57] This was refined in *Hansen v. Denckla*, 357 U.S. (1958).

[58] *Burger King Corp. v. Rudzewicz*, 471 U.S. 462, 475 (1985). See also D.L. Stott, Personal Jurisdiction in Cyberspace: the Constitutional Boundary of Minimum Contacts Limited to a Web Site, 15 *J. Marshall J. of Computer & Info. L.*, 824–825 (1997).

[59] *Bensusan Restaurant Corp. v. King*, 937 F.Supp. 310 (S.D.N.Y. 1996). Similar holdings can be found in *McDonough v. Fallon McElligott*, Inc., 1996 U.S. Dist. LEXIS 15139, No. 95-4037, slip op. (S.D.Cal. Aug. 6, 1996).

[60] J.C. Henry, *Establishing Personal Jurisdiction for Internet Transactions*, <http://www.law.stetson.edu/courses/computerlaw/papers/jhenryf97.htm>.

[61] A.F. Lowenfeld, *International Litigation and the Quest for Reasonableness* 19 (1996).

[62] *World-Wide Volkswagen Corp. v. Woodson*, 444 U.S. 286, 297 [1000 S.Ct. 559, 567, 62 L.Ed.2d 490] (1980).

[63] *International Shoe*, 326 U.S. 310, 316 [66 S.Ct. 154, 158, 90 L.Ed. 95] (1945).

[64] See *World-Wide Volkswagen Corp. v. Woodson*, 444 U.S. 286 (1980); see also *Burger*

identified five items for analysis: the burden on the defendant; the forum state's interest in adjudicating the dispute; the plaintiff's interest in obtaining convenient and effective relief; the interstate judicial system's interest in obtaining the most efficient resolution of controversies; and shared state interest in furthering fundamental substantive social policies.[65] In general practice, these items prove complementary. Once the first requirement is reached, the second one shall also be satisfied.[66]

As online interactivity between business partners becomes commonplace, the need for physical presence in a state is slowly disappearing.[67] In line with these developments, traditional jurisprudence is evolving as the courts grapple with the new medium for business.[68]

Regarding purposeful availment, the stream of commerce theory was developed in *Asahi v. Superior Court of California* Case. Traditionally, the theory dealt with product liability lawsuits where manufacturers and distributors and products were across state and international borders.[69] When a defendant placed its product in a nationwide stream of commerce, he was subject to the jurisdiction of the forum where his product caused harm, even though he neither directly sold the product in the forum nor was he aware that the product was sold there.[70] However, Judge O'Connor explained in the *Asahi* Case that the awareness of a defendant that its product has entered a forum state by the stream of commerce does not equate to an act purposefully offering oneself to a forum state.[71] Additional activities

---

King, 471 U.S. 462 (1985). See also G.L. Gassman, Internet Defamation: Jurisdiction in Cyberspace and the Public Figure Doctrine, 14 *J. Marshall J. of Computer & Info. L.*, 572 (1996).

[65] *Burger King*, 471 U.S. at 477.

[66] This could be explained, as the first requirement includes reasonableness, and thus has to a certain extent considers the issue of fairness as well.

[67] R.H. Trangsrud, The Federal Common Law of Personal Jurisdiction, 57 *Geo. Wash. L. Rev.* 849, 892 (1989).

[68] S. Cohen, Jurisdiction Over Cross Border Internet Infringements, *20 European Intellectual Property Review*, 296 (1998).

[69] See for example, *Gray v. American radiator & Standard Sanitary Corp.*, 176 N.E.2d 761 (Ill. 1961); *Asahi Metal industry Co. v. Superior Court of Cal.*, 480 U.S. 102 (1987). See also M.F. Noonan, Civil Procedure—Personal Jurisdiction: Evolution and Current Interpretation of the Stream of Commerce Test in the Third Circuit, 40 *Villanova Law Review* 779 (1995).

[70] M.H. Redish, Of New Wine and Old Bottles: Personal Jurisdiction, The Internet, and the Nature of Constitutional Evolution, 38 *Jurimetrics Journal*, 584 (1998).

[71] *Asahi*, 480 U.S. at 112.

by the defendant towards the forum state are required to satisfy minimum contact.[72] This approach might be appropriately characterized as a type of "stream-of-commerce plus" standard.[73] It has been widely supported by scholars and since become the main guiding theory for jurisdiction in electronic commerce cases, with *CompuServe v. Paterson* serving as a primary example.[74]

The remaining problem is determining what type of Internet activities could sufficiently justify jurisdiction by a court. American courts have grouped cases into three categories of activities along a "sliding scale,"[75] the basis for which is the level of interactivity and commercial activity involved in the case. The first case to make a distinction between a passive and an interactive web site was *Zippo Manufacturing Co. v. Zippo Dot Com, Inc.*[76]

The first category is clearly interactive in nature. It may involve repeated transmission of files or even contracts with consumers in the forum state, which constitutes doing business in the forum state and is thus indisputably under its jurisdiction.[77] Most cases that fall into this type concern the defendants receipt of a direct economic benefit from the Internet communications. The second category is the so-called case of the passive web site. The defendant merely posts advertisement or information online. He has no intention or reasonable expectation of being haled into the forum state, so no jurisdiction shall be asserted. The most problematic category of activities rests in the middle of these two sorts.[78] Players range from sites that

---

72 The "additional conduct" required in Judge O'Connor's view is actively indicating an intent or purpose to serve the market in the forum state, thus putting the defendant on notice that he may be susceptible to a particular forum's laws. See further *Asahi*, 480 U.S. at 112.

73 Redish, *supra* note 70, at 585.

74 *CompuServe, Inc. v. Paterson*, 89 F.3d 1257 (6th Cir. 1996).

75 R.L. Hoegle & C.P. Boam, The Internet and Jurisdiction: International Principles Emerge but Confrontation Looms, 3 *Journal of World Intellectual Property*, No. 1, 33 (2000). See also W.E. Agin, *Jurisdiction over Web Sites, or "Where Will I be Sued Next?"*, <http://www.agin.com/aigc/tic84.html>.

76 952 F.Supp. (W.D. Pa. 1997).

77 If a merchant knowingly conducts business with foreign residents, a court located in a foreign venue may exercise jurisdiction. Further elaboration of this point can be found in *Burger King*, 471 U.S. 475 (1985).

78 The general division line can be found in *CompuServe*, 89 F. 3d 1257, 1264–1265 (6th Cir. 1996). The "interactive" web site differs substantially from a "passive" web site in that it can engage in communications with potential consumers who are situated in a particular geographic location and can establish a pattern of geographically-specific activity through its contacts with those persons.

allow a user to send email to the company to sites that allow users to order products via an Internet transaction.[79] They are not passive since they involve information exchange, but cannot be categorized as businesses because the level of interaction is not high enough.[80] The condition for minimum contact requires that the defendants conduct business in the forum state. Accordingly, it is vital to understand what constitutes "conduct of business". We can know more from the following discussions.

The defendant in *Bensusan restaurant Corporation v. Richard B. King* owned a small bar in Missouri with the name of "The Blue Note" and set up a website under that name. The plaintiffs owned the famous New York Jazz Club called the Blue Note, a federally registered trademark. The defendant applied to dismiss the case for lack of personal jurisdiction. In dismissing the case, the court held that the defendant did not conduct his Internet activity with the intention of attracting the plaintiff's customers. Furthermore, the court held that although the web site was globally accessible, it was the intention of the defendant to attract local consumers. The court has no personal jurisdiction over non-residents when they do not intend to purposefully support the facilities of the forum state.[81] This case reveals court processes for evaluating interactivity and the meaning of conducting business.[82]

The choice between asserting jurisdiction or not asserting jurisdiction is not sufficient for dealing with cases involving the third type of activities. Realizing this problem, the court has further listed this hierarchy of activity types: (a) actual financial transaction over the Internet; (b) purchase and downloading of software via the Internet; (c) purchase information in the form of web pages; (d) sites that

[79] G.R. Cummins, Esq. & C.M. Cerasale, *Jurisdiction in Cyberspace: User Beware*, <http:/./www.gcwf.com/articles/interest/interest_23.html>.

[80] *Zippo*, 952 F. Supp. 1124 (W.D. Pa. 1997).

[81] *Bensusan*, 937 F.Supp. (S.D.N.Y.), confirmed by the U.S. Court of Appeals (2nd. Cir.) on Sept. 10, 1997. See also O. Renault, *Jurisdiction and the Internet: Are Traditional Rules Enough?* <http://www.law.ualberta.ca/alri/ulc/current/ejurisd.htm>.

[82] See also a recent case *American Information Corporation v. American Infometrics, Inc.*, Memorandum Opinion delivered on April 12, 2001, by Motz, District Judge; F.R.Civ.P.Sec. 12 (b)(2). It concludes that maintenance of a web site that permits basic inquiries through a form and accepts job applications does not establish minimum contacts sufficient for personal jurisdiction in the absence of any evidence that any resident of the forum state has ever contracted with or even contacted the company. For discussion, see further U.S. District Court for Maryland: Targeting Approach to Internet Jurisdiction, *Computer Und Recht International*, No. 3, 79–81 (2001).

solicit and obtain user information; (e) sites through which the viewer can browse; (f) static home pages.[83] As regards interactivity and commercial nature, the court shall have jurisdiction based on either of the first three types of activities, while no jurisdiction for the next three types.

Even with a standardized list of activities, the courts shall have to look at the extent of interaction possible at each web site individually to decide upon appropriate jurisdiction. In practice, the court may consider the following factors in evaluating the nature of a web site:[84] (a) whether the web site is commercial in nature;[85] (2) whether the defendant has entered contracts with residents of the forum;[86] (3) whether the web site allows users to register online for a commercial mailing list;[87] (4) whether the defendant gains profits out of its contacts with the forum residents;[88] (5) whether the web site attracts a high number of actual hits from forum residents;[89] (6) whether the defendant has contacted the forum through several different means;[90] (7) whether the defendant advertises elsewhere on the Internet;[91] and (8) whether the web site provides a toll-free telephone number.[92] These factors have been considered in different cases focusing on the web site operator's intent and conduct,[93] the goal of which has

[83] This was another approach to evaluating whether a party has sufficient minimum contacts with a forum State. This six-tier hierarchy was proposed by E. Schneiderman & R. Kornreich in their article Personal Jurisdiction and Internet Commerce, *New York Law Journal*, (June 4th, 1997). See also *The Law of Internet Jurisdiction*, <http://www.unc.edu/~deweyma/law.html>.

[84] See further E.G. Gunnells & A.G. Mersereau, *Personal Jurisdiction Issues in Conducting Business Over the Internet*, <http://www.hicksmaloof.com/ln7.html>.

[85] International Star Registry of Illinois, No. 98-C-6823, 1999 WL 300285; *ESAB Group, Inc. v. Centricut, LLC*, 34F. Supp. 2d323, 330–331 (D.S.C. 1999); *Mieczkowski v. Masco Corp.*, 997 F.Supp. 782, 786 (E.D. Tex. 1998); *Gary Scott International, Inc. v. Baroudi*, 981 F.Supp. 714, 717 (D. Mass. 1997); *Superguide Corp. v. Kegan*, 987 F. Supp. 481, 485–486 (W.D.N.C. 1997).

[86] *Digital Equip. Corp. v. Altavista Tech., Inc.*, 960 F.Supp. 456, 464 (D. Mass. 1997).

[87] *Maritz, Inc. v. Cybergold, Inc.*, 947 F. Supp. 1328, 1333 (E.D. Mo. 1996).

[88] *Bluementhal v. Drudge*, 992 F.Supp. 44, 55 (D.D.C. 1998); *Scherr v. Abrahama*, No. 97-C-5453, 1998 WL 299678, 4–5 (N.D. Ill. 1998).

[89] *Plus System, Inc. v. New England Network, inc.*, 804 F.Supp. 111, 118–119 (D. Col. 1992).

[90] *Superguide Corp.*, 987 F.Supp. 487 (D.N. Cal. 1997).

[91] *Cody v. Ward*, 954 F.Supp. 43, 47 (D. Conn. 1997); *Edias Software International, L.L.C. v. Basis International, Ltd.*, 947 F.Supp. 413, 419–420 (D. Ariz. 1996).

[92] *Telco communications v. An Apple a Day*, 977 F.Supp. 404, 406–407 (E.D. Va. 1997).

[93] E.S. Freibrun, Esq., *Out-of-State Jurisdiction Over Web Site Operators and Junk E-Mail: Legal Developments on the Internet*, <http://www.cl.ais.net/lawmsf/artic125.htm>.

been to determine whether or not, per the stream of commerce plus approach, the defendant has minimum contacts.

While a large part of this section has been spent dealing with contractual disputes, some words should be said about international tort arising out of electronic commerce. Some scholars have suggested that "effects test" shall take the place of "minimum contact tests,"[94] and the practice of courts gives further credence to this suggestion. In *Calder v. Jones*,[95] for example, the court decided jurisdiction based on finding that the defendant performed an intentional act which was aimed at the forum and which caused foreseeable harm in the forum.[96] In the case of international tort, affirmative acts are not a decisive factor for the court in determining jurisdiction; the mere action of allowing a viewer to contact a site host shall be sufficient.

To take another case, the New York-based defendant in *The People in the State of New York v. Kevin Jay Lipsitz*, ran an online magazine subscription service and routinely distribute false and misleading email advertisements to other users across the US. The plaintiffs were Internet users or consumers in several states who became angry at the defendant's abuse of their rights and filed action in a New York court. The court held that the facts that the defendant was a resident of New York and his Internet activities were conducted there were enough to assert jurisdiction.[97] This analysis has implications for cases concerning torts where a defendant may have no other contacts with a forum but has targeted a resident with the knowledge that the extent of the injury will be incurred in that forum.[98] In such situations, the point is to determine whether passive postings alone qualify as tortuous acts.

In *Yahoo! Inc. v. La Ligue Contre Le Racisme Et L'Antisemitisme et al.*,[99] Yahoo Inc. operates a number of web sites, including an auction

[94] S. Tita & G. Scamby, The "Effects Test": Unifying Personal Jurisdiction Case Law in Internet Defamation Cases, 33 *Law/Technology*, World Jurist Association No. 1 at 1–30 (2000).

[95] 465 U.S. 783 (1984).

[96] *Calder v. Jones*, 465 U.S. 788–789 (1984). See also D.L. Kidd, Jr., Note, Casting the Net: Another Confusing Analysis of Personal Jurisdiction and Internet Contacts in Telco Communications v. An Apple a Day, 32 *University of Richmond Law Review*, 505, 517 (1998).

[97] <http://www.oag.sate.ny.us/press/june/lebedeff.html>.

[98] *Naxos Resources Ltd. V. Southam Inc.*, No. CV 96–2134 WJR, 1996 WL 66241 (C.D. Cal. August 16 1996).

[99] The order was issued on June 7, 2001 by Fogel, District Judge, Fed.R.Civ.P. Sec. 12 (b)(2).

site and search engine directory at Yahoo.com and a regional site at Yahoo.fr. The site operated at Yahoo.fr is written in French. Various third parties posted for sale on Yahoo's auction site Nazi-related propaganda and third Reich related memorabilia. The French court ordered Yahoo! Inc. to re-engineer its site located in the United States to comply with French criminal law forbidding the display and sale of Nazi objects under Penal Code Article R645–1. Subsequently, Yahoo! Inc. brought an action in the federal district court of California. As to the issue of jurisdiction, the court decided that Yahoo! has made a sufficient *prima facie* showing of purposeful availment alleging that defendants knowingly engaged in actions intentionally targeted at its headquarters for the express purpose of ensuring California would feel the consequences of such actions. And the balance of factors determining reasonableness weighs in favor of this court's exercise of personal jurisdiction over defendants who have failed to make a compelling case necessary to refute the presumption that jurisdiction is reasonable.[100]

2.2.3.3. Tag Jurisdiction

Tag Jurisdiction is based on purported service of process on a person only transitorily present in the territory of the state or the United States. Is "tag" jurisdiction appropriate in electronic commerce? Is jurisdiction proper when an Internet communication is "tagged" while passing through a particular state en route to its final destination?[101] Under traditional tag jurisdiction, the served party has at least some tangible connection with the forum state. This is not the case in situations involving electronic commerce. Ultimately, this means there is little hope of support for such jurisdiction. If this view were to prove incorrect, the adoption of tag jurisdiction in electronic commerce would fundamentally change the whole concept of jurisdiction.[102]

---

[100] For further discussion of this case, see M.H. Wittow, U.S. District Court for the Northern District of California: Personal Jurisdiction over Nonresidents, *Computer Und Recht International*, No. 4, 111–117 (2001); M. Love, International Jurisdiction over the Internet: A Case Analysis of Yahoo!, Inc. v. La Ligue Contre le Racisme et L'antisemitisme, 17 *Temple International and Comparative Law Journal* 261–275 (Spring 2003).

[101] *Internet Jurisdiction: Policy Issues*, <http://www.unc.edu/~deweyma/policy.html>.

[102] If this were to happen, tag jurisdiction would extend to telephone and mail communications, which is unrealistic.

2.2.4. *Comments*

The nature of cyberspace is at odds with standards for jurisdiction. Though the Internet by definition lacks a location, the court, in considering its jurisdiction, will be moved to decide the "location of the act or omission."[103] Determining whether an act or contact is strong enough to assert jurisdiction in electronic commerce is a difficult task and, as they face new phenomena, courts can make contradictions in judgments.[104] The Supreme Court has acknowledged that a personal jurisdiction analysis is an imprecise inquiry, and that the "minimum contacts" test is not susceptible to "mechanical application".[105]

The court has been successful at adapting the traditional commercial theory to accommodate electronic commerce. The scaling approach is rather creative in explaining the essence of different activities in the Internet, whose different levels of activity can cause different results. US case law suggests that the interactive nature of activities within a particular forum can be determinative in asserting adjudicative jurisdiction; accessibility to web sites cannot. The risk of liability in a remote jurisdiction can be reduced by limiting interaction on the site (by way of avoiding the inclusion of ordering functionality, 800 telephone numbers, or other means by which users can make direct contact with the site operators).[106]

---

[103] A.H. Ravia, *Local and International Jurisdiction on the Internet (Part I)*, <http://www.law.co.il/articles/juris1.htm>. It would not be unfair to subject a person to jurisdiction because that person's actions gave rise to jurisdiction. See also *Asahi*, 480 U.S. 117 (1987); N.Y. C.P.L.R. 302 (Consol. 1978).

[104] The Internet's ubiquitous, yet intangible, reach has led courts to inconsistent conclusions about the Internet's role in the traditional personal jurisdiction framework. These disparate decisions hinder efforts to predict the precise legal consequences a company faces when doing business on the Internet. See P.J. Whalen, *Internet Jurisdiction*, <http://www.spencerfane.com/publica . . . Commerce/internet-jurisdiction.html>; as asserted by Ponte, personal jurisdiction is a thorny issue in international commercial transaction. See further L.M. Ponte, Boosting Consumer Confidence in E-Business: Recommendations for Establishing Fair and Effective Dispute Resolution Programs for B2C Online Transactions, 12 *Albany Law Journal of Science & Technology* 482 (2002).

[105] *Kulko v. Superior Court*, 436 U.S. 84, 92 (1978).

[106] See further *Electronic Commerce: An International Overview*, <http://www.inter-leges.com/Archive/1999/1/18–1066.html>. See also G.M. Perry, *Personal Jurisdiction in Cyberspace: Where can You be Sued, and Whose Laws Apply?* December 1998, <http://www.llgm.com/FIRM/article14.htm>. See also M.K. Dyer, *Omnipresence "Persona"-Fied: A Review of Personal Jurisdiction Principles and Their Application to Cyberspace*, <http://www.emitech.com/dyer/persjur.html> Remote jurisdiction can be avoided by including in the contract a clause which nominates the jurisdiction to which the parties will submit or a disclaimer which states that the web site operator is not

However, there are problems with putting the scaling approach into practice. First of all, not all courts give meaningful attention to the difference between "passive" and "interactive" web sites and their differing capacities to "contact" persons in a particular forum.[107] This causes inconsistent and sometimes flawed court rulings.

Secondly, the scaling approach is rather flexible and the court's discretion may greatly influence final results. Justice Marshall noted in *Kulko v. Superior Court* that the "minimum contacts test" is "one in which few answers will be written in black and white. The greys are dominant and even among them the shades are innumerable."[108] Minor changes in focus can drastically alter decisions regarding the nature of interactivity.[109] Not surprisingly, various courts have disagreed on what activity will be necessary to provide a court with personal jurisdiction.[110] Some courts have declared that the site alone provides enough contact with the state to establish jurisdiction,[111] while several district courts have refused jurisdiction over defendants whose only contact is the web site.[112]

Lawyers have criticized these declarations.[113] But more time shall be had for adjustment. Likely, though the scaling approach has been quite influential to date, it is ultimately an interim framework that

---

soliciting trade anywhere other than certain countries. However, there is discussion on the validity of such declaration.

[107] Y.A. Tamayo, Who? What? When? Where? Personal Jurisdiction and the World Wide Web, 4 *Richmond Journal of Law & Technology*, 7 (Spring 1998), <http://www.richmond.edu/~jolt/v4i3/tamayo.html>.

[108] 436 U.S. 84, 92 (1978); see also *Estin v. Estin*, 334 U.S. 541, 545 (1948).

[109] For example, in *Blumenthal v. Drudge*, No. 97–1968, 1998 U.S. Dist. LEXIS 5606 (D.D.C. Apr. 22, 1998), the defendant's web site was considered interactive since users who access the web site may request subscriptions to the report by emailing their requests and it sent each new report to those listed in its mailing list. If no reports were sent, the judgement may have been different.

[110] For the analysis of contradiction of decisions, see further Stott, *supra* note 58, at 843–852.

[111] See for example *Maritz, Inc. v. Cybergold, Inc.*, 947 F.Supp. 1328 (E.D. Mo. 1996); *Digital Equip. Corp. v. Altavista Tech., Inc.*, 960 F.Supp. (D. Mass. 1997).

[112] See for example *Esab Group, Inc. v. centricut, LLC*, 34 F.Supp. (D.S.C. 1999); *Desktop Technologies, Inc. v. Reprod. & Design, Inc.*, 1999 WL 98572 (E.D. Pa. Feb. 25, 1999); *Origin Instruments Corp. v. Adaptive Computer Systems, inc.* 1999 WL 76794 (N.D. Tex. Jan. 4, 1999); *Millennium Enterprises, Inc. v. Millennium Music, LP*, 33 F.Supp. (D. Ore. 1999).

[113] Much criticism arose out of *United States v. Thomas*, 74 F.3d 701 (6th Cir. 1996), cert. denied, 117 S. Ct. 74 (1996). For analysis, see further A.G. Mirzaian, Y2K . . . Who Cares? We Have Bigger Problems: Choice of Law in Electronic Commerce, 6 *Richmond Journal of Law & Technology*, 20 (Winter 1999–2000), <http://www.richmond.edu/jolt/v6i4/article3.html>.

should be abandoned as the commercial use of the Internet evolves and judicial understanding becomes clearer.[114]

The need to adapt and evolve the doctrine of personal jurisdiction consistent with technological advances has been widely recognized in the US. However, the US courts have continued to rely on the notion of "minimum contacts" to establish personal jurisdiction. By creating concrete guidelines like the scaling approach, the courts tried to justify the use of minimum contacts. Nevertheless, implementing these guidelines has resulted in inconsistent consequences. The Internet does not exist in a vacuum, but exists as a product of human volition. The courts should also treat it as such. An individual should not be subjected to all existing jurisdictions when entering cyberspace, but should be assured that he or she will receive the benefits of constitutional due process.[115]

Another issue that concerns us is the limited nature of US case law, which deals with cases within the US borders. Determining how to extend established principles to international practice presents a two-part problem.

Firstly, how should American courts implement principles used in international cases? Considering the complexity of international cases, courts shall act with great care when adjudicating cases involving foreigners.[116] They shall have to take into consideration the procedural and substantive policies of other countries whose interests are affected by the court's assertion of jurisdiction.[117]

Asserting jurisdiction in international cases shall pose problems. Even though minimum contacts can be found in the international cases, the assertion of jurisdiction can still be called unreasonable and unfair.[118] Generally speaking, seven items must be balanced to assure fair play and substantial justice: the extent of the defendant's purposeful injection into the forum state's affairs; the burden on the

---

[114] M.A. Willard, *Personal Jurisdiction and the Internet*, <wysiwyg://358/http://www.escm.com/new/art/JURISDICTION.html>.

[115] R.T. Krueger, Traditional Notions of Fair Play and Substantial Justice Lost in Cyberspace: Personal Jurisdiction and On-Line Defamatory Statements, 51 *Cath. U.L. Rev.* 334 (Fall 2001).

[116] *Asahi*, 480 U.S. 102 (1987).

[117] G. Zeviar-Geese, *The State of the Law on Cyberjurisdiction and Cybercrime on the Internet*, <http://www.law.gonzaga.edu/borders/documents/cyberlaw.htm>.

[118] *Core-Vent Corp. v. Nobel Industries*, AB, 11 F.3d 1482, 1490 (9th Cir. 1993). See also E.M. Maltz, Unraveling the Conundrum of the Law of Personal Jurisdiction: A Comment on Asahi Metal Industry Co. v. Superior Court of California, *Duke Law Journal* 669, 689–690 (1987).

defendants of defending in the forum; the extent of conflict with the sovereignty of the defendant's state; the forum state's interest in adjudicating the dispute; the most efficient judicial resolution of the controversy; the importance of the forum to the plaintiff's interest in convenient and effective relief; and the existence of an alternative forum.[119] Balancing these items will be the challenge.

Secondly, how should US principles be implemented at an international level? This depends on the attitudes of the international actors. Considering the pioneering position of the U.S. in the field of the Internet and its strong economic influence, other countries may adopt the principles and use them in their judicial systems. Canada, for one, has already done so.[120]

The implementation of US principles in international cases still has many issues to be resolved. For example, whether any Web activity by anyone without commercial intent, absent the potentially foreseeable harm of trademark infringement, would be sufficient to assert personal jurisdiction over a foreign defendant?[121] Whether a user at one website creating a document with a hyperlink into another person's website would be sufficient to create jurisdiction over the owner of the linked site?[122]

To sum up, the American case law indicates that for personal jurisdiction to be asserted in electronic commerce the defendants shall have done more than post advertisements. Web activity by itself shall not subject a party to jurisdiction.[123] This seems reasonable in light of the alternative. If the mere posting of a web site created more than minimum contacts in every forum in which it can be accessed, every court in America would gain nationwide (indeed, worldwide) jurisdiction over almost everyone.[124] Advertising can only

---

[119] *Core-Vent Corp. v. Nobel Industries*, AB, 11 F.3d 1488–1490.

[120] To date, Canadian courts have had few occasions to consider the issue of jurisdiction in electronic commerce, but there is consensus among e-commerce lawyers that evolving U.S. principles will be applied in Canada. See further D. Young, *Jurisdiction Remains a Work in Progress*, eBusiness Journal, October 1999, <http://news.globetechnology.com/site/ebusiness/102799_01.html>.

[121] *Digital Equipment Corporation v. Altavista Technology, Inc.*, Civ. Action 96–12192 NG (D. Mass. March 12, 1997).

[122] *Playboy Enterprises, Inc. v. Frene*, 839 F.Supp. 1552 (M.D. Fla. 1993).

[123] See further Kelly & Hieber, Untangling a Web of Minimum Contacts: The Internet and Personal Jurisdiction in Trademark and Unfair Competition Cases, 18 *The Trademark Reporter*, No. 5, at 576 (1997).

[124] See *Hearst Corp. v. Goldberger*, No. 96 Civ. 3620, 1997 WL 97097, at 1 (S.D.N.Y. Feb. 26, 1997). Defendant, a New Jersey resident, created a web site in New Jersey

be considered as one component of a bundle of means of contact for consideration when related to the cause of action directed to persons in the forum state.[125] Because of sovereignty concerns, there is a higher jurisdictional barrier when litigating against a foreign national.[126] As a result, when adjudicating cases involving foreign nationals, the court must act with great care, balancing several factors on a case by case basis.

2.3. *European Attitudes towards Adjudicative Jurisdiction*

2.3.1. *General Introduction to European Practice*

Though it has decided no case concerning jurisdiction in electronic commerce so far, the EU takes a more formal and rigorous approach to the issue of adjudicative jurisdiction than its US counterpart.[127] To understand European philosophy we need look at the Brussels (1968)[128] and Lugano (1988)[129] conventions on Jurisdiction and Enforcement of Judgments in Civil and Commercial Matters (the Brussels Convention and the Lugano Convention). The two conventions present similar views concerning jurisdiction, but each deals with a different area of application. The Brussels convention explores issues of jurisdiction between and among the EU States; the Lugano Conven-

at "esqwire.com" which was accessible to and had been accessed by New York residents. While the site featured a description of legal support services, the defendant had not performed such services to anyone by the commencement of the suit. Plaintiff commenced suit in New York charging that the defendant's use of "esqwire" infringed its mark in "esquire". The court held that it lacked personal jurisdiction over the defendant, saying that: "Where, as here, defendant has not contracted to sell or actually sold any goods or services to New Yorkers, a finding of personal jurisdiction in New York based on [the mere availability of] an Internet web site would mean that there would be nationwide (indeed, worldwide) personal jurisdiction over anyone and everyone who establishes an Internet web site. Such nationwide jurisdiction is not consistent with traditional personal jurisdiction case law nor acceptable to the Court as a matter of policy."

[125] See, for example, *Digital Equipment Corp. v. AltaVista Technology, Inc.*, Civil Action No. 96–12192NG, BNA's Electronic Information Policy & Law Report, 21 March 1997, at 343.

[126] *Sinatra v. National Enquirer*, 854 F.2d, at 1199.

[127] See H.L. Korn, Development of Judicial Jurisdiction in the United States, 65 *Brooklyn L. Rev.* 935 (1999).

[128] It has been amended several times. The 1996 version is currently in force. See [1998] OJEC 37, at 1.

[129] This convention joins Switzerland, Norway and Iceland with the countries included in the Brussels Convention. See [1998] OJEC L319, at 9.

tion concerned jurisdiction in the European Free Trade Association (EFTA) states as well as between those states and the EU states.

Due to the fact that the conventions were held much earlier than electronic commerce appeared in the European market, neither specifically treated such commerce. They do not suit today's commercial world well. For example, the conventions pay special attention to consumer contracts and afford consumers the right to sue in their own state of residence: a right that may be inappropriate in a case concerning electronic commerce. Furthermore, while the conventions' principles aim to unify jurisdictional procedures in the EU, national rules still play an all-to-important important role in implementing those principles.

Recently, attention has focused on electronic commerce. This has been evidenced by the adoption of the Directive on Electronic Commerce to regulate Internet transactions, which upholds the country of origin principle.[130] According to this directive, a company operating in any member state is able to operate anywhere within the union's territory as long as it complies with the regulations of the country in which it is based.[131] While this directive does not deal with the specific application of the Brussels convention principles, it does influence interpretations of Article 5 (5) on disputes arising out of establishment. It establishes the basis for jurisdiction as the forum where the consumer pursues an activity through a "fixed establishment" (a web site).[132]

At its meeting held 4 and 5 December 1997, the European Council made seemingly unsatisfactory revisions to the Brussels Conventions.[133] A regulation (later named "Brussels I Regulation")[134] by the European

---

[130] *Electronic commerce: Commission Welcomes Final Adoption of Legal Framework Directive*, Brussels, 4 May 2000, <http://europa.eu.int/rapid/start/c . . . txt=gt&doc=IP/00/442I0IRAPID&Ig=EN>.

[131] M. Frendo, Legal Aspects of E-commerce, 32 *Law/Technology*, World Jurist Association 12 (1999).

[132] See Articles 7–9, Amended Proposal for a European Parliament and Council Directive, in Certain Legal Aspects of Electronic Commerce in the Internal Market, 98–0325, COM (17 August 1999), 427 final. <http://europa.eu.int/comm/dg15/en/media/eleccomm/com_427en.pdf>.

[133] Article 15 (c) together with Recital 13 of the Regulation completely undermines the freedom to provide services based on the principle of the country of origin control and mutual recognition.

[134] Draft Regulation on Jurisdiction, Recognition and Enforcement of Judgments in Civil and Commercial Matters, ref IP/99/510. The Regulation will not apply to the United Kingdom, Ireland, and Denmark. However, the United Kingdom

Commission was submitted and successfully replaced the Brussels Convention as of March 1, 2002 with a view *inter alia* to new forms of commerce that did not exist in 1968. Nevertheless, the Brussels Convention will continue to apply to Member States bound by the Convention that are excluded from the new Regulation. In addition, the Regulation will not affect rules governing jurisdiction and recognition of judgments contained in specific Community instruments and rules contained in conventions relating to specific matters to which Member States are party.[135]

2.3.2. *The Brussels Convention and the Lugano Convention*

The primary rule on jurisdiction laid down by the Brussels and Lugano Conventions is Article 2, which refers to a defendant's domicile. Persons domiciled in a contracting state shall, whatever their nationality, be sued in the courts of that state.[136] In order to determine whether a party is domiciled in a contracting state, a court shall apply its internal rules.[137]

There are several exceptions to this rule. According to Article 5 to 18, persons domiciled in a contracting state may be sued in the courts of another contracting state. The state of performance can be supplementary rule for contractual disputes. In matters relating to a contract, a person domiciled in a contracting state may be sued in the state where the stipulations of the contract should be met.[138] In matters relating to tort, delict or quasi-delict, the case can be brought to courts of the state wherein the harmful events occurred.[139] Disputes arising out of the operations of a branch, agency or other establishment can be taken to court where the branch, agency or other establishment is situated.[140] Article 6 further provides this opportunity for a case being heard in another contracting state: a person domiciled in a contracting state may be sued in another state in

and Ireland seem prepared to opt into the regulation. See further S. Dutson, *Transnational E-Commerce, Computers and Law*, 25 (February/March 2000).

[135] See further *Jurisdiction, Recognition and Enforcement of Judgments in Civil and Commercial Matters*, available at <http://europa.eu.int> (viewed on October 23, 2003).

[136] Article 2 of the two Conventions.

[137] A. Lindberg, *Jurisdiction on the Internet—The European Perspective: An Analysis of Conventions, Statutes and Case Law*, American Bar Association, 20 July 1997, <http://www.abanet.org/buslaw/cyber/initiatives/eujuris.html>.

[138] Article 5 (1) of the Conventions

[139] Article 5 (2) of the Conventions.

[140] Article 5 (3) of the Conventions.

multi-party disputes, on a counterclaim, and where a contractual dispute relates to rights over immovable property.

The conventions involve concerned parties in determining jurisdiction. The parties to a contract have the right to make an agreement on the issue of adjudicative jurisdiction.[141] To agree in advance as to which state shall have jurisdiction, they must first satisfy certain formal conditions.[142] Additionally, Article 17 demands real consent on the choice of court on the part of the persons concerned so as to protect the weaker party.[143]

There are limitations to the parties' choice of jurisdiction.[144] Based on the principle of consumer protection, the conventions provide that a consumer may choose between filing an action either in the country where he is domiciled or the seller's state of domicile.[145] For the seller, only the consumer's state of domicile can be sued.[146]

2.3.3. *The Brussels I Regulation*

The basic principle of the Regulation is that jurisdiction is exercised by the Member State in which the defendant is domiciled, regardless of his or her nationality. Domicile is determined in accordance with the domestic law of the Member State where the court has been seized.[147] In particular, Article 15 (1) (c) of the Brussels Convention is replaced by the prerequisite that the contract be concluded by a person who pursues commercial or professional activities in the country where the consumer is domiciled, or who by some means has directed such activities to that country or to several states including that country, and the contract falls within the scope of such activities.[148] This provision clearly covers electronic commerce.

The Regulation covers jurisdiction over all consumer contracts and outlines a new section on individual contracts of employment; a new

---

[141] Article 17 of the Conventions.

[142] There are three conditions: (a) the agreement is in writing or evidenced in writing; (b) the agreement is in a form which accords with practices established between the parties; or (c) in international trade or commerce, the agreement is in a form which accords with a usage of certain dignity.

[143] See further L. Katz, Jurisdiction and E-Commerce Disputes, 3 (2) *Journal of World Intellectual Property*, 292 (2000).

[144] References can be made to Article 15 (3) of the two Conventions.

[145] Article 2 (1), 5 No. 5, 13 (1), 14 (1) of the Conventions.

[146] Article 14 (2) of the Conventions.

[147] Article 2, 3, 4 of the Regulation.

[148] M. Lubitz, Jurisdiction and Choice of Law for Electronic Contracts: An English Perspective, *Computer Und Recht International* No. 2, at 42 (2001).

general rule indicates when "*lis pendance*"[149] takes place.[150] In cases concerning the sale of goods or provision of services, the place of performance shall be where goods or services were or should have been delivered or provided. Accordingly, the place of performance for downloaded software shall be the place where the software was downloaded. It further states that in cases of international contract disputes concerning online practices, customers can seek justice in their country of residence, as long as the merchant actively solicited the consumers business in the consumer's home country.[151]

The Brussels I Regulation has been met with various criticisms. First, suggested regulations pose problems for online merchants. Online advertisements are viewable anywhere in the world the Internet can be accessed. The so-called country of destination principle means that merchants will have to make sure that they comply with up to 15 national laws on consumer protection in order to avoid problems in the EU alone.[152] The fact is that they cannot be expected to be knowledgeable about the plethora of consumer protection regulations and laws in 15 member states, much less the state and local regulations that also govern consumer transactions.[153] Nevertheless, the consumer groups had argued that anything other than what the Commission had proposed would lead to a denial of justice as consumers cannot

[149] It is meant to determine which jurisdiction is competent when a case is pending in two or more courts.

[150] See further Commission Adopts Draft Regulation on Jurisdiction, Recognition and Enforcement of Judgments in Civil and Commercial Matters, Brussels, 14 July 1999, IP/99/510.

[151] Article 15 (c) of the Brussels Regulation when a contract has been concluded by a person who pursues commercial or professional activities in the state of the consumer's habitual residence or, by any means, directs such activities to that state or to several states including that state the contract falls within the scope of such activities. See also *Electronic Commerce: Legal Jurisdiction and Applicable Law*, at 3, in Details of Questions to be Addressed, Secretariat-General of the European Commission, 8 October 1999, <http://europa.eu.int/comm/sg/tfjai/events/index_en.htm>; EU Initiatives on Electronic Commerce, Coudert Brothers, May 5, 2000, at <http://www.coudert.com/practice/euinitiatives.htm>.

[152] As reported by the European Consumers' Organization, after more than one year of struggle between industry and consumer interests, the country of destination principle was confirmed in September 2000. All the "bad" amendments were rejected, including the amendments which would have permitted businesses to use choice of jurisdiction clauses in consumer contracts. See further *Brussels Regulation on Jurisdiction*, available at <http://lists, essential.org> (viewed on October 22, 2003); see also E. de Bony, *EU Tackles Jurisdiction in E-commerce Disputes*, 14 July 1999, <http://www.idg.net/ec?external=1&c . . . 3DWW%26oq%3Ddispute%257Celectronic>.

[153] *Jurisdiction in Cyberspace*, September 1999, <http://www.gip.org/gipjuris.htm>.

be expected to sue abroad.[154] While the perspective of the consumer groups prevailed at last, it is necessary to further study other views presented during the discussions to better accommodate the demands from both merchants and the consumers. Secondly, a recent report holds that court procedures only have positive economic effects for consumers when the value of the litigation is above 2000 ECU. The fact that the majority of online transactions involve small amounts means the Brussels I Regulation will not offer effective protection to online consumers.[155] This may have a negative effect on electronic commerce generally. Furthermore, the regulation runs counter to Mr. Blair's hope that electronic commerce shall be "lightly regulated," the European Commission's initiative to create a single market, and the Directive on Electronic Commerce.[156] Therefore, further consideration of its programs is requisite.[157]

On the one hand, the EU has taken care to advance European initiatives in electronic commerce cases.[158] On the other hand, it has taken particular care to avoid incompatibility and inconsistency with legal developments in other parts of the world so as to avoid obstacles to global electronic commerce. Their efforts in reaching agreement on the Directive on Electronic Commerce and the Brussels I Regulation might serve as a model for international players and thus

---

[154] See further *European Parliament: The Answer is Yes!*, available at <http://www.eurofinals.org> (viewed on October 23, 2003).

[155] See further M. Pullen, *On the Proposal to Adopt the Amended Brussels Convention and the Draft Rome II Convention as EU Regulations Pursuant to Article 65 of the Amsterdam Treaty*, EU version, Position Paper Prepared for the Advertising Association, <http://www.ilpf.org/confer/present99/pullen_posit.htm>.

[156] J. Warchus, *E-commerce: A Choice of Laws?* <http://www.wiredsussex.org.uk/ecommerce/ecomm11.htm>.

[157] Two issues have identified for further discussion: whether electronic commerce is better fostered by the existing Brussels Convention rules on jurisdiction or whether additional safeguards in favor of consumers are necessary; whether it is reasonable to take the view that commercial activities are directed at a particular state merely because a web site can be accessed from that state.

[158] Four key objectives are emphasized by the European Commission. Firstly, widespread, affordable access to the infrastructure, products and services needed for electronic commerce must be provided through secure and easy-to-use technologies and services and reliable, high-capacity telecommunications networks. Secondly, a coherent regulatory structure within the EU, based on single market principles, must be ensured. Thirdly, a favorable business environment must be fostered by promoting relevant skills and raising awareness. And fourthly, there must be a compatible and coherent regulatory framework at the global level. See *further Electronic Commerce: Commission Presents Framework for Future Action*, <http://europa.eu.int/comm/internal_market/en/media/infso/313.htm>.

reinforce Europe's influence on the development of international legal framework.[159]

2.4. *Observations*

2.4.1. *Self-Regulation in Adjudicative Jurisdiction*

Liberalization is well underway. Market force shall play a fundamental role in promoting the healthy development of the commercial world. But while stressing the importance of market force and competition to realize maximum economic gains, governments shall not lose their role in guaranteeing and balancing interests in society.

Experience shows us that the community of online users and service providers is up to the task of developing a self-governing system.[160] While the Internet may not have borders and is invisible, it does have users located in many physical locations that may be able to decide for themselves which regulatory systems they wish to utilize.[161] Indeed, Internet users have established many enforcement weapons to persuade wrongdoers to comply and service providers do their part by imposing conditions for access. In the area of online dispute resolution, self-regulation seems certain to prosper.

Online parties will do better to self-regulate than to leave regulation to national governments. However, just as one scholar commented, governments will inevitably impose additional restrictions on online activities, as governments, frustrated and embarrassed[162] by their

---

[159] *Electronic Commerce: Commission Welcomes Final Adoption of Legal Framework Directive*, <http://europa.eu.int/comm/internal_market/en/media/eleccomm/2k-442.htm>.

[160] When speaking of self-regulation, the "self" generally refers to the business sector alone, which fails to recognize individual users of Internet services and participants in electronic commerce as independent Internet stakeholders and possible administrators in a larger self-regulatory regime.

[161] M. Geist, *Internet Jurisdiction: The SEC "Opts Out"*, <http://lawschool.mtcibs.com/lawtech/archive/199705.htm>.

[162] Alarmed by the apparent prevalence of various forms of objectionable on-line content, as well as by the Internet's enormous potential for misuse, several governments have already responded by implementing restrictions. For example, Chinese government envisions a system oriented entirely towards business to serve as a tool to spur China's economic development. On-line communications beyond this scope are not granted any special protection. The restrictions on expression which govern in other contacts continue to apply. However, this regime is not technologically feasible. The Internet is far too large for any monitoring efforts to be even vaguely comprehensive. This fact is confirmed by the Chinese government's own efforts to limit access to a manageable number of users, which include limiting access to certain professions and keeping the cost of local Internet service artificially

inability to enforce existing limitations on online communication, are forced to resort to more repressive measures.[163] In the end, they shall cause damage to relevant parties. The basic premise of self-regulation is continuous improvement to meet the needs of the particular business in the most efficient manner.[164] The market can meet the needs of the market better than governmental regulation can. Only the market shall decide which court shall be more reasonable for disputing players.

Standards concerning self-regulation and jurisdiction in the cybercommunity may soon be adopted. While bearing in mind the benefits of the groups they represent, some organizations are already trying to formulate appropriate rules for general Internet society. Their research and ongoing practice may serve as models for future practice.

Freedom of contract serves to facilitate self-regulation in the commercial world, with particularly positive implications for dispute resolution and jurisdiction. Parties should be free to express their will in establishing guarantees that represent the real interests of relevant parties. Potential resolutions that take into account party preferences will likely gain the support of the Internet world.

Self-regulation and litigation in electronic commerce reach an amicable compromise: a consensual regime of user self-regulation with backup from state-run litigation. Market performance may provide the principles for adjudicative jurisdiction; the state shall adopt the rules.[165] The only question regards determining under what circumstance self-regulation suffices and when regulation by governments is necessary. Relevant governments will need time to react.[166]

---

high. Such efforts are also counter-productive since any economic development attributable to the Internet is correspondingly minimized. See further *Great Firewall of China?: Beijing Slaps Restrictions on Internet Access*, available at <http://www.asiaweek.com> (viewed on October 23, 2003).

[163] J.T. Delacourt, The International Impact of Internet Regulation, 38 *Harvard International Law Journal*, 234 (1997).

[164] Observations on the State of Self-Regulation of Internet, Prepared for the Ministerial Conference of the Organization for Economic Cooperation and Development (OECD): A Borderless World: Realizing the Potential for Global Electronic Commerce, Ottawa, Canada, October 7–9, 1998. <http://www.ilpf.org/selfreg/whitepaper.htm>.

[165] It is the position of Alliance for Global Business in its Global Action Plan for Electronic Commerce that any premature regulation could inhibit the growth of electronic commerce and that government should rely on voluntary business self-regulatory practices and market pressures to develop more flexible and balanced solutions.

[166] European telecommunications ministers backed a combination of self-regulation

2.4.2. *Free Choice by Parties and Consumer Protection*

In civil and commercial matters, free will is highly respected. In a freely negotiated agreement, the selection of a forum may become the most important term of the contract.[167] Both parties are in the position to freely express their views on which court shall govern their dispute and which law shall be applicable. In electronic commerce, which transcends national borders and exacerbates the already complicated issue of choosing appropriate jurisdiction, this freedom cannot be underestimated. Only when concerned parties fail to make a choice should the court decide the jurisdiction based on rules or case laws.

The idea of free will of the parties originated in Europe and different ways can realize this idea. However, one way is subjected to controversy: the so-called "adhesion contracts". Such are enforceable under US law, although some have argued they are "unfair" or "unconscionable." The terms "unfair" and "unconscionable" have flexible meanings.[168] This has caused much concern about the issue of consumer protection.

Jurisdictional rules (particularly regulatory applications of consumer protection laws) sometimes reflect presumed power imbalances between buyers and sellers. But some presumptions may need to be reevaluated given the manner in which the Internet empowers consumers *vis-à-vis* merchants.[169] Historically, consumers have been considered the weaker party in business transactions and special rules and regulations have thus been passed to protect consumer interests. For example, consumer transaction disputes have traditionally been tried within the exclusive jurisdiction of the state wherein the consumer resides.

When disputes arise over online consumer transactions, is it appropriate for two parties to reach agreements to bring the case to other

---

and government controls for the development of electronic commerce in the EU, but remained divided about whether regulation or voluntary codes of conduct should take precedence. See further E. de Bony, *EU Differs on E-commerce Regulation*, <http://www.idg.net/ec?external=1&c . . . earchbox%26sv%3DIS%26ik%3Dnoframes>.

[167] G. Born & D. Westin, *International Civil Litigation in the United States Courts*, 223–224 (Deventer, 1993); N. Guthrie, A Good Place to Shop: Choice of Forum and the Conflict of Laws, 27 *Ottawa Law Review*, 216–223, 231–232 (1995).

[168] See further Achieving Legal and Business Order in Cyberspace: A Report on Global Jurisdiction Issues Created by the Internet, London Meeting Draft, Report of the American Bar Association Jurisdiction in Cyberspace Project.

[169] T.P. Vartanian, *A Global Approach to the Laws of Jurisdiction in Cyberspace*, <http://www.kentlaw.edu/cyberlaw/housetestimony.html>.

courts? Most scholars advance a positive answer. In electronic commerce, consumers have the freedom to actively discriminate between products and merchants, whose more passive job is to disseminate information. In this environment, they have cast off their former passive role. On the other hand, merchants facing stricter competition than ever before must offer more favorable conditions for their customers, often transparent product information, and thus give up their power to them. As a result, the consumer protection principle needs further restructuring in this new business environment, balancing the interests of both parties.[170]

The process of realizing the free will of both parties in electronic commerce is simple. Generally speaking, merchants offer information related to forum choice on their web site. Consumers who read this information either accept available forums by clicking on an Accept Button or continue to search the web for further information. Electronic commerce both justifies free will and makes it realistic.

2.5. *International Efforts in Regulating Adjudicative Jurisdiction*

2.5.1. *International Regulation of Jurisdiction*

With the emergence of the Internet, nations cannot truly hide behind the international scene. One unique feature of the Internet is that a computer in one region of the world can access a computer in another part of the world in an instant.[171] National borders are easily bypassed and interconnection is becoming closer than ever before. In consequence, any regulation from an individual state can influence other states.

The Internet represents a network of networks, not a single system as the term may connote.[172] A state cannot make its own business without taking into account the interoperation of states.[173] Similarly,

---

[170] Consumers are much more empowered. See further J. Schack, Cost Containment, 33 *Institutional Investor* 43 (1999); see also *infra* notes 152–157 and accompanying text.

[171] B. Robin, E. Keeler & R. Miller, *Educator's Guide to the Web* 1–2 (1997).

[172] S.M. Hanley, International Internet Regulation: A Multinational Approach, 16 *J. Marshall J. of Computer & Info. L.*, 1010 (1998).

[173] This can be seen from the European attitude. The European Commission acknowledges that new national legislation in diverse areas can create trade barriers that will hamper the development of electronic commerce at a global level. The community should work through appropriate international forum and bilaterally

a state cannot develop its own regulatory policy for electronic commerce and cut itself off from the rest of the world. International cooperation is urgent. Regulation of the Internet should provide global coverage within a secure framework fostering the growth of electronic commerce in the world market.[174]

This is also true for adjudicative jurisdiction in electronic commerce. To avoid conflicts in jurisdiction in the international scene, international bodies must cooperate in developing a policy. Some organizations have already taken the initiative. The American Bar Association (ABA) has launched one project on transnational jurisdiction and published research results.[175] ICC, OECD and other international organizations[176] have also put effort into this issue.

The current problem is determining who can act as the appropriate regulatory body for adjudicative jurisdiction. The Hague Conference on Private International Law rightly appeals to the self-regulatory nature of jurisdiction and is garnering industry support.

2.5.2. *Draft Hague Convention*[177]

Long before the international community was considering the impact of the Internet on jurisdiction, a project to work on the future of the Hague Convention on Jurisdiction and Foreign Judgments in Civil and Commercial matters was first proposed in 1992.[178] Formal

with its major trading partners to establish a coherent global regulatory framework. 5 December 1997, <http://www.qlinks.net/comdocs/eu-us.htm>.

[174] Frendo, *supra* note 131, at 30.

[175] The Cyber Law Committee of the ABA compiled an inventory of how different national rules and requirements deal with jurisdiction in cyberspace.

[176] For example, the Global Business Dialogue for Electronic commerce (GBDe), an international group of leading online businesses, outlined the emerging industry consensus in a paper on jurisdiction; the Internet Law and Policy Forum (ILPF), a forum of legal and policy experts, has recently held an important conference on jurisdiction and the Internet and is developing a work program to address legal and policy issues related to jurisdiction on the Internet; the ICC has put together a cross-functional task force on jurisdiction and electronic commerce. For analysis of international regulation of jurisdiction, see further R. Wai, Transnational Liftoff and Juridical Touchdown: The Regulatory Function of Private International law in an Era of Globalization, 40 *Columbia Journal of Transnational Law* 219–220 (2002).

[177] The Preliminary Draft Convention on Jurisdiction and Foreign Judgments in Civil and Commercial Matters was adopted by the Special Commission on 30 October 1999. The text could be obtained in <http://www.hcch.net/e/conventions/draft36e.html>. For a general discussion, see further R.A. Brand, Intellectual Property, Electronic Commerce and the Preliminary Draft Hague Jurisdiction and Judgments Convention, 62 *U. Pitts. L. Rev. Issue* 4, 581–603 (2001).

[178] In May 1992, Edwin Williamson, Legal Advisor at the US Department of

negotiations started in 1996 and since then, the committee has paid much attention to the electronic commerce provisions.[179] One preliminary draft specifically attends to electronic commerce.

According to Article 4 (1), parties can agree on any court. The agreement can be reached by any means and take any form so long as it is usable for subsequent reference.[180] The agreement shall take the priority in determining adjudicative jurisdiction. When no choice is made, the defendant's habitual residence shall be the relevant connecting factor; legal persons can be sued in the state of statutory seat, the state of incorporation, the state of central management, or the state of the corporation's principal place of business.[181]

The Draft Hague Convention gives electronic commerce a special position within its framework. Concerning business-to-business transactions, a plaintiff may bring an action to the courts of a state in which the goods or services were provided in whole or in part. In matters relating both to the supply of goods and the provision of services, the forum state shall be the one where performance of the principal obligation took place in whole or in part.[182]

The position of electronic commerce becomes complicated when contracts are concluded and performed online.[183] Traditional jurisdictional theories can be used in situations where contracts are concluded online, but performed offline. The performance of the contract remains the primary factor in deciding jurisdiction. When it comes to contracts both concluded and performed online, it is difficult to identify the contracting place and the place of performance. In such cases, a presumption has to suffice for the place of performance or more precisely, the place of delivery of the information.[184]

State, wrote to Georges Dorz, Secretary General of the Hague Conference on Private International Law, proposing that the organization take up the negotiation of a multilateral convention on the recognition and enforcement of judgments.

[179] Meeting in Ottawa on the Hague Convention on Jurisdiction and Foreign Judgments in Civil and Commercial matters, <http://www.cptech.org/ecom/hague-march-2000.html>.

[180] Article 4 of the Draft Hague Convention.

[181] Article 3 of the Draft Hague Convention.

[182] Article 6 of the Draft Hague Convention.

[183] Goods and services are blurred in cyberspace, but the distinction has become increasingly important. See further *Doing Business On-line in the Digital Millennium: the Law Looks Ahead*, <http://www.chapmantripp.co.nz/publish/c040500.htm>.

[184] Electronic Commerce and International Jurisdiction, Ottawa, 28 February to 1 March 2000, summary of discussions prepared by C. Kessedjian with the cooperation of the Private International Law team of the Ministry of Justice of Canada, <C:\WINDOWS\TEMP\jdgmpd12.doc>.

In consumer contracts, the consumer shall be able to take proceedings to the courts of his habitual residence once (a) the conclusion of the consumer contract is linked to the activities of the business in the state of the consumer's residence, or directed at that state in particular by soliciting business through means of publicity; and (b) the consumer has taken the necessary steps to conclude the contract in his state of residence.[185] These two conditions serve to balance the interests of merchants and consumers. Again, free will of parties is advocated in a cautious way.[186] The problem is determining whether there shall be some limitation for choice, which shall deserve further consideration.[187]

The last type refers to torts in electronic commerce. Two types of courts can satisfy jurisdiction in such cases. The courts of the place where the tortuous act arises shall have jurisdiction unless it can be shown that the perpetrator could not reasonably foresee the tortuous act or a similar consequence. The courts of the place where the injury occurs will be competent to rule on all the injury suffered anywhere by the injured party, as long as the injured party is a habitual resident of the state in which the court is situated. If the latter condition cannot be met, then the jurisdiction of the courts of the place where the injury occurs is limited to dealing with that specific injury.[188]

2.5.3. *Comments*

The Draft Convention is the most ambitious project undertaken by the Hague Conference so far. However, the negotiations were suspended when the drafters reached an impasse in June 2001. A new drafting committee was set up to prepare a new proposal in April

---

[185] Article 7 of the Draft Hague Convention. For analysis, see T.P. Lester, Globalized Automatic Choice of Forum: Where Do Internet Consumers Sue?: Proposed Article 7 of the Hague Convention on International Jurisdiction and Foreign Judgments in Civil and Commercial Matters and its Possible Effects on e-Commerce, 9 *New England Journal of International and Comparative Law* 431–488 (2003).

[186] Article 7 (3) of the Draft Hague Convention.

[187] Disagreements concerning consumer protection involve issues like whether or not and under what circumstances to allow adhesion contracts. See further J. Love, *Views of the Consumer Project on Technology*, March 1, 2000, <http://www.cptech.org/ecom/hague-march-2000.html>.

[188] See further Article 10 of the Draft Hague Convention. See further Electronic Commerce and International Jurisdiction, Ottawa, 28 February to 1 March 2000, Summary of discussion prepared by C. Kessedjian, preliminary Document No. 12 of August 2000, at 8, <H:\RB_DOC\DPU\00011271.DOC>.

2002. Many controversial issues are left for further negotiations. Two of the most important issues involve jurisdiction to hear e-commerce and other Internet-related disputes, and disputes involving intellectual property rights. A new draft was addressed in April 2003, awaiting the official views from governments.[189]

The road to the adoption of the Convention has been bumpy. Nevertheless, the Draft Hague Convention has meanwhile provided an arena in which the international community can work to coordinate rules for adjudicative jurisdiction. It has taken into consideration some of the various situations that shall be confronted in electronic commerce and, importantly, distinguished between contracts concluded online but performed offline and those concluded and performed totally online. With further technological development, the latter distinction shall become even more important.

Theoretically, party identification and localization to the contract could substitute for territorial connections. Identification would disrupt the traditional allowance that persons can remain anonymous in the transaction.[190] The localization of the parties is more important in that it could substitute for the location of performance. Because parties can act in any location where connection to the Internet can be accessed, their offering information about their residence and place of business shall be helpful. These issues will become more important after the Draft Hague Convention takes effect.

Clear conditions have been provided in the Draft Hague Convention for the courts to assert jurisdiction legally. Application is another matter and more work needs to be done. Electronic commerce is increasingly complicated and it requires time to form a complete picture of the possible framework for jurisdiction. One issue to be treated later is that of online employment contracts. Determining how to accommodate the rules[191] to this online situation can be vital

189 The new draft has been technically narrowed to "choice of forum" clauses in B2B contracts; it also seeks to exclude patents and trademarks from the treaty. See further CPTech's Page on the Hague Conference on Private International Law's Proposed Convention on Jurisdiction and Foreign Judgments in Civil and Commercial Matters, available at <http://www.cptech.org> (view on 22 October, 2003).

190 But some kind of transparency or control should remain. Thus, the use of certification methods proposed by private entities is encouraged.

191 Rules concerning individual contracts of employment are provided in Article 8 of the Draft Convention. Some experts claim the rules shall cause a fragmentation of the jurisdiction.

to electronic commerce's further development. Can the choice of court provision be applied here?

Some have argued for the convention's abandoning the issue of jurisdiction in electronic commerce altogether. But we understand the importance of jurisdiction in electronic commerce. Though the issue is complicated, there is no excuse for deleting electronic commerce from the basic framework of jurisdiction law. The convention must not shirk from the task of addressing, as it is set out to do, "civil and commercial matters" in which the role of jurisdiction for electronic commerce is vital.

3. *Choice of Law*

3.1. *Basic Understanding of Choice of Law in Electronic Commerce*

After the court has justified its power to hear one case, the substantive part of the litigation shall start. When the case involves foreign (or international) factors, applicable law must be determined. The adequacy of this determination is vital to the successful outcome of the case. Presently, different countries have regulations of their own based on particular national interests.[192] These different national laws can occasion different judgments for the same case.

Choice-of-law issues are notoriously difficult to resolve, even in relatively simple contexts.[193] The character of internationalization in electronic commerce cases is much more complicated than in normal international transactions, which in turn makes the issue of choice of law in such cases a huge task for judges and lawyers alike.[194]

Traditionally, applicable law depends on physical location. But cyberspace is indifferent to the physical world and there is no necessary connection between an Internet address and a physical juris-

---

[192] National laws are developed which do not well consider the transnational dimensions of global computer networks and thus are ineffective to deal with multinational issues. See further M. Kirby, Legal Aspects of Transborder Data Flows, 9 *Computer L.J.* 233 (1991).

[193] S.F. Kreimer, The Source of Law in Civil Rights Actions: Some Old Light on Section 1988, 133 *U. Pa. L. Rev.* 601 (1985).

[194] See further A.H. Boss, The Jurisdiction of Commercial Law: Party Autonomy in Choosing Applicable Law and Forum Under Proposed Revisions to the Uniform Commercial Code, 32 *Int'l Law.* 1067–1068 (1998).

diction.[195] You can find Internet users everywhere,[196] but at the same time nowhere.[197] No one can really determine where a specific act takes place.[198] Not surprisingly, then, applying strictly territorial choice of law rules to global digital networks creates formidable problems.[199]

Having acknowledged such problems, some scholars have suggested ways to totally block the issue of choice of law from the arena of electronic commerce. One suggestion is the formation of a new law for cyberspace, the so-called *lex cyberalty* or cyberlaw.[200] With cyber-jargon developing to the point of quasi-language, cyberspace has obviously developed a distinct culture.[201] Supporters believe that since

---

[195] Johnson, *supra* note 15, at 1367, 1371; T. Puurunen, The Legislative Jurisdiction of States Over Transactions in International Electronic Commerce, 18 *J. Marshall J. Computer & Info. L.* 689–690 (2000).

[196] A person logging onto the Internet has a presence on it, which can be observed by any computer linked to the Internet. See D.L. Burk, Transborder Intellectual Property Issues on the Electronic Frontier, 6 *Stan. L. & Pol'y Rev.* 9–10 (1994).

[197] Encryption may be used to conceal the identity of the user. See R.F. Pollack, Creating the Standards of a Global Community: Regulating Pornography on the Internet—An International Concern, 10 *Temp. Int'l & Comp. L.J.* 467, 480 (1996); M.A. Pike, *Using the Internet* 49 (2nd Ed. 1995).

[198] One can talk of the location of events and transactions in cyberspace, but only in reference to a virtual space consisting of the "address" of the machines between which messages and information are routed; this machine addressing system is entirely independent of the physical address or location of those machines. See further D.L. Burk, Trademarks Along the Infobahn: A First Look at the Emerging Law of Cybermarks, 1 *U. Rich. J.L. & Tech.* 1, 12–14 (1995), at <http://www.urich.edu/jolt/vlil/burk.html>.

[199] Many commentators argue that the old choice-of-law doctrines fail to provide any meaningful guidance in the virtual world because these doctrines depend on notions of physical locations. The issues created by the growth of the Internet are *sui generis* and must ultimately be addressed by legislative action recognizing the unique attributes of cyberspace. See R.T. Muth, Old Doctrines on a New Frontier: Defamation and Jurisdiction in Cyberspace, 68 *Wisconsin Lawyer*, 11 (1995).

[200] See for example, Legal Advisory Board (LAB), reply to the Green Paper on Copyright and Related Rights in the Information Society, <http://www2.echo.lu/legal/en/ipr/reply/reply.html>; see also P. Samuelson, *Legally Speaking, the NII Intellectual Property Report, Communications of the ACM*, Dec. 1994, at 21. *Lex informatica* is also suggested corresponding to *Lex Mercatoria*, see generally J.R. Reidenberg, *Lex Informatica*: The Formulation of Information Policy Rules Through Technology, *76 Texas Law Review 553 (1998)*; A. Mefford, *Lex Informatica*: Foundations of Law on the Internet, 5 *Indiana Journal of Global Legal Studies*, 211 (Fall 1997); W.H. van Boom & J.H.M. van Erp, Electronic Highways: On the Road to Liability, in V. Bekkers et al. (Eds.), *Emerging Electronic Highways: New Challenges for Politics and Law*, 153, 156 (1996).

[201] See further R.L. Dunne, Deterring Unauthorized Access to Computers: Controlling Behavior in Cyberspace through a Contract Law Paradigm, 35 *Jurimet. Journal*, 8–10 (Fall 1994).

lex merchant exists specifically for a commercial world so should a specific law exist for a unique cyberspace.[202] Uniform law should resolve conflict regarding choice of law totally and ultimately. This suggestion shall be more fully explored in Chapter Six.

Other ambitious ideas include a separate cyberlaw, which would harmonize different national laws to best serve Internet society.[203] The suggestion of a cyber law seems reasonable, but harmonization should probably be a gradual process. Considering the uncertainties produced by rapidly changing technologies and industrial structures, it would be inappropriate to quickly adopt broad new legal rules. A gradual adjustment is more desirable in light of the potentially contentious questions arising in connection with the new technology.[204] *Lex* merchant came out of a special arrangement for settling commercial disputes.[205] In electronic commerce, there have also arisen

---

[202] *Id.*

[203] See for example, R.T. Nimmer, Licensing on the Global Information Infrastructure: Disharmony in Cyberspace, 16 Nw. *J. Int'l L. Bus.* 224, 246–247 (1995); J. Goldring, Netting the Cybershark: Consumer Protection, Cyberspace, the Nation-State, and Democracy, in B. Kahin & C. Nesson (Eds.), *Borders in Cyberspace: Information Policy and the Global Information Infrastructure* 322, 340–344 (Cambridge, MA: MIT Press, 1996); L.A. Herscha, Is There a Doctor in the House? Licensing and Malpractice Issues Involved in Telemedicine, 2 *B.U.J. Sci. & Tech. L.* 8 (1996); M. Rustad & L. Eisenschmidt, The Commercial Law of Internet Security, 10 *High Tech. L.J.* 213, 300 (1995); J. Ritter & J. Gliniecki, International Electronic Commerce and Administrative Law: The Need for Harmonized National Reforms, 6 *Harv. J.L. & Tech.* 263 (1993); L. Solomon & L. Corso, The Impact of Technology on the Trading of Securities: The Emerging Global Market and the Implications for Regulation, 24 *J. Marshall L. Rev.* 299, 330 (1991); D. Wilson, Viewing Computer Crime: Where Does the Systems Error Really Exist?, 11 *Computer/L.J.* 265 (1991); J. Grundfest, Internationalization of the World's Securities Markets: Economic Causes and Regulatory Consequences, 4 *J. Fin. Svcs. Res.* 349 (1990).

[204] See further Denver Area Educ. *Telecomm. Consortium, Inc. v. FCC,* 116 S. Ct. 2374, 2385 (1996). This has been evidenced by practice on the EU side. The foremost purpose of the European Communities Green Paper, "Copyright and Related Rights in the Information Society," appears to be the solicitation of comments from interested parties regarding how copyright law should be extended to the Internet in the EU. See further S. Fraser, The Copyright Battle: Emerging International Rules and Roadblocks on the Global Information Infrastructure, 15 *J. Marshall J. of Computer & Info. L.,* 759, 783 (1997); see also A.A. Caviedes, International Copyright Law: Should the European Union Dictate Its Development? 16 *B.U. International Law Journal,* 165, 228 (1998).

[205] However, there is doubt concerning whether there are such norms of international business transactions that are independent of national laws. See further G. Delaume, Comparative Analysis as a Basis of Law in State Contracts: The Myth of the *Lex Mercatoria,* 63 *Tulane Law Review,* 575 (1989); see also K. Highet, The Enigma of the *Lex Mercatoria,* 63 *Tulane Law Review,* 613 (1989).

such arrangements, for example, Cybercourt and Virtual Magistrate.[206] Their activities can have some gradual influence on the further development of *Lex cyberalty*.

The policy of self-regulation in cyberspace has been advocated, but time is needed for Internet society to reach certain agreements. As an open-ended group with an exponential growth rate, the "cyber-community" is too large and heterogeneous to achieve commonly accepted rules in a short period of time.[207]

While encouraging the development of *lex cyberalty* by the Internet society, we should further improve the choice of law system to accommodate the present situation. While there is no easy way to decide upon the location of relevant activities in electronic commerce, people are certainly manipulating electronic processes in the physical world. The task at hand is to involve physical contexts in the choice of law. This study will take up the issue and suggest an appropriate system for national states, which may gain acceptance in the international community. Two types of disputes arising out of electronic commerce shall be further dealt with in the following two sections: contractual disputes and torts.[208]

3.2. *Choice of Law in Contractual Disputes*

As electronic commerce deals with international transactions in the digital era, contractual relationships in electronic commerce are far more complicated than in traditional international commerce. Dealing with electronic commerce contract disputes is likewise problematic. To elucidate the nature of such dealings, this study will address US and EU cases. With them as its models, it should then analyze the

---

[206] For information on Virtual Magistrate Project, see <http://vmag.law.vill.edu:8080/>. For further discussion, see M.E. Staib & M. Yablonski, "Virtual Magistrate" Offers Alternative Dispute Resolution for Internet Disputes: Project Offers Parties a Chance to Avoid the Uncharted Terrain of "Cyber" Law, *Litigation News*, September 1996, at 6.

[207] See further R. Mergers, Intellectual Property and Digital Content: Notes on a Scorecard, *Cyberspace Lawyer*, June 1996, at 15.

[208] See further D.R. Johnson & K.A. Marks, Mapping Electronic Data Communications onto Existing Legal Metaphors: Should We Let Our Conscience (and Our Contracts) Be Our Guide?, *38 Vill. Law Review*, 487, 490–491 (1993). Possible legal disputes in cyberspace are listed in this article. It reveals the difficulty of characterizing a case as either tort or contract. See further E.F. Scoles & P. Hay, *Conflict of Laws* 3.8, 42 (2nd Ed. 1992).

feasibility of an international system and finally suggest a reasonable system for contractual disputes.

3.2.1. *International Practice*

3.2.1.1. The US

The US provides the most complete system for choice of law in contractual issues. When developing this system, American scholars advocated different theories, which were later applied in practice.

Forum selection clauses contained in contracts are generally recognized in the US. For such clauses to be valid, the choice of law should be reasonable.[209] For contracts reached through the Internet, there are two determinants of reasonableness: the requirement of "connecting factors" to the forum selected, which holds that there must be some connection between the chosen law and the parties or the transaction;[210] and the requirement of the lack of a gross inequality of bargaining power.[211]

When there are no forum selection clauses present, two roads are generally followed. These are suggested in the First and Second Restatement of Conflict of Laws.[212]

According to the First Restatement, the law where the contract was made governs the validity of the contract; the law of the place where performance occurs governs the contractual performance.[213] These are clear provisions for applicable law[214] and once represented the universal American approach to the issue of choice of law.[215] But with the development of new means of communication, location and along with it these provisions have lost their relevance.

---

[209] See for example, *Carnival Cruise Lines v. Shute*, 499 U.S. 585, 593–594 (1991).

[210] See G.B. Born, *International Civil Litigation in United States Courts*, 655 (3rd Ed. 1996).

[211] See further Section 187 of Restatement (Second) of Conflict of Laws.

[212] See further J.P. Donohue, *Litigation in Cyberspace: Jurisdiction and Choice of Law, A United States Perspective*, <http://www.abanet.org/buslaw/cyber/initiatives/usjuris.html>.

[213] Restatement (First) of Conflict of Laws, 495 U.S., section 377–397 (1990); see also J. Story, *Commentaries on Conflict of Laws*, 242 (2nd Ed. 1841).

[214] It has been claimed that application of a law other than that dictated by the First Restatement would impose a criterion that would not have been foreseen by at least one of the two parties to the suit. See further H.F. Goodrich, *Handbook of the Conflict of Laws* 92, at 261–262 (3rd Ed. 1949).

[215] See L. Brilmayer, *Conflict of Laws: Cases and Materials*, at 1 (4th Ed. 1995).

Even in normal international transactions, they have been discarded in most states.[216]

As a reaction to the rigidity of the rules in the First Restatement,[217] governmental interest analysis was introduced in the legal practice in the 1950s.[218] Professor Currie intended to use this analysis to ensure the realization of the essential purpose of the law chosen. One of its greatest virtues is its ability to reveal false conflicts of laws[219] and thereby facilitate the selection of law that has substantial connection.

Of course, there are instances of real conflict. According to the theory of governmental interest analysis, in case of a real conflict, a court must apply the forum's law, determine whether "a more moderate and restrained interpretation" of the forum law reveals that its application does not accord with the purposes underlying it, apply the law with the most significant interest, or to apply a myriad of other choice of law principles.[220]

In most situations, the forum law is given favorable consideration.[221] The court is not in an objective position to interpret underlying policy in other laws.[222] The theory of governmental interest analysis has

---

[216] In the years after the *Babcock* decision, courts have become increasingly reluctant to apply the First Restatement when looking at choice of law issues. See further Born, *supra* note 210, 674. For criticism against the First Restatement, see further W.W. Cook, *The Logical and Legal Bases of the Conflict of Laws* (1942); F.V. Harper, Policy Bases of the Conflict of Laws: Reflections on Rereading Professor Lorenzen's Essays, 56 *Yale L.J.* 1155 (1947); R.J. Traynor, Law and Social Change in a Democratic Society, *U. Ill. L. Rev.* 230 (1956); P. Dane, Vested Rights, "Vestedness," and Choice of Laws, 96 *Yale L.J.* 1191, 1197 (1987).

[217] B. Currie, On the Displacement of the Law of the Forum, 58 *Columbia Law Review*, 964, 967 (1958).

[218] See generally B. Currie, The Constitution and the Choice of Law: Governmental Interests and the Judicial Function, in B. Currie, *Selected Essays on the Conflict of Laws*, 183–184 (1963).

[219] False conflict exists when only one state has a policy interest in the application of its law and all others have no interests. See W.L.M. Reese et al., *Cases and Materials on Conflict of Laws*, 488 (9th Ed. 1990); see also *Babcock v. Jackson*, 191 N.E. 2d 279 (N.Y. 1963); L. Brilmayer, *Conflict of Laws: Foundations and Future Directions*, 145–189 (1991); L. Kramer, Rethinking Choice of Law, 90 *Colum. L. Rev.* 277, 315–344 (1990); J.P. Trachtman, Conflict of Laws and Accuracy in the Allocation of Government Responsibility, 26 *Vand. J. Transnational L.* 975, 1017–1022 (1994).

[220] See further Mirzaian, *supra* note 113, at 20.

[221] Thus, it can often lead to unjust results and the law of other states shall be in an inferior position.

[222] See further L. Brilmayer, Interest Analysis and the Myth of Legislative Intent, *78 Michigan Law Review*, 392 (1980); see also J. Hill & J.E. Brazier, Constraining

proven to be an unreliable school of thought in the conflict of laws.[223] The theory of comparative impairment[224] suffers the same defects and is thus ill suited to electronic commerce.[225]

The Second Restatement later adopted the most significant relationship theory, according to which the court shall examine several factors to see whether the chosen law has a most significant relationship with the case in point. These include the place of contracting; the place of negotiation of the contract; the place of performance; the location of the subject matter of the contract; and the domicile, residence, nationality, place of incorporation, and place of business of the parties.[226] In carrying out this exam, the court shall give relevant weight to the following issues: the needs of interstate and international systems; the relevant policies of the forum; the relevant policies of other interested states and their interests in the issue; protection of justified expectation; basic policies of the field of law; certainty, predictability, and uniformity of result; and ease in the determination and application of the law to be applied.[227]

This theory is the favorite of scholars and judges who delight in the large measure of judicial discretion that results when judges are asked to catalog and weigh a number of usually incommensurable

---

Administrative Decisions: A Critical Examination of the Structure and Process Hypothesis, 7 *Journal of Law, Economics & Organization*, No. 2, 373, 398 (1991); P.S. Berman, The Globalization of Jurisdiction, 151 *U.Pa. L. Rev.* 422–423 (December 2002).

[223] F.K. Juenger, Conflict of Laws: A Critique of Interest Analysis, 32 *American Journal of Comparative Law*, 48 (1984).

[224] See generally W.F. Baxter, Choice of Law and the Federal System, 16 *Stanford Law Review*, 1 (1963). Under this theory, the court applies the substantive rule of the state whose policy goals would suffer most if the court used another state's law.

[225] See F.K. Juenger, Mass Disaster and the Conflict of Laws, *University of Illinois Law Review*, No. 1, 105, 113 (1989).

[226] Restatement (Second) of Conflict of Laws 188 (2), (1971). For further discussion on the factors in the context of the global information infrastructure, see H.H. Perritt, Jr., *Law and the Information Superhighway* 527–533 (1996).

[227] Restatement (Second) of Conflict of Laws 6, 145 (1971). Professor Leflar listed another five factors for consideration in making choice of law, namely: predictability of results; maintenance of interstate and international order; simplification of the judicial task; advancement of the forum's governmental interest; and application of the better rule of law. This offers little guidance. Furthermore, this theory tends to favor application of the forum law, which shall unfairly damage non-forum litigants, exhibit disrespect to non-forum governments and undermine principles of order and uniformity in choice of law. See further R.A. Leflar, *American Conflict of Law*, 193–195 (3rd Ed. 1977); see also G.R. Shreve, Choice of Law and the Forgiving Constitution, 71 *Indiana Law Review*, No. 2, 271 (1996).

factors.[228] Discarding the mechanic use of the applicable law, this flexible theory seriously attempts to find out the real law with the most significant connection with the case.

Yet what some see as its merits, others see as its shortcomings. It has been claimed that the criteria offer too little direction. With so much flexibility afforded to the court, no one can guess at which law will be applied: judges with different interests can achieve different results. Furthermore, when two laws have the same strength, it is impossible to make a legitimate decision between them.

Notable, too, are the rules adopted in the Uniform Computer Information Transactions Act (UCITA),[229] which reflects the updated trend for dealing with transactions in cyberspace. This commercial statute provides rules for contracting in furtherance of the contract law values of contract freedom and facilitation of commercial practice.[230] It deals with typical online transactions that involve the complete delivery of goods online. Rather than adopting a particular approach to choice of law, its provisions combine various choice-of-law rules to obtain a more particularized balance of relevant interests.[231]

First, party autonomy is encouraged. Both parties are to agree on the laws applied in their particular case,[232] and no limitations are

[228] W.H. Allen & E.A. O'Hara, Second Generation Law and Economics of Conflict of Laws: Baxter's Comparative Impairment and Beyond, 51 *Stanford Law Review*, 1019 (1999).

[229] This document can be found in <http://www.law.upenn.edu/bll/ulc_frame.htm>. It was drafted by the National Conference of Commissioners on Uniform State Laws (NCCUSL) and approved at its annual conference meeting in its one-hundred-and-ninth year in St. Augustine, Florida in 2000. In 2003, NCCUSL submitted resolution to the ABA House of Delegates for "approval" of UCITA. None of the six ABA sections and two committees charged with considering the resolution voted to approve it. Seven of the nine members of the ABA UCITA Working Group advised the House of Delegates that UCITA should not be approved. Accordingly, NCCUSL withdrew the UCITA resolution from consideration at the ABA House of Delegates. For controversies concerning the UCITA, see further C.L. Mann. The Uniform Computer Information Transactions Act and Electronic Commerce: Balancing Issues and Overlapping Jurisdiction in the Global Electronic Marketplace: The UCITA Example, 8 *Washington University Journal of Law & Policy* 218–220 (2002).

[230] See further R.T. Nimmer, *UCITA: Modern Contract Law for a Modern Information Economy*, in Patents, Copyrights, Trademarks, and Literary Property Course Handbook Series, 232–233 (1999).

[231] See further K. Patchel, Choice of Law and Software Licenses: A Framework for Discussion, 26 *Brooklyn Journal of International Law*, 160 (2000).

[232] Subsection 109 (a) of the UCITA provides that the parties in their agreements may choose the applicable law.

placed on the laws chosen. Comment 2 indicates that any limits on the autonomy of parties with a reasonable relationship to the jurisdiction whose law is selected were inappropriate, especially in cyberspace transactions where physical locations are often irrelevant or unknown.[233] However, in consumer transactions, relevant consumer protection provisions should not be omitted. Mandatory rules of the forum state should be respected. Two limits are listed in Comment 2: general limitations such as the doctrine of unconscionability and the public policy exception of UCITA section 105.[234]

If no choice of law has been made, three types of law are relevant. Firstly, an access contract or a contract providing for electronic delivery of a copy is governed by the law of the jurisdiction where the licensor was located when the agreement was entered into.[235] The location of the licensor is the connecting point; depending on the circumstances, this can be the licensor's place of business, chief executive office, place of incorporation or primary registration, or primary residence.[236]

Secondly, a consumer contract that requires delivery of a copy on a tangible medium is governed by the law of the jurisdiction where the copy is or should have been delivered to the consumer.[237] This provision relates to the transactions reached through the Internet but consummated in the physical world.

The principle of the most significant relationship is applied for all other cases.[238] Comment 4 states both that this rule is similar to the rule of the Second Restatement and that interpretations of the restatement are applicable.[239] The main achievement of the UCITA is that

---

[233] See further Section 109 of the UCITA. Comment 2 states that the information economy accentuates the importance of contractual choice of law provisions because it allows remote parties to enter and perform contracts spanning multiple jurisdictions and operating in circumstances that do not depend on physical location of either party or the information. Subsection (a) enables small companies to actively engage in multinational business; if the agreement could not designate applicable law, even the smallest business could be subject to the law of all fifty States and all countries in the world. That would impose large costs and uncertainty on an otherwise efficient system of commerce; it would raise barriers to entry.

[234] UCITA d109 cmt.2b.

[235] Subsection 109 (b) (1) of the UCITA.

[236] Subsection 109 (d) of the UCITA.

[237] Subsection 109 (b) (2) of the UCITA.

[238] Subsection 109 (b) (3) of the UCITA.

[239] Comment 4 of UCITA b 109 (b).

it clarifies the connecting factors for electronic commerce by applying the most significant relationship test.

3.2.1.2. The EU

Dealing with "contractual obligations in any situation involving a choice between the laws of different countries,"[240] the Rome Convention on the Law Applicable to Contractual Obligations (Rome Convention)[241] provides the best guide for understanding the attitude of the EU.[242] With the harmony of member states of the EU in mind, it works to eliminate differences between national conflict rules that impede the free movement of persons, services and capital.[243] In practice, there are important limitations on their general applicability,[244] but the convention's rules should serve as a model for handling contractual relationships within the EU.

First of all, it highly advocates the principle of party autonomy.[245] The law chosen by the parties shall govern the contract, and the parties are free to choose whatever law they like, even the law of a country not party to the convention.[246] The choice does not have to be made in writing, but it must be expressed or demonstrated with reasonable certainty by the terms of the contract or the circumstances of the case.[247] One limitation lies in the public policy requirement.[248]

---

240 Rome Convention, Article 1 (1).

241 80/934/EEC. This Convention, entered into force on April 1, 1991, is set up by the EU and applied to members of the Union. As it takes the form of an international agreement rather than a Community instrument proper, the European Court of Justice has no jurisdiction to interpret it. On January 14, 2003, the European Commission presented a Green Paper on the question of whether it should be converted into a Community instrument proper and modernized on the substance.

242 See further Lindberg, *supra* note 137.

243 C. Saf, *A Study of the Interplay between the Conventions Governing International Contracts of Sale*, September 1999, <http://www.cisg.law.pace.edu/cisg/text/saf1.html>.

244 Firstly, the convention does not take precedence over rules included in the EU legislation; secondly, it does not apply where a member state has joined an international convention on a certain topic; thirdly, the convention exempts from coverage certain substantial areas, including wills and succession, domestic relations, commercial paper, corporate law, and trust.

245 Rome Convention, Article 3 (1).

246 Rome Convention, Article 2, Article 3 (1).

247 Rome Convention, Article 2.

248 The parties cannot choose to avoid the mandatory rules of a country if all parts of the contract are closely connected to that country. See Rome Convention, Article 3 (3).

In the absence of party autonomy, the court shall look to see whether the parties' implied choice has been demonstrated with reasonable certainty.[249] If no implied choice can be deduced, the convention provides that the law of the state with which the contract is most closely connected shall govern the contract.[250] The convention assumes that the contract is most closely connected with the state where at the time of the conclusion of the contract, the party who effects the performance characteristic of the contract habitually resides, or, in the case of a corporate body, is centrally administered.[251]

Characteristic performance refers to the performance for which the payment is due. Depending on the type of the contract, this could include the delivery of goods, the granting of the right to make use of an item of property, the provision of a service, transport, insurance, banking operations, security, etc., which usually constitutes the center of gravity[252] and the socio-economic function of the contractual transaction.[253]

In the EU, consumers are highly protected[254] and a special part of the convention is reserved for consumer contracts.[255] Party autonomy is still upheld, but autonomous arrangements are not to deprive the consumer of the protection provided by mandatory rules of the state where he habitually resides.[256] Exemptions are applicable if, firstly, the consumer is subject to special invitation or advertising in the state of his habitual residence before concluding the contract; and secondly, if he has taken all necessary steps for the conclusion of the contract in that state.[257] Where the parties have not agreed on the applicable law in advance, the law of the consumers' habitual residence will apply.

---

[249] Article 3 (1).

[250] Article 4 (1).

[251] Article 4 (2) of Rome Convention.

[252] Instead of establishing clear choice-of-law rules that dictate a *priori* the law that will apply to a particular category of transactions based on the occurrence of a particular event or the location of one of the parties within the chosen jurisdiction, the center of gravity approach directs the forum to apply the law of the jurisdiction that has the closest connection with the particular transaction or, in some cases, the particular issue before it.

[253] See further M. Giuliano & P. Lagarde, *Report on the Convention on the Law Applicable to Contractual Obligations*, 1980 O.J. (C 282) 1, 20.

[254] See further V. Kendall, *EC Consumer Law* (1995).

[255] According to Article 5 (1), this refers to where the consumer is acting outside of his or her "trade or profession", that is, acting as a private person.

[256] Article 5 (2).

[257] *Id.*

The appropriateness of the consumer protection rules in the light of the development of electronic commerce were further evaluated in the Green Paper on the conversion of the Rome Convention of 1980 on the law applicable to contractual obligations into a Community instrument and its modernization.[258] With the development of new distance selling techniques, Article 5 of the Rome Convention is criticized for the criteria of distinguishing consumers eligible for specific protection from those subject to the general system. Guidelines are provided for the debate, bearing in mind the general concerns for the protection for the consumer and the need to preserve balance in the interests of the parties.[259]

While there are no special rules contained in the Rome Convention for electronic commerce, the EU has adopted several directives to deal with specific issues arising out of digital communications. The EU Data Protection Directive[260] was adopted in 1995 and took effect on October 25, 1998. It applies to all processing of personal data, with only limited exceptions.[261] Though harmonization is far from complete, its initial intention was to harmonize the data protection laws.[262]

With a view to areas lacking harmonization, Article 4 of the directive lays out the rules for choice of law. The principle rule is that each member state shall apply its own data protection laws where the processing is carried out in the context of the activities of an establishment of the controller on the territory of the member state.[263] The location of the controller determines choice of law. As far as the directive is concerned, a controller is the person who alone or jointly with others determines the purposes and means of the processing of personal data.[264] In electronic commerce, this can mean the seller who is doing business. The seller is the person who is making

---

[258] Green Paper, presented by the Commission of the European Communities, Brussels, January 14, 2003, COM (2002) 654 final.

[259] *Id.*

[260] Directive 95/46/EC of the European Parliament and the Council, October 24, 1995, Official Journal of the European Community, L1281 (November 23, 1995), at 31, <http://europa.eu.int/comm/dg15/en>.

[261] See Article 2, 3; and P.P. Swire & R.E. Litan, *None of Your Business: World Data Flows, Electronic Commerce, and European Privacy Directive*, Chapter 2 (1998).

[262] See further P.P. Swire, *Of Elephants, Mice, and Privacy: International Choice of Law and the Internet*, <http://www.acs.ohio-state.edu/units/law/swire1/elephants.htm>.

[263] Directive, Article 4 (1) (a).

[264] Directive, Article 2 (d).

use of the digital information and thus the law of the seller should be applied in such cases.

The EU Distance Selling Directive is another representative of EU policy. The choice of law rules contained in the directive concern the policy of consumer protection.[265] This directive is applicable to organized sales efforts that use a means of distance communication, including telephones, the mail, or the Internet.[266] The directive requires member states to take measures to ensure consumers do not lose the protection granted by this directive in virtue of the choice of law of a non-member country as the law applicable to the contract if this contract has a close connection with the territory of one or more of the member states.[267] No matter what law is chosen for the contract, the consumers shall still be protected by their home-country law.[268]

3.2.1.3. The 1985 Hague Convention

The Hague Convention on the Law Applicable to Contracts of International Sales of Movable Goods[269] is an important international agreement on uniform conflict-of-laws rules in contracts.[270] The purpose of the convention is to mitigate that legal unpredictability suffered due to differing national rules by unifying law in international sales. To date, it has not entered into force; only five states have ratified the convention,[271] which largely limits its meaningfulness in practice. Furthermore, its scope excludes its application to several sales contracts. Still, it serves as a useful model.

---

[265] It grants the consumer the right to withdraw from a distant contract for at least seven working days, without giving any reason and without penalty except for the cost of returning the goods. See further Article 6 (1) of the Distance Selling Directive.

[266] See further Article 2 (1) & (4) and Annex I of the Directive concerning the covered means of communications.

[267] Distance Selling Directive, Article 12 (2).

[268] See further P. Meller, Online Buyers Gain Ability to Sue, N.Y. Times, December 1, 2000, at <http://www.nytimes.com/2000/12/01/technology/01NET.html>; and M.A. O'Rourke, Progressing Towards a Uniform Commercial Code for Electronic Commerce or Racing Towards Nonuniformity?, 14 *Berkeley Tech. L.J.* 635, 654–655 (1999).

[269] The convention can be found in <http://www.hcch.net/e/conventions/text31e.html>. It concluded on December 22, 1986.

[270] The Hague Convention is a permanent multinational group charged with preparing texts that unify choice of law rules. See further P. Winship, Private International Law and the U.N. Sales Convention, 21 *Cornell International Law Review*, No. 3, 487–488 (1988).

[271] Argentina, Czech Republic, Moldova, the Netherlands, and Slovakia.

The convention acknowledges the law chosen by the parties.[272] It further provides several external conditions for this chosen law.[273] Importantly, the parties should choose a law applicable to part of the contract.[274] But there is no limitation in essence when it comes to defining contractual connections. Parties are free to choose applicable law as long as connection is expressed or clearly demonstrated by the terms of the contract and the conduct of the parties, viewed in their entirety.[275]

Where no choice of law is made, the law of the state where the seller has his place of business at the time of conclusion of the contract shall govern.[276] In certain situations, the law of the state of the buyer also has power.[277] The appropriate law shall ultimately be determined by the principle of the law with closest connection.[278]

The Hague Convention occurred well before the wide use of the Internet and no consideration was at that time paid to electronic commerce. However, its principles for international practice represent an overview of conditions acceptable to most states.

3.2.2. *Analysis of the Present Applicable Law Regime and Suggestions*

To sum up, the descriptions above reveal present legal attitudes in the EU. The Second Restatement sets out a list of factors to guide the forum's decision and, further, lists items to be taken into account in applying those factors to contracts.[279] According to the Second Restatement, the forum shall have a broad discretion. The EU takes a different position. The Rome Convention sets more limits for the forum in choosing the applicable law. It has a bright line rule, which sets out rebuttable presumptions regarding the country that has the closet connection.[280] We will discuss in the following part whether and how such principles will fit into the digital world.

---

272 Article 7 (1) of the Hague Convention.

273 *Id.*

274 *Id.* Article 7 (2).

275 *Id.* Article 7 (1).

276 *Id.* Article 8 (1).

277 See further *Id.* Article 8 (2).

278 *Id.* Article 8 (3).

279 See further Section 6 and 188 of the Second Restatement. For example, it provides that when the place of negotiating the contract and the place of performance are in the same state, the law of that state usually will apply.

280 It is claimed that the Rome Convention is more state-selective and less approach-oriented, than the Second Restatement. See further E.F. Scoles & P. Hay, *Conflict of Laws*, 2.18, *supra* note 208, at 47.

3.2.2.1. Party Autonomy

Reflecting democratic values, all the legal regimes recognize the importance of party autonomy: parties should have the right to choose the law regulating their contractual relationship. Granting party autonomy is also the easiest way of settling the issues of applicable law.[281] The court can easily determine applicable law. And when involved in the process of determination, parties gain a clearer perspective on the present business and take a more serious attitude towards possible actions.[282] Party autonomy shall be even more strongly encouraged in the case of electronic commerce because of these two key factors: the possibility of doing business on the Internet without knowing the other party's physical location; and the simultaneous presentation of information on the Internet to all jurisdictions.[283]

Should parties be free to choose any law they wish, even a law with no clear relationship to the contract? Apparently, the parties can choose any law they wish, provided their choice reflects their real intentions. When a law is not well adaptable to a case, another, more advanced law should govern.[284] The freedom of law is particularly important in electronic commerce cases, as many states lag behind in making updated legislation to accommodate the new situation.

Choice of law in consumer transactions is another important issue. Most legislation gives consumers special protection because they have traditionally been in a weak position in transacting relationships. But traditional circumstances have changed with the emergence of electronic commerce. That the Internet is both limiting the ability of a seller to confine its market and dramatically widening the options available to consumers invalidates the presumption of inequality in consumer transactions. As power to decide rests in the hands of the consumer, policy reasons for refusing to enforce party autonomy in

---

[281] See further L.O. Smiddy, Choosing the Law and Forum for the Litigation of Disputes, in A.W. Branscomb (Ed.), *Toward a Law of Global Communications Networks*, 303 (1986).

[282] Party autonomy that recognizes the ability of the parties to choose for themselves the law that will apply to their transaction values most highly the parties' planning-related interests, and, in particular, their interest in certainty and predictability. See further Restatement (Second) of Conflict of Laws, r187cmt. e (1971).

[283] This is in accordance with the idea of self-governance in cyberspace. One view of cyberspace is that sovereigns should refrain from regulation of the Internet and the Internet society should take up this job so that distinct law and legal institutions are well designed.

[284] Restatement (Second) of Conflict of Laws, 187, cmt. f (1971).

such commercial contexts are weakened.[285] The characteristics of electronic commerce and the needs of Internet entrepreneurs justify party autonomy.[286] Reality justifies party autonomy. Contractual choice of law clauses in the sale agreements set out by the merchants are generally enforced, even when a clause looks like, acts like, and is part of an adhesive consumer contract.[287]

To avoid any possible adverse result, it is also advisable to add the provision that party autonomy not conflict with the public policy of relevant states. Strong public policies must be taken into account, or else enforcement be called into question.

Historically, courts have viewed the choice of law in adhesion contracts[288] suspiciously.[289] But with the emergence of electronic commerce, views are changing. The way to reach agreements in electronic commerce is of course different from the way to reach agreements in traditional transactions. Advertisements including choice of law provisions may be put on the web. Consumers can look through the advertisements and if they agree with the provisions, they can click on an Agree Button.[290] In such cases, consumers should know what they are getting into. Those who are dissatisfied with choice-of-law provision may simply "vote with his or her mouse" and seek a new party.[291] The definition of what constitutes an appropriate contract is changing. Recent cases[292] suggest that standardized forms or even

---

285 Vartanian, *supra* note 169.

286 Although this rationale focuses primarily on the needs of electronic commerce, the present trend and ongoing practice show that the broad contractual choice-of-law provision applies to all transactions, not just those conducted electronically.

287 L.S. Mullenix, Another Easy Case, Some More Bad Law: Carnival Cruise Lines and Contractual Personal Jurisdiction, 27 *Tex. Int'l L.J.* 323, 325 (1992); P.D. Carrington, Regulating Dispute Resolution Provisions in Adhesion Contracts, 35 *Harv. J. on Legis.* 225–226 (1998).

288 An adhesive contract is a standardized contract offered exclusively on a "take it or leave it" basis without giving the consumer an opportunity to bargain. *Black's Law Dictionary* 40 (6th Ed. 1990).

289 The forum shall scrutinize adhesive contracts with care and will refuse to apply any choice-of-law provision they may contain if to do so would result in substantial injustice to the adherent. See further Restatement (Second) of Conflict of Laws 187 cmt. b (1971); see also Scoles, *supra* note 208, at 671–672.

290 See further M. Burnstein, A Global Network in a Compartmentalized Legal Environment, in K. Boele-Woelki & C. Kessedjian (Eds.), *Internet: Which Court Decides? Which Law Applies?* 31–32 (Kluwer Law International, 1998).

291 *Id.*

292 See for example, *Carnival Cruise Lines v. Shute*, 499 U.S. 585, 593–594 (1991). The U.S. Supreme Court upheld the choice-of-law provision even though bargaining parity between the two parties was lacking. Justice Brennan acknowledged that a

simple visual notices on log-on screens are acceptable contracts. It is very likely that further development of electronic commerce will give rise to generally accepted practice concerning applicable law, which shall best balance the interests of and be well accepted by the public.[293]

3.2.2.2. Applicable Law in Absence of Party Autonomy

In electronic commerce cases where parties fail to choose applicable law, we must settle on appropriate connecting factors for determining applicable law.

As transborder transactions have become commonplace, the former stringent physicality requirement has been abandoned in general practice,[294] and the principle of the most significant relationship has been adopted by most states. This controversial principle is applicable to transactions through the Internet as well as to normal transactions. The present author believes it offers good general guidelines for determining the final applicable law, but holds that its flexibility necessitates an element of certainty. When it comes to electronic commerce, the real problem resides in the choice of connecting factors for deciding applicable law.

Electronic commerce can be further divided into two types of transactions based on methods of distribution: dealings reached through the Internet with physical delivery and dealings totally done through the Internet.[295]

There cannot be much disagreement as regards the first type. Though it may be difficult to determine the location of contractual dealings, the place of the delivery of goods should be an effective territorial link. Practices for dealing with traditional transactions are thus still relevant.

Transactions completed in cyberspace pose a bigger problem. If a product is downloaded, the merchant lacks even a delivery address.

---

complaining party, by satisfying a "heavy burden of proof", could show that a forum selection clause should not stand because it would be grossly onerous to that party.

[293] See further H.H. Perritt, Jr., Dispute Resolution in Electronic Network Communities, *38 Vill. L. Rev*. 391 (1993); see also E. Katsh, Law in a Digital World: Computer Networks and Cyberspace, 38 *Vill. L. Rev*. 403 (1993).

[294] See generally W.M. Richman & W.L. Reynolds, *Understanding Conflict of Laws* (1984).

[295] This delivery can take the form of actual downloading of a copy of the software product, or merely the provision of access to the software for its use online.

The intangible nature of exchanged property renders certain connecting factors, such as location of contracting and performance, meaningless in determining the jurisdiction of whose law should apply to the contract.[296]

A connecting factor can be personal or of a particular action. Traditionally, when the location of a particular action has lost its meaning, we can still rely on the location of relevant parties. To protect consumers, the law of the state where the consumers reside is usually applied.[297] But electronic commerce demands a change in such practice. It would be unfair to request an online merchant, whose customer base could easily span the globe, to face so many disparate international laws.[298] Particularly in light of the changing power dynamic within electronic commerce today, it is advisable to apply the law of the state of the merchant's residence or place of business. This has been testified by the position of the US and the EU discussed above.

3.3. *Choice of Law in Tort*

Torts arise in electronic commerce in the form of intellectual property rights infringement, defamation, etc. As the Internet has made information on the web easily viewable to a large number of people around the world, torts can result in even more adverse consequence than ever before.[299] Plaintiffs are often left without a clear forum or effective law since many cyber-torts occur without prior contractual relations that would settle issues of jurisdiction and applicable law.[300] Thus, the issue of torts is likely to be much more significant in cyberspace than it has been to date in real space.[301] Many cases

[296] See further E. Ulmer, *Intellectual Property Rights and the Conflict of Laws*, 7 (1976).

[297] See, for example, Rome Convention, Article 5 (2).

[298] For example, when a UK company conducting lawful business activities under English law could face the risk of prosecution in a country as a result of a complaint by a consumer or by a competitor in that country merely because the web site is accessed in that country. What the company can do is to take measures to restrict its trading activities in certain countries or simply take the risk of needing to comply with various national laws.

[299] Digital networks make possible multinational infringements that are simultaneous and pervasive. See further J.C. Ginsburg, Copyright Without Borders? Choice of Forum and Choice of Law for Copyright Infringement in Cyberspace, 15 *Cardozo Arts & Entertainment Law Journal*, 155 (1997).

[300] Resnick, *supra* note 13, at A21.

[301] T. Hardy, The Proper Legal Regime for "Cyberspace", 55 *U. Pitts. L. Rev.*, 1053 (1994).

have already arisen with regard to torts on the Internet.[302] It is expected that even more cases will arise with the increasingly wider application of electronic commerce.

Not surprisingly, the issue of choice of law arises with respect to torts committed via the Internet.[303] As different applicable laws can result in dramatically different results, choosing the right law is important to ensuring a justified judicial decision.

3.3.1. *International Practice*

3.3.1.1. The US

In general, two major doctrines exist for resolving choice of law. The First Restatement uses the simple rule of *lex loci delicti*, or the law of the place of the wrong,[304] i.e., the place where the last event necessary to make an actor liable arises.[305] In most situations, this place is where the injury occurs.[306]

This simple way of deciding applicable law is often lauded for providing certainty, uniformity and predictability of the outcome.[307] Indeed, it is obvious to us that the law of place is appropriate for real space on account of its certainty and ease of application.[308] But its implications for cyberspace are problematic. Since information on the Internet can be reached from any location and torts arising in

---

[302] See for example, *Daniel v. Dow Jones & Co.*, 137 Misc. 2d 94 (N.Y. Sup. Ct. 1987); *Cubby, Inc. v. CompuServe, Inc.*, 776 F.Supp. 135 (S.D.N.Y. 1991).

[303] C.P. Beall, The Scientological Defenestration of Choice-of-law Doctrines for Publication Torts on the Internet, 15 *J. Marshall J. of Computer & Info. L.*, 365 (1997).

[304] *Black's Law Dictionary* 911 (West, 6th Ed. 1990).

[305] See further J.D. Lee & B.A. Lindahl, *Modern Tort Law: Liability & Litigation* 13.03 (Rev. Ed. 1994).

[306] When a person shoots another one in State A, A shall be the place of wrong since this is where the force infringed upon his body. See further Restatement (First) of the Conflict of Laws, section 377, illustration 1 and 4. To conflict scholars, this rule seemed largely arbitrary, indeed counterintuitive. See for example, B. Currie, Survival of Actions: Adjudication versus Automation in the Conflict of Laws, reprinted in Currie, *supra* note 218, at 128, 158; B. Currie, Married Woman's Contracts: A Study in Conflict-of-Laws Method, reprinted in Currie, *supra* note 218, at 77, 116 (1963).

[307] *Boudreau v. Baughman*, 322 NC 331, 368 SE2d 849, 854 (1988). It was once widely accepted among the States. See H.H. Kay, Theory into Practice: Choice of Law in the Courts, *34 Mercer Law Review*, 521, 586 (1983); see also D.F. Cavers, *The Choice-of-Law Process* 6 (1965).

[308] M.R. Burnstein, Conflicts on the Net: Choice of Law in Transnational Cyberspace, 29 *Vanderbit Journal of Transnational Law*, 94 (1996).

cyberspace can be felt in almost every state, this law would justify the use of the law of any state connected to the Internet. Ironically, this would mean no *lex loci delicti* at all.[309] The law of place flounders on the Internet where there are no boundaries to demarcate the site of harm.[310] A judge using the First Restatement rule would end up no closer to a decision than before applying the choice-of-law rule.[311] To an extent, the expectation of internet players may suffer as they often are unaware of the physical locations of the Internet addresses they visit and may know even less about the residency of their fellow sojourners in cyberspace.[312] Or, the Internet could offer the plaintiff in the case the opportunity to forum-shop by securing the choice of law through skillful use of allegations at the pleading stage,[313] which would directly result in injustice.

In response to changes in modes of communication and transportation, the emphasis of the choice of law has shifted away from territoriality presumptions towards a more flexible legal theory.[314] The Second Restatement initially directs the court to consider where the injury occurred, but when another state has a more significant relationship, the court should look to it.[315] The court has to examine several contacts to find out the place with the most significant relationship:[316] the place where the conduct causing the injury occurred;

[309] See further H. DeSaussure & P.P.C. Haanappel, A Unified Multinational Approach to the Application of Tort and Contract Principles to Outer Space, 6 *Syracuse J. International L. & Com.* No. 1, 12 (1978).

[310] F.K. Juenger, *Choice of Law and Multistate Justice*, 51 (1993).

[311] J.D. Faucher, Let the Chips Fall Where They May: Choice of Law in Computer Bulletin Board Defamation Cases, 26 *U.C. Davis Law Review*, 1056–1057 (1993).

[312] See further R.H. Acker, Choice-of-Law Questions in Cyberfraud, *The University of Chicago Legal Forum*, 446 (1996).

[313] See further *Keeton v. Hustler Magazine, Inc.*, 465 U.S. 770 (1984).

[314] This can be demonstrated by statistics: in 1983, 21 States applied this rule; since 1994, only 13 States followed it. See further Kay, *supra* note 307, at 591–592; see also S.C. Symeonides, Choice of Law in the American Courts in 1993 (and in the Six Previous Years), 42 *American Journal of Comparative Law*, 599, 606 (1994); S.C. Symeonides, Choice of Law in the American Courts in 1994: A View "From the Trenches", 43 *American Journal of Comparative Law*, 1 (1995); P.J. Borchers, The Choice-of-Law Revolution: An Empirical Study, 49 *Wash. & Lee L. Rev.* 357, 373–374 (1992).

[315] Restatement (Second) of Conflict of Laws, 145 (2) (a) (1971). The court is not idly choosing a law, but resolving a controversy. See G.R. Shreve (Ed.), *A Conflict-of-Laws Anthology* 55 (Cincinnati: Anderson Publishing Co., 1997); D.F. Cavers, A Critique of the Choice of Law Problem, 47 *Harv. L. Rev.* 173, 189 (1933).

[316] *Id.* 145.

the place of the domicile or residence of the parties; and the place where the parties' relationship is centered.[317] The analysis shall also consider the factors relevant to contractual issues.[318] These factors are intended to help courts answer the question of whether or not justice is furthered by the application of one state's law to events that occurred in a different state.[319] Applicable law results from a careful balancing of all relevant considerations regarding fairness, efficiency, conflicting needs, and appropriate legal principles.[320]

Having acknowledged that a defendant risks becoming subject to another state's laws when his conduct causes effects in the other state, the earlier territorial emphasis has been broken, and a new flexible approach to choice of law is put in place.[321] However, it sacrifices simplicity and certainty expected by the involved parties,[322] which are important considerations for choice of law.[323]

With the flexible elaboration, the Second Restatement offers little substantive guidance concerning detailed choice-of-law decisions,[324] especially when the factors relied upon are geared towards a real-space world of easily drawn political boundaries. Per these guidelines, the choice-of-law process is administered on a case-by-case, ad-hoc basis with no clear-cut rules. Balancing the various factors in cyberspace and determining relevant locations in the digital world is daunting.[325]

Equally as daunting is implementing other US conflict-of-law approaches, which include center of gravity approach, interest analysis approach, and the Leflar better law approach.[326]

---

[317] *Id.* 145 (2).

[318] *Id.* 6, 145.

[319] *Id.* 6 cmt. c.

[320] See further Acker, *supra* note 312, 456–457.

[321] P. Stone, *The Conflict of Laws*, 2–3 (1995).

[322] Restatement (Second) of Conflict of Laws, 6 cmt. g.

[323] *Id.* 6 cmt. g & cmt. I; see also L. Brilmayer, The Role of Substantive and Choice of Law Policies in the Formation and Applicable of Choice of Law Rules, in 252 *Recueil des Cours* 9, 57 (Hague Academy of International Law, Ed. 1995).

[324] As judge has wide discretion in choosing a law with the most significant relationship, this principle means nothing except, perhaps, that the answer is not ready at hand. See for example, W.L.M. Reese, The Law Governing Airplane Accidents, *39 Washington & Lee Law Review*, 1303–1304 (1982); see also R. David, The International Unification of Private Law, 2 *International Encyclopedia of Comparative Law*, 8 (1969).

[325] For further criticisms, see F.K. Juenger, Choice of Law in Interstate Torts, 118 *U. Pa. L. Rev.* 202, 212 (1969).

[326] For further discussions, see S. Wilske, Conflict of Laws in Cyber Torts, *Computer Und Recht International*, No. 3, 70–71 (2001).

Nevertheless, at the present stage, no other principles or approaches can be found to accommodate the new demands of choice of law in cyberspace. State courts usually apply *lex fori* whenever they feel that interests of residents in their jurisdiction are at stake, in particular when activities in cyberspace result in a certain negative effect in their state.[327] Actually, significant advances in mobility have led to more cases involving interests of several states, and the flexible approach contained in this principle can better meet the demands of the complexity entailed therein. The chosen applicable law should ultimately be justified by its close relationship with the case. Accordingly, while further work shall be done to add clarity to the choice-of-law, this principle shall not be abandoned.

3.3.1.2. The EU

No conventions have harmonized this area in the EU, and the member states are free to adopt their own rules. Most states follow the same rule: *lex loci delicti*, or the law of the place where the tort was committed.[328] However, there are still disagreements when the action causing the tort and the harm occur in different places. Since no unified rules exist at the EU level, choice of law is up to the national rule where the suit is brought.[329]

That said, recent legislation at the EU level suggests a trend with implications for choice of law. Looking at such legislation is important because it applies directly to the member states and takes precedence over pre-existing national laws. Such legislation is flexible and specifically tailored to meet new situations.

In September 1993, the European Council adopted a Directive on Copyright and related Rights as they pertain to satellite and cable broadcasts.[330] This proposal was based on the EU's Satellite Broadcasting Council Directive,[331] which applies the broadcasting country

[327] Beall, *supra* note 303, at 361, III; J.H. Ely, Choice of Law and the State's Interest in Protecting Its Own, 23 *Wm. & Mary L. Rev.* 173 (1981); M.E. Solimine, An Economic and Empirical Analysis of Choice of Law, 24 *Ga. L. Rev.* 49–50 (1989).

[328] See M. Reimann, *Conflict of Laws in Western Europe: A Guide Through the Jungle*, 135 (1995); see also *Black's Law Dictionary* 923 (7th Ed. 1999).

[329] See further Swire, *supra* note 262.

[330] Council Directive No. 93/83/EEC on the Coordination of Certain Rules Concerning Copyright and Rights Related to Copyright Applicable to Satellite Broadcasting and Cable Retransmission, 1993 O.J. (L 248) 15.

[331] See Official Gazette of the EU No. L 248/15 (October 6th, 1993).

theory[332] and is seen as a divergence from the traditional principle of territoriality. This directive provides that if a satellite transmission infringed a copyrighted work, the law of the nation where the physical uplink occurred would determine the legal penalty for infringement.[333] This is a demonstration of the rule of origin, which better serves the goal of predictability and ease of determination of the applicable law than do choice of law rules that rely predominantly or exclusively on the economic impact of an act of exploitation.[334] When applied to the Internet, this approach could mean the law of the state where the Internet server is located would be applied.[335] However, this is only a deduction from the extant EU legislation.

The EU is now considering expanding the Rome Convention to deal with the applicable law with respect to non-contractual obligations.[336] Draft Council Convention on the Law Applicable to Non-Contractual Obligations (Rome II Convention)[337] establishes the principle of the closest connection,[338] which is usually the place where the action caused the damage.[339] However, the debate has not led to a definite consensus regarding whether the law of the country of domicile of the defendant or the plaintiff, or the law of the country where damage is actually suffered, or some other law should be adopted. Justifying a position will take time.[340]

---

[332] Article 1 (2) (b) of the Broadcasting Council Directive provides that the authoritative country for acquiring broadcasting rights is the country from where the broadcast is being conducted.

[333] See *Id.* P 15.

[334] See further L.G.C. Kaplan & J.R. Bankoff, Of Satellites and Copyrights: Problems of Overspill and Choice of Law, 7 *Emory International Law Review*, 727, 741 (1993).

[335] See further J.M. Driscoll, It's a Small World After All: Conflict of Laws and Copyright Infringement on the Information Superhighway, 20 *U. Pa. J. Int'l Econ. L.*, 978–979 (1999).

[336] Warchus, *supra* note 156.

[337] H.C. Dethloff, European Conflict-of-Law Provisions Governing Unfair Competition, Commercial Communications, December 1999, at 2.

[338] Article 3 (1) of the Rome II Convention.

[339] Article 3 (6) of the Convention.

[340] This provision has aroused attention from advertisers, publishers and online commerce companies, in particular in the US, and is still in discussion with the European Commission, who also prepared a green paper (COM 18 January 2001) to promote discussion. See further P. Meller, Proposed Law Stirs Concern on Europe E-Commerce, N.Y. Times, February 8, 2001.

3.3.2. *Analysis of the Possible Applicable Law*

According to traditional theory, the applicable law can be either that of the country where the tort originated or that of the residence of the defendant.[341] When it comes to tort in cyberspace, this can cause problems.

Determining territorial connection is vital to traditional theory. But when it comes to torts in cyberspace, we lack physical information. It is difficult not only to specify the location of those who take actions to originate the tort, but also to identify those defendants. Anyone can initiate a tort in electronic commerce from any location.

How can we determine location and best balance the interests of both parties? The present author believes the EU Directive discussed above takes the lead in answering this question. The US has not elaborated such a position, but the judgments of *Religious Tech. Ctr. V. Lerma*[342] and *Religious Tech. Ctr. V. F.A.C.T.Net, Inc.*[343] suggest support for a law of origin. Officially, they chose the law of the defendants' residence, which was the exact place where the Internet transmissions originated.

The location of the server is important to the initiation of the tort and easy to determine, which is relevant to the choice of law. Moreover, Internet servers are in themselves vital to the origination and existence of tort in cyberspace. Thus, the law of the state where the Internet server is located can best suit the case of tort in electronic commerce.

The law of the server equates to the country of origin rule in electronic commerce jargon.[344] At first, determining the origin of the tort seems difficult. Presumably, the action of tort in electronic commerce arises firstly in the place where the information is made public.[345] But as determining the location of the user or the computer

---

[341] See further Restatement (First) of the Conflict of Laws, section 377, illustration 1 and 4.

[342] 897 F.Supp. 260 (E.D. Va. 1995).

[343] 901 F.Supp. 1519 (D. Colo. 1995).

[344] This rule is officially adopted by the EU in its Ecommerce Directive, which frees trades from the needs to comply with the national laws of 15 Member States. See further *European Parliament Passes the Ecommerce Directive*, 4th May 1000, <http://www.silicon.com/bin/bladeru . . . EVENT=&REQINT1=37294&REQAUTH=21046>.

[345] See R.T. Nimmer & P.A. Krauthaus, The Global Information Superhighway Challenges Virtually all of the Premises of Copyright Law, 6 *Stanford Law & Policy*

can be difficult, the location of the server is the best mark. The law of the location of the server fulfils the requirement of foreseeability: the parties shall be able to foresee the law that shall be applied in their particular case.[346] In consequence, it supports the notion of fairness and protection of individual rights.[347] The law of the country of the server has the added benefit of helping to hold Internet Service Providers, with the knowledge of relevant activities performed by users, liable for misdeeds concerning third-party activities.[348]

Various questions have been raised concerning the application of the rule of origin.[349] As might be expected, no one approach is likely

---

Review, 25, 32–39 (1994); N. Elkin-koren, Copyright Law and Social Dialogue on the Information Superhighway: The Case Against Copyright Liability of Bulletin Board Operators, 13 *Cardozo Arts & Ent. L. J.*, 345, 387 (1995); T. Dreier, Copyright Digitized: Philosophical Impacts and Practical Implications for Information Exchanges in Digital Networks, in *WIPO Worldwide Symposium on the Impact of Digital Technology on Copyright and Neighboring Rights*, 187, 198 (1993).

[346] This can be illustrated by the example of product liability. Foreseeability safeguards the interest of a manufacturer by ensuring he will avoid liability under the law of countries if he demonstrates that he could not have foreseen that product would be marketed or used there. See further P.J. Kozyris, Values and Methods in Choice of Law for Products Liability: A Comparative Comment on Statutory Solutions, 38 *American Journal of Comparative Law*, 475, 501–507 (1990); R.J. Weintraub, Methods for Resolving Conflict-of-Laws Problems in Mass Tort Litigation, *U. Ill.L.Rev.* 129, 148 (1989); Hague Conference on Private International Law: Convention on the Law Applicable to Products Liability, October 12, 1972, Article 7, 11 I.L.M. 1283. This article provides that the place of injury or the plaintiff's residence is inapplicable if the manufacturer could not reasonably foresee that the injury causing product would be available in those places through ordinary commerce.

[347] Foreseeability is closely related to fairness and protection of individual rights. See further L. Brilmayer, *Conflict of Laws*, 210–230 (1991); and Brilmayer, *supra* note 323, at 60.

[348] See for example, M. Racicot et al., *The Cyberspace is not a "No Law Land"*, <http://www.strategis.ic.gc.ca/SSG/it03315e.html>; see also *Gershwin Publ'g Corp. v. Columbia Artists Management*, 443 F.2d 1159 (2d Cir. 1971); *Screen Gems-Columbia Music, Inc. v. Mark-Fi Records, Inc.*, 256 F.Supp. 399 (S.D.N.Y. 1996); J. I. Rojas, Liability of ISPs, Content Providers and End-Users on the Internet, in *18th Annual Institute on Computer Law*, at 1009, 1029 (PLI Pats., Copyrights, Trademarks, and Literary Prop. Course Handbook Series No. 507, 1998); J.P. Cunard & A.L. Wells, The Evolving Standard of Copyright Liability Online, *in Litigating Copyright, Trademark and Unfair Competition Cases for the Experienced Practitioner* 1997, at 365, 394 (PLI Pats., Copyrights, Trademarks, and Literary prop. Course Handbook Series No. 497, 1997).

[349] It is claimed that the application of this rule could be problematic in digitally generated networks where transmitting and receiving computers, scattered and even moving among myriad countries, can interactively change roles with ease; with this rule, pirates shall seek the least protective country to act; and lastly, there is the problem of recognition and enforcement of the judgments. See further R. Fentiman, *Conflict of Laws in Cyberspace*, paper submitted to the Symposium: Multimedia and the Internet: Global Challenges for Law, organized by International

to introduce absolute stability and secure the protection of legitimate rights.[350] But a territorial connecting point should be formulated to decide upon applicable law and at present it appears that location of origin is the most appropriate. Notably, while we admit the law of the state where the server is located, the principle of the most significant relationship still prevails as the guiding theory.

3.4. *General Observations*

The issue of choice of law is one of the most challenging aspects of law, both in theory and practice. It is not new, nor so long as there are different rules in different states will it ever go away.

The advent of electronic commerce has raised new issues for choice of law, which have become the foci of many recent discussions.[351] The Internet is particularly problematic for the traditional territorial choice of law regime because a single online action might lead to effects in a number of different countries.[352] Indeed, cyberspace has been aptly described as a "world unto itself,"[353] so dramatically redefining conceptions of community that the geographic locus of its members becomes largely irrelevant.[354] Choice of law is particularly difficult in the case of international computer networks where, because of dispersed location and rapid movement of data, and geographically dispersed data processing activities, several connecting factors could

---

Federation of Computer Law Associations, the Computer Law Association, Inc., and Belgian Association for Computer & Law, held in Brussels: June 27–28, 1996, at 3, 9; see also J.C. Ginsburg, *Global Use, Territorial Rights, Private International Law Questions of the Global Information Infrastructure*, paper submitted to WIPO Worldwide Symposium on Copyright in the Global Information Infrastructure, organized by WIPO, held in Mexico City, May 22–24, 1995, at 386, 396, 398, 401.

[350] K. Ishiguro, *International Copyright Infringements in Cyberspace: A Conflict-of-laws Analysis*, paper submitted to Session F-1 of the SOFTIC Symposium on a Balance between Protection and Exploitation of Digital Content, held in Tokyo: November 13–14, 1997, <http://www.ilpf.org/confer/present99/ishiguro_a1.htm>.

[351] See for example, J.L. Goldsmith, Against Cyberanarchy, 65 *University of Chicago Law Review*, 1199 (1998); J.C. Ginsburg, The Cyberian Captivity of Copyright: Territoriality and Authors' Rights in a Networked World, 15 *Santa Clara Computer & High Technology Law Journal*, 347 (1999); Ginsburg, *supra* note 299, at 153.

[352] K. Burmeister, Jurisdiction, Choice of Law, Copyright, and the Internet: Protection against Framing in an International Setting, 9 *Fordham Intellectual Property, Media & Entertainment Law Journal*, 658–659 (Winter, 1999).

[353] Modern communication has reduced the world's vastness into mere geographical lines, crossed over millions of times each second, without either a sovereign's or traveler's awareness. See Zembek, *supra* note 40, at 339, 343.

[354] See further Salbu, *supra* note 24, at 454; see also UCITA 109 cmt. 2 (2000).

occur in a complex manner, involving elements of legal novelty.[355] How can we choose a single governing law for activities having multi-jurisdictional connections, and how can we best deal with problems of *situs* in determining how to choose governing law when the locus of activity cannot easily be pinpointed in geographical space?[356] Choice of law must respond to the inherent features of the Global Information Infrastructure (GII) and most importantly, to the possibility of making documents simultaneously and instantaneously available throughout the world.[357]

Above all, the choice of law regime for electronic commerce should serve the twin goals of conflict of laws: certainty and fairness.[358] While recognizing the importance of flexibility in deciding applicable law, some element of determinacy should be imposed. In contractual disputes and tort, the significant relationship principle is the standard in resolving choice of law.

While cyberspace is intangible, it exists in the smallest bursts of matter and energy called forth by the presence of man in a particular location through an Internet provider.[359] It is not self-contained: cyberspace infractions that are disconnected from particularized physical space nonetheless entail injuries to people in the real space.[360] Thus, physical connections can still be loosely found and they can serve as connections for deciding applicable law. In particular, the location of the Internet server, a typical physical connection to cyberspace, could be most helpful in deciding applicable law not only in tort, but also in other possible issues.

---

[355] D.L. Burk, Patents in Cyberspace: Territoriality and Infringement on Global Computer Networks, 68 *Tulane Law Review* 5 (1993); see also OECD, explanatory memorandum, *in Guidelines on the Protection of Privacy and Transborder Data Flows of Personal Data*, 13, 36 (1980).

[356] See further Boss, *supra* note 194, at 1234.

[357] A.P. Reindl, Choosing Law in Cyberspace: Copyright Conflicts on Global Networks, 19 *Michigan Journal of International Law*, 870 (1998).

[358] G.A. Zaphiriou, Basis of the Conflict of Laws: Fairness and Effectiveness, 10 *Geo. Mason U. L. Rev.* 302–303 (1988). The parties themselves shall value primary predictability, which also promotes social utility. If the parties have clearly established legal rights, then presumably they are much better able to bargain privately and reach more efficient outcomes. See further R.H. Coase, The Problem of Social Cost, 3 *Journal of Law & Economics* 1, 19 (1960); see also C.L. Ingrim, Choice-of-Law Clauses: Their Effect on Extraterritorial Analysis—A Scholar's Dream, A Practitioner's Nightmare, 28 *Creighton Law Review*, 663, 677 (1995).

[359] D. Menthe, Jurisdiction in Cyberspace: A Theory of International Spaces, 4 *Michigan Telecommunications Technology Law Review*, 69 (1998), <http://www.mttlr.org/volfour/menthe.html>.

[360] See further Zembek, *supra* note 40, at 341, 347, 367.

In addition to principles for choice of law, uniform rules for dealing with disputes in electronic commerce are requisite. A model law made by experts in cyberspace shall be welcomed by states at large trying to advocate electronic commerce or in the process of initiating electronic commerce. The efforts of the UNCITRAL[361] and the EU are exemplary.[362]

4. *Conclusion*

Nothing that has such fundamental influence on the society has ever developed at such a rapid pace and was accepted in such a short period of time as electronic commerce. Alongside its speedy development, attention has been paid to its implications for legal proceedings. Litigation is the traditional tool for deciding legal results once there are conflicts. With the explosion of computer technology, national courts have taken advantage of its benefits; there is even a Computer Integrated Courtroom (CIC).[363] But as using modern technology to facilitate litigation is one issue, resolving disputes smoothly is another. Two problem areas for litigation are adjudicative jurisdiction and choice of law.

Both are actually old topics with new faces. The fundamental characteristics of the Internet that support its seemingly limitless use as a

---

361 UNCITRAL Model Law on Electronic Commerce <http://www.infojus.com.br/leiuncitral.htm>. adopted in December 1996 provides a nice basis for initiating business and harmonizes the rules in this field. However, it has yet to be adopted by the states and possible loopholes are to be dealt with on other occasions. The goal of the law was two-fold. It sought to offer national legislators a set of internationally acceptable rules that would remove statutory obstacles from the free flow of legally significant electronic data across international borders. It also sought to facilitate harmonious international economic relations by fulfilling the purposes and functions of traditional paper-based requirements via a "functionally equivalent approach," which made use of electronic commerce techniques. See further K. Gautier, Electronic Commerce: Confronting the Legal Challenge of Building E-Dentities in Cyberspace, 20 *Miss. C. L. Rev.* 128 (Fall, 1999); T.D. Casey & J. Magenau, A Hybrid Model of Self-Regulation and Governmental Regulation of Electronic Commerce, 19 *Santa Clara Computer & High Technology Law Journal* 25 (December 2002); J. Hughes, The Internet and the Persistence of Law, 44 *B.C.L. Rev.* 376 (March 2003).

362 The European Parliament and Council Directive on Certain Legal Aspects of Electronic Commerce in the Internal Market was adopted in 2000; see further Official Journal of the European Communities, 17 July 2000, L 178/1. It intends to unify the rules within the market of the EU, but has implications for other markets, too.

363 For further discussion, see R.F. Madden, Developments in the Electronic Courtroom, 6 *International Yearbook of Law Computers and Technology*, 203–208 (1992).

tool for commerce present significant new challenges to the application of traditional legal concepts.[364] The Internet is multi-jurisdictional in the sense that messages can travel among networks anywhere on the globe where there are computers with access to it.[365] On the other hand, it is nearly a-jurisdictional: physical location and physical boundaries are irrelevant in this networked environment.[366] It thus makes adjudicative jurisdiction and choice of law new again to the world of business and law.

When considering how to modify the existing legal framework for dealing with commercial issues, governments shall seek to ensure that the framework provides fairness to consumers and business, facilitates electronic commerce, results in consumers having a level of protection not less than that afforded in other forms of commerce, and provides consumers with meaningful access to fair and timely dispute resolution and redress without undue cost or burden.[367] The framework must take into account international character of the tool of electronic commerce, the Internet, which is so insensitive to geography that it is often impossible to determine the physical location of a user and whose scope is so pervasive that impacts of activities performed in one state are automatically felt in others. While no simple solution to the issues of adjudicative jurisdiction and choice of law can be reached, support from the Internet industry and cooperation among international society shall work to improve the legal framework of which they are apart, providing so far as possible certainty and predictability.[368]

---

[364] Hoegle, *supra* note 75, at 48.

[365] See further Henry, *supra* note 60.

[366] See further D.G. Post, Anarchy, State, and the Internet: An Essay on Law-Making in Cyberspace, 1995 *Journal of Online Law*, article 3, paragraph 36, <http://www.law.cornell.edu/jol/post.html>.

[367] This could be found in the OECD Guideline for Consumer Protection in the Context of electronic Commerce. <http://www.uscib.org/policy/jurrdfin.htm>.

[368] Predictability requires a legal infrastructure that allows the participants to an electronic transaction to consummate it without undue concern over the risk of repudiation, the means of enforcement or the rules of dispute resolution. See further a presentation by T.P. Vartanian, *Whose Internet is it Anyway? The Law of Jurisdiction in Cyberspace: Achieving Legal Order Among the World's Nations*, 2000 Global Internet Summit, Vienna, Virginia, March 13–14, 2000, <http://www.ffhsj.com/bancmail/bancpage.htm>.

CHAPTER FIVE

ATTEMPTS AT FORMULATING A NEW MECHANISM

Realizing the necessity of formulating a new mechanism specifically for electronic commerce, many are in pursuit of one.[1] According to recent surveys and inventories, the OECD, ICC and CI have identified more than 40 online ADR mechanisms for electronic commerce. These mechanisms vary in terms of procedural and technical aspects. Among those, 26 offer informal, non-binding types of dispute resolution, such as assisted negotiation, mediation, or ombuds-type services; 14 offer more formal, binding arbitration procedures; 11 feature automated dispute resolution; and 14 offer multiple ADR methods.[2] This chapter shall examine these projects and determine their appropriateness for disputes in electronic commerce.

1. *Projects Arising out of Self-Regulation Initiatives*

1.1. *Virtual Magistrate Project*

The idea for Virtual Magistrate originated in a meeting held on October 25, 1995, in Washington, DC, sponsored by the National Center for Automated Information Research (NCAIR) and the Cyberspace Law Institute (CLI).[3] Initially, the designers of the project

---

[1] For example, DG INFSO presented the IST R&D Program for collaborative research and the TEN-Telecom program for demonstrations of innovative services as possible routes for co-financing projects to deploy cross-border on-line dispute settlement systems. See <http://europa.eu.int/comm/information_society/ist/index_en.htm>; <http://www.ispo.cec.be/tentelecom>. The US Department of Commerce/Federal Trade Commission announced the workshop on the issue of "Alternative Dispute Resolution for Consumer Transactions in the Borderless Online Marketplace" held on June 6–7, 2000. See <http://www.ita.doc.gov/ita_home/adr-frn.htm>.

[2] See further Building Trust in the Online Environment: Business to Consumer Dispute Resolution, Joint Conference of the OECD, HCOPIL, ICC, the Hague, 11–12 December 2000, Orientation Document, DSTI/ICCP/REG/CP(2000)1–UPDATED as of 7 December 2000, at 4.

[3] These were the participants in the working group discussion: T.C. Lexiner

sought to fabricate a mechanism to determine whether or not materials accused of copyright infringement should be removed immediately from the host site.[4] In such cases, "one party (the complainant) asserts that a second party has posted a message or a file on a system under the control of another party (system operators, or sysops) containing 'wrongful content' of some kind, *e.g.*, material that infringes complainant's copyright or trademark rights, misappropriates trade secrets belonging to complainant, is defamatory or fraudulent or inappropriate (obscene, lewd, or otherwise violative of system rules), and demands that the offending posting be removed from the system under sysop's control".[5] The project's larger intention, determined after delicate deliberation, is to provide an online arbitration system resolving disputes on the Internet in a fast and efficient manner. After obtaining consensus on the role, jurisdiction, and procedures of the project, it was made publicly known on March 4, 1996 and implemented in the fall of the same year.

Several bodies are involved in the Virtual Magistrate Project. NCAIR committed the first donation to finance a pilot project. The American Arbitration Association (AAA)[6] serves as administrative clerk to the project, undertaking the task of receiving cases, reviewing them for suitability, and assigning them to the magistrate. Additionally, it shall defend and indemnify those involved in the project in case of litigation over their activities for the project. CLI and the AAA jointly select magistrates, who must be familiar with law and online systems. The Villanova Center for Information Law and Practice operates the home page for the project, maintaining the discussion groups for cases.

The project aims to resolve disputes involving users of online systems, or those who claim to be harmed by wrongful messages, postings or files, or system operators (to the extent that complaints or

(NCAIR); A. Sloane (NCAIR); E. Kirsh (America Online); W. Marmon (MCI); D.R. Johnson (CLI/Lexis Counsel Connect); D. Post (CLI/Georgetown Law School); R. Gellman (CLI Fellow); J.B. Buur (CLI Fellow/Federal Trade Commission); and G.H. Friedman (AAA).

[4] The participants were concerned about the controversial issue of liability for online service providers accused of allowing access to illegal material, such as postings or e-mail messages that infringe copyright, invade privacy, constitute consumer fraud, or are defamatory. Dealing with liability and the legality of materials in these cases is urgent.

[5] D. Post, *Dispute Resolution in Cyberspace: Engineering a Virtual Magistrate System* (May 1996), <http://www.law.vill.edu/ncair/disres/DGP2.HTM>.

[6] <http://adr.com>.

demands for remedies are directed at system operators).[7] Bearing this in mind, accepted cases involve complaints about messages, postings, and files claiming copyright or trademark infringement, misappropriation of trade secrets, defamation, fraud, deceptive trade practices, inappropriate materials, invasion of privacy and other wrongful content.[8] The issue of infringement of intellectual property rights is of particular significance.[9] The project might receive cases concerning the disclosure of the identity of an individual to non-governmental persons or the appropriateness of refusing access to online systems by the system operator.[10] However, problems about billing or financial obligations between users and system operators will not be addressed.[11]

Eight basic goals have been singled out for the online arbitration project: to establish the feasibility of using online dispute resolution for disputes that originate online; to provide system operators with informed and neutral responses to complaints about allegedly wrongful postings; to provide users and others with a rapid, low-cost, and readily accessible remedy for complaints about online postings; to lay the groundwork for a self-sustaining, online dispute resolution system as a feature of contracts between system operators and users and content suppliers (and others concerned about wrongful postings); to help to define the reasonable duties of a system operator confronted with a complaint; to explore the possibility of using the Virtual Magistrate Project to resolve disputes related to computer networks; to develop a formal governing structure for an ongoing Virtual Magistrate operation;[12] and to make the project easy to understand and accessible to all.[13] It is understood that the project's goals are subject to timely change in order to well serve the demands of the Internet society.[14]

---

[7] See *The Virtual Magistrate Project: Concept Paper*, paragraph 4 (last modified on July 24, 1996), <http://vmag.vclip.org/docs/vmpaper.html>.

[8] *Id.* Concept paper, paragraph 10.

[9] This is closely connected with the heated discussion concerning online service provider liability. See further Y. Zhao, Internet Service Providers and Their Liability, 34 *Law/Technology*, World Jurist Association, No. 1, at 1–19 (2001).

[10] See *supra* note 7, concept paper, paragraph 10.

[11] See *id.*

[12] *The Virtual Magistrate Project: Pilot Project Goals*, paragraph 1 (last modified on February 26, 1996), <http://vmag.vclip.org/docs/vmaggoals.html>.

[13] R. Gellman, *A Brief History of the Virtual Magistrate Project: The Early Months*, paragraph 23 (last modified on May 22, 1996), <http://www.law.vill.edu/ncair/disres/GELLMAN.HTM>.

[14] *Supra* note 7, concept paper, paragraph 11.

The Virtual Magistrate Project makes full use of modern technology. Most communication among the participants takes the shape of electronic mailings and telephone calls.[15] This is further characterized by the dispute resolution procedures.[16] Available to any computer network worldwide,[17] the project receives complaints via regular electronic mail.[18] An AAA staff member first screens complaints and decides whether they are within the project's jurisdiction[19] and then waits agreement by the parties.[20] Once a positive decision is made, the AAA staff member shall select one magistrate from a roster maintained by the AAA and forward the complaint to the defendant and any possibly affected third parties, such as an online service provider or the originator of the accused materials.[21] Most proceedings are held online. No procedures involve paper submissions or face-to-face contact. The parties do not need to travel to meet personally, nor even have to speak to each other on the telephone. A listserv/newsgroup (grist) is created for each case, where the parties can post their views or ideas. The magistrate is supposed to receive and resolve complaints within seventy-two hours (three business days) after acceptance.[22]

Confidentiality is highly advocated, which comports with accepted arbitral practice and procedures. Upon request and at the discretion of the magistrate, any party to a case could proceed without revealing his name, address, or affiliation.[23] The grist shall only be acces-

---

[15] The October, 1995 meeting was the only face-to-face meeting. The project was implemented through the World Wide Web, with electronic mail as a backup.

[16] See *Chicago-Kent College of Law, Illinois Institute of Technology, The Virtual Magistrate Project: Basic Rules*, <http://www.vmag.org/docs/rules.html>.

[17] See *supra* note 7, concept Paper, paragraph 4.

[18] The general practice is to click on an e-mail button on the project's web site to post a complaint. See further *Chicago-Kent College of Law, Illinois Institute of Technology, VMAG: Online Dispute Resolution*, <http://www.vmag.org>.

[19] *Supra* note 16, Basic Rules, paragraph 10. The staff of the AAA shall carefully review the complaint and requests additional information from the complainant when necessary.

[20] *Id.* The complaint shall be accepted only when all the parties have agreed to participate and hold harmless from liability the Virtual Magistrate Project, the AAA, the Magistrate, and all other persons connected with the Virtual Magistrate Project for any act of commission or omission in connection with the Virtual Magistrate Project.

[21] *Supra* note 7.

[22] It was originally expected to make decisions within forty-eight hours. However, more time than this has been needed for the exchange of messages. Three business days is the usual time period for making a decision, but even more time than this could be needed to ensure a fair result. The magistrate may need more time to collect all points of view. See further *supra* note 16, Basic Rules, paragraph 10.

[23] See *supra* note 16, Basic Rules, paragraph 4.

sible by password and only the participants shall be able to read the posted messages during the proceedings.[24] The record of the proceedings is not open to the public until a decision is made.[25]

Reasonableness is the legal standard for the magistrate while making decisions. This flexible standard offers the magistrate a wide discretion. Considering the present lack of specific rules on the Internet and the character of arbitration, this flexible approach is understandable. Decisions made shall not have any binding effect for future decisions, but may serve as a guide for future legislation or dispute resolution.[26]

While making a decision, several factors shall be considered to ensure reasonableness: network etiquette; applicable contracts; appropriate substantive laws; and whether a system operator would be acting reasonably if it withheld messages, files, or postings from public access pending resolution of claims between the parties.[27] Before applying a specific law, the magistrate should also consider the circumstance of each complaint, the views of the parties about applicable legal principles and remedies, and the likely outcome in any ultimate litigation or traditional dispute resolution mechanism.[28]

The Virtual Magistrate Project is creative in making full use of the Internet and the web for dispute resolution and was originally welcomed by the Internet world. However, since its establishment, Tierney and Email America[29] is the only case that has been decided.[30]

---

[24] See further *supra* note 16, Basic Rules, paragraph 15.

[25] *Supra* note 16, Basic Rules, paragraph 6,7; See also *supra* note 7, Concept Paper, paragraph 26. Although the public can access the Virtual Magistrate Project Home Page and see the pending cases listed on the docket, they will not be able to access case information until the time of a final decision. After the decision is made, the complaint, the response, the decision, and any other pertinent materials will automatically be made public. However, upon the request of any party and at the discretion of the magistrate, information pertaining to the complaint, such as names, addresses, and affiliations may be kept confidential.

[26] See *supra* note 7, Concept Paper, paragraph 28.

[27] See *supra* note 7, Concept Paper, paragraph 16.

[28] See *supra* note 7, Concept Paper, paragraph 17.

[29] The AAA identifies cases by the name of the principal parties, using "and" rather than "vs."; the Virtual Magistrate Project adopted this practice. This particular case was resolved without the participation of Email America, which did not recognize the authority of the project. See *Virtual Magistrate Handbook for Magistrates*, paragraph 27 (last updated Feb. 26, 1996), <http://vmag.vclip.org/magis/vmhdbook.html>. For further discussion of Email America's absence, see further *Tierney and Email America: Case Information* (last modified May 8, 1996), paragraph 1, at <http://vmag.vclip.org/doksys/96-0001>. See further *A "Good" Case, Not An "Ideal" Case: Virtual Justice: The No-Show Case Showcases: Promise and Peril of the Virtual Magistrate Project*, Voorhees Report, June 3, 1996, at *3, available in 1996 WL 8913605.

[30] See *Chicago-Kent College of Law, Illinois Institute of Technology, The Virtual Magistrate:*

Problems involved in this case cast doubt on the credibility and efficacy of the project.

Firstly, the sole defendant, Email America, was absent from the proceedings. Only the third party, America Online (AOL), responded to the case. As arbitration needs the agreement of both parties, or else the decision be given default-like qualities, the defendant's absence called the decision into question.

Secondly, AOL, a strong original proponent of the project later found out that its own internal terms-of-service (TOS) complaint mechanisms[31] were enough to resolve most disputes successfully.[32] AOL could also have taken actions in the same case without the magistrate's direction.

Thirdly, the decision reached in this case cannot be executed. The fact that the message turned out to be direct email means that there was nothing to enforce it against.[33] This problem results from the magistrate's rushing too quickly to judgment.

The last problem with the case could be the identity of the complainant, who serves as an advisor to the project on consumer fraud issues[34] and a forum moderator on Counsel Connect.[35] The complexity of his role raised high suspicion concerning the trustworthiness of the proceedings.

Sample Opinion, <http://www.vmag.org/sample.html>. The complainant, J.E. Tierney requested an advertisement posted by Email America be removed from the system of America Online. See further Docket No. 96–0001 (May 8, 1996), <http://vmag.vclip.org/doksys/96–0001>; see also *Tierney and Email America: Case Information*, *supra* note 29; see also *Tierney and Email America: Final Decision*, (last modified May 21, 1996), <http://vmag.clip.org/doksys/96–0001/index.html?6>.

[31] Paragraph 4 (a) of AOL's TOS specifically reserves the right to remove content which is deemed harmful, offensive, or otherwise in violation of the TOS. See Response & Affidavit of America Online, paragraph 32 (last modified May 15, 1996), <http://vmag.vclip.org/doksys/96–0001/index.html>.

[32] See further H.H. Perritt, Jr., Dispute Resolution in Cyberspace: Demand for New Forms of ADR, 15 *Ohio State Journal on Dispute Resolution*, 687 (2000).

[33] See A.E. Almaguer & R.W. Baggott III, Shaping New Legal Frontiers: Dispute Resolution for the Internet, 13 *Ohio St. J. on Disp. Resol.* 732–733 (1998). The magistrate thought he was dealing with a posting in AOL's classified section; this assumption was proved erroneous only after the decision was rendered.

[34] See D.J. Loundy, Virtual Magistrate Becomes a Reality, Sort of, *Chi. Daily L. Bull.*, June 16, 1996, at 5; see also Gellman, *supra* note 13, paragraph 7.

[35] Counsel Connect is not directly affiliated with the Virtual Magistrate Project, but its co-director did help to develop the project. See further D. Post, Virtual Magistrates, Virtual Law, Am. Law., July/August, 1996, at 104; see also D. Thom, E-Mail Arbitration System takes ADR to Cyberspace, *N.J.L.J.*, April 15, 1996, at 22.

Several other complaints were submitted, but have been determined to be outside the jurisdiction of the project, or the responding party has refused to participate.[36] In some occasions, discussions between the parties and the magistrate led to a satisfactory resolution of the disputes without further direct action by the magistrate.

The issue of enforcement of the decisions is problematic. The New York Convention[37] covers normal arbitral decisions, but it is of no use here.[38] The enforcement shall totally depend upon the willingness of the parties. Ideally, enforcement shall run smoothly as a voluntary process. When a problem arises, the winning party can go to court to start a formal procedure. The decision does not have to be a substitute for traditional judicial remedies as the parties can choose to make the arbitration decision nonbinding, leaving open the possibility of traditional litigation.[39] However, the decision above could still exert some weight on the court and facilitate the whole procedure in deciding upon the merits of both parties.

From this experience, we can draw at least three conclusions regarding the Virtual Magistrate's future success. Firstly, online procedures must be made known as widely as possible. Until now many disputes have been resolved through the internal mechanism[40] of online service providers, whose web sites are much easier to identify

[36] In the first six weeks of operation, three complaints were submitted. The fist one concerned a retail transaction involving a computer purchase, but did not involve any computer network activities. The other two submissions received no support from the other parties. According to R. Gellman, the cases were rejected because considerable effort would be required to contact all parties and convince them to submit to the jurisdiction of the Virtual Magistrate. See further Gellman, *supra* note 13, paragraph 32.

[37] See Convention on the Recognition and Enforcement of Foreign Arbitral Awards, June 10, 1958, 21 U.S.T., at 2517, 330 U.N.T.S., at 38.

[38] The Virtual Magistrate arbitrator expects system operators to support and enforce decisions. Third parties (copyright owners) will be asked to comply with a decision in return for use of the Virtual Magistrate services. Decisions may be reconsidered, but will not be subject to appeal. See further *The Virtual Magistrate Project: Concept Paper*, July 24, 1996, available at <http://www.vmag.org> (viewed on October 23, 2003). Meanwhile, suggestions have been made to make decisions binding. One suggestion is to modify the New York Convention to serve the project. It would require modification of the writing requirement and certain geographical requirements in a manner similar to national laws. See further J. Goldsmith & L. Lessig, *Grounding the Virtual Magistrate*, available at <http://www.lessig.org> (viewed on October 23, 2003).

[39] See further *The Virtual Magistrate Project: Basic Rules*, paragraph 1 (last modified July 24, 1996), <http://vmag.vclip.org/docs/vmrules.html>.

[40] See *infra* notes 96–98 and accompanying text.

and are known to the users.[41] Parties will only involve a project in their agenda when it is well known to the public and its web site is easy to access.

Secondly, the scope of the project's jurisdiction should not be too limited. Too many limitations would prove disastrous to the project, particularly at the initial stage. Of course, the project should not expect to resolve all legal disputes between parties, and certainly could not do so within a short timeframe. Based on several considerations, disputes involving relatively simple facts and several other types of cases should be excluded from the project's mission. The basic question for most disputes will concern whether a message, file, or posting should remain publicly available on the Internet. But at the same time jurisdiction should not be so narrow that chances of cases being brought to the project are limited. Fortunately, Professor Kentra at Chicago-Kent has recently revised the rules to make the project available for a wider range of disputes.

Publicity and expanded jurisdiction alone will not ensure success. The fact is that while the Virtual Magistrate Project has received extensive publicity, service providers still neglect to add actual links on their own sites to the project. After the recent expansion of jurisdiction to include a wider range of cases, few complaints have been filed and no additional disputes have been decided.[42] With these points in mind, the third conclusion we can draw is that the public's confidence in the project should be built up. Its refusal to participate in the project reveals that a party still has doubts. Improving confidence shall involve both legal issues and technical issues, from the security of email services to the accessibility of relevant web sites. Exploiting modern technology shall be especially important. Only with necessary facilities in place can the disputing parties trust the project and its results.

---

[41] Another reason could be that there are not enough real online disputes. According to Assistant General Counsel for AOL, W. Burrington, AOL only handles a few on-line disputes each month. See further D. Thom, ADR in Cyberspace, *Am. Law.*, May 1996, at supp. 19.

[42] See further Perritt, *supra* note 32, at 686–687.

1.2. *The University of Massachusetts Online Ombuds Office*

The Online Ombuds Office[43] was established in June 1996 with the financial support of NCAIR.[44] In 1997, the office became part of the Center for Information Technology and Dispute Resolution at the University of Massachusetts, which was established with the help of Hewlett Foundation, the NCAIR, and the Department of Legal Studies of the University of Massachusetts.[45]

Ombudsman has its origin in Sweden in the early eighteenth century, where it was meant to fight against abuses of governmental and bureaucratic authority and administration and to make further corrections.[46] Historically, ombudsmen have been independent officials, who receive complaints, conduct investigations, and make recommendations.[47] Occasionally they adjudicate disputes, or write a reflective column for a newspaper's editorial page.[48] The new Online Ombuds Office has the same objective of offering information and expertise. But it exists on the World Wide Web and attempts to bring the resources of the office to resolve disputes arising out of online activities.

The Online Ombuds Office provides mediation to parties involved in conflict and has indeed carried out several successful online mediations.[49] Its informal and user-friendly nature has attracted a lot of

---

[43] Located at <http://www.ombuds.org>.

[44] See *Center for Information Technology and Dispute Resolution, University of Massachusetts, Online Ombuds Office*, <http://aaron.sbs.umass.edu/center/ombuds/default.htm>.

[45] *Center for Information Technology and Dispute Resolution, University of Massachusetts*, <http://aaron.sbs.umass.edu/center/Default.htm>.

[46] The Ombudsman concept was originated in Sweden by Charles XII in 1713. King Charles, concerned that his monarchy was lethargic and unresponsive to the concerns of the citizenry, appointed a trusted advisor and established the concept, making that advisor the history's first Ombudsman. The independent Ombudsman concept was established by the Swedish Parliament in 1809 and continues today in this independent form. See further *The City of Detroit Ombudsman Quick Facts*, <http://www3.ci.detroit.mi.us> (viewed on October 22, 2003).

[47] See further M.P. Roew, Options, Functions, and Skills: What an Organizational Ombudsperson Might Want to Know, 11 *Negotiation Journal*, 103–114 (1995). The ombudsperson's role is a varied one, but generally includes responsive listening, providing and receiving information, reframing issues and developing options, making referrals, and assisting persons to help themselves. An ombudsperson is not an authoritative or final decision maker, but is a confidential and informal information resource, communications channel, complaint-handler and dispute-resolver.

[48] See further L. Brown, *The Reluctant Reformation: On Criticizing the Press in America* 66 (1974).

[49] During March of 1999, the office worked with the online auction sites eBay and Up4Sale to mediate disputes arising out of online auctions. Later it mediated

public attention. Online and as well as non-online communication facilitates the exchange of information and thereby the proper functioning of mediation.[50] Parties wishing to get assistance from ombudsman shall first get access to a project web site that offers both relevant information and tools for self-help,[51] which could in one or another way help parties resolve disputes early on.[52]

Technical experts are always on hand to interpret the relevance of the environment out of which the disputes emerged. While making full use of modern technology, such persons assist ombudsman in speedily reaching quality resolution to disputes. Considering that the Internet is still a new and complicated matter for many ombudsmen, these experts are particularly important in electronic commerce cases.

As a result of several factors, the Online Ombuds Office has been more successful than the Virtual Magistrate Project. For one, its so-called Center plays an important role in procuring the workload, while the former project largely depends on the interest of personnel.[53] More important than this is its general informal nature, which gives parties more freedom and control over of the cases and the results than is possible in arbitration. This element of control is particularly attractive to strong economic powers, such as online service providers, who have often depended upon internal mechanisms to resolve disputes.

---

a domain name case involving the site Netique.com, and it is now working with the World Organization of Webmasters to resolve disputes involving webmasters. The first case involved a local newspaper's claim that an Internet user was committing copyright infringement by posting excerpts from his stories on the Internet. The case was resolved successfully with little difficulty or acrimony. See further *Transcript of a Dispute: The Web Site Developer and the Newspaper*, <http://aaron.sbs.umass.edu/center/ombuds/narrative1.html>.

[50] This could include face-to-face meetings, telephone calls, handwritten notes, emails, video conferences, etc. As it is important that mediators have appropriate means of communication once the need for them arises, various communication tools should be made available to them. See further S.S. Silbey & S.E. Merry, Mediator Settlement Strategies, 8 *Law & Policy*, 7, 14 (1986); see also M.C. Aaron, The Value of Decision Analysis in Mediation Practice, 11 *Negotiation Journal*, 123, 126 (1995).

[51] See further E. Katsh, *The Online Ombuds Office: Adapting Dispute Resolution to Cyberspace*, <http://mantle.sbs.umass.edu/vmag/katsh.htm>.

[52] The web site contains a data base of online disputes and cases and materials that might promote resolution of the dispute without formal intervention.

[53] The fact is that AAA's interest in the Project has waned with personnel changes at AAA.

1.3. *eBay's Escrow Arrangement and Dispute Resolution Services*[54]

Online auction houses are some of the most successful e-businesses. eBay is the world's first, biggest and best person-to-person online trading community, which provides a Web-based forum in which individuals and small businesses can auction goods and services.[55] The rule of such online auctions is that the site owner, in this instance eBay, assumes no responsibility for the transaction between bidder and seller.[56] To develop consumer confidence, eBay offers several built-in safeguards for avoiding or resolving disputes.

An escrow service is typical for an online auction site: the purchaser holds payment until goods or services are accepted, and the seller is offered the opportunity of inspecting and approving returned items before making reimbursement.[57] This free service helps to avoid disputes. eBay also provides a feedback and complaint service, which can help to informally resolve disputes. Without intervention from third parties, users can contact each other directly through email or telephone to resolve disputes at the initial stage. The online feedback service has the added benefit of ensuring intended customers have some knowledge about their possible trading partner.

Once a dispute arises, users can refer to SafeHarbor, a comprehensive safety resource, which aids in the resolution of issues within eBay's internal mechanism. At the same time, an independent dispute resolution service will work to resolve disputes quickly and fairly.[58]

SquareTrade is eBay's preferred dispute resolution provider. SquareTrade's Online Dispute Resolution offers a fast and convenient way of resolving disputes either independently, using SquareTrade's Web-based Direct Negotiation tool, or through mediation. To guarantee users that sellers will respond to their complaints, the SquareTrade

---

[54] Various sites offer online auctions. eBay, one of the most successful sites, successfully obtained the trust from consumers by providing various dispute resolution services. Yahoo closely follows the practice adopted by eBay, its cultural counterpart in online auctions. See further M.S. Donahey, Online Auctions and Dispute Resolution, International Conference on Dispute Resolution in Electronic Commerce, WIPO, November 2000, ARB/ECOM/00/13.

[55] See further eBay, <http://www.ebay.com>.

[56] See eBay, Inc., User Agreement, at <http://pages.ebay.com/help/community/png-user.html>.

[57] See further *eBay, Inc., Services: Escrow Overview*, <http://pages.ebay.com/help/community/escrow.htm>.

[58] *Why eBay is Safe*, <http://pages.ebay.com/help/basics/n-is-ebay-safe.htm>.

Seal is provided for a seller to show that they are committed to high selling standards and have had their identity verified by a third party. The condition for retaining a SquareTrade Seal is that a seller must agree to participate in SquareTrade's Dispute resolution should a problem arise, have their identity verified by SquareTrade, and commit to SquareTrade's standards for online selling.[59] During dispute resolution, online facilities shall be used. Email, of course, is an important communicative tool; SquareTrade's free negotiation tool on its secure servers is useful for online discussions.

It is notable that Up4Sale, an online auction site purchased by eBay,[60] approached the Center for Information Technology and Dispute Resolution of University of Massachusetts for services on dispute resolution[61] and mediation was applied.[62] A combination of internal and external resources available for dispute resolution serves to promote consumer confidence.

1.4. *Credit Card Chargeback*

Credit Card Chargeback is believed to be the most common form of ADR for consumer disputes at present.[63] According to the Fair Credit Billing Act,[64] credit card issuers, retaining limited authority to adjudicate the dispute,[65] must investigate cardholder claims of billing errors in writing.[66] Bill errors could include those for which a cardholder requests documentation as to the validity of the charge,[67] or a reflection on a statement of goods or services not accepted by the obligor or his designee or not delivered to the obligor or his

---

[59] *SquareTrade: Building Trust in Transactions*, <http://www.squaretra . . . tplace_name=ebay&campaign=EBY_OD_2>.

[60] See About Up4Sale, at <http://www.up4sale.com/about1.htm>.

[61] For further discussion, see E. Katsh, J. Rifkin & A. Gaitenby, E-Commerce, E-Disputes, and E-Dispute Resolution: In the Shadow of "eBay Law", 15 *Ohio St. J. on Disp. Resol.* 705–734 (2000).

[62] See Up4Sale, at <http://www.up4sale.com>.

[63] 12 C.F.R. section 226.3(1999); see also 15 U.S.C. section 1666(a)(3)(B) (1994). Under Regulation Z and the Fair Credit Billing Act, chargebacks extend only to consumers and not to business transactions.

[64] 15 U.S.C. section 1666 et seq. (1994).

[65] The authority of card issuers is defined by the merchant and cardholder agreements.

[66] 15 U.S.C. section 1666 (a); see also *Himelfarb v. American Express Co.*, 484 A.2d 1013, 1018–1019 (Md. 1984).

[67] 12 C.F.R. section 226.13(a)(6) (1999).

designee in accordance with the agreement made at the time of a transaction.[68] The card issuers will not charge cardholders without determining that such goods are actually delivered, mailed, or otherwise sent to the obligor and providing the obligor with a statement of such determination.[69]

The service of chargebacks is comparatively cheap and easy for the cardholder; no dispute resolution fees are involved and the only obligation for consumers is that they speedily call or write the card issuer in protest of charges. It offers the customers the opportunity to protect their own rights, thus balancing to a certain extent the bargaining power. When many claims are brought against the same merchant, his membership in the credit card network shall be jeopardized. To avoid this danger, merchants will do their best to conduct fair business. When a chargeback does occur, informal negotiations shall usually ensue directly between the merchant and the consumer, which provides them with the somewhat independent opportunity to resolve the dispute. This practice is accepted by most credit card networks,[70] as well as consumers and merchants.[71] Major credit card networks extend chargeback protection internationally and have adopted special consumer protection chargeback rules for electronic commerce.[72]

The OECD has issued a draft recommendation on the question of chargeback, laying down principles that should be taken into account by member states to guarantee the chargeback principle for

---

[68] 15 U.S.C. section 1666(b)(3) (1994); see also 12 C.F.R. section 226.13(a)(3) (1999).

[69] 15 U.S.C. section 1666(a)(3)(B)(ii).

[70] As stated by Visa officials, Visa's chargeback rules do not accommodate all of the possible consumer protection laws around the world, although some chargeback rights do correspond with statutory rights granted to consumers in particular countries, such as the rights granted under federal Reserve Board Regulation Z for dispute certain credit card transactions. The reasons for chargeback being offered under Visa's rules for international transactions enable issuers of Visa cards to address the fundamental consumer concerns of their cardholders, and incidentally reinforce the reputation of Visa Cards as the best way to pay. See further Latter from B.W. Peterson, Senior Vice President and Associate General Counsel, Visa International Service Association, to the Secretary of the Federal Trade Commission, in Federal Trade Commission, *U.S. Perspectives on Consumer Protection in the Global Electronic Commerce Marketplace*, <http://www.ftc.gov/bcp/icpw/comments/visa.htm>.

[71] Merchants are in a better position with this practice than they are when payment is stopped on checks. Merchants in the latter situation can only sue the consumer or cut the consumer off from further check-payment privileges.

[72] See further Perritt, *supra* note 32, at 690.

consumers.[73] This practice is very common in the US, but in some European countries, chargebacks are not required.[74] As the proportion of consumer transactions through debit cards is higher than the number of transactions through credit cards in such countries, the availability of chargebacks in debit card agreements is much more important than it is in credit card agreements.[75] Nevertheless, this practice suggests an important way of thinking about consumer protection in an ADR mechanism for electronic commerce.[76]

1.5. *CyberTribunal*[77]

CyberTribunal was developed by the Center de Recherché de Droit Publique (CRDP) of the University of Montreal to address the needs of both merchants and consumers and assist parties in both the prevention and resolution of disputes arising in electronic commerce. It employs mediation and arbitration to resolve the disputes concerning a number of topics, including copyright, freedom of expression, and privacy. The proceedings are conducted in French or English, with Spanish to follow.[78] And because it is to function as an experiment, all services are offered free of charge. Many believe in the future of this experiment, but practice shows that increased computer confidence is vital to ensuring its success. Presently, an effort must be made to advance its popularity.

---

[73] See further OECD Draft Recommendation on Charge-back Mechanisms, DAFFE/CP(97)13.

[74] It is not provided in France. Though chargebacks are required by law in the United Kingdom, however, this law is inapplicable to certain types of international transactions. See Organization for Economic Co-operation & Development, Consumer Redress in the Global Marketplace: Chargebacks (visited April 15, 2000), <http://www.oecd.org/dsti/sti/it/consumer/prod/e_96–142.htm>.

[75] See Organization for Economic Co-operation & Development, Consumer Redress in the Global Marketplace: Chargebacks (visited April 15, 2000), <http://www.oecd.org/dsti/sti/it/consumer/prod/e_96–142.htm>.

[76] It is seen as a means of enabling consumers to get refunds in dispute cases, thus avoiding redress mechanisms. However, understood in a broader sense, ADR is itself a dispute resolution mechanism.

[77] Recently renamed as eResolution, this project markets itself as a provider of conflict resolution services for transactions conducted on the Internet. See Cyber Tribunal, Cyber Conflict Resolution Center, at <http://www.cybertribunal.org/english/defaulting.htm>.

[78] CyberTribunal General Arbitration Procedure, Article 10.

1.5.1. *CyberTribunal Mediation*

The mediators have complete freedom since no rules are provided for their purpose. The goal behind this omission is to enhance the flexibility of the procedure and encourage the parties to take full advantage of the electronic medium.

1.5.2. *CyberTribunal Arbitration*

Rules adopted for arbitration are based on the UNCITRAL Arbitration Rules and the ICC Arbitration Rules, with possible modifications regarding the special nature of electronic commerce.[79] The parties are requested to use standardized forms for communications. Only in situations when no such forms are provided, shall the parties communicate by means of email or any other means.[80]

CyberTribunal Arbitration is carried out as follows. A party initiates arbitration by transmitting an application to the secretariat. The secretariat determines the admissibility of the complaint within five days of receipt and further transmits acknowledgement of receipt to the complainant and notification of receipt to the defendant.[81] At this stage, mediation can be suggested. If it is accepted, arbitration shall be suspended. If no result is reached through mediation, then the arbitration shall restart by the filing of a new application for arbitration.[82] A web site shall be set up to exchange and store data, documents, and information related to this case, which shall be accessible only to the parties and the tribunal.[83] The tribunal shall consist of one or three arbitrators appointed by the secretariat and subject to the approval of the parties.[84] The tribunal has power to rule on its own jurisdiction and take provisional measures with respect to the substance of the dispute.[85] If the parties fail to choose applicable law, the tribunal shall select the national law with which the dispute has the closest link, with the exception that the national law of a consumer shall be applied when a consumer is a party.[86] In

---

[79] CyberTribunal General Arbitration Procedure, Article 16.
[80] CyberTribunal General Arbitration Procedure, Article 3.
[81] CyberTribunal General Arbitration Procedure, Article 4.
[82] CyberTribunal General Arbitration Procedure, Article 4 (4).
[83] CyberTribunal General Arbitration Procedure, Article 1 (f), 5 (4), and 15 (2).
[84] See further CyberTribunal General Arbitration Procedure, Article 6.
[85] CyberTribunal Arbitration Procedure, Article 11 and 14.
[86] CyberTribunal Arbitration Procedure, Article 17 (1) and (4).

choosing applicable law, the tribunal shall take into account the contract and prevailing cyberspace parties.[87] The tribunal further decides upon the appropriateness of testimony and computerized documents and whether to hear witnesses or experts in person or via other means.[88] It engenders its award within 30 days of the declaration of closure, unless extended by the secretariat.[89] The award, made by a majority of the arbitrators, contains full explanations and electronic signatures and is transmitted to the parties by encrypted email and filed in the site of the case in question.[90] This award is final. Unless opposed by the parties, the award shall be posted on the CyberTribunal web site 60 days after its rendering.[91] In case of opposition, the secretariat shall propose to the parties that the award be redacted of identifying characteristics and then posted.[92]

1.6. *Miscellaneous Projects*

Several other projects have offered dispute resolution services for specific disputes connected with electronic commerce. Though not so influential as the projects discussed above, their existence adds to the richness of our reference for dealing with future disputes.

The services run by the Council of Better Business Bureau (BBB) benefit from BBB's widespread reputation and physical presence. Established to help foster consumer trust and confidence in electronic commerce, the BBBonline Privacy program offers a comprehensive assessment process measuring a company's ability to stand behind the promises it makes in its online privacy statement. It further provides for a dispute resolution mechanism over privacy issues for consumers. Complaints shall be handled firstly by the business and, if this handling is not successful, then transferred to ADR with a BBB mediator.

TRUSTe is a well-known initiative under which consumers can resolve issues related to their individual privacy rights and other consumer issues.[93] Web site owners wishing to participate in the TRUSTe

---

[87] CyberTribunal Arbitration Procedure, Article 17 (2).
[88] See further CyberTribunal Arbitration Procedure, Article 18.
[89] CyberTribunal Arbitration Procedure, Article 21.
[90] CyberTribunal Arbitration Procedure, Article 22 and 23 (1)–(3).
[91] CyberTribunal Arbitration Procedure, Article 23 (6).
[92] CyberTribunal Arbitration Procedure, Article 23 (6).
[93] <http://www.truste.org>.

program shall sign a one-year contract with TRUSTe, which binds the user to certain privacy principles and provides for escalation procedures in the event a dispute cannot be resolved. Once a dispute arises between a consumer and a web site that carries the TRUSTe seal or trademark, a dispute resolution mechanism shall enable TRUSTe to review and later escalate procedures, if necessary.

1.7. *Analysis*

The above projects and others, like dispute resolution services provided by the Janzen Group[94] and Cyberjury,[95] concern to some extent self-regulation and provide some evidence of the advantages and disadvantages of this practice. The Internet is largely a privatized world, and private actors are creating frameworks under which governments and their courts are increasingly irrelevant.[96] Indeed, many business groups prefer to deal with disputes in electronic commerce through voluntary regimes designed and controlled by Internet society.

1.7.1. *Internal Mechanisms*

Internal mechanisms for handling consumer complaints could effectively prevent and resolve disputes at the earliest stage. Some such existing mechanisms are required by law, like the chargeback practice; some are provided voluntarily as a result of commercial considerations, such as the escrow services offer by eBay. Though such mechanisms can be regarded as dispute resolution mechanisms in the broadest sense, we tend to treat them as dispute avoidance techniques.

Internal mechanisms are important. While disputes over low values are expected to arise more frequently than ever before, resolution made possible by the internal side of business shall largely cut down the burden of the outside mechanisms. Outside mechanisms may refrain from intervening if businesses show the willingness and capacity

---

[94] The Janzen Group sells online ombudsman services to companies which engage in online business, promising to resolve disputes with these companies' customers as they may arise. See The Janzen Group, Business and Workplace Mediation and Conflict Resolution, at <http://www.janzengroup.com>.

[95] Cyberjury, a web site, presents readers with the facets of "real life" cases and asks them to express their verdict based on the affidavits and facts of the parties. See R.J. Konray, Cyberjury, at <http://www.cyberjury.com>.

[96] P.D. Carrington, Virtual Civil Litigation: A Visit to John Bunyan's Celestial City, 98 *Colum. L. Rev.* 1516 (1998).

to offer reasonable remedies for consumers, including remedies for complaints arising from both small and large purchases. Moreover, by providing consumers with procurement in the first instance, such mechanisms may successfully promote consumer confidence in merchant reliability. Efficient internal mechanisms, compatible with or modeled on a recognized standard, can thereby benefit merchants of any size. Feedback attained from internal complaining mechanisms can additionally help to shape an organization's marketing program and future.[97]

Internal mechanisms should be developed. A business web site could include clear information on their complaining procedures, explaining to consumers how to go about making a complaint, detailing the contacting methods and suggesting possible responses. The internal mechanisms shall have the capacity to determine and implement remedies. A merchant can decide whether a person has a legal right to a remedy or not; it is good customer relations practice to give a customer some redress in defined situations.[98] While not all complaints can be settled amicably, those spilling over the line into disputes shall resort to external mechanisms.

1.7.2. *External Mechanisms*

One ostensible benefit of self-regulation is that it can provide a testing forum.[99] As dispute resolution in electronic commerce remains a new program, relevant rules are under construction and will improve with trial-and-error.

Practice thus far has proven self-regulation to have its merits, all the more evident in light of outsider's shortcomings. Though the projects discussed earlier would not have been possible without the support, both financial and technical, of experts in the fields of online commerce and law, their role in these projects did not guarantee them success. That the first decision by the Virtual Magistrate Project is not enforceable in large part because of the carelessness of the

[97] A. McChesney, Feasibility Studies for New Standards Relating to Consumers and Electronic Commerce, February 14, 2000, for the Office of Consumer Affairs, Industry Canada, at <http://strategis.ic.gc.ca/SSG/ca01275e.html>.

[98] McChesney, *Id.*

[99] See further D.K. Mulligan & J. Goldman, The Limits and the Necessity of Self-Regulation: The Case for Both, in *Privacy and Self-Regulation in the Information Age*, U.S. Department of Commerce, NTIA 1997, at 67–68; <http://www.ntia.doc.gov/reports/privacy/privacy_rpt.htm>.

magistrate, for example, may present a case for further party involvement in regulation.

Its practice has also warranted criticisms against self-regulation. The program casts objectivity in doubt. For instance, in the first case decided in the Virtual Magistrate Project, the relationship of the complainant with the project posed a challenge to the final decision. Compliance from relevant parties is another big issue. In the same case, the defendant refused to recognize the authority of the project, which had direct implications for the later enforcement of the project's decision.

The substantial value of the projects described above is determined by the expertise of those involved in the dispute resolution process and, most importantly, the speed and convenience with which they resolve disputes. To be more effective, all the programs make full use of online facilities and thereby prove the point that an online mechanism is feasible in dispute resolution. As the Internet does not readily facilitate the safe dissemination of confidential information, present concerns involve determining how to complement online facilities with, for example, secure email communications and encryption techniques.

An assurance of confidentiality, a general feature of alternative dispute resolution, is particularly important to building consumer confidence. Currently, the issue of confidentiality is problematic for those using the online mechanism. Not making documents public until a final determination has been made is often advocated,[100] but then, too, all email communications delivered through the parties' Internet Service Providers may be intercepted by a sysop; hopefully, advances in encryption software will resolve this threat.[101] Presently important to the formulation of an objective view, which would make possible an appropriate decision in resolving disputes in electronic commerce, is the use of other means of communication. Involved parties and the delegated mediator or arbitrator must be presented alternative ways to communicate with each other and other relevant

[100] The Virtual Magistrate Project does not reveal any communications until the last stage of a case, which reveals its concern over the confidentiality of involved parties. See further *supra* note 7, Concept Paper, paragraph 26.

[101] One advance could be the use of confidential chat-rooms, which allow Internet users to communicate through text in real time. See further Virtual Magistrate Project Providers Dispute Resolution in Cyberspace, *World Arbitration & Mediation Rep.*, March 1996, at 77.

persons, as the complexity of the dispute requires, to reach a better understanding of the interests at stake.

The issue of consumer confidence will also remain troublesome until consumers have the knowledge necessary to understand electronic commerce. Web sites, advertisements, educational programs, and so forth, should be developed in order to educate, lead, and make the pubic comfortable.

Web sites can be gateways to dispute resolution services. They can advertise the availability of services on the Internet; contain information about the procedures for prospective parties; collect contact information from prospective consumers in order to assess their suitability for participation in the services; contain rules of the services and necessary documents to submit; present information about the backgrounds of the arbitrators or mediators; etc. They could also be used for other purposes. One web site could provide legal rules and advice on a particular field, another could offer library services, another could accomplish long-distance education, and so forth.

eBay's site serves as a good example. If the site at which a dispute arises is linked to a famous dispute resolution site, complainants are more likely to make use of the mechanism. The link should serve at once to improve consumer confidence in the business with the link and to publicize the dispute resolution site, thus bolstering business and online dispute resolution.

Furthermore, to have an array of experts who are familiar with legal issues and technology shall remain vital to supporting consumer confidence and the final success of the mechanism. In the Online Ombuds Project, it was decided that each ombudsman shall be paired with someone who had some technical expertise and considerable familiarity with the Internet. This was a temporary measure. In the long run, the ombudsman should posses such expertise for himself.

Ultimately, experts can help to expedite decisions at a low cost. At present, internal channels enforce decisions, but in the future a new framework should be formulated to enforce decisions if necessary.

2. *World Intellectual Property Organization (WIPO)*

The WIPO Mediation and Arbitration Center (the Center), an important provider of dispute resolution services, has been made even more conspicuous since it developed new services for resolving domain name disputes. Its practice in this area has implications for disputes in electronic commerce as a whole.

2.1. *Background*

After the emergence of the Internet, the Internet Assigned Numbers Authority (IANA) was established to maintain the root server and act as the Internet's central coordination, allocation, and registration body for addresses, names, and protocol parameters.[102] On June 10, 1998, the US government issued a Statement of Policy on Management of Internet Names and Addresses, known as the White Paper,[103] inviting the private sector to form a global consensus entity to take over the responsibility for Internet Protocols, domain names, IP addresses, and the Internet root server system.[104] Four months later, a new corporation known as ICANN[105] was created to perform the administrative duties like those involved in the assignment of IP addresses, Autonomous System Numbers, TLDs, and other unique parameters of the DNS and its protocols.[106] ICANN, a nonprofit corporation supported by the US department of Commerce, is the primary entity through which Internet policy is established.[107] While administrative in nature, its important goal is to preserve the central coordinating functions of the global Internet for the public good.[108] One of its first charges was to create a dispute resolution policy to allow cheap and fast resolution of conflicts regarding rights to domain names.

[102] See IANA Press Release, October 19, 1998, at <http://www.postel.org/iana-pr102098.html>; see also D. Flint, Much Confusion in Cyberspace—A Personal View of the Proposals for Internet Regulation, 19 *Business Law Review*, 112–115 (May 1998).

[103] Statement of Policy on Management of Internet Names and Addresses, 63 *Federal Register*, 31741 (1998).

[104] Electronic Signatures in Global and National Commerce Act on H.R. 1714 Before the Subcomm. On the Courts and Intellectual Property of the House Comm. on the Judiciary, 106th Cong. (1999) (Prepared testimony of M.M. Roberts, Interim President and Chief Executive Officer of the Internet Corporation for Assigned Names and Numbers).

[105] For a full description of the transfer of authority to ICANN, see further L. Pearlman, Truth, Justice and the Dot-Com Wars, *Law News Network*, at <http://www.lawnewsnetwork.com/practice/techlaw/news/A20216-2000Mar31.html>; see also D.C. Nunziato, Freedom of Expression, Democratic Norms, and Internet Governance, 52 *Emory Law Journal* 196–201 (Winter 2003); A.M. Froomkin, Habermas@Discourse.net: Toward a Critical Theory of Cyberspace, 116 *Harvard Law Review* 838–855 (January 2003).

[106] Introduction to the IANA TLD Delegation Practices Document or ICP-1 paper, May 21, 1999, at <http://www.iana.org/icp1.html>.

[107] See further ICANN, Approved Agreements among ICANN, the US Department of Commerce, and Network Solutions, Inc., at <http://www.icann.org/nsi/nsi-agreements.htm>.

[108] See further IANA, Frequently Asked Questions (FAQ) #2, at <http://www.iana.org/faqs.html>.

The US government's White Paper[109] charged ICANN with the selection of five new domain name registrar companies to compete with Network Solutions, Inc. (NSI), who was the sole agency responsible for the registration of domain names until the spring of 1999. Domain names themselves are problematic. While numbers and IP addresses are potentially infinite, there is only a limited pool of meaningful words from which agents can create a domain name. In a specific line of business, this pool gets even smaller.[110] Many seek to exploit this situation by registering domains with no intention of using them, but with the idea of negotiating the sale of the name later on in order to profit.[111] This leads to many disputes,[112] for example, those between the registrants and major trademark holders, somewhat late to the Internet themselves, who find their marks registered as domain names when they attempt to take up shop online.[113] Though NSI created a procedure[114] under which a third party can challenge the rights of a domain name owner to use a particular domain name,[115] its limited protection[116] and the passive

---

[109] The US Green Paper, A Proposal to Improve the Technical Management of Internet Names and Addresses, issued by the Department of Commerce's National Telecommunications and Information Administration (NTIA) on January 30, 1998, became the White Paper on June 5, 1998. See further NTIA, at <http://www.ntia.doc.gov/ntiahome/domainname/domainhome.htm#3>.

[110] S. Niyogi, *The Future of Domain Names*, at <http://www.siliconindia.com>.

[111] *Panavision Int'l, L.P. v. Toeppen*, 945 F.Supp. 1296, 1300 (C.D. Cal. 1996); *Intermatic, Inc. v. Toeppen*, 947 F. Supp. 1227, 1233 (N.D. Ill. 1996); see also A.M. Froomkin, Symposium: The Legal and Policy Framework for Global Electronic Commerce: A Progress Report of Governments and Governance, 14 *Berkeley Tech. L.J.*, 617, 626 (Spring 1999).

[112] For the emergence of disputes, see further C. Oppedahl, Internet Domain Names that Infringe Trademarks, at <http://www.patents.com>; see also The Internet is Running out of Addresses, at <http://www.economist.com>.

[113] J. Zittrain, ICANN: Between the Public and the Private—Comments Before Congress, *14 Berkeley Tech. L.J.* 1071. 1079 (1999).

[114] See further C. Oppedahl, Analysis and Suggestions Regarding NSI Domain Name Trademark Dispute Policy, 7 *Fordham Intell. Prop. Media & Ent. L.J.* 73, 77–81 (1996).

[115] The most spectacular characteristic is the "on hold" procedure: the owner of a registered trademark that is identical to a later-registered domain name can apply to have the domain name placed "on hold" so that no one can use the domain name until the dispute is resolved, either amicably or judicially. See further the Network Solutions Domain Name Dispute Resolution Policy, Revision 03 (effective February 25, 1998), at <http://www.networksolutions.com>.

[116] This procedure only works effectively for the owners of federal or national trademarks. See further C. Clough, *The Only Way to Fully Protect your Domain Name under Our Current "Dispute Policy" is with a Federal Trademark!*, at <http://blaze.net/search/internic.html>; see also C. Oppedahl, *Changes in Domain Name Rules could Result in Ownership Loss*, at <http://www.patents.com>.

action of NSI[117] has caused rather than curbed cybersquatting.[118] Criticisms of NSI and its policies are abundant and have implications for policy change for the domain name system.[119]

Following the ICANN request for opinions and suggestions from interested parties, and from WIPO in particular,[120] the ICANN Uniform Domain Name Dispute Resolution Policy and Rules were adopted on October 24, 1999. ICANN designated several bodies as dispute resolution service providers. Based on its experience with intellectual property rights and dispute resolution, the WIPO was the first one to be designated.[121] A supplemental rule was later implemented by the WIPO Center for the resolution of disputes.

2.2. *Combating Cybersquatting*

As we all know, a domain name is the name or address of a web site identifying a computer or network connected to the Internet.[122] What constitutes a domain name dispute, however, is not so clear.

---

[117] The trademark owner simply sends a letter of complaint to the domain name holder and then sends the NSI a copy of that complaint with the evidence of delivery plus a copy of the trademark registration certificate. NSI shall contact the domain name holder asking for evidence of federal mark protection that pre-dates the complaint. If none is provided, NSI will put the domain name on hold until the dispute is resolved.

[118] See, for example, C. Oppedahl, *NSI Domain Name Dispute Policy Puts Owners at Significant Risk*, at <http://www.patents.com>; see also G.G. Davis, III, Internet Domain Names and Trademarks, A Growing Area of Domestic and International Disputes, 532 PLI/Pat 383, 393 (1998); S. Kouretchian, Revised Rules Govern Domain-Name Disputes: To Adequately Preserve Their Rights, New Registrants Should File for Trademark Protection, *Nat'l L.J.*, October 28, 1996, at C20.

[119] For further discussion, see D. Lock, Toll-Free Vanity Telephone Numbers: Structuring a Trademark Registration and Dispute Settlement Regime, 87 *Calif. L. Rev.* 408 (March 1999); S.B. Sterling, Comment, New Age Bandits in Cyberspace: Domain Names Held Hostage on the Internet, *17 Loy. L.A. Ent. L.J.*, 746–747 (1997).

[120] Realizing the need for a new way to hear and decide domain name disputes that offers a more economical and efficient alternative to the court system, WIPO conducted studies to draft a Final Report on the Domain Name Process into which was incorporated a new UDRP as an alternative to litigation.

[121] Two others have been approved, namely, the National Arbitration Forum (Minneapolis, Minnesota) and the Disputes.org/eResolution Consortium (Amherst, Massachusetts, and Montreal, Canada), which take different approaches to the background of their panellists. Additional centers might be approved at a later date. See further Providers Take Different Approaches, 2 *World Telecom Law Report*, No. 2, 23 (2000); see also E-conflicts Find an eResolution Creation of a Canadian Virtual Tribunal to Settle Domain Name Disputes, at <http://www.newswire.ca>.

[122] See further *Your Own Domain Name*, <http://www.pharamond.com>.

Some of the literature on such disputes simplifies domain name disputes into cybersquat disputes or, even worse, simply mistakes domain name disputes for cybersquats. It is true that cybersquatting is the most important and most common form of dispute involving domain names, and most mechanisms dealing with domain name cases deal exclusively with cybersquats, but domain name disputes are not limited to cybersquats. This study will address various forms of domain name disputes.

Generally speaking, cybersquatting refers to the practice of stockpiling domain names for future resale to the general public.[123] It happens to the SLDs only, as this part shapes the distinct characteristics of a business. According to the WIPO Final Report,[124] there are important three pre-conditions that should be met for a case to be deemed a cybersquat.

First of all, the domain name is identical or confusingly similar to a trade or service mark in which the complainant has rights, including being confusingly similar to those activities the complainant intends to pursue. The weight of a domain name is especially significant to businesses. Like a trade or service mark, a domain name can effectively represent a business, but it is also more unique than such a mark. While we can find the same mark representing, for example, different categories of goods or services, the same domain name can never refer to different online businesses. This we may consider an exterior requirement for cybersquatting; the key conditions are to follow.

Secondly, the registrant has no rights or legitimate interests with respect to the domain name. To prove such interests, the registrant must be able to show that he/she is commonly known by the name; or has made prior use of the name in connection with a good faith offer of goods/services (or made prior demonstrable preparations for such use of the name); or is making a legitimate non-commercial or fair use of the domain name without intent for commercial gain or to otherwise misleadingly divert consumers or tarnish the mark.[125]

---

[123] D. Cabell, *Name Conflicts in Cyberspace*, <http://www.mama-tech.com>, viewed on 3 September 1999.

[124] See further, Final Report of the WIPO Internet Domain Name Process: The Management of Internet Names and Addresses: Intellectual Property Issues (hereinafter WIPO Final Report), <http://www.ecommerce.wipo.int>, viewed on 30 April 1999.

[125] See further Section 4(c) of the UDRP accepted by the ICANN at its Annual Meeting in Los Angeles on 4 November 1999, <http://www.icann.org>. The

Thirdly, the domain name has been registered and is being used in bad faith. This is the most substantial factor in determining the act of cybersquatting; using a domain name in good faith shall not be deemed as cybersquatting. Thus, it is very important to clarify what exactly constitutes bad faith. The job of clarification was initially taken up by the Internet Corporation for Assigned Names and Numbers Uniform Domain Name Dispute Resolution Policy (the ICANN UDRP) and later tackled in the first case dealt with by the WIPO Center.[126] Broadly put, determining bad faith requires showing that both the registration and the use of the domain name have been misdeeds.[127]

The UDRP gives a list of specific requirements for determining a bad faith registration: there are circumstances indicating that the domain name was registered primarily for the purpose of selling, renting, or otherwise transferring the domain name to the complainant, who is the owner of the trademark or service mark, or to a competitor of that complainant, for a sum in excess of the costs related to registering the domain name; the domain name was registered in order to prevent the complainant from using a mark in a corresponding domain name, provided that there is a pattern of such a conduct; the domain name was registered primarily for the purpose of disrupting the business of the complainant; the registrant intentionally attempted to attract Internet users to his web site or other online location, with the goal of commercial profit, by creating in them confusion regarding the complainant's mark.[128] Obviously, this is not a definitive list. Intensive analysis will still be needed to clarify what indeed constitutes bad faith.

Network Solution, Inc. (NSI) Policy singles out two possible defenses: domain registration prior to the effective date of the complainant's trademark; or the ownership by the domain holder of a federal or national trademark for the identical name.

[126] The first case, *World Wrestling Federation Entertainment, Inc. v. Michael Bosman*, was submitted electronically to the WIPO Arbitration and Mediation Center on 2 December 1999. The Administrative Panel Decision has a nice elaboration of bad faith.

[127] D. Cabell, *Trademark Disputes Online—ICANN's New Uniform Dispute Resolution Policy*, <http://www.mama-tech.com>, viewed on 18 November 1999.

[128] See further the ICANN UDRP, Section 4 (B), *supra* note 125. S. 1225, a new Bill passed by the U.S. Senate, says that bad faith intent could be determined from a number of factors, including intent to divert customers, offers to sell domain names for a substantial consideration, and multiple domain registrations using others' trademarks. See further *New Bill Would Provide Remedies for Domain Name Hijacking*, <http://www.mbc.com>.

Section 4(a) of ICANN UDRP states that only when a complainant proves that the above three conditions are met can the act be defined as cybersquatting; a registrant who incorporates an unauthorized trademark into his or her domain name without authorization as such is correspondingly a cybersquatter.[129] Actually, the three conditions are interconnected, each being necessary to reach a fair and complete judgement of cybersquatting. Just as internal requirements should be balanced with external requirements, positive requirements should be complemented by negative requirements. For instance, to defend himself against the accusation of bad faith, a respondent should be able to show that he has rights or legitimate interests. Thus, the second condition is complementary to the third condition. Furthermore, standards for proof of actual intent are left to the approved resolution providers.[130]

Domain name disputes are not to be equated with cybersquatting, as cybersquatting is only one category of domain name disputes. There are two other important categories of disputes: parasites, and twins/poachers. Although all these three categories are closely connected and, to a certain extent, similar to each other, there is a clear line to be drawn between them.

Like cybersquatters, parasites also expect to gain profits, but the parasites' profits are specifically earned through the use of the domain names, for example, a famous name or a name that connects multiple businesses. We can easily imagine how domain name disputes could arise between those in similar lines of business, or between those who simply wish to trade off a name's fame. In the case of twins, where the domain name registrant and the complainant may have the same name or nearly identical names, the involved parties may actually both have a legitimate claim to the name.[131] Perhaps, to resolve such difficult disputes, we must add new categories of gTLDs as is suggested in the Final Report of the WIPO Internet Domain Name Process. Here, the condition of bad faith is irrelevant, which sets these types of domain name disputes apart from

---

[129] A. Baum & M. Epstein, New Dilution Act Used to Evict "Cybersquatters", *Nat'l L. J.*, January 27, 1997, at C03.

[130] Section 4 (b) of the UDRP, *supra* note 125.

[131] See further I.S. Nathenson, Showdown at the Domain Name Corral: Property Rights and Personal Jurisdiction over Squatters, Poachers and Other Parasites, 58 *University of Pittsburgh Law Review*, 991 (1997), <http://www.pitt.edu>.

cybersquatting and points to a need for new methods and guidelines for dealing with a variety of such disputes.

Why have we neglected these other types of disputes? For one, cybersquatting cases are more prevalent. Another reason for emphasizing cybersquatting might be that labeling the wrongfulness in such cases is easier than it is in cases of parasites and twins/poachers. A third reason may be that the characteristic of bad faith means cybersquatting demands urgent resolution. Whatever the case, dealings with each of these three types of domain name disputes has helped to shed light on the proprietary rights that trademark owners have in the domain name version of their trademarks. It is to protect these rights that an efficient mechanism is urgently needed to resolve domain name disputes in general.

As analyze above, cybersquatting can bring about serious social disturbances. In resolving cybersquatting disputes, it is necessary to determine in the first place whether it could be categorized as a civil offence or a criminal one, and then provide the corresponding measures.

While it has become commonplace for a cybersquater to be subjected to civil procedures, there is some evidence that cybersquatting should be subject to criminal jurisdiction. The US House Judiciary Committee unanimously agreed to outlaw cybersquatting.[132] Moreover, it proposed a Bill[133] that would make the willful dilution of famous marks or trade on the owner's reputation a crime for whomever knowingly and fraudulently or in bad faith registers or uses the trademark of another. Although the White House has indicated that it would not pass this legislation,[134] the proposal has spurred further discussion regarding ways to curb cybersquatting. As the proposal suggests, proving criminality in domain name disputes (more specifically, the requirement for bad faith) involves more than the three conditions discussed above.[135] If the act is serious enough, perhaps it shall

---

[132] On 29 November 1999, President Clinton signed into law the "Intellectual Property and Communications Omnibus Reform Act of 1999", which resulted in the amendment of the Federal Trademark Act. The new provisions of the Trademark Act target the cybersquat. See further S.D. Littlepage, *Anti-Cybersquatting Act: Federal Protection for Trademarks and Personal Names on the Internet*, <http://www.dickinson-wright.com>.

[133] For the draft version of this Bill, see further <http://www.senate.gov>.

[134] See further I.J. Kaufman, The Domain Name System: Dispute Resolution and the Nice Classification System, 28 *International Business Lawyer*, No. 1, 39, (2000).

[135] According to the proposal, the following conditions (requirements of bad faith)

qualify as criminal in nature. As some states have already passed legislation on crimes connected with computers, and consideration of the criminal nature of cybersquatting is likely to underpin further legislation. At the present time, however, the mechanism in place to deal with cyersquating disputes does not concern the issue of criminality.

2.3. *Procedures for the Mechanism*

The whole procedure shall be initiated by a complaint[136] from an aggrieved mark holder who believes it is the victim of bad faith, abusive registration of a domain name in one or more TLDs.[137] A request that the complaint be referred to a panel operating under the Abusive Registration Rules, contact information for the complainant, the respondent, and the complainant's representative, if any,[138] the domain name or names at issue, the name of the registrar or registrars involved, an allegation that the registration is abusive and a description of the grounds for such a contention, any documentary evidence on which the complaint intends to reply and a schedule of such documents, and a statement of the determination sought shall be included in the complaint.[139] Meanwhile, the submitted complaint shall be accompanied by the payment of a nonrefundable adminis-

---

shall be met to qualify criminality: (a) the defendant registered or used an identifier to cause confusion or mistake, deceive, or cause dilution of the distinctive quality of a famous trademark; or with the intention of diverting consumers from the trademark owner to the defendant; (b) the defendant provided false information in its application to register the identifier or offered to transfer the identifier's registration to the trademark owner or other person or entity for something of value; and (c) the identifier is not the defendant's legal first name or surname or the defendant had not used the identifier in legitimate commerce prior to either the first use of the registered trademark or the effective date of the registration.

[136] The WIPO web site contains s standard complaint form, which can be submitted online. The Final Report contains a recommendation that provision be made in the procedural rules for the secure electronic filing of all pleadings in cases. However, the WIPO Abusive Registration Rules provide that communications should be expedited postal or courier service, transmitted by telefax, or sent, where the provider has the appropriate technical facilities, by electronic transmission through the Internet.

[137] WIPO Policy on Dispute Resolution for Abusive Domain Name Registration, Article 3 and 6.

[138] A party may be represented by any person, irrespective of nationality or professional qualifications. *Id.*, Article 4 (a).

[139] *Id.* Article 6.

tration fee.[140] If necessary, an advanced deposit for the costs of the proceedings could also be required.[141] For failure to pay the fee within seven days after a second reminder, the complaint shall be deemed withdrawn.[142]

After receiving the complaint, the WIPO Center shall check the complaint to ensure that it complies with the basic requirements of the UDRP. If it does, then the center shall transmit the complaint to the respondent and notify both parties of the date of the commencement of the proceedings, *i.e.*, the date on which the center initially received the complaint.[143] The respondent shall have 10 days from the date of commencement to submit a statement of defense including comments on any of the elements of the complaint and providing any documentary evidence on which the respondent intends to rely, as well as a schedule of such documents.[144] The center shall transmit the defense to the complainant immediately after receiving it.[145] Failing to submit the defense shall not obstruct the process of resolution; the panel may proceed with its determination on an *ex parte* basis.[146]

The WIPO Center shall then appoint a three-person panel and designate a presiding panelist.[147] Following the appointment, the center shall transmit the file to each member of the panel[148] and notify the disputing parties of the identities of the panel and the presiding member.[149] The parties can challenge a panelist who appears to lack impartiality or independence, assuming the challenged panelist declines to withdraw.[150] In such a situation, the center shall make the final

[140] *Id.*, Article 37 (a)–(c). No action shall be taken on the complaint until the administration fee has been paid.

[141] *Id.*, Article 39.

[142] *Id.*, Article 37 (d) and 39.

[143] *Id.*, Article 7.

[144] *Id.*, Article 8 (a).

[145] *Id.*, Article 8 (b).

[146] *Id.*, Article 28 (a).

[147] *Id.*, Article 9 (a). Unless the parties have the same nationality, the presiding member, excluding special circumstances, shall be a national of a country other than the country of either of the parties.

[148] *Id.*, Article 20.

[149] *Id.*, Article 9 (b).

[150] *Id.*, Article 10 (a), (b). Each panelist is required to be impartial and independent and must confirm that there are no circumstances that might give rise to justifiable doubt as to such impartiality or independence or must disclose such circumstances.

decision concerning the qualification of the panelist.[151] The proceedings shall be declared closed within 10 days of the delivery of the response or the establishment of the panel, whichever occurs later.[152]

The panel shall have complete discretion during the procedures.[153] It can decide on applicable language,[154] the production of further statements and additional documents, and the admissibility, relevance, materiality, and weight of any evidence submitted.[155] It can also choose to hold a hearing, though the general practice has been to determine the merits based on the documents alone.[156]

The panel shall resolve the dispute in accordance with the Abusive Registration Policy,[157] together with the laws that it determines appropriate in light of all the relevant circumstances.[158] The decision shall be made within 10 days of the closure of the proceedings by a majority of the panel, or else the presiding member makes the decision as if acting as a sole panelist.[159] The date of decision, the signature of the panelists,[160] the cost of the proceedings[161] and, most importantly, the reasons for giving such a decision shall be included in the final decision.

The panel shall communicate the decision to the WIPO Center, who then transfers it to the parties.[162] Seven days after the transfer, the center shall communicate the decision to the registrar, who continues with detailed implementation measures. The decision shall be

[151] *Id.*, Article 12–17.

[152] *Id.*, Article 34.

[153] *Id.*, Article 21 (a) (b). This is based on the fact that the parties are treated with equality and that each is given a fair opportunity to present its case.

[154] *Id.*, Article 22 (a). Unless otherwise agreed, the language of the proceeding shall be consistent with the domain name registration agreement, subject to the panel's power to determine otherwise. Meanwhile, according to Article 22 (b), the panel may order translations of documents that are not in the language of the proceeding.

[155] *Id.*, Article 25.

[156] *Id.*, Article 27 (a).

[157] *Id.*, Article 31.

[158] *Id.*, Section 15.

[159] *Id.*, Article 32 (a).

[160] *Id.*, Article 33 (a)–(c). At minimum, the signature of the majority or of the presiding member, when acting alone, must appear, and a brief explanation should be given for the absence of any signature.

[161] *Id.*, Article 40. This could include the panel's fees, expenses of the panel, and other expenses necessary to the conduct of the proceedings, such as the cost of hearing facilities.

[162] *Id.*, Article 33 (e).

effective and binding as of the date it is communicated to the registrar.[163] Further, the center shall communicate the decision to the WIPO to publish on a publicly available web site.[164] This marks the end of the whole procedure.

2.4. *Character of the Mechanism*

Just one day after the UDRP rules took effect the WIPO mechanism was put to work resolving a case.[165] To date, hundreds of cases have been brought forward for resolution.[166] In order to deliver quality services, the WIPO Center maintains an extensive legal, administrative and information technology infrastructure. An international team of legal and paralegal staff spanning six continents has been supported by a secretariat to ensure the professional administration of the cases. This network of disparate bodies enables the smooth functioning of mechanism. The mechanism has several unique characteristics.

Firstly, the nature of the mechanism has been clearly defined as administrative. The WIPO Center was established to offer arbitration and mediation services for international commercial disputes between private parties.[167] But though the services provided by the center are apparently legal or adjudicative in nature, the center is not a legal authority. Technically, it establishes administrative panels that evaluate domain name issues.[168]

The administrative function of the WIPO Center is evidenced by the initiation of the mechanism. As stated in the ICANN UDRP, disputes over the registration and use of an Internet domain name must be submitted to an administrative body. In practice, this submission puts into focus a prior registration agreement and the relevant

[163] *Id.*, Article 35 (b).

[164] *Id.*, Article 33 (f).

[165] The first case was received on December 2, 1999, and was decided and partially published by January 14, 2000. This case concerned an abusive domain name registration by a cybersquatter of <http://www.worldwrestlingfederation.com> accepted by Melbourne IT. See further WIPO Press Release 2000/204, at <http://www.wipo.org/eng/main.htm>.

[166] See further <http://www.arbiter.wipo.int>.

[167] See further The WIPO Arbitration and Mediation Center, <http://www.arbiter.wipo.int>.

[168] See further Substantive Guidelines Concerning Administrative Domain Name Challenge Panels, Interim Policy Oversight Committee, <http://www.gtld-mou.org>, viewed on 23 May 1997.

procedures offered therein. The so-called Registration Agreement entails implicit consent on the part of the registrant regarding arbitration: domain name holders that are deemed to be cybersquatters are subject to mandatory and binding arbitration, possibly resulting in loss of the domain name, and a fee to cover the arbitration expenses. The implementation of this administratively driven mechanism thus differs from traditional arbitration, which attains jurisdiction from the agreement to arbitrate by both parties. The passive role of the registrar in the dispute will be addressed later.

Secondly, litigation is not excluded from the new mechanism. Once a complaint is filed in the WIPO Center, it will be processed unless the complaint is settled or withdrawn. Failing to respond, the domain name holder will almost certainly lose. But though decisions are reached, they are not legally binding. No decision made by an administrative body could affect the power of the appropriate national or regional sovereign court to hear cases interpreting and enforcing intellectual property rights that fall within its jurisdiction.[169] Litigation can be particularly important when it comes to enforcement, as it is governed by the mandatory law of a state and its decisions are enforceable based on the power of a state. Litigation can thus serve as a safety valve for the administrative procedure. A trademark owner who believes litigation would be advantageous to him may resort to this mechanism. Furthermore, it is claimed that under the new mechanism, the panels are to apply streamlined, quick and cost-effective procedures to review multiple claims and eliminate cases of clear abuse of trademark holders' rights, leaving the more complex cases to the courts.[170]

This does not mean litigation is the rule. For the WIPO Center to be successful, it is important to limit registrants' freedom to turn to litigation. Some registrants would exploit too much freedom in bad faith, purposefully prolonging the period of resolution and adding to the indeterminacy of the results by requiring litigation. Considering the swiftly changing technology and the potential profit-gain entailed

[169] Final Report of the International *Ad Hoc* Committee: Recommendations for Administration and Management of gTLDs, <http://www.iahc.org>, viewed on 4 February 1997. Likewise, this procedure would not prevent any party from initiating arbitration or mediation procedures that are otherwise available.

[170] WIPO Processes First Case under New Dispute Resolution Procedure, 3 *World Telecom Law Report*, No. 1, 23 (2000).

by the use of domain name, it would be most detrimental to the justified party in keeping the case too long in court. To limit participants' capacity for maliciousness and make more certain jurisdiction in domain name disputes, so-called mutual jurisdiction[171] has been advanced. The domain name applicant shall be required in the domain name registration agreement to submit without prejudice to other potentially applicable jurisdictions,[172] to the jurisdiction of the courts of the country of domicile of the domain name applicant, and the country where the registrant is located.[173]

Thirdly, this mechanism can be characterized by its extensive use of online facilities, which may pave the way for future dispute resolution mechanisms. The WIPO Center's case management is supported by an online filing facility, email communication facilities for parties and panelists, and systemized documents that include a model complaint and a model response.[174] Once a case is brought to the WIPO Center, a secure online space in which all relevant communication will take place shall be created. The complaint and response and later relevant evidence are exchanged online through secure channels. Hearings shall be available using an electronic chat room, if deemed necessary by the panel.[175]

This mechanism should effectively reduce the time and cost entailed by traditional dispute resolution mechanisms,[176] particularly because of its time limit and set fee features.[177] As indicated, the whole procedure

[171] For the definition of Mutual Jurisdiction, see Article 1 of the UDRP Rules, <http://www.icann.org>.

[172] This shall mean that the *situs* of the tort shall also be included. See further I.J. Kaufman, *The Domain Name System—Act Now or Regret Later*, <http://www.icanndomainnames>.

[173] See further WIPO Final Report, *supra* note 124.

[174] Domain Name Dispute Resolution Service in 2000, WIPO Arbitration and Mediation Center, at <http://arbiter.wipo.int/domains>.

[175] As provided in Article 27 (a) of the WIPO Rules for Administrative Procedure Concerning Domain Name Registrations (the complete text is available at <http://www.wipo2.wipo.int>), the hearing can take the form of a physical meeting, a telephone or video conference, or a simultaneous exchange of electronic communications that allows the parties and the panel to exchange information in real time.

[176] The main point of this mechanism is that it is fast and cheap. See further E.H. Tiller, ICANN's Uniform Domain Name Dispute Resolution Policy: An Overview and Critique, 1 *Internet L. & Bus.* 589, 591–593 (2000).

[177] The filing fee ranges from $750 to $6000 or more, depending on the provider, the number of domain names at issue and the number of panelists. The typical UDRP proceeding costs less than US $10,000, including the filing fee and attorneys' fees.

shall be terminated within forty-five days, which is rather fast compared to the period needed for litigation and most arbitrations. Moreover, because the entire process is conducted by email, litigants save significant time that would otherwise be spent responding to documents and requests, sitting for depositions, and preparing for trial.[178] Many people have argued that the low registration fee accounts for the proliferation of cybersquatting and that the relatively high fee for combating cybersquatting through litigation and arbitration has further deterred the effective resolution of potential cybersquat disputes. The same people would agree that to curb cybersquatting, a case fee affordable for complainants is necessary.

Unlike traditional mechanisms, the WIPO Center's mechanism for resolving domain name disputes calls for a specific breed of expert analysts and places heavy demands on them. As indicated in the ICANN rules, the panel shall have very broad powers over the manner in which the proceeding is to be handled.[179] Their power is justified by knowledge and expertise in both the matters of the case and the procedures of the mechanism, in which any abuse of power should be frowned upon. They must be reputed not simply for knowledge in their particular field, but also for their impartiality, sound judgment, experience as decision-makers, and substantive experience in the areas of intellectual property law, electronic commerce and the Internet. As they control online communications in the case, with some administrative support, it is especially important that they have both knowledge of and are well equipped with relevant technology. The selected panelists should be able to both communicate with the parties in an efficient, modern way and also, as circumstances require, pick up speed. There is a lot to expect from panelists without offering them educational opportunities. To improve the services offered by the panelists, an exchange of experiences among the panelists with regard to the mechanism was facilitated by the center.[180]

---

[178] D.H. Bernstein, Domain Name Dispute Resolution: A Model for the Future?, International Conference on Dispute Resolution in Electronic Commerce, WIPO, November 2000, ARB/ECOM/00/22.

[179] Section 10 of the ICANN Rules. For further analysis, see D. Cabell, Domain Name: World Standard Set for Key Internet Disputes, 6 *Dispute Resolution Magazine*, No. 2, 2000, <http://www.mama-tech.com>.

[180] The Center successfully organized the first Domain Name Panelist meeting on November 7, 2000 at the WIPO Headquarters.

The registrar is uniquely characterized by his passivity. With the introduction of competition into the Internet world, administrating the registration of domain names is an increasingly important job. But despite their influence, it is generally acknowledged that registrars shall not bear liability in domain name disputes, and registration agreements[181] invariably provide as such.[182] Nor do registrars have any responsibility to transfer or remove a domain name in dispute; the *status quo* prevails pending the dispute and the domain name is not put on hold or otherwise blocked until a decision is rendered.[183] Their most important role in the dispute mechanism is to implement the decision while providing information, such as verification of the relevant registration, for the panel when necessary.[184] Provided that registrars act responsibly within the ICANN system and, in particular, carry out their responsibilities under the UDRP, any question of direct or indirect infringement is of no serious concern to them.[185]

Lastly, no damages are awarded. Unlike the remedies available through litigation, the remedies available under online procedure shall be limited to either the cancellation or transfer of the domain name registration or the rejection of the claim. There are no provisions for damages, attorneys' fees, or other injunctive relief. This is reasonable. The mechanism is intended to be a simple and efficient one, and the determination of monetary damages would add uncertainty and complexity to both submissions and the panel's decision. It is, after all, administrative in nature and lacks the judicial capacity of traditional methods. Where damages should be determined, litigation may play its role as a complementary mechanism.

---

[181] See, for example, Network Solutions, Inc. Domain Name Registration Agreement, Article G, <http://www.quickstart.rccis.com>.

[182] See further M. Barry, Is the InterNIC's Dispute Policy Unconstitutional?, <http://www.mids.org>, viewed on 1 August 1997.

[183] See further Cabell, *supra* note 123.

[184] During the procedure, the registrar shall be required to confirm relevant information about the disputed domain name. For typical interactions between WIPO and a registrar during the administrative procedure, see <http://www.arbiter.wipo.int>.

[185] C. Gibson, Digital Dispute Resolution: Internet Domain Names and WIPO's Role, *Computer Und Recht International*, No. 2, 35 (2001).

2.5. *Analysis*

While largely based on international initiative, the WIPO mechanism emphasizes self-regulation. Though it serves a public function[186] and requires the concurrence of every powerful party with an interest in domain name policy,[187] ICANN is a private corporation. Furthermore, the service provider is a private body with its own pleading rule, service rule, time limits, and decision-makers.

This mechanism got to its feet on 8 December 1999 and has since achieved great international success. The service offered allows an aggrieved trademark owner located anywhere in the world to challenge a third party's registration of a domain name that incorporates or is confusingly similar to its trademark. There are no territorial limitations for its players; anyone, anywhere can file the suit and the case may be arbitrated by someone located anywhere on the globe. There is also no limit to its scope. At the moment, the center is working to offer services for disputes both for multilingual domain names[188] and in new gTLDs.[189] Presumably, with the increasing caseload and the broadened scope,[190] the center's responsibilities shall expand further. Its international success is dependent upon two items: the uniform application of the UDRP to all potential respondents and the automatic execution of an effective remedy for successful complainants.[191] Just as Francis Gurry, Assistant Director General,

---

[186] Management of Internet Names and Addresses, 63 *Fed. Reg.* 31, 741 (Department of Commerce, June 10, 1998), available at 1998 WL 298883.

[187] K. McCarthy, Who the Hell Does WIPO Think It Is?, *The Register*, August 16, 2000, at <http://www.theregister.co.uk/content/5/12638.html>.

[188] Registration of multilingual domain names was made possible after testing in Chinese, Japanese, and Korean.

[189] New gTLDs were introduced in 2001, which include .aero, .biz, .coop, .info, .museum, .name, .pro. This idea has been proposed by the IAHC, see J.B. Lucas, IAHC Announces New Top-Level Domains: Recommends New Challenge Procedures, 2 *BNA's Elec. Info. Pol'y & L. Rep.* 152–153 (February 7, 1997); H.N. Mewes, Note, Memorandum of Understanding on the Generic Top-Level Domain Name Space of the Internet Domain Name System, 13 *Berkeley Tech. L.J.* 235, 245 (1998).

[190] The scope encompasses domain name disputes affecting other intellectual property-related rights. See further the Second WIPO Internet Domain Name Process, at <http://wipo2.wipo.int/process2>.

[191] A. Christie, The ICANN Domain Name Dispute Resolution System: A Model for Other Transborder Intellectual Property Disputes on the Internet?, International Conference on Dispute Resolution in Electronic Commerce, WIPO, November 2000, ARB/ECOM/00/23. As said in the paper, the features derive from the fact that ICANN has control over the "root zone" file on the "A root" server containing the authoritative list of all TLDs, and has the sole power to decide on the registrar for these TLDs.

stated, "The aim is to make sure that parties are treated fairly and equally and that balanced decisions providing practical guidelines are taken, which shall help bring some clarity in a relatively quick and cheap manner."[192]

The advantages of this online mechanism over traditional mechanisms are easily discernable. Many have come to laud the mechanism, which they expect, and which has been shown to be able to reduce the need for other potentially time-consuming and expensive means of communications, in-person meetings, and hearings.[193] Its many advantages can be outlined as follows. Firstly, disputes can be resolved fast, usually within about 45–60 days, which is remarkable when compared to the time generally involved in litigation. Secondly, the low fee is a plus. The online nature of the communications involved and the reduction in document production have contributed to its low cost. Simplicity is the third advantage this service offers. Parties can easily access a web site, which provides guiding rules, model complaints and responses, and other relevant information. The clearly detailed nature of the rules in play, which set standards for the relief possible, etc., makes the workings of the process both evident to involved parties and simple for the arbitrators to accomplish.

Because of its many advantages, some have suggested this mechanism should serve as a model for dealing with dispute resolution in electronic commerce in general. Is this suggestion appropriate? While facts at hand in abusive domain name registration cases, like cybersquatting in three gTLDs and a few ccTLDs,[194] are generally cut and dry, it may be that where disputes in electronic commerce

---

[192] P.M. Swamy, WIPO Handling First Cybersquatting Case, *Bus. Line*, December 15, 1999.

[193] See further C. Gibson & J. Fulton, *A Legal Technical Framework for the Online Resolution of Domain Name Disputes*, <http://www.ibm.nsysu.edu>.

[194] After due consideration of the views expressed on the subject, the WIPO elected to limit its mandatory general administrative procedure for the resolution of domain name disputes to instances involving deliberate bad faith and abusive domain name registration. These limitations were made in light of the weight of opinion against mandatory submission to such a procedure in respect of disputes over good faith rights to the use of the name in question. See further M.S. Donahey, Resolving Certain Domain Name Disputes: The WIPO Recommendations, Journal of Internet Law, <Http://www.gcwf.com>. The three gTLDs covered are: ".com", ".net", and ".org"; the ccTLDs covered are: ".ac"(Ascension Island), ".io"(British Indian Ocean Territory), ".nu"(Niue), ".sh"(St. Helena), ".tt"(Trinidad and Tabago), ".tv"(Tuvalu), ".ws"(Western Samoa). In addition, a number of parties who have filed proposals with ICANN for new generic TLDs have agreed to adopt the UDRP for the resolution of domain name disputes in their registries.

in general are concerned, the disputed facts are complicated. If that assumption is accurate, then the expansion of the mechanism would involve financial and time-oriented challenges in terms of adjusting for, at the minimum, the discovery of facts. That said, the mechanism is still at its beginning stage and its application could be extended once proven operable. Both its successes and problem areas should indicate opportunities for a future mechanism. Looking at its shortcomings alone may not only reveal warning signs but also give rise to ideas for improving the approach taken towards future disputes in electronic comments.

As with any new procedure, this mechanism has experienced a few hiccups during its initial period of operations. They mostly concern procedural issues. One point of contention has been the possibility of complainants submitting a reply following initial response of the domain name registrant, which the ICANN rules do not mention. Most panels shall refuse to consider such replies: on the one hand, to save time, and on the other hand, to reach balance between the two parties. Their thinking is that the complainant should have arranged all documents containing relevant facts and arguments when initially submitting the case and, moreover, that limiting the time for respondents has already served to balance party interests. Others have been more lenient. One of the four service providers,[195] National Arbitration Forum (NAF) based in Minneapolis, Minnesota, revised its supplemental rules to explicitly permit replies so long as they are filed within 5 days and accompanied by a $ 150 filing fee. As this inconsistent application of the UDRP rules may cause forum shopping, UDRP rules should be amended to incorporate guidelines concerning replies. Somewhat brighter guidelines should be promulgated for ensuring consistent standards to govern domain name disputes.

Another problematic area for this mechanism is the elaboration and effect of its final decisions. According to UDRP rules, the panel's

[195] For further information on NAF, see further <http://www.arbforum.com/domains>. The other two providers are Disputes.org/eResolution Consortium (Amherst, Massachusetts, and Montreal, Canada) and the CPR Institute for Dispute Resolution. Additional centers might be approved at a later date. It is notable that the new providers take differing approaches to the background of their panelists. See further Providers Take Different Approaches, 2 *World Telecom Law Report* 2, 23 (2000); see also E-Conflicts Find an eResolution! Creation of a Canadian Virtual Tribunal to Settle Domain Name Disputes, at <http://www.newswire.ca>.

decision shall provide the reasons on which it is based.[196] This is important to the whole mechanism. Although no precedent shall be followed, the former decisions shall still provide an insight into the dispute resolution procedures. The disputing parties could have some guidance from the old cases and act in accordance with them. Considering time limitations and similarities between the cases, insight into past cases could help the panelists formulate decisions. Otherwise, when there have been contradictory decisions made, panelists can seek to gain a broad understanding of the different decisions made and form a new attitude with which to make a new decision. Furthermore, consistency among the cases could help to build confidence in the system.

Some have suggested an appellate panel be made available as part of this online mechanism. The present author believes the adoption of such a panel to deal with cybersquatting cases would be inappropriate for several reasons. For one, the adoption of appellate panels would unnecessarily extend the time spent on individual cases and raise their costs. Secondly, the relatively simple facts involved in such disputes make the appellate panels unnecessary. Even when injustice arises, litigation is available as the last resort. With that said, in the case of the disputes in electronic commerce in general, it could be beneficial to have such as a backing.

Several other criticisms of the online mechanism have been raised.[197] Some are reasonable, some are not. Many criticize ICANN for a lack of openness, accountability, and membership.[198] Of course, the need to maintain transparency and openness within the governance of the Internet and associated dispute resolution process is significant, but it is the view of the present author that the present mechanism has largely accommodated this need. Its web site makes the process for dispute resolution self-explanatory for involved parties by providing complete information including the UDRP procedures and WIPO's administrative services, relevant documents, the practical

---

[196] UDRP Rules 15 (d).

[197] See, for example, A.M. Froomkin, *Major Flaws in the WIPO Domain Name Proposal—A Quick Guide*, <http://www.law.miami.edu>. Also, see Domain Name System Information and News, at <http://www.isoc.org>.

[198] See, for example, K. Coughlin, What a Tangled Web the Federal Government Wove—ICANN Has the Unwieldy Task of Sorting Out Net Addresses, *Start-Ledger*, October 3, 1999.

flowchart and guide, a FAQ (frequently asked questions) section, model forms, notice of pending cases, and full texts of published decisions. It shall further provide multilingual presentations.[199] The fear of anti-trust is not justifiable based what was discussed above regarding a uniform mechanism. Furthermore, it is claimed that the mechanism is balanced towards the complainant since he shall have time to prepare for the case before initiating it, while the respondent will have a very limited time to prepare for the case. However, as far as cybersquatting is concerned, this should not be a big problem. When registering the domain name in the first place, the registrant should have already considered its position.

It is true that basic privacy must be protected on the Internet. However, the disclosure of the background information of the domain name registrant is also important for locating the potential infringing party. It is thus advisable to keep the registrant's file confidential, except when justified requests arise. Ultimately the registrar will have to determine what constitutes a valid request, but such requests should include a request to file a complaint or to determining the validity of the details of the registrant.

The mechanism is fast and inexpensive compared to litigation, but it cannot award monetary damages or make discovery. Litigation could provide all of the discovery and protection of parties' rights one would expect in dispute resolution, but at a much higher cost and in not so nearly an expeditious proceeding.[200] Thus, both methods have their shortcomings. It is up to the complainant to decide which aspect of the mechanism is most important to them and to choose a mechanism accordingly.

There has been some concern about the potential favoring of trademark holders.[201] By the end of May 2000, 175 cases had been resolved. Among these cases, 143 resulted in the transfer of a domain name to the complainant; only 32 complaints were decided in favor

---

[199] See further Gibson, *supra* note 185, at 36.

[200] See further Information About Trademark and Domain Names, <http://www.ladas.com>.

[201] R. O'Keefe, *Alternative Resolution for Domain Name Disputes*, <http://infoeagle.bc.edu>; see also Letter from F. Paul Bland, Jr., Staff Attorney, Trial Lawyers for Public Justice, to Secretary, Federal Trade Commission, at 6 (March 20, 2000), at <http://www.ftc.gov/bcp/altdisresolution/comments/blandjr.pdf>; L. Naylor, Individuals Getting Wiped Out by WIPO, The Standard, September 5, 2000, at <http://www.thestandard,net/article/display/0,1151,18239.00.html>.

of the respondents.[202] Still, whether or not there is a bias has yet to be proven. Interestingly enough, trademark owners complain that the UDRP is fatally flawed since it requires complainants to undertake the heavy burden of showing that the domain name holder's primary purpose is to extract money in order to support his own arguments.[203] A mechanism that involved parties would be equally satisfied with is unlikely. We can only attempt to meet as many demands as possible.

All in all, the present author wholeheartedly approves of the progress this mechanism has brought about and also welcomes possible improvements to it. Particularly imperative to its success is ensuring the WIPO Center can provide necessary technical support to the whole mechanism by continually equipping it with the necessary staff and facilities. At present, it is especially important that the center also concentrate on promoting the clarification of relevant rules for dispute resolution, as there is as yet no complete legal guide for the processing of the cases. Although the new mechanism is not legal in nature, as it does not have the power to legislate, it the WIPO Center is still the leading dispute resolution service provider for disputes arising out of the registration and use of Internet domain names. As such, it should be able to exert an important influence on the formation of new laws in this area.

3. *Conclusion*

When asked whether or not they would like to resolve disputes in court or via traditional ADR mechanisms such as offline arbitration, the users in electronic commerce respond in the negative. They would prefer to resolve disputes entirely online—to have their complaint filed online, their documents considered online, their hearing held online, and their decision made online.[204]

---

[202] See <http://arbiter.wipo.int>.

[203] ICANN's Dispute Policy Seen too Tough on Trademark Holders, *Comm. Daily*, November 16, 1999.

[204] W.K. Slate II, Challenges and Opportunities for Dispute Resolution in the Era of Electronic Commerce, International Conference on Dispute Resolution in Electronic Commerce, WIPO, November 2000, ARB/ECOM/00/7.

Online facilities offer major opportunities for dispute resolution. Some people are still in doubt as to whether online communications can live up to their expectation.[205] They may feel, for example, that the intense chemistry experienced in situations of personal confrontation cannot be duplicated through the computer screen. But those who know the Internet well believe online system can be used both to assist the rational evaluation of the parties' positions and ultimately, to convey emotion, assess credibility, and form newly enhanced relationships.[206] Indeed, as the Internet is used more widely and persons become more comfortable with it, traditional mechanisms will fall behind online mechanism and ultimately fail to meet the customers' demands. New phenomena bring new demands. It is thus wise to have an online mechanism to accommodate disputes arising out of online business. Most international organizations have realized this and are advocating an online environment for dispute resolution.

Ongoing projects are leading the way ahead for a future mechanism to deal with disputes in general. Although we would not blindly advocate a complete substitution of the arbitral process by online procedures in any situation, which would be totally unrealistic, there are certain elements, at least in the ordinary arbitral process, which could be conducted with the use of the modern technologies.[207] Current projects are the specialized results of certain groups of people,[208] and there is at present no very coordinated effort among the ADR community to study, address and respond to disputes in electronic commerce.[209] Without such competition, the present author can take liberties in conducting further research on governance and regulation and making suggestions for the design of a new mechanism for electronic commerce.

---

[205] For further discussion of the advantages and disadvantages on online mechanisms, see L.Q. Hang, Comments: Online Dispute Resolution Systems: The Future of Cyberspace Law, *41 Santa Clara L. Rev.* 853–863 (2001); R.M. Victorio, Internet Dispute Resolution (iDR): Bringing ADR into the 21st Century 1 *Pepp. Disp. Resol. L.J.* 289–298 (2001).

[206] D.R. Johnson, *The Promise of Online Dispute Resolution*, at <http://www.toolbox.org/Tvtools/app-onlinedr.html>.

[207] F. Gurry, The Dispute Resolution Services of the World Intellectual Property Organization, 2 *Journal of International Economic Law*, No. 2, 397, 1999.

[208] These efforts do not generally involve substantial input from consumer organizations.

[209] R.C. Bordone, Electronic Online Dispute Resolution: A Systems Approach—Potential, Problems, and a Proposal, 3 *Harv. Negotiation L. Rev.* 188 (Spring 1998).

CHAPTER SIX

A NEW MECHANISM FOR ELECTRONIC COMMERCE

1. *Introduction*

It is without doubt that electronic commerce shall constitute a major part of future commercial transactions. With more and more transactions consummated through the Internet, disputes shall definitely arise more often and in a more diversified form than they have in traditional business. At present, there are various levels of mechanisms to resolve such disputes, the most formal one being litigation. However, ADR mechanisms have been in existence since the widespread emergence of international transactions. The advantages entailed by ADR mechanisms are attractive to most transacting parties. While litigation still takes an important position in dispute resolution, ADR mechanisms have become more and more frequently employed. This is explained by the quantity of cases resolved, the amounts entailed, the frequency of provision of such services in contracts, etc. Furthermore, it is illustrated by a flourishing of projects providing such services. In a word, ADR mechanisms are now on the right track.

It is true that many cases concerning electronic commerce have been resolved in the present dispute resolution mechanisms. However, the problems entailed in the present mechanisms have adversely effected the final resolution of disputes in various aspects. Common weaknesses identified by Consumer International (CI) include linguistic limitations (most were English only); availability to certain merchants only; consumer fees, which are higher than typical transaction values; lack of ability to fit the type of dispute resolution with the type of dispute; limited incentives for compliance with online ADR results; lack of transparency in respect of both dispute resolution results and the credentials of dispute resolution officers; and failure to include adequate consumer representation on the service's governing board.[1] With the rapid development of electronic commerce, a new

[1] Press Release: Consumer Redress in E-Commerce in Need of Attention: No

mechanism accommodating the character of the new commerce is urgently needed to serve the Internet society.

As discussed in former Chapters, various bodies have pursued a new mechanism for electronic commerce, and some have achieved great success. All their efforts constitute the basis for the present study.

2. *Online Mechanism for Electronic Commerce*

For merchants, internal mechanisms can resolve complaints and prevent disputes to a certain extent. However, when disputes do arise, an external mechanism shall be necessary. The existence of a mechanism to specifically deal with disputes in electronic commerce shall increase consumer confidence in the merchants' credibility and thereby enhance their reputation.

2.1. *The Requirements of the New Mechanism*

With the wide application of the Internet, transactions can be completed online much more efficiently, requiring less time and cost, than transactions completed offline. The rapid development of online consumer transactions is a result of this fact.

In line with this new development, ADR mechanisms should be reformulated. Several requirements should be respected in formulating a new mechanism. Technical criteria should be established and used as rules, guidelines or definitions of characteristics to ensure that certain services are fit for their purpose. The mechanism's compliance with requirements can provide assurance about the reliability or other characteristics of services. As far as a mechanism for electronic commerce is concerned, the following requirements should be met.

First of all, the new mechanism should be able to resolve disputes in a relatively inexpensive way.[2] As we know, consumer transactions

---

Online Dispute Resolution Service Meets All Criteria for Good Practice, 11 December 2000, at <http://www.consumersinternational.org>.

[2] Just as suggested in the recitals of Article 17 of the European Commission Proposal on Certain Legal Aspects of Electronic Commerce in the Internal Market, out of court dispute resolution should be particularly useful for some disputes on the Internet because of their low transactional value and the size of the parties,

shall become an increasingly important form of future commercial dealings. Generally speaking, the amount of money exchanged in such transactions is rather low. A mechanism shall be meaningless if the fee for resolving disputes is higher than the disputing amount, which would deter consumers from submitting to dispute resolution.

Secondly, disputes shall be resolved in an efficient way. This efficiency is economic, social, and practical in nature. Economic efficiency concerns the first principle of cost minimization. Social efficiency refers to the peaceful and quick resolution of disputes through an environment from which the disputes arise. Practical efficiency concerns speed. This mechanism should be able to handle disputes in an expeditious manner. An efficient mechanism will facilitate simple and fast proceedings.

The new mechanism shall be easy for both consumers and businesses to utilize, in complicity with the requisite procedures for filing and resolving claims and, most importantly, expeditious in fulfilling the task of resolution. With the development of modern technology, the pace of modern society has become faster. Time means money. When drawn out for too long, the value of a decision in a certain dispute shall be minimized. Consumers shall also be reluctant to submit a case if it is expected to last very long. Thus, it is vital to emphasize efficiency in creating the new mechanism. Reasonable time limits should be set for considering disputes, submitting documents, rendering decisions, and complying with decisions.

Thirdly, the principle of fairness shall be applied to formulate relevant procedures. While emphasizing efficiency, procedural fairness and the protection of the rights of both parties should not be overlooked. A balance should be reached between fairness and effectiveness. This mechanism should treat both parties equitably and fairly. Once deemed necessary, oral hearings, or the examination of witnesses should not be excluded. But it should also be noted that if too many procedural rules are added in an attempt to make the mechanism fair, the mechanism could be too expensive or burdensome to be effective. It seems that a balance should be struck. Actually, procuring fairness shall not cause problem in realizing time and cost efficiency.[3]

---

who might be deterred from using legal procedures because of their cost. This article can be found at <http://www.ispo.cec.be/ecommerce/legal.htm>.

[3] See, for example, M.E. Schneider, Lean Arbitration, 10 *Arbitration International*, No. 2, at 119 (1994).

The principle of efficiency should be based on procedural fairness; if fairness cannot be reached, efficiency shall mean nothing.

Fourthly, the principle of enforceability should be upheld. This point is supported by former efforts to obtain a convention in recognizing and enforcing foreign decisions. The decision-making process is important, but this process shall mean nothing if the final decision is not recognized or cannot be enforced. Rules intended to regulate decisions in a traditional way are unsuitable for the present situation. Enforcement should be tailored to the online environment and integrated into the whole dispute resolution mechanism. Fully realizing final decisions will require international efforts.

Fifthly, in order to be successful, the new mechanism should also incorporate the values and concerns of those who actually live in cyberspace. The Internet has improved the traditionally weak position maintained by the consumers. Consequently, while protecting consumers on the one hand, the mechanism must on the other hand turn its attention to the protecting the interests of merchants more than dispute resolution mechanisms have in the past. The balancing of powers and the underlying interests of participants in the dealings shall be vital to the fate of electronic commerce, which shall be influential to the final adoption of the mechanism by both parties. An interest-based approach should be taken. While the "real world" dispute resolution mechanism remains a rights-and-power-based system, an interest-based approach would prove more mutually satisfying, value-creating, and "win-win" than any polarized, zero-sum rights-based approach.[4]

Sixthly, the new mechanism should be made easily accessible and convenient. Businesses participating in the mechanisms should provide links from their web sites; governments, consumer organizations, trade associations, and other groups should also provide links to make it easy for consumers to find help.[5] The mechanism shall be viewable in different ways and barriers to entry to this mechanism shall not exist. Complainants shall have no problems in locating the mechanism and filing suits.

---

[4] See L.R. Singer, *Settling Disputes: Conflict Resolution in Business, Families, and the Legal System*, 1–14 (1994).

[5] Alternative Dispute Resolution in the Context of Electronic Commerce, Trans Atlantic Consumer Dialogue (TACD), Doc No. ECOM-12–00, February 2000.

Finally, modern technology shall be applied. The new mechanism should be responsive to the peculiarities of life in cyberspace and cognizant of the fact that life in cyberspace is different from life in real space. It should make use of modern technology to realize the former principles. The purpose of raising this recommendation to the level of principle is to emphasize the influential status of technology in the new mechanism. The new mechanism must exploit this status, while not invalidating real space.

2.2. *The Form of the New Mechanism*

Online electronic dispute resolution is intriguing. This process shall allow for greater flexibility, more creative solutions, and quick decisions. Moreover, its indirect nature will preserve the relationship between the parties once the dispute is resolved. Efforts to do so will bring to the forefront ADR options such mediation, arbitration, and mini-trials.[6]

There is no doubt that the new mechanism is an interest-based model of ADR. As the choice of ADR vehicle shall have a strong bearing on the success of the new mechanism, it is important to decide whether the initial target for this mechanism should be arbitration, mediation, etc. The choice among those forms shall depend on what the parties hope to achieve and what they are willing to do to achieve the desired end. The features of cyberspace and technology shall have an influence on the choice of a specific ADR vehicle.

To date, arbitration has proven more successful than other vehicles because of its binding nature. Processes producing unbinding or non-final decisions are not so attractive to either party and could if parties are acrimonious and not willing to work together prove dangerous. While they can agree to such processes, they can also break such processes with no detrimental results.[7] The evidence or reasoning in the decisions of such cases could have some positive effect on later possible adjudicative procedures, but such processes have adverse implications for the confidence of their participants.

---

[6] R.J. Poslums, The Trillion Dollar Risk, Best's Rev., September 1998, at 36, 110. See also H.H. Perritt, Jr., President Clinton's National Information Infrastructure Initiative: Community Regained?, 69 *Chi.-Kent L. Rev.* 1012 (1994).

[7] See, for example, W.I. Fagan, Overcoming Impass: Are There Limits to Online Mediation?, International Conference on Dispute Resolution in Electronic Commerce, WIPO, November 2000, ARB/ECOM/00/15.

The legal position of arbitration is representative of the legal position of most kinds of contractual dispute resolution procedures.[8] However, arbitration also applies to non-contractual issues. Indeed, arbitrators have been broadly interpreting the parties' agreement to arbitrate all disputes arising out of or related to the contract to include non-contractual issues. And national laws are increasingly construed to permit the arbitrability of non-contractual issues.[9] Thus, in most situations, once valid agreements requiring arbitration in case of disputes exist, both parties are obliged to arbitrate.[10] The court shall have no right to adjudicate in the first instance when a valid agreement is in place. The decisions made afterwards shall be binding and final.[11] Only in limited situations can the court dismiss such decisions.[12]

Arbitration has several notable advantages. For one, the application of arbitration shall avoid the issue of deciding adjudicative jurisdiction, which simplifies the whole dispute resolution process. Another point is that arbitration decisions may be more predictably recognized and enforced in the territory of all trading nations on the globe than judgments made by national courts.[13] The neutrality of international arbitration is generally recognized. Arbitration has developed a relatively complete set of more or less legally based rules that offer a better guide than other dispute resolution mechanisms do. As arbitration is largely a process in which information is obtained and evaluated, online tools shall provide especially significant opportunities for online arbitration. Another phenomenon is that courts are increasingly willing to enforce arbitration agreements, even those contained in consumer contracts of adhesion.[14] For all of these reasons, arbitration is appropriate for the new mechanism.

---

[8] H.H. Perritt, Jr., Dispute Resolution in Electronic Network Communities, 38 *Vill. L. Rev.* 392 (1993).

[9] J. Goldsmith & L. Lessig, *Grounding the Virtual Magistrate*, at <http://mantle.sbs.umass.edu/vmag/groundvm.htm>.

[10] See, for example, U.S. Arbitration Act 9 U.S.C. 2 (1990); Uniform Arbitration Act 1, 7 U.L.A. 5 (1985); Restatement (Second) of Judgments 84 (1982).

[11] See, for example, U.S. Arbitration Act (USAA), 9 U.S.C. 1–10 (1990); Uniform Arbitration Act 1, 7 U.L.A. 5 (1985). See further A.W. Shilston, The Evolution of Modern Commercial Arbitration, 4 *Journal of International Arbitration*, 45, 55 (1987); A. Redfern & M. Hunter, *Law and Practice of International Commercial Arbitration*, 27 (London, 1991); H. Golsong, A Guide to Procedural Issues in International Arbitration, 18 *International Lawyer*, 633 (1984).

[12] See, for example, Uniform Arbitration Act 2, 7 U.L.A. 60–68.

[13] See, for example, *Scherk v. Alberto-Culver*, 417 U.S. 506 (1974).

[14] See M.E. Budnitz, Arbitration of Disputes Between Consumers and Financial

While a lot of existing mechanisms take the form of arbitration, they are not very well suited for the present situation. Criticism has arisen concerning the high fee and increasingly lengthy processes of arbitration. The traditional approach to international arbitration must evolve if it is to be considered useful and applicable for electronic commerce. As a result, international commercial entities are searching for ways to increase management participation, eliminate procedural and other ancillary issues, and open up dialogue between the parties on the business issues in dispute.[15]

2.3. *The Conception of the New Mechanism*

The designing of a new mechanism is a systematic project, which requires cooperation from various related bodies. Many existing mechanisms are resolving disputes based on their original objectives. In designing a new mechanism, it is vital to make it new.

There is no doubt that the new mechanism should be well suited to disputes arising out of electronic commerce, which requires their having a low administrative cost and sufficient effectiveness. The present author believes this could be realized through the establishment of an "international" center, like the present arbitration bodies, offering administrative support for merchants and consumers. This center shall be private and not-for-profit in nature. The term "international" should be emphasized here. The mechanism should be truly effective in the borderless online marketplace, ensuring effective resolution of disputes between parties in distant locations. Currently, the ICC is examining its role as an international online ADR service provider and plans to submit a proposal to its national committees in the near future.[16] Given that the ICC hosts an international commercial arbitration court, the new task could fit in the ICC's existing functions and profiles. Thus, instead of formulating a complete new body, the ICC could take up this position.

Institutions: A Serious Threat to Consumer Protection, 10 *Ohio St. J. on Disp. Resol.* 267 (1995); B.G. Garth, Privatization and the New Market for Disputes: A Framework for Analysis and a Preliminary Assessment, in S.S. Silbey & A. Sarat (Eds.), *Studies in Law, Politics, and Society*, No. 12, at 367 (1992); J.R. Sternlight, Panacea or Corporate Tool?: Debunking the Supreme Court's Preference for Binding Arbitration, 74 *Wash. U.L.Q.* 637 (1996).

[15] S.B. Goldberg, E.D. Green & F.E.A. Sander, *Dispute Resolution*, 445 (Little, Brown & Company (Canada) Limited, 1985).

[16] See further Comments of the USCIB: Online ADR: the Business Community is Acting Now!, April 17, 2000, at <http://www.uscib.org/policy/adrusgfl.htm>.

Different from the existing mechanisms, this center shall intensively employ a computerized, online system.[17] The information technology represented by desktop computers, the Internet and other wide area networking techniques, email,[18] electronic discussion groups, and electronic publishing through the WWW shall be fully applied in this mechanism. Unlike the ongoing projects discussed in Chapter Five, this mechanism shall be comprehensive in nature, offering an array of public online dispute resolution processes. Everything that was previously done on paper and through slow and complex mechanisms could be done in a digital format, through standardized processes which are easy for users to use and which will be automated in most stages.[19] This idea has been reiterated on various occasions by different bodies. For example, the United States Council for International Business (USCIB) applauds the efforts of the US Government to promote effective online ADR as the appropriate means to resolve consumer complaints online.[20] Furthermore, since in most cases full-blown proceedings are not in the interests of both parties in electronic commerce, a "simplified" arbitration process shall be employed.

This center shall undertake the same administrative tasks as other arbitration bodies do: the receipt and registration of claims; the administration of the claims throughout the proceedings;[21] the maintenance of a list of qualified "arbitrators" and the selection, by applying agreed criteria, of a sole arbitrator or arbitrators from the list; the provision of legal, technical, and administrative support to the arbitrators during the proceedings, etc.[22] For the time being, various

[17] For general discussion on online mechanism, see E. Katsh, Online Dispute Resolution: Some Lessons from the E-Commerce Revolution, 28 *N. Ky. L. Rev.* 816–818 (2001).

[18] Email has great potential as a mechanism for intra-organizational dispute resolution or group problem solving.

[19] Electronic Arbitration Tribunal an Alternative Dispute Resolution for SMEs (E-Arbitration-T), Technical Annex: Part B, at <http://www.diritto.it/articoli/informatica/arbitration.html>.

[20] With a membership of over 300 global corporations, professional firms, and business associations, USCIB advances the global interests of American business both at home and abroad. It officially represents US business positions in the main intergovernmental bodies, and *vis-à-vis* foreign business communities and their governments.

[21] This could include services such as arranging for spaces for conducting the hearings, obtaining stenographers, and receiving and distributing the arbitrators' fees.

[22] See further V. Heiskanen, Dispute Resolution in International Economic Commerce, 16 *Journal of International Arbitration*, 38–39 (1999).

rules can be chosen to govern procedural issues, for example, the rule of ICC or AAA international arbitration rules; the center could also formulate its own rules.

Thus, once a dispute arises, a complainant could, making use of the filing form in the web site, bring the case to the center. The center shall review the case first to decide whether this case belongs to its scope. If it does, then the center shall on the one hand send a list of arbitrators to the complainant and, on the other hand, inform the defendant of the suit and the selection of an arbitrator. The arbitral tribunal shall consist of one or three arbitrators selected by both parties. In the case where there are three arbitrators, each party shall choose one and the center shall appoint a chairing arbitrator with the consent of both parties. In case of one arbitrator, the center shall appoint the arbitrator with the consent of the parties. If no agreement can be reached between the disputing parties concerning the sole arbitrator or the chairing arbitrator, then the center can make final decisions taking into account the preference of the parties and relevant circumstances. Depending on the circumstances, the parties may challenge the appointment of an arbitrator.[23] Once the arbitrators have been chosen, the documents shall be transferred and a formal procedure shall start. This procedure shall largely exist in the form of online written documents, but if the situation requires it, then teleconferencing or electronic forms of communication shall be used.

The decision shall be made within a few days, whatever the imposed time-frame demands. However, the proceedings may draw to a close for different reasons: for example, the two parties reach an agreement and the complaint is withdrawn. Once a decision is made, the losing party is obliged to comply with this decision. The coercive nature of the decision shall be ensured through the relevant national courts.

The decision shall be considered final in effect, but this procedure shall not take the place of litigation. Theoretically, either party can choose any method to resolve disputes, but this right is actually reserved for consumers. Once accepting the service of the mechanism, merchants shall make this clear on their web sites; only consumers

[23] For example, the relationship of the arbitrator with one of the parties, the neutrality of the arbitrator, etc.

can then decide which means to apply in their disputes. The validity of the decision made could be reversed by a court decision at a later stage based on legal grounds. This is reasonable considering the fundamental position maintained by the system of litigation.

2.4. *How to Realize the "Online Mechanism"*

An online mechanism offers a lot of advantages to traditional mechanisms. First of all, so long as they have the necessary facilities, access to this mechanism shall be provided to every individual in dispute. Provided transmission is efficient, the process is fast, which ultimately cuts down on costs: the traditional courtroom is not necessary; traveling shall be significantly minimized;[24] the amount of hiring and retaining of lawyers is reduced. The procedures can be carried out without the presence of both parties. Passing documents back and forth through the Internet, parties can reserve time for thinking over specific issues and formulating rational opinions. The persistence of a record of every communication shall also make parties think seriously about what they send.[25]

To design an online mechanism is not a novel or revolutionary idea, and plenty have developed such mechanisms for limited purposes. Adjudication is no more difficult to implement electronically than rulemaking. The novelty resides in the extended application of online facilities to potentially all disputes arising out of electronic commerce.

Publicity is necessary to ensure a smooth transition to the new online mechanism. No matter how brilliant the mechanism may be in theory, if it cannot garner legitimacy from those who will be recommending it, it will fail in the end. Users should have basic knowledge of the center or this center shall be opted out of the game. Furthermore, this mechanism should be respected by national sovereigns, which could afford immeasurable support. Accordingly, dis-

---

[24] See I.T. Hardy, Symposium: Electronic Communications and Legal Change: Electronic Conferences: The Report of an Experiment, 6 *Harv. J. Law and Tech.* 233 (Spring 1993).

[25] An online dispute resolution process shall produce an automatic record and transcript of the conversations and serve to keep both parties honest. See further M. Lauritsen, Settling Differences Through Interactive Multimedia Networks, at <http://www.law.vill.edu/ncair/disres/LAURIT.HTM>.

semination of information concerning the mechanism should go well before the whole mechanism takes foot. The center should at once formulate arbitration protocols, covering the nature of the mechanism, participants, procedures, etc., and prepare guidelines and codes of conduct to make the mechanism understandable for consumers and merchants. Publicity should involve bulk brochure mailings, propaganda through TV, radio or the Internet, etc.

Along with propaganda, it is important to cultivate a pool of personnel who have enough legal training and, more importantly, are equipped with necessary technical knowledge. The fate of this mechanism is in the hands of its personnel, from those who provide administrative services on a daily basis to the arbitrators making decisions.

With preparatory work out of the way, a web site should be developed to announce the center. Information provided on the site should include the idea, activities, procedures, costs, manner of decision making, and other relevant legal information regarding the mechanism.[26] Most importantly, it should provide users with knowledge of how to file a suit as well as subsequent procedures. It should offer guidance in a transparent way, preventing confusion related to the eventual proliferation of competing schemes.

Furthermore, relevant arrangements shall be made to ensure this mechanism has a widespread presence on the web. Some symbol should be developed to make this mechanism distinct and easily identifiable. Merchants should be required to post a warning message on their own web sites concerning whether they accept this mechanism or not. The web site of the center shall be connected to the site of merchants if the merchant's agree upon it. When consumers click on the button accepting this mechanism, the agreement to arbitrate is reached. Such an implied agreement shall cause no problem in legal sense. Furthermore, governments, consumer organizations, trade associations, and others should also provide links to make it easy for complainants to locate this web site. Even individuals could be encouraged to place this web site as a link on their web pages to ensure easy access when dispute arises.[27]

---

[26] For this purpose, an online library can be created to house documents relevant to the mechanism.

[27] This resembles the idea promoted by the Electronic Frontier Foundation (EEF) which was for producers of web pages to place a little blue ribbon in the corner of their page serving as a link to the EEF. As a result of this publicity, the EEF

The methods for the filing, pleading, discovery, etc. shall be formulated. To realize online filing is not difficult. A complete set of complaining forms, replying forms, forms for selecting arbitrators, etc., shall be provided on the web site and all of these can be downloaded for practical purposes. Pleading is also easy since it simply involves the exchange of electronic materials providing facts and legal theories supporting or refuting a claim and the response. Nor should a problem exist in realizing discovery online, at least in the form of interrogatories.

The trial function should be easily formulated as well. While modern litigation is becoming more and more focused on discrete issues decided largely on paper submissions,[28] online trials should step in to make modern technology when paper cannot do the job. Besides online graphics, images, charts, heat maps, timelines, decision trees and graphs, multimedia facilities like multithreaded forum or group software, document software, Internet relay chat, list servers, web server hosting, teleconference,[29] recorded audio and video testimony should be made use of in online trials.[30] When technical or legal expert opinions are needed, they can be submitted by E-mails. The exchange of documents between parties online is the first step towards the final adoption of this online mechanism. Of course, all of these tasks will still need to be performed by people in a physical location.

Once a case is submitted, a separate cyber-room is created for all the cyber-procedures to follow this submission. To ensure security, several techniques can be used. The web site can be established by using currently available software. For example, a software environment called MUDs or Multi-User Dimensions can be created. Each MUD has a unique Internet address. Procedures can be implemented

became the fourth most linked-to site on the entire World Wide Web by February 1997. See *further The Electronic Frontier Foundation, Action Alerts-Local, State, Non-US & Global*, at <http://www.eff.org>.

[28] See further R.L. Marcus, Completing Equity's Conquest? Reflections on the Future of Trial Under the Federal Rules of Civil Procedure, 50 *U. Pitt. L. Rev.* 725, 731–735 (1989).

[29] Each party shall sit before a computer equipped with sound facilities and a video camera. On their screen appear frames containing the faces of the other parties, while the audio software receives one party's spoken words and relays everyone else's.

[30] Internet applications include e-mail, bulletin boards, file transfer protocol, telnet, WWW, etc. For a concise description of each, see further N. Nathanson, *The Laws of the Internet* 4–8 (1997).

to prohibit entry to those who are undesirable and allow entry to those who have met the minimum qualifications. Meanwhile, a separate place can be created wherein people can give comments.[31] More than one space can be organized to deal with particular issues or to allow particular persons to interact.[32] Topics may be organized by a designated facilitator or be self-selected by participants. Participants can choose to respond in one or more spaces.[33] Access and participation can be controlled with several parameters.[34] Secure discussion shall possibly help both parties and the arbitrators gain deeper insight into the case. Furthermore, this space can provide the opportunity to air and discuss some issues not considered relevant in the case but important to the parties.[35]

Since the parties would like to ensure their confidentiality in the procedures, a neutral description of involved parties, with their names excluded, could be posted. Anyone interested in the discussion could have no problem accessing this place. To further secure the discussion, the postings can be edited first or an offline dialogue can be conducted for clarification. In this space, two specific groups of people could be identified. One group is the experts, who can give advice or decisive opinions for a particular case. Another group could be the users of similar or the same goods or services, who can share their experience. The exchange of information among them improves the understanding of certain goods or services. Once concern over these services appears serious enough, pressure could be exerted on behalf of the interests of this group. Individual disputes could thus be raised to a collective process, which could well protect consumers

---

[31] This could be like a Usenet newsgroup, a discussion area designed to allow the exchange of ideas. See E.B. Davis, A Look at One of the Most Popular Services in Cyberspace: Usenet, 42 *Fed. Law.* 15 (July 1995).

[32] One possible function is to realize collective action. If one consumer has a problem with the merchant, it might be not wise for him to seek damages of $ 50 through a process that would cost him $1000 or more. But it shall be reasonable if more consumers are attracted to take collective action against the merchant.

[33] W.J. Olmstead, Electronic Dispute Resolution, an NCAIR Conference, Washington, DC, May 22, 1996, at <http://mantle.sbs.umass.edu/vmag/OLMST.HTM>.

[34] For example, participation in the electronic forum can be limited to a particular group. The ability to read or write can be controlled. The entire public can be allowed to see a dialogue, but participation can be limited.

[35] See further Alternative Dispute Resolution in the Context of Electronic Commerce, Trans-Atlantic Consumer Dialogue (TACD), Doc No. ECOM-12-00, issued in February, 2000.

at large.[36] This could in turn reduce the possibility of similar cases arising in the future.

2.5. *The Ensuing Arrangement for the Online Mechanism*

It is very important to make this mechanism acceptable to the Internet society as a whole. Gaining user confidence is vital. One way of gaining confidence could involve attaining government certification of the program. A governmental seal could be displayed on the program's web site to prove it meets government-set accreditation criteria. Of course, as an ADR mechanism, government intervention shall be limited. In the present case, government works simply to provide reassurance to users and thereby to promote the mechanism. Ultimately, however, it is the mechanism itself that will determine its fate. Making reasonable arrangements for the mechanism is essential and it is the purpose of this chapter to look further into such arrangements.

2.5.1. *Committee of the Center*

This mechanism should be independent. Bearing this in mind, a problem involves determining who should be represented in the center and who should be responsible for setting up this mechanism. A mechanism set up unilaterally by a specific group of participants in the network may appear to benefit this group. As discussed in the principles for establishing the new mechanism, interest-balancing shall be necessary in detailing the procedures.

If the interests of all parties involved in the networks are taken into account, collective dispute resolution processes will have better standing and shall in the end be well accepted by the Internet society in general. In order to gain concurrence in the new mechanism, coalitions should be built.[37] Two specific groups should be represented in the mechanism. A consumer protection group is of course

---

[36] See further M.E. Schneider & C. Kuner, Dispute Settlement in International Electronic Commerce, 14 *Journal of International Arbitration*, No. 3, at 25–27, (1997).

[37] Coalitions could involve cyberspace citizens, to system operators, to national governments, etc. See further W.L. Ury et al., *Getting Disputes Resolved: Designing Systems to Cut the Costs of Conflict*, 69 (1988); see also C.A. Costantino & C.S. Merchant, *Designing Conflict Management Systems: A Guide to Creating Productive and Healthy Organizations*, 76 (1996).

an important group; stakeholders of the Internet society shall be another important group. The latter involves several different types of sub-groups, which include Internet Service Providers, electronic commerce companies (credit card companies, telecommunications companies, airlines, tourism companies, etc). Besides the groups above, other parties not directly involved in the disputes, like nonprofit organizations, or for-profit entities could also be represented in the center.

Should representatives from governments be listed? Representatives from governments shall strengthen the basis of the center. The private sector's voluntary efforts for resolving disputes could lack sufficient persuasion in generating strong confidence from consumers. The representatives from governments are neutral in the center, but could be a sign showing the support from the governments, which shall add to the confidence of consumers. This mechanism shall not thrive in an atmosphere deprived of the threat of state-imposed sanctions.[38]

2.5.2. *Location*

Normally, the attitude of the location and the legal atmosphere shall influence the choice of the parties. In the present case, most procedures are carried out in cyberspace, so location is not so important. However, the parties shall sometimes still have certain anxieties regarding location. It is thus sensible to station this center in a neutral state, like Switzerland, while facilitating arbitration anywhere in the world. Just like the practice of the ICC, such arbitration shall have no "home base."

2.5.3. *Language*

Language shall not cause any problem during this procedure. The language used in the transaction could be applied in this mechanism as well. While this could be burdensome for the center, necessary networks could be formed to undertake some of the translating tasks. The representatives of a consumer protection group sitting in the committee of the center shall also provide necessary assistance during

[38] As some disputes can be resolved voluntarily only because of the possibility of judicial remedies, the effectiveness of ADR mechanisms may depend on the practical availability of more conventional courts as a last resort. See further H.H. Perritt, Jr., Jurisdiction in Cyberspace: The Role of Intermediaries, in B. Kahin & C. Nesson (Eds.), *Borders in Cyberspace: Information Policy and the Global Information Infrastructure* 164 (Cambridge, MA: MIT Press 1997).

the whole procedure, which could involve language services. Furthermore, the mechanism could be linked to automatic translation facilities, which with the present technology should not cause any problem. This is evidenced by the experience of the Federation of European Direct Marketing (FEDMA).[39]

2.5.4. *Administrative Fees and Other Relevant Expenses*

This mechanism shall not be tremendously costly. As almost all the activities shall be done online, the ensuing fee for processing a case shall be much lower than the cost of normal procedures. Furthermore, the traditional secretary stationed in a state could be replaced by online facilities, which could largely reduce administrative fees. Expenses shall include the fee paid to arbitrators and administrators of the center and the fee for training and maintaining the center's web page. Other miscellaneous fees could include advertising and propaganda fees, evaluation fees, etc.

Obtaining the necessary finances for carrying out its online activities has been important to this mechanism. Of course, service shall be free to the users at the initial stage to encourage the adoption of the mechanism. But like most other arbitration centers, this center should be able to support itself financially. The center must receive the relatively low fee to maintain normal operation and pay arbitrators.

Levying on service providers and state funding could help to develop the mechanism. The system operators could be charged some amount. The national sovereigns could be persuaded to pay a small price to lessen the burden their national judicial systems feel due to the service of the center. Additionally, the center should have a well-organized financial framework, accomplished with the following goals in mind.

Firstly, the center could charge companies carrying out electronic commerce certain fees. As the center could provide companies with a guarantee attractive to their consumers, thus pushing consumers to transact with these companies, it deserves these companies' financial support. For its periodic maintenance and publicity, both important to related businesses, the center should be supported by the world of electronic commerce merchants.

---

[39] For information on FEDMA, see <http://www.fedma.org>.

Secondly, consumers should take some responsibility for supporting the center. When purchasing a product online, consumers shall have the right to decide whether or not they will enjoy this service. The same good or service should be more expensive if this service is adopted than if it is not. If the service is not chosen and disputes arise, consumers shall either seek other means of resolution, which are likely to require high fees, or resort to using the center's services at a raised price. Since in the latter case consumers would need to undertake the legal risks and costs associated with crossborder litigation, they are likely to initially opt for relevant service by clicking on the appropriate button. Companies send the customers' fees onto the service at regular basis, forming a pool to cover its expenses.

Once proved successful for disputes in electronic commerce, the mechanism shall develop further. The private, not-for-profit nature of the center could change. While above means for obtaining fees can be maintained, the users could also be obliged to pay a certain fee when filing a complaint. The fee shall be kept low, commensurate with the value of the disputes. Once the complaint is accepted for arbitration, fees in addition to those already discussed shall be requested of all involved parties.

2.5.5. *Selection of Decision-makers*

As discussed above, decision-makers or so-called arbitrators can be important in this mechanism. One or three arbitrators shall be appointed to a case. In case of three, equal representation should be given to both parties. If one is appointed to the case, both parties should be consulted. Upon appointment, the arbitrators shall have full power regarding the case and have a final say in the whole procedure. Arbitrators should obviously be qualified, but what shall their qualifications be? As disputes in electronic commerce could involve various states, candidates should represent many countries. If the parties can choose arbitrators who understand their own language and culture, time and money shall be saved and efficiency can be realized.

The efficiency of the whole mechanism largely depends on the arbitrators. They should not be too rigid in their approach to the procedures. While observing the basic principles of due process, they should be able to make use of other possible solutions. Besides having basic professional knowledge, the present arbitrators should be familiar with cyberspace and be able to skillfully apply modern technology. Arbitrators could be lawyers, but it would be preferable for them to have a significant involvement in business and technical communities.[40] If arbitrators are not familiar with cyberspace, it will be difficult for them to make rulings reflective of the customs and practice that has developed there. This, in turn, will undermine the legitimacy of the mechanism in the same way that traditional territorial law has lost credibility in its attempt to resolve disputes arising in virtual communities.[41] Indeed, with further development of modern technology and its further impact on everyone's daily life, such requirements will become meaningful to all other dispute resolution mechanisms.

Another important quality for arbitrators is their neutrality[42] and independence, especially since in the new mechanism parties cannot personally evaluate the arbitrators. Arbitrators shall have considerable discretion with respect to procedural details in the new mechanism. To deal with complicated situations in a way that will garner the trust of the users of this mechanisms, their neutrality is key. Their independence could be procured by various means, for example, by security of tenure through a long-term contract.

One other factor to note is that all the legal traditions and cultures from around the world shall be represented in the list of arbitrators. With enough choices available, differences in existing systems could be reconciled. A specific group of experts experienced in all manners and forms of disputes shall further ensure fair and complete adjudication.

A training program could be created to develop a pool of qualified arbitrators. A handbook could be published to give an overview of training requirements, complaint and decision handling procedures, and issues of jurisdiction, enforceability, and the like.[43]

---

[40] U.S. Gen. Accounting Office, *Employment Discrimination: How Registered Representatives Fair in Discrimination Disputes* 2 (1994).

[41] See M.E. Katsh, *The Electronic Media and the Transformation of Law*, 53–54 (1989).

[42] *Goldberg v. Kelly*, 397 US 254, 271 (1970); see also R.C. Reuben, Constitutional Gravity: A Unitary Theory of Alternative Dispute Resolution and Public Civil Justice, 47 *UCLA L. Rev.* 949, 1058 (2000).

[43] See further The Virtual Magistrate Project, Virtual Magistrate Handbook for Magistrates, at <http://vmag.vcilp.org/magis/vmhdbook.html>.

2.5.6. *Possible Remedies*

There are no universal rules establishing the remedies for an international arbitration. The remedies to be included in the award have to be considered in the light of: (a) the parties' arbitration agreement, including the rules which they have agreed should apply to the arbitration; (b) the law applicable to the substance of the dispute; (c) the law applicable to the arbitration proceedings.[44] Applicable law to the dispute is the most important in determining possible remedies. There are several possibilities for an applicable law regime. One possibility is to let the arbitrators apply extant national choice-of-law rules to determine applicable law. This is not a good idea since it is unclear which country's choice-of-law rules would apply to any particular dispute. A different solution is a uniform choice-of-law regime. This can also cause problems since a choice-of-law process in cyberspace will invariably be difficult. Rather than establishing a choice-of-law regime, a third solution seems more feasible by establishing a uniform law—the so-called "*lex informatica*". This solution shall be further discussed in Part 3.2 of the same Chapter.

Generally speaking, the following remedies could be employed: removing a post; forbidding a party from sending or posting messages for a specific amount of time;[45] imposing permanent banishment; forcing a disputant to post an apology or a correction of some specified sort; injunctions; remedial or/and punitive damages; terminating access; publication of improper conduct; antitrust action,[46] etc. Arbitrators can choose one or more of these remedies.

---

[44] M. Huleatt-James & N. Gould, *International Commercial Arbitration: A Handbook* 97 (2nd Ed., LLP Asia, 1999).

[45] Expulsion is the ultimate mechanism of compliance where membership in a trade association is a prerequisite to the right to pursue a trade.

[46] This could be caused when a certain act leads others to avoid services. For example, Microsoft developed a browser, Internet Explorer, incorporated in its Windows operating system. This led to the now well-known antitrust case that the government successfully brought against the company. United *States v. Microsoft Corp.*, 97 F. Supp. 2d 59 (D.D.C. 2000) (order); *United States v. Microsoft Corp.*, 87 F. Supp. 2d 30 (D.D.C. 2000) (conclusions of law); *United States v. Microsoft Corp.*, 84 F. Supp. 2d 9 (D.D.C. 2000) (findings of fact); *Microsoft Corp. v. United States*, 121 S. Ct. 25, 25 (2000).

2.5.7. *Technical Support*

This mechanism is highly technology-oriented. Just as the quality of a teleconference, for example, depends upon the standard of the audio and video production equipment connected to the network, the application of relevant technology shall largely determine this mechanism's success. As shown by the existing projects, privacy[47] and authentication, confidentiality and security, identification of origin of problems, and the integrity of the process shall become issues of great importance while applying this mechanism. With the new mechanism combining all available technology, the entirety of the proceedings shall be fully recorded and replayed anywhere at any time by parties having the ability to decrypt them.[48] A secure multi-agent platform shall be designed for this purpose. Thus, while offering legal services, the center should be well equipped with technical experts.

2.5.8. *Arbitration Agreements*

Arbitration agreements constitute the basis of arbitral procedure.[49] In electronic commerce, arbitration agreements are also necessary. For the present mechanism, merchants in the first place accept the procedure and declare that they have done so. Consumers are in the passive position of agreeing with or refusing the merchant's choice. They have the right to use this mechanism or any others from the outset and are not restricted or blocked from resorting to other recourse available if they are not satisfied with the outcome. However, once consumers choose this mechanism, merchants shall be obliged to follow its procedure.

Internet technology makes arbitration agreements extremely easy to impose. To constitute lawful arbitration agreements merchants should list the declaration of the mechanism in the "Terms and Conditions" section of their web sites; include the agreements with

---

[47] For discussion of online privacy issues, see generally A. Bacard, *The Computer Privacy Handbook* (1995); J.R. Reidenberg & F.O. Gamet-Pol, The Fundamental Role of Privacy and Confidence in the Network, 30 *Wake Forest L. Rev.* 105 (1995); H. Green et al., A Little Privacy, Please, *Bus. Weekly*, March 16, 1998, at 98; National Info. Infrastructure Task Force, Options for Promoting Privacy on the National Information Infrastructure , April 1997, at <http://www.iitf.nist.gov/ipc/privacy.htm>.

[48] See further J. Arsíc, International Commercial Arbitration on the Internet: Has the Future Come Too Early?, 14 *Journal of International Arbitration*, 213 (1997).

[49] Perritt, *supra* note 38, at 186.

the product, for example, in the product's box; and enable "click-wrap"—a process that involves a consumer clicking an "I agree" button in a pop-up box on a computer screen before downloading or installing software.[50] The three means above can be used individually or collectively in transactions and each means shall be considered as constituting valid and enforceable arbitration agreements.[51]

2.5.9. *Discovery*

Clearly accounting for various aspects of the case shall help in reaching a fair and accurate trial outcome.[52] This account appears even more meaningful in the case when one party is equipped with a bulk of relevant information, while the other party is lacking such information.[53] Consumer transactions typically give rise to such cases. Consumers know that goods are in some way or another defective, but they do not have access to records concerning the design or manufacturing of the goods, etc. Merchants usually have such records on hand and can thus easily compile information for their case. Discovery is necessary for consumers who are in the weak position in this case. No other mechanisms have permitted the extent of discovery that litigation has, which has called into question the extent of discovery in ADR mechanisms.

In the present mechanism, necessary discovery should be provided, but within a limit. However, the approach to discovery differs enormously around the world. The situation becomes even more difficult when the parties' legal advisers try to insist on adhering to procedures relating to discovery which are applicable to proceedings in

---

[50] See further R.N. Dreben & J.L. Werbach, Top 10 Things to Consider in Developing an Electronic Commerce Web Site, 16 *Computer Lawyer* No. 5, at 19 (1999).

[51] Some scholars might argue that some of the means are unenforceable, but many software licensing lawyers take the opposite attitude. For further discussion, see M.A. Lemley, Beyond Preemption: The Law and Policy of Intellectual Property Licensing, 87 *Calif. L. Rev.* at 120 n. 20 (January, 1999); see also *Klocek v. Gateway, Inc.*, 104 F. Supp. 2d 1332 (D. Kan. 2000); B. Kuklin, On the Knowing Inclusion of Unenforceable Contract and Lease Terms, 56 *U. Cin. L. Rev.* 845 (1988). Concerning the issue of compliance with Article II of New York Convention, see *infra* notes 69–77 and accompanying text.

[52] *Hickman v. Taylor*, 329 US 495 (1947).

[53] C.A. Wright & K.W. Graham, Jr., *Federal Practice and Procedure: Federal Rules of Evidence*, 5422, at 674 (1980); E.G. Thornburg, Sanctifying Secrecy: The Mythology of the Corporate Attorney-Client Privilege, 69 *Notre Dame L. Rev.* 157, 203 (1993).

courts in their home countries. The practice of NAF could provide a good example: formulation of rules governing discovery.[54] According to the NAF Code of Procedure, discovery is allowed, but should be filed within a certain period of time.[55] A party may request the disclosure of documents, sworn answers to not more than twenty-five written questions, or one or more depositions or any other discovery before a hearing where (1) the information sought is relevant to a Claim or Response, reliable, and informative to the arbitrator; (2) the cost is commensurate with the amount of the Claim; and (3) the Request is reasonable and not unduly burdensome and expensive.[56]

2.5.10. *Formulation of Final Decision*

A final and well-reasoned decision shall be made within a certain time limit. Arbitrators should present at least some of their reasoning in the final decision.[57] The AAA Statement of Principles, for example, suggests that the arbitrator should offer a brief written explanation of the basis for the decision at the timely request of either party.[58] It is true that written reasoning shall help people understand the final decision and guide their conduct in the future. As there are still no generally recognized rules in electronic commerce, this reasoning shall be especially helpful in clarifying the rules. The extent of reasoning shall be at the discretion of the arbitrators.

2.5.11. *Enforcement of Decisions*

An indispensable element of arbitral culture is the expectation that arbitral awards are final and will be honored by the parties.[59] Though

---

[54] Another example is the IBA Rules on the Taking of Evidence in International Commercial Arbitration adopted in June 1999. The document is available at <http://www.ibanet.org>.

[55] As identified in the NAF Code of Procedure, the requesting Party shall serve on all other parties with a copy of the Request no later than thirty days before the date of a participatory Hearing or for a Document Hearing, ten days from the date of the notice of the selection of an Arbitrator.

[56] See further NAF Code of Procedure, Rule 29 (B), (C).

[57] See, for example, Better Business Bureau, Rules of Arbitration, 20 (1998), at <http://www.bbb.org/complaints/bindarb.asp>; see also the CPR Institute for Dispute Resolution Rules, which require that the arbitrator shall state the reasoning on which the award rests unless the parties agree otherwise.

[58] American Arbitration Association, Consumer Due Process Protocol: Statement of Principles of the National Consumer Disputes Advisory Committee, Principle 15 (1998), at <http://www.adr.org/education/consumer_protocol.html>.

[59] H.M. Holtzmann, The Permanent Court of Arbitration and the Evolution of

appeals can be made to the court on grounds of mathematical mistakes or other technical problems, decisions made by this mechanism should be binding for both parties. Thus, once a decision is made, we expect the losing party shall take corresponding actions to implement the decision voluntarily. Failing to do so could be damaging to his business insofar as negative publicity could call into question his trustworthiness and his future connections to the site of the center shall be more expensive. However, we should not always take volunteerism for granted. Experience has shown that the availability of mandatory enforcement prompts compliance. Two issues can arise in enforcement. Firstly, can the arbitration agreement be enforced if one party seeks litigation? Secondly, once arbitration leads to an award, will this award be enforced by the courts?

As far as the first issue is concerned, the agreement to arbitrate depends on certain activities of the parties. As discussed above, the center's being linked to the site of the merchant or containing obvious statements concerning his association with the service shall constitute offers of service in the sense of contract law; consumers' clicking on a certain button constitutes the acceptance of the offers in the legal sense.[60] Merchant shall be obliged to enter the procedure of arbitration by their prior actions. Thus, such agreements shall be generally recognized.

The present discussion shall concentrate on the second issue. According to legal theories, the losing party should pay the expenses and amount in due. Once a monetary remedy is decided as such, the center itself could swiftly compensate the winning party in order to ensure this party's satisfaction. The center is then entitled reimbursement from the losing party. To function smoothly, a foundation

---

a Worldwide Arbitration Culture, in The International Bureau of the Permanent Court of Arbitration (Ed.), *International Alternative Dispute Resolution: Past, Present and Future*, 105 (Kluwer Law International, 2000).

[60] C. Li, Tentative Discussion on the Challenge of the Internet against Traditional Conflict of Laws, 11 *Legal Science*, 53 (1999). For discussion of offer and acceptance in contract, see R. Craswell, Offer, Acceptance, and Efficient Reliance, 48 *Stan. L. Rev.* 481 (1996); M.A. Eisenberg, Expression Rules in Contract Law and Problems of Offer and Acceptance, 82 *Cal. L. Rev.* 1127 (1994); A. Katz, The Strategic Structure of Offer and Acceptance: Game Theory and the Law of Contract Formation, 89 *Mich. L. Rev.* 215 (1990); P.M. Tiersma, Comment, The Language of Offer and Acceptance: Speech Acts and the Question of Intent, 74 *Cal. L. Rev.* 189 (1986); N.G. Williams, Offer, Acceptance, and Improper Considerations: A Common-Law Model for the Prohibition of Racial Discrimination in the Contracting Process, 62 *Geo. Wash. L. Rev.* 183 (1994).

could be formed to deal with compensation under the control of the center. The amount to be paid by the company shall be decided by their annual profits. If the company fails to pay its due, the center should seek legal recourse; furthermore, it could publish such facts on the web sites and levy heavy fees for offering services in the future.

The system operators could also serve as the functional equivalent of local government enforcement agencies.[61] Further, an association of networks, or networks and system administrators, or system administrators and users, or simply system administrators, could contractually establish the validity of the center and its decisions.[62] This contractual approach shall be most beneficial.[63] If one party fails to comply with the award, it shall potentially be cut off from the whole system—deprived of membership in trade associations or other industry groups and denied services from online auction sites or operators of billing systems, etc. The self-regulatory effort of the Internet society could be realized through cooperation among different sections.

Enforcement of such decisions is occasionally more problematic, particularly when decisions involve more than monetary remedies or technical considerations. Though if the defendant has identifiable assets within the territory of the forum state then enforcement shall not be a problem, but of course, there are not always such assets. What should be done in cases where the assets are unavailable? Enforcement of Foreign Arbitral Awards (1958 New York Convention)[64] has proposed guidelines for recognizing and enforcing foreign arbitral decisions.[65] It directly focuses on two elements of arbitral procedure: the validity of the arbitration agreement and the enforcement of the arbitration award,[66] leaving a more comprehensive regulatory

---

[61] See further H.S. Reeves, Property in Cyberspace, 63 *U. Chi. L. Rev.* 778 (1996).

[62] Perritt, *supra* note 8, at 361 (1993).

[63] R.L. Dunne, Deterring Unauthorized Access to Computers: Controlling Behavior in Cyberspace through a Contract Law Paradigm, 35 *Jurimetrics Journal*, No. 1, at 2 (Fall 1994).

[64] Since 1958, 131 countries (as of March 30, 2003) have become parties to the New York Convention.

[65] For commentary on the New York Convention, see W.W. Park, A User's Guide to The New York Arbitration Convention, in B. Barin (Ed.), *Carswell's Handbook of International Dispute Resolution Rules*, 526–538 (Carswell, 1999).

[66] T.E. Carbonneau, Arbitral Adjudication: A Comparative Assessment of Its Remedial and Substantive Status in Transnational Commerce, 19 *Tex. Int'l L.J.* 33, 39–56 (1984).

scheme to be implied from its express principles. Essentially, this convention requires member states to recognize and enforce any arbitral award made in any other country which is a party to the convention or which is rendered in the country where enforcement is sought, but which is not considered as a "domestic" award.[67] Does it apply to dispute resolution cases in electronic commerce? This convention contains many traps for the unwary.[68]

The feasibility of this convention in the present case must be more extensively examined. As the present mechanism applies arbitration as the basic vehicle, the application of this convention shall cause no contradiction. The wide acceptance of this convention by international society can also further facilitate its application to mechanism. What should be noted are points related to this mechanisms' application of awards.

First of all, the New York Convention specifies that arbitration agreements should be in writing.[69] There is no uniform agreement as to what constitutes "writing."[70] However, the term is later specified to include agreements contained in an exchange of letters or telegrams.[71] In most countries, writing is understood "normally by the reference to the mode of imposition of the medium rather than by the reference to the medium itself."[72] In practice, some courts have interpreted the term "telegram" to include other modern means of telecommunications.[73] One important sign in extending the term "writing" to electronic form is the UNCITRAL Model Law on Electronic Commerce. According to the Model Law, "(1) Where the law requires information to be in writing, that requirement is met by a data message if the information contained therein is accessible so as to be

---

[67] Article I (1) of the New York Convention.

[68] For problems in applying the New York Convention, see further R.M. Lucash, Esq., *Arbitration in International Computer Contracts*, at <http://www.lgu.com/in43.htm>.

[69] See Article II of the New York Convention.

[70] R.R. Jueneman & R.J. Robertson, Jr., Biometrics and Digital Signatures in Electronic Commerce, 38 *Jurimetrics Journal* 434 (1998).

[71] Article II (2) of New York Convention.

[72] H.B. Thomsen & B.S. Wheble, *Trading with EDI—The Legal Issues*, IBC Financial Books, 136 (London, 1989). This could be testified to by some national rules. For example, the US Uniform Commercial Code provides in Section 1–201 (46) that "written or writing" includes printing, typewriting, or any other international reduction to tangible form.

[73] See further G. Born, *International Commercial Arbitration in the United States*, 292 (1994).

usable for subsequent reference; (2) Paragraph (1) applies whether the requirement therein is in the form of an obligation or whether the law simply provides consequences for the information not being in writing."[74] This broad interpretation, which would also encompass communications by the Internet, could be helpful in applying the New York Convention.[75] We can also expect future conventions to encompass new means of communications within the scope of "writing."[76] The underlying objective behind doing so is to facilitate international trade and improve the possibility of concluding arbitration agreements in international trade.[77]

Secondly, the New York Convention requires that a party applying for enforcement of an award must present the duly authenticated original award or a duly certified copy thereof.[78] Similarly, in online cases the decision could be issued on hard copy, or a "trusted third party" could serve to confirm that the digital signatures on an electronic decision are those of the arbitrators.[79]

Thirdly, the New York Convention's rules apply to foreign arbitral awards, but how does the term "foreign" fit cases involving Internet players? The convention makes enforcement of an award dependent on the award having been made in a country party to the convention, regardless of the home countries of either party to the arbitration.[80] It is difficult to determine a physical location when procedures are carried out online, so the "foreignness" factor is not so relevant. Still, one could say that decisions made by the center should fall within the scope of the convention insofar as they are in keeping with forms of delocalized and denationalized international

---

[74] See the Report of UNCITRAL on the work of its 29th Session, UN General Assembly Official Records Supplement No. 17 (A/51/17), Annex I, Article 6.

[75] See further R. Hill & I. Walden, The Draft UNCITRAL Model Law for Electronic Commerce: Issues and Solutions, 13 *Computer Lawyers*, No. 3, at 18 (1996).

[76] See further F.A. Cona, Application of Online Systems in Alternative Dispute Resolution, 45 *Buff. L. Rev.* 975, 993 (1997); J. Rosener, *Cyberlaw: The Law of the Internet* 237–241 (London 1997).

[77] See further A.J. van den Berg, *The New York Convention of 1958—Towards a Uniform Judicial Interpretation*, 191 (Asser / Kluwer—The Hague Deventer, 1981); N. Kaplan, Is the Need for Writing as Expressed in the New York Convention and the Model Law out of Step with Commercial Practice?, 12 *Arbitration International*, 27–43 (1996).

[78] Article IV of New York Convention.

[79] J. Arsíc, International Commercial Arbitration on the Internet: Has the Future Come Too Early?, 14 *Journal of International Arbitration*, 217 (1997).

[80] Article I(1) of New York Convention.

arbitration that have been in existence for a long time.[81] Theoretically, international arbitration shall float without attachment to the place of arbitration.[82] When applied to the present mechanism, the arbitration shall be delocalized and the awards shall be recognized everywhere and enforceable in accordance with the New York Convention.

There are other problems, for example, the exclusion of consumer contracts from the convention,[83] the validity of online notice,[84] and the issue of compliance with the law of the country where the arbitration took place.[85] All these issues are minor, but in order to ensure the online mechanism is viable, member states should examine and amend these existing rules to deal with all types of potential problem areas. The unique character of cyberspace should be kept in mind when making modifications.

One trend to note is an increase in judicial recognition and enforcement of ADR decisions.[86] As long as the procedure is fair, few problems shall arise. Furthermore, contract law shall play a large role in this process. General contract law principles fit well with the emergent culture of the Internet, which eschews involuntary obligations, whether imposed from the state or from tort law.[87] Thus, with various efforts, enforcement of arbitral awards should not be a problematic issue.

---

[81] See further P. Mayer, the Trend Towards Delocalization in the Last 100 Years, in M. Hunter, A. Marriot & Veeder (Eds.), *The Internationalization of International Arbitration: The LCIA Centenary Conference*, 37–45 (London: Graham & Trotman, 1995). This idea has been heatedly discussion and various opinions have been presented. See further J. Paulsson, Delocalization of International Commercial Arbitration: When and Why It Matters?, 32 *Int'l & Comp. L.Q.*, 53–61 (1983); J. Paulsson, Arbitration Unbound: Award Detached from the Law of the Country of Origin, 30 *Int'l & Comp. L.Q.*, 358–387 (1981); W.W. Park, The *Lex Loci Arbitri* and International Commercial Arbitration, 32 *Int'l & Comp. L.Q.*, 21–52 (1983); W.W. Park, Judicial Control in the Arbitral Process, 5 *Arbitration International* No. 3, 230–245 (1989); W.L. Craig, Some Trends and Developments in the Laws and Practice of International Commercial Arbitration, 30 *Tex. Int'l L.J.*, 1–58 (1995); H. Smit, A-national Arbitration, 63 *Tulane Law Review*, 629–645 (1989).

[82] See further F. de Ly, The Place of Arbitration in the Conflict of Laws of International Commercial Arbitration: An Exercise in Arbitration Planning, in M. Storme & F. de Ly (Eds.), *The Place of Arbitration*, 113 (Mys & Breesch, Gent, 1993).

[83] Article V(1)(a) of New York Convention.

[84] Article V(1)(b) of New York Convention.

[85] Article V(1)(d) of New York Convention.

[86] S.G. Dick, ADR at the Crossroads, *Disp. Resol. J.*, March 1994, at 52–53.

[87] M. Rustad & L.E. Eisenscmidt, The Commercial Law of Internet Security, 10 *High Tech. L.J.* 263 (1995).

3. *The Law for Electronic Commerce in the New Mechanism*

The application of the Internet creates the mysterious so-called cyberspace. Though the space is invisible to all, various activities that take place in it directly influence modern society in real space. There is an obvious connection between mysterious online activities and the real world. While actions are performed in cyberspace, the actors involved are in the physical world. The necessary facilities initiating those activities are also in specific real-world locations. But difficulties incurred in tracing the actors are problematic for the application of law. As more and more commercial transactions take place through the Internet, commercial society more urgently needs to answer these questions: What shall be the result of certain activity? What rule should be followed when conducting the transaction? Do the normal transaction rules apply well to electronic commerce? Such questions show that it is necessary to look further into the legal side of electronic commerce, especially the legal rules to be applied during the transactions and the possible ensuing disputes.

3.1. *Cyberspace as an "International Space"?*

3.1.1. *Cyberspace as a Space*

The search for the right metaphor for the Internet occupies some of the best minds.[88] Indeed, several metaphors have been used to describe the Internet, but these metaphors concern how the Internet functions as a medium of communications[89] and not as a space with implications for law. As stated in the purpose of this study, all the analysis shall be carried out with respect to the legal framework.[90]

For a long time, we have taken for granted that geographical borders are of primary importance in determining legal rights and respon-

---

[88] See further A. Ginsburg, Howl, in A. Ginsburg, *Howl and Other Poems* (1956); at <http://www.ginzy.com>.

[89] See, for example, C. Kozar & A. Lockhart, *Service Provider Liability*, April 24, 1997, at <http://www.ashelockhart.com/isp>; see also J. Litman, The Exclusive Right to Read, 13 *Cardozo Arts & Ent. L.J.*, 29 (1994); as said, Internet communication is quite simple, a print medium.

[90] Many observers have treated cyberspace as a "place" for analytical purposes. See, for example, L.M. Harasim, Networlds: Networks as Social Space, in L.M. Harasim (Ed.), *Global Networks* 15–34 (1993).

sibilities: all law is *prima facie* territorial.[91] That means a space should be located for the formulation and application of law. However, the Internet cannot be located. No one can feel or touch cyberspace,[92] cyberspace can never be controlled by anyone, and anyone with the necessary facilities can visit cyberspace without restriction. Lacking in obvious territorial connections, cyberspace creates difficulties in employing legal analysis. Obviously, it is outside the sovereignty of states. Geographic boundaries are not meaningful in defining a legal regime for cyberspace. However, a more legally significant border for the "law space" of the Internet could be imposed.

Some scholars have suggested conceiving cyberspace as a distinct space[93] for purposes of legal analysis by recognizing a legally significant border between cyberspace and the real world.[94] Defining cyberspace as a "place"[95] has had the curious consequence of creating a need for a term that describes every place else.[96] Notably, the International Ad Hoc Committee (IAHC)[97] used "public resource"[98] to describe the Internet top-level domain space. Some scholars have suggested that cyberspace shall take a similar legal role to outer space, Antarctica, or the international sea.[99] This suggestion is beneficial to further elaboration

[91] *American Banana Co. v. United Fruit Co.* 213 US 347, 357 (1909).

[92] And the reality is that no one lives in cyberspace. See D.L. Burk, Trademark Doctrines for Global Electronic Commerce, 49 *S.C. L. Rev.* 733 (1998); A.R. Stein, The Unexceptional Problem of Jurisdiction in Cyberspace, 32 *Int'l Law.* 1175 (1998).

[93] The Internet, as cyberspace, was introduced as a place where people could go join a cyber-community and adopt a cyber-identity. However, some scholars consider the metaphor of the Internet as place did not exactly stand the test of time. See further T. Wu, When Law & the Internet First Met, 3 *Green Bag* 2d, 171–173 (Winter, 2000).

[94] D.R. Johnson & D.G. Post, Law and Borders—The Rise of Law in Cyberspace, 48 *Stanford L. Rev.* (1996), at <http://www.cli.org/X0025_LBFIN.html>.

[95] Some scholars argue that the net is not a separate space. See further J.L. Goldsmith, Symposium on the Internet and Legal Theory: Regulation of the Internet: Three Persistent Fallacies, 73 *Chi.-Kent. L. Rev.* 1121 (1998).

[96] See W. Rodger, *Read Their Lips: No Net Taxes*, Wired, May 1998, at 101.

[97] The IAHC was formed in November 1996 by the Internet Society (ISOC), the Internet Assigned Numbers Authority (IANA), the Internet Architecture Board (IAB), the Federal Networking Council (FNC), the World Intellectual Property Organization (WIPO), the International Telecommunications Union (ITU), and the International Trademark Association (INTA) to deal with the domain name system on an international level.

[98] The IAHC declared that top level Internet domain space is a public resource and is subject to public trust. See *Final Report of the International Ad Hoc Committee: Recommendations for Administration and Management of gTLD's*, Executive Summary, 19 February 1997. <http://www.iahc.org/draft-iahc-recommend-00.html>.

[99] See further D. Menthe, Jurisdiction in Cyberspace: A Theory of International

of the role of cyberspace for electronic commerce. Along this line, in July 1997 American President Clinton suggested that the Internet should be a global-free trade zone.[100] The law of this space shall take into account the special characteristics of the environment it regulates and the types of persons, places, and things found therein.

First of all, cyberspace is a place[101] that divides the tangible and virtual worlds. As the law for electronic commerce is the area of law that deals most directly with contacts between the two "worlds,"[102] recognizing a legally significant border between cyberspace and the real world is relevant. You should treat cyberspace as a separate space because there are places within it where you can access information and you know that you are there.[103] One vital feature of this space is that groups and activities found at various online locations possess their own unique qualities, which shall likely demand their having unique sets of rules. It is probably easier to determine which rules should apply to your online activities than to determine which territorial authority might apply its laws to your conduct.[104]

3.1.2. *Cyberspace as an International Space*

Before entering into further discussion about cyberspace and electronic commerce, it is very important to find out the status of cyberspace in the legal framework, as this shall provide a basic understanding of the present position of cyberspace. First of all, it is necessary to determine whether cyberspace involves national or international legal systems. We have all known that cyberspace transcends national bor-

---

Spaces, *4 Michigan Telecommunications and Technology Law Review*, 69 (1998), at <http://www.mttlr.org/volfour/menthe,html>. This paper deals with the issue of prescriptive jurisdiction. However, this idea could be a hint to the future elaboration of the status of cyberspace on the issue of adjudicative jurisdiction.

[100] Remarks by the President of the USA in Announcement of Electronic Commerce Initiative, White House Press Secretary, 1 July 1997, <http://www.whitehouse.gov>.

[101] Some argue that cyberspace is not a place and is instead many places. See further L. Lessig, *Code and Other Laws of Cyberspace*, 82 (1999), which the present author finds to offer wisdom into the nature of cyberspace. While cyberspace is considered as a space as a whole, it can be further divided into different spaces. See also D. Hunter, Cyberspace as Place and the Tragedy of the Digital Anticommons, 91 *California Law Review* 446–452 (March 2003).

[102] C.L. Conner, *Compuserve v. Patterson*: Creating Jurisdiction Through Internet Contacts, 4 *Richmond Journal of Law & Technology*, 9 (Spring 1998), <http://www.richmond.edu/~jolt/v4i3/conner.html>.

[103] See further Hardy, *supra* note 24, at 213, 232–234.

[104] Johnson, *supra* note 94, at 1372–1373.

ders and that an action taken in a state could be felt in most states in the world. A state can make legislation concerning activities in cyberspace out of its own economic, cultural, and political interests. However, the effectiveness of such legislation shall be largely limited, as states will be required to refrain from actions that encroach on another state's sovereignty.[105] Because the spillover effect of the Internet[106] significantly limits the feasibility of national regulation, we shall tend to discuss the status of cyberspace in the international legal framework.[107]

Before going further, we should note that although international systems are preferred in cyberspace, national regulation maintains an important rule. While there are issues beyond government's reach, government shall still be able to take steps to affect the regulability of the Internet.[108] Though with legally restricted powers, national government can perform relevant tasks concerning those within its reach.

The international system is multi-leveled. A state shall have full sovereignty over its own territory, including territorial sea; certain sovereignty over exclusive economic zones in the sea; and no sovereignty over so-called "international space". The history of international space begins at sea,[109] and law of the high seas remains the dominating voice in the discussion of this theory.[110] Later, the discovery of Antarctica and man's entrance into outer space has added

---

[105] See I. Brownlie, *Principles of Public International Law* 301 (5th Ed. 1998).

[106] Since copying is essential for the net to function, copyright is one example. See, for example, M.A. Lemley, Dealing With Overlapping Copyrights on the Internet, 22 *U. Dayton L. Rev.* 547 (1997); Litman, *supra* note 89, at 29; E. Dyson, Intellectual Value, Wired, July 1995, at 136, 137; J.P. Barlow, The Economy of Ideas, Wired, March 1994, at 85.

[107] Thus, it is said that the Internet shall strengthen international law. See further H.H. Perritt, Jr., The Internet is Changing International Law, 73 *Chi.-Kent L. Rev.* 997 (1998); B. Cohen, Note, A Proposed Regime for Copyright Protection on the Internet, 22 *Brook. J. Int'l L.* 401, 428 (1996); J.B. Ritter & J.Y. Gliniecki, Electronic Communications and Legal Change: International Electronic Commerce and Administrative Law: The Need for Harmonized National Reforms, 6 *Harv. J.L. & Tech.* 263, 265 (1993); O. Schachter, Philip Jessup's Life and Ideas, 80 *AJIL* 878, 894 (1986).

[108] See further L. Lessig, The Law of the Horse: What Cyberlaw Might teach, 113 *Harvard Law Review*, 514–515 (1999).

[109] In 1609, Hugo Grotius postulated that no state could legitimately exercise jurisdiction over the open sea. See further H. Grotius, *Mare Liberum; Sive, de Iure Quod Batavis Competit ad Indicana Commercia Dissertio* (1609).

[110] See further B. Anderson, *Imagined Communities: Reflections on the Origin and Spread of Nationalism*, 14 (1983).

to the discussion. Along with the discovery of international space, the theory of "the Common Heritage of Mankind (CHM)" came into being.[111] It asserts that all nations should benefit from the resources that are recovered from areas in which all nations have an interest[112] and that no one nation can claim sovereignty over such areas.[113]

Today may be the "twilight of sovereignty."[114] When it comes to cyberspace, states cannot claim sovereignty. Furthermore, even with the intention of claiming sovereignty they would not be able to control cyberspace.[115] Accordingly, from the angle of international law, cyberspace should be categorized as international space. What are the implications of this categorization for the present study?

Traditionally, sovereignty and territory have been the bases of international law. However, international law is also determined by the nature of its subjects. The way people communicate and the nature of the environment or nation in which they communicate may be more important than territory.[116]

The theory of international space and CHM begins with one proposition: nationality, not territory, is the basis for the jurisdiction to prescribe.[117] Three international spaces have been identified: Antarc-

---

[111] G.M. Danilenko, The Concept of the "Common Heritage of Mankind" in International Law, 13 *Annals of Air & Space Law* 247–249 (1988).

[112] J. Eltman, A Peace Zone on the High Seas: Managing the Commons for Equitable Use, 5 *Int'l Legal Persp.* 47, 64 (1993); P.E. Wilson, Jr., Barking Up the Right Tree: Proposals for Enhancing the Effectiveness of the International Tropical Timber Agreement, 10 *Temp. Int'l & Comp. L.J.* 229, 232 (1996).

[113] C.C. Joyner, Legal Implications of the Concept of the Common Heritage of Mankind, 35 *Int'l & Comp. L.Q.* 190–191 (1986).

[114] It is quite possibly the final days of a governance system relying on individual sovereign states as primary law-making authority. See generally W. Wriston, *The Twilight of Sovereignty* (1992).

[115] Some scholars argue that sovereignty could still exist in cyberspace. According to the analysis, cyberspace could be controlled by cyberspace residents and application designers. However, the understanding of sovereignty is not the same as the one used in international law and should, according to the present author, be refuted. For the argument concerning sovereignty, see further T. Wu, Note, Cyberspace Sovereignty? The Internet and the International System, 10 *Harv. J.L. & Tech.* 647 (1997); see also J.H. Saltzer et al., End-to-End Arguments in System Design, 2 *ACM Transactions in Computer Systems* 277 (1984).

[116] J.M. Rogers, Forward: The Internet and Public International Law: The Internet and International Law, 88 *Ky. L.J.* 808 (Summer, 1999/Summer, 2000). Thus, some scholars argue that traditional notions of sovereignty have been undermined. See further Symposium, The Decline of the National State and Its Effects on Constitutional and International Economic Law, 18 *Cardozo L. Rev.* 903 (1996).

[117] Menthe, *supra* note 99, at 69; B.E. Heim, Note, Exploring the Last Frontiers for Mineral Resources: A Comparison of International Law Regarding the Deep Seabed, Outer Space, and Antarctica, 23 *Vand. J. Transnat'l L.* 819, 827 (1990).

tica,[118] outer space[119] and the high seas.[120] Cyberspace obviously transcends territorial borders, and territoriality loses its meaning in this space. The theory of international space and CHM rightly fill up this loophole for cyberspace.[121]

Of course, there are many differences between cyberspace and the other three international spaces. For one, the three international spaces are all in physical existence (albeit an existence that takes many varied forms), while cyberspace is nonphysical. The vital point in categorizing spaces as international spaces lies not in their physical similarities, but in their international, sovereignless quality.[122] Appropriate conceptual analogies to the notion of cyberspace are found in regions where states may not typically assert sovereignty.[123]

While no state can claim sovereignty over international space, the specter of international conflicts has been a prime factor behind the formation of treaty regimes, which are only one, albeit the primary source, of international law.[124] Treaties concerning each of the former three international spaces have been formulated. This is not the case for cyberspace. It emerged during the 1970s and 1980s as the apparatus of the Internet took root, but it was not until the early 1990s that an explosion in users and uses, including commercial uses, introduced a virtual community and achieved worldwide attention.

---

[118] See, for example, J. Blum, The Deep Freeze: Torts, Choice of Law, and the Antarctic Treaty Regime, 8 *Emory Int'l L. Rev.* 667–668 (1994).

[119] See, for example, I.H.Ph. Diederiks-Verschoor, *An Introduction to Space Law*, 4–5 (2nd Ed. Kluwer Law International, 1999); H. Shin, Oh, I Have Slipped the Surly Bonds of Earth: Multinational Space Stations and Choice of Law, 78 *Cali. L. Rev.* 1379–1381 (1990); H. Keefe, Essay, Making the Final Frontier Feasible: A Critical Look at the Current Body of Outer Space Law, *11 Santa Clara Computer & High Tech. L.J.* 366–367 (1995); S. Gorove, Interpreting Article II of the Outer Space Treaty, 37 *Fordham L. Rev.* 349–352 (1969); N. Jasentuliyana, Space Law and the United Nations, 17 *Annals of Air & Space Law* 137, 147 (1992); C.C. Okolie, International Law Principle of Jurisdiction in Regard to Settlements of Humankind on the Moon and Mars, in *Proc. Thirty-Fourth Colloquium L. Outer Space* 64–65 (1991).

[120] See further Shin, *id.*, at 1381.

[121] E.A. Posner, Law, Economics and Inefficient Norms, 144 *U. Pa. L. Rev.* 1741 (1996); H.S. Rana, The "Common Heritage of Mankind" & The Frontier: A Revaluation of Values Constituting the International Legal Regime for Outer Space Activities, 26 *Rutgers L.J.* 245 (1994).

[122] Menthe, *supra* note 99.

[123] See further M.R. Burnstein, Conflicts on the Net: Choice of Law in Transnational Cyberspace, 29 *Vand. J. Transnat'l L.* 103 (1996).

[124] See further Menthe, *supra* note 99. For example, concerns over the Antarctica "pie" during the Cold War led to a treaty freezing national claims to polar wedges. See further Antarctica Treaty, Article IV, 12 U.S.T. 794, 402 U.N.T.S. 71, 75.

National states have been trying to formulate new rules and transform traditional regulations to accommodate it, but it shall still take some time for all the states to reach consensus on a treaty to regulate Internet activities.[125] For the time being, national rules shall take the primary position in regulation.

In cyberspace, it would be meaningless to argue for sovereignty. However, with more and more business carried out in cyberspace, a standardized rule for assigning bodies the power to regulate is requisite. The theory of international space rightly acknowledges the importance of public law, which itself defines contours of private law.[126] The purpose of defining international space is to use the standard of nationality to characterize certain activity and claim national jurisdiction.[127] For example, in outer space, the nationality of the registry of the vessel, manned or unmanned, is the relevant category; in Antarctica, the nationality of the base governs. A version of this principle shall also apply to activities in cyberspace.

Just as one would apply the law of the flag to the high seas, one should apply the law of a "vessel" in cyberspace. What constitutes this vessel? While the nationality of a web page may be important, the nationality of the person or entity who undertakes the tasks, or the ones who controls him, could be important as well.[128] Not only is determining which standard to be used to identify significant materials or actions difficult, but determining the nationality of those items is also a dubious task.

To a certain extent, the problem of choice of law could be solved by this principle, but not at all finally or resolutely. And the law chosen as such is only a procedural part. What shall be the sub-

---

[125] For this reason, it is suggested that international treaties should be crafted not as rules but rather as standards, which shall be left for legal interpretation in implementation. See for further A. Schwartz & R.E. Scott, The Political Economy of Private Legislatures, 143 *U. Pa. L. Rev.* 595, 597, 651 (1995).

[126] The globalization of trade, and the issue of conflict of laws, require solutions from the public international law system. See further H.H. Perritt, Jr., The Internet and Public International Law: The Internet is Changing the Public International Legal System, 88 *Ky. L.J.* 885, 892 (Summer, 1999/Summer, 2000).

[127] For example, the general principle in the high seas is to adopt the law of the ship's flag to govern in nearly all matters relating to a vessel, its captain, and its crew. See further W. Tetley, The Law of the Flag, "Flag Shopping," and Choice of Law, 17 *Tul. Maritime L.J.* 140 (1993); see also E. Lafleur, *The Choice of Laws in the Province of Quebec*, 185 (1898).

[128] See further Menthe, *supra* note 99.

stantial law for electronic commerce? Furthermore, this suggestion only exacerbates conflicts among states concerning which organ is up to the task of executing appropriate international law and which organ shall have the final say.[129] A comprehensive framework based on accepted legal norms[130] is needed to endow the Internet with settled status.

There is a demand for law in cyberspace, or more specifically for commercial activities carried out therein. A long-term solution to the problems raised by this limitless space will include rules specifically governing tort and contracts among individuals of different nations.

3.2. *The Law for Electronic Commerce*

3.2.1. *The Necessity of "New" Law for Electronic Commerce*

Some scholars wholeheartedly promote the development of a law for cyberspace.[131] Drastically different from physical space and a facilitator of activities that impact individuals around the globe, cyberspace is not well suited to a legal framework based on territoriality. To be successful, electronic commerce needs a new legal system to support it.[132]

Others believe that this idea may place too much weight on the influence the Internet could exert on social life. The Internet is after all simply a means of communication, whose functions differs nothing from other forms of communications.[133] It is only a tool to realize a certain objective.[134] Basic commercial theories stay the same. Moreover,

---

[129] This has been discussed in relation to the IAHC's efforts. See further A. Gigante, Blackhole in Cyberspace: The Legal Void in the Internet, 15 *J. Marshall J. of Computer & Info. L.*, 433 (1997).

[130] M.S. Yeo & M. Berliri, Conflict Looms Over Choice of Law in Internet Transactions, 4 *Electronic Com. & L. Rep.* 89 (1998).

[131] For general description, see D.R. Johnson & D. Post, The Rise of Law on the Global Network, in Kahin, *supra* note 38.

[132] See further J.C. Ginsburg, The Cyberian Captivity of Copyright: Territoriality and Authors' Rights in a Networked World, 15 *Santa Clara Computer & High Tech. L.J.* 347–348 (1999); J.R. Reidenberg, Governing Networks and Rule-Making in Cyberspace, 45 *Emory L.J.* 911–912 (1996).

[133] A.L. Shapiro, The Disappearance of Cyberspace and the Risk of Code, 8 *Seton Hall Const. L.J.* 703 (1998).

[134] Judge Easterbrook argued that there was no reason to teach the law of cyberspace any more than there was reason to teach the law of the horse since neither would illuminate the entirety of law. See further F.H. Easterbrook, Cyberspace and the Law of the Horse, *U. Chi. Legal F.*, 207 (1996).

major technological changes may have major legal effects without their needing to generate a unique body of law.[135] If you were to devise one law for the Internet, would you have to make another set of laws once new forms of communication appeared?[136] All that needs to be done is a modification of old rules to accommodate the character of the new tool; cyberspace is a delightful new playground for old games.[137] Traditional legal approaches alone will be enough to cope with the Internet.[138]

While both discussions are reasonable to a certain extent, the issue of the necessity of new law is not so black and white. We still need to look further into the activities in cyberspace and their connection with law to form an appropriately colored approach.

Some refer to the Internet phenomena as "new." But what is new? Actually, from some angles, the Internet looks new; from others, it does not. We must analyze its newness when justifying a legal approach.[139] There are different levels of laws. In the upper level, there are laws generally applicable to all situations, which include general legal conceptions and general principles flexible to change. These laws are not appropriate for the Internet. While accommodating new situations, those flexible rules can at the same time be too general to give specific guidance, a problem which might lead to inconsistent outcomes and make it difficult for citizens to comply

[135] See, for example, M.J. Horwitz, *The Transformation of American Law* 1780–1860 (1977).

[136] It is argued that such a body of regulatory law is a category, but not an exclusive category of law. See further M.A. Geist, The Reality of Bytes: Regulating Economic Activity in the Age of the Internet, 73 *Wash. L. Rev.* 521, 568–569 (1998); see also T. Wu, Application-Centered Internet Analysis, 85 *Va. L. Rev.* 1163, 1183 (1999).

[137] See further J.H. Sommer, Against Cyberlaw, 15 *Berkeley Tech. L.J.* 1231 (Fall, 2000).

[138] As discussed, it is not necessary or constructive to treat the Internet as a source of new legal issues that create a new legal discipline called "Internet law". Instead, the Internet is a new medium in which traditional legal principles are analyzed in novel contexts. There is no "Internet Law" as such and so no such specially designed law is required. See further G.B. Delta & J.H. Matsuura, *Law of the Internet*, at xix (Aspen Law & Business, New York, 1998).

[139] As discussed by T. Hardy, newness could mean that some sort of legal solution tailored to the cyberspace problem will bring clarity and predictability to the rules attending cyberspace conduct, the benefits of which outweigh the additional complexity thereby added to the legal system, or that the underlying policy concerns of "real space" law are inappropriate when applied to activities in cyberspace. See T. Hardy, The Proper Legal Regime for "Cyberspace", *55 University of Pittsburgh Law Review*, 1053–1054 (1994).

with the law. More specific laws generally take into account specific situations and apply to specific activities, and it is these laws that we should pay attention to.

At a shallow level of analysis, every medium is fraught with complex new legal questions, the most fundamental one being whether or not existing laws designed with other media in mind could be applied to this new medium as well.[140] Generally speaking, means of communications are not the basis for laws. We should distinguish the difference between technological and substantive innovation. Some issues appear just because the Internet creates new contexts for old problems rather than new problems *per se*. Sending a defamatory message online, for example, has no substantially different consequence from that of sending such a message through the mail. The traditional rule regarding defamation could serve both cases well. New laws are not necessary since the old laws for other media could do as well.[141]

Furthermore, it is not sensible to create laws for the Internet just because it promotes convergence and thereby breaks down fixed special boundaries around the treatment of one medium.[142] Or else new laws shall always come out when new technological developments make new media possible, which would occasion overlapping legislation and cause confusion in further applications. Moreover, the fact is that statutory law written for high-technology issues is often only relevant to (and includes a detailed account of) the technology of the time and thus has a short shelf life.[143] When uncertainty regarding applicable law is minor and not a significant clog in routine behavior, then a specific rule will not be worth adding complexity to our legal system.[144]

---

[140] See further Hardy, *id.*, at 996.

[141] Easterbrook, *supra* note 134, at 207; Lessig, *supra* note 108, at 501.

[142] OFTEL, *Beyond the Telephone, the TV and the PC* (London, 1995), para. 1.1.4.; see also European Commission, Green Paper on the Convergence of the Telecommunications, Media and Information Technology Sectors, and the Implications for Regulation: Towards an Information Society Approach (COM (97)623). See also G.J.H. Smith, *Internet Law and Regulation* (FT Law and Tax, London, 1996), Chapter 6.

[143] A. Petkofsky, *Cyber-Cases Present Challenge: Some Legal Issues Stretching Jurisdiction of Traditional Courts, Richmond Times-Dispatch*, 18 December 1994, at A1; J.P. Barlow, Crime and Puzzlement: Desperados of the Data Sphere, *Whole Earth Rev.* 56 (Fall 1990).

[144] Hardy, *supra* note 139, at 998.

Nevertheless, there are indeed situations when the use of the Internet could pose serious challenges to the existing laws.[145] The mere extension of physical world laws and government jurisdiction to cyberspace shall ultimately prove ineffective. Changes in science and technology have transformative power because the prevalent ideas in science and technology today are central to the material conditions in which those ideas arise.[146] New technologies shall create opportunities for new kinds of behavior as well as new legal questions.[147] With the use of the Internet, which is so different from other media, new relationships and transactions are forged by modalities novel to most people.[148] For example, when business is conducted online, there is the problem of digital signature. What shall be the effect of signature? Again, the use of the Internet shall give rise to cyberspace intermediaries. There have been long discussions

---

[145] There is growing recognition that traditional forms of regulation are unsuitable for many of the economic and political transactions that occur on the Internet. For general discussion, see Lessig, *supra* note 101; I.K. Gotts & A.D. Rutenberg, Navigating the Global Information Superhighway: A Bumpy Road Lies Ahead, 8 *Harv. J.L. & Tech.* 275 (1995); F.H. Cate, Comment, Law in Cyberspace, 9 *How. L.J.* 565, 567 (1996).

[146] The influence of science and technology on the ends pursued by international law has been pervasive, posing new problems or exacerbating old problems that transcend national boundaries. See further J.W. Dellapenna, Law in a Shrinking World: The Interaction of Science and Technology with International Law, 88 *Ky. L.J.* 830, 852 (1999–2000); see also J.K. Gamble, International Law and the Information Age, 17 *Mich. J. Int'l L.* 747 (1996); M. Lachs, Views From the Bench: Thoughts on Science, Technology and World Law, 86 *AJIL.* 673 (1992).

[147] See, for example, A.W. Branscombe, Cyberspaces: Familiar Territory or Lawless Frontiers, 2 *J. Computer-Mediated Comm.* (June 1996), at <http://www.usc.edu/dept/annenberg/vol2/issue1/intro.html>; A.W. Branscombe, Jurisdictional Quandaries for Global Networks, in Harasim, *supra* note 90, at 83–104; I.T. Hardy, Property (and Copyright) in Cyberspace, 1996 *U. Chi. Legal F.* 217 (Fall 1996), at <http://www.lib.uchicago.edu/forum/hardy.html>; D.R. Johnson, Due Process and Cyberjurisdiction, 2 *J. Computer-Mediated Comm.* (June 1996), at <http://www.usc.edu/dept/annenberg/vol2/issue1/due.html>; H.H. Perritt, Jr., Property and Innovation in the Global Information Infrastructure, *U. Chi. Legal F.* (Fall 1996), at <http://law.lib.uchicago.edu/forum/perritt.txt>; D.G. Post, Anarchy, State, and the Internet: An Essay on Law-Making in Cyberspace, *J. Online L.* 3 (1995), at <http://www.law.cornell.edu/jol/post.html>; J.M. Oberding & T. Norderhaug, A Separate Jurisdiction for Cyberspace?, *2 J. Computer-Mediated Comm.* (June 1996), at <http://www.usc.edu/dept/annenberg/vol2/issue1/juris.html>; A. Johnson-Laird, *The Anatomy of the Internet Meets the Body of Law* 23–25 (1996); R.D. Cooter, Decentralized Law for a Complex Economy: The Structural Approach to Adjudicating the New Law Merchant, 144 *U. Pa. L. Rev.* 1643 (1996); M.J. Radin, Property Evolving in Cyberspace, 15 *J.L. & Com.* 509 (1996).

[148] Y. Akdeniz, C. Walker & D. Wall (Eds.), *The Internet, Law and Society*, 17 (Pearson Education Limited, 2000).

about the liability of those intermediaries.[149] Should intermediaries be held liable for the wrong made by the third party? Under what conditions shall they be held liable? No laws exist concerning these problems. When the policy considerations that underlie an existing rule no longer make sense as applied to cyberspace,[150] a new law shall be needed to define the status of digital signature.

Different ways of realizing electronic commerce have been suggested. For those who insist on maintaining existing law, there is the problem of adaptation. One way to adapt legislation is to reinterpret the laws' wording. As we have seen in the case of "writing," the traditional interpretation concerns the writing of touchable, paper documents; the new interpretation encompasses digital documents. Thus, electronic commerce can be regulated without formulating new laws.[151]

Since there is the looming prospect of a vast array of new services and relationships in cyberspace, much effort shall have to be spent on the formulation of new rules for electronic commerce. Considering the international nature of the Internet, an international treaty could be the best choice for electronic commerce. However, since electronic commerce is a relatively new event, drafting a new convention at the present stage might be too hasty. Other measures have been suggested for the time being. First of all, *lex informatica* has been specifically proposed for electronic commerce.[152] It is kind of autonomous body of law emerging from the chaotic legal reality for cyberspace.[153] We shall discuss this body of law further presently.

---

[149] See further B.W. Sanford, *Libel and Privacy*, 48 Section 2.7.4. (2nd Ed., 1991). For general discussion, see further Y. Zhao, Internet Service Providers and Their Liability, 34 *Law/Technology*, World Jurist Association, No. 1, 1–19 (2001).

[150] See further Hardy, *supra* note 139, at 998.

[151] This is considered to be an adaptation of existing law, augmented by techniques of governance. See further J.L. Goldsmith, Against Cyberanarchy, 65 *University of Chicago Law Review*, 1199 (1998).

[152] See, for example, A.W. Branscombe, Overview: Global Governance of Global Networks, in A.W. Branscombe (Ed.), *Toward a Law of Global Communications Networks*, 1, 21 (1986).

[153] Some scholars have offered emergent norms as an alternative to legal rule-making, particularly in developing countries that lack an established legal system. See, for example, R.D. Cooter, The Theory of Market Modernization of Law, 16 *Int'l Rev. L. & Econ.* 141 (1996); R.D. Cooter, Against Legal Centrism, 81 *Cal. L. Rev.* 417 (1993); D.G. Post & D.R. Johnson, "Chaos Prevailing on Every Continent": Towards A New Theory of Decentralized Decision-Making in Complex Systems, 73 *Chi.-Kent L. Rev.* 1087–1088 (1998).

Other suggestions have also been made concerning the principle of respect within national legal systems for multi-national communities within the Internet.[154]

3.2.2. Lex Informatica[155]

This suggestion originates from the idea of *lex mercatoria* or Law Merchant.[156] In the Middle Ages, transactions were carried out across Europe, which required common rules to provide a basis for transactions between those from different states with different local, feudal, royal and ecclesiastical laws.[157] No common laws were passed, but an enforceable set of customary practices took effect, which promoted the benefits of merchants and was reasonably uniform across all the jurisdictions involved in the transactions.[158] It was independent of local sovereign rules and assured commercial participants of basic fairness in their relationships.[159] To enforce these practices, special

[154] See further Akdeniz, *supra* note 148, at 16. It is also defined as the principle of comity, which is the recognition one nation allows within its territory of the legislative, executive, or judicial acts of another nation, having due regard both to international duty and convenience, and to the rights of its own citizens or of other persons who are under the protections of its law. See further *Hilton v. Guyot*, 115 U.S. 113, 163–164 (1995); see also *Lauritzen v. Larsen*, 345 U.S. 571, 582 (1953); *Mitsubishi Motors v. Soler Chrysler-Plymouth*, 473 U.S. 614 (1985); *The Bremen v. Zapata Off-Shore Co.*, 407 U.S. 1 (1972); for detailed discussion on this principle, see also S.R. Swanson, Comity, International Disputes Resolution Agreements, and the Supreme Court, 21 *Law & Policy in International Business*, 333 (1990); J.R. Paul, Comity in International Law, 32 *Harv. Int'l L.J.* 1–44 (1991); H.E. Yntema, The Comity Doctrine, 65 *Mich. L. Rev.* 9 (1966).

[155] This term is taken from W.H. van Boom & J.H.M. van Erp, Electronic Highways: On the Road to Liability, in V. Bekkers et al. (Eds.), *Emerging Electronic Highways: New Challenges for Politics and Law* 153, 156 (1996).

[156] For discussions on *Lex Mercatoria*, see J. Wiener, *Globalization and the Harmonization of Law* 151–183 (Pinter: London and New York, 1999).

[157] With the fall of the Roman Empire, commercial activities in Europe were almost nonexistent relative to what had occurred before and what would come later, when professional merchants arose in the 11th and 12th centuries. There were significant barriers to overcome before substantial interregional and inter-national trade could develop: multilingualism, distance barriers, a lack of interpersonal bonds, etc. Localized and contradictory laws and business practices produced local hostilities towards foreign commercial customs and led to mercantile confrontations. Thus, there was a clear need for law as a language of interaction. See further B.L. Benson, The Spontaneous Evolution of Commercial Law, 55 *Southern Econ. J.* 644, 646–647 (1989).

[158] See further W.A. Bewes, *The Romance of the Law Merchant*, 15–25 (1923); see also L.E. Trakman, From the Medieval Law Merchant to E-Merchant Law, 53 *University of Toronto Law Journal* 276–283 (Summer 2003).

[159] See further H.J. Berman & C. Kaufman, The Law of International Commercial *Transactions (Lex Mercatoria)*, 19 *Harv. Intl L.J.*, 221, 274–277 (1978).

courts grew up whose jurisdiction was that of commercial transactions, and judges were drawn from the ranks of the merchant class itself on the basis of experience and seniority.[160] They adjudicated disputes by reference to customary trade practice. The determinations of these courts were valid and enforceable under national laws because the lords of the day recognized the benefits that would accrue from efficient trade.[161]

Today, there are some disputes concerning the existence of Law Mercatoria.[162] There can be no proof of the practice without written documentation; if there were written documents, then the legitimacy of *lex mercatoria* as customs rather than rules is called into question. Further, it is difficult to determine whether the flexible Law Mercatoria should be considered as an independent body of law, or just a gap-filler.[163]

As regards the present situation, some customs have been codified in the national legal system. To achieve stability while preserving the customs' flexibility, customs were required to have been well established. Legal documents can define the content of certain customs, while allowing for their continued development in practice. Customs are developing in cyberspace as they might be in any community, and rapid growth in computer communications[164] suggests that there may be a great many such customs before long.[165] Also, when we look into the present arbitration system, which is actually the modern form of the former special courts,[166] we find that customs are applicable to the adjudication of cases and, more importantly, the enforcement of final decisions based on such customs has received world recognition.[167]

---

[160] Adjudicators were generally selected from the ranks of the merchant class on the basis of their commercial experience, their objectivity and their seniority within the community of merchants. See further L.E. Trakman, *The Law Merchant: The Evolution of Commercial Law*, 11, 15 (1983).

[161] Trakman, *id.*, at 2, 9.

[162] See further F. de Ly, *International Business Law and Lex Mercatoria*, 8 (1992).

[163] See H.J. Berman & F.J. Dasser, The "New" Law Merchant and the "Old": Sources, Content, and Legitimacy, in T.E. Carbonneau (Ed.), *Lex Mercatoria and Arbitration*, 21, 22 (1990).

[164] K.D. Suzan, Comment, Tapping to the Beat of a Digital Drummer: Fine Tuning U.S. Copyright Law for Music Distribution on the Internet, 59 *Alb. L. Rev.* 789, 828 (1995).

[165] Hardy, *supra* note 139, at 1010.

[166] See further Trakman, *supra* note 160, at 42.

[167] See further Berman, *supra* note 163, at 21, 22.

Evidently, *lex mercatoria* still exists and still has meaning today for international business transactions. Founded on the shared legal understandings of an international community composed principally of commercial, shipping, insurance, and banking enterprises, it is an autonomous international body of law, which is binding in appropriate cases in national courts.[168] Accordingly, *lex mercatoria* could serve as a starting point in determining how the goals of *lex informatica* can be attained.[169]

Two important elements distinguish *lex mercatoria* from other types of law. Firstly, no statute or other authoritative pronouncement of law gave rise to its existence; secondly, *lex mercatoria* exists in some sense apart from and in addition to the ordinary rules of law that apply to non-merchant transactions.[170] Special courts and the application of *lex mercatoria* speedily resolve disputes.

This discussion of *lex mercatoria* is relevant to the situation of cyberspace. There is a need to have uniform guiding rules for transactions carried out in cyberspace. At present, there are no such rules and reaching a uniform convention will not be realistic in the short-term. Furthermore, the idea that an ADR mechanism could be devised to resolve disputes at a speedy pace gives rise to the possibility of *lex informatica.*

Since custom is the foundation of the *lex mercatoria,* custom shall naturally be the essential source of *lex informatica.*[171] Since the appearance of the Internet, more and more activities have taken place in cyberspace. Customary rules called "netiquette" or "nethics"[172] have been developed. Such norms generally reflect the common real-life community concerns that most are worried about preserving on the Internet, provide the basic rules on the information highway, and allow netizens to effectively punish those who breach the established norms.[173]

---

[168] See further Berman, *id.*, at 21–24.

[169] See further A. Mefford, Lex Informatica: Foundations of Law on the Internet, 5 *Ind. J. Global Leg. Stud.* 225 (Fall, 1997).

[170] Hardy, *supra* note 139, at 1020; see also A.F. Lowenfeld, *Lex Mercatoria*: An Arbitrator's View, in Carbonneau, *supra* note 163, at 37, 54–55.

[171] Mefford, *supra* note 169, at 228.

[172] When the Net was much smaller, "high-minded" academics were able to foster a communitarian ethic that substituted cooperation for compulsory law, and these were summed as "netiquette". See further A. Rinaldi, *Netiquette Home Page: Questions and Answers*, at <http://www.fau.edu/rinaldi/netiquette.html>.

[173] G.B. Allison, *The Lawyer's Guide to the Internet*, 338 (1995).

The parallels between *lex mercatoria* and *lex informatica* are strong. In each case, national governments are not in the position of making unilateral regulation and international regulation is preferable to governmental interference. Today we can accept that developing an international regulatory system shall require sufficient time and energy. As there is not authoritative guidance at hand, the rules to be applied in cyberspace could be those considered as customs among the users in the Internet society: those practices generally observed in cyberspace and voluntarily accepted as binding by users.

That said, *lex informatica* has no intention of displacing existing rules and shall not take priority once new rules are reached among states. Some scholars argue that *lex informatica* and legal rules parallel and overlap one another.[174] The present author holds the opposite position. It is true that *lex informatica* is an important guide when there are no rules to fill the gap in the legal society. Nevertheless, once new rules are made, they shall take the place of *lex informatica*, except in the situation when states have imposed certain restrictions on such rules.

In the field of international law, customs occupy an important position.[175] They are a source for international law and directly applicable to adjudicating cases.[176] There are two important factors based on which certain practices can be defined as customs. A custom is both objectively deemed so because of its general practice and subjectively assumed customary as law, the so-called *opinio iuris*.[177] With

---

[174] See further J.R. Reidenberg, Lex Informatica: The Formulation of Information Policy Rules Through Technology, 76 *Texas Law Review*, No. 3, 583–586 (February 1998). As discussed, the relationship between *Lex Informatica* and legal rules shall be that policymakers must add *Lex Informatica* to their set of policy instruments and should pursue *Lex Informatica* norms as an effective substitute for law where self-executing, customized rules are desirable.

[175] For general discussion of customary law, see R.P. Dhokalia, *Codification of Public International Law* (1970); H.W.A. Thirlway, *International Customary Law and Codification* (1972); G.M. Danilenko & H. Lauterpacht, Codification and Development of International Law, 49 *AJIL* 16 (1955); O. Schachter, International Law in Theory and Practice, 178 *Recueil des Cours* 9 (1982); P.C. Szasz, The Role of the U.N. Secretary-General: Some Legal Aspects, 24 *N.Y.U.J. Int'l L. & Pol.* 161 (1991); P.R. Trimble, A Revisionist View of Customary International Law, 33 *UCLA L. Rev.* 665 (1986).

[176] The sources of international law include treaty, custom, and general principles of law. See further Statute of the International Court of Justice, June 26, 1945, Art. 38; see also P. Malanczuk, *Akehurst's Modern Introduction to International Law*, 36 (7th Ed., 1997); M.W. Janis, *An Introduction to International Law*, 4–6, 10 (1988).

[177] Customary international law emerges from state practice backed by *opinio juris*.

more and more activities taking place in cyberspace, certain uniform rules to regulate activities in different locations are urgent. Internet society is able to generate practices which appear most appropriate for users in cyberspace. With the benefits in plain view, such practices are automatically followed, like customs.[178]

As states are not the best bodies to regulate, self-regulation groups,[179] like commissions and panels of experts, take the place of such bodies in forming rules to avoid chaos, which take into account existing practices.[180] Such groups and associations are formed with charters and by-laws.[181] Made by those who well understand cyberspace, the

---

Opinio juris signifies that state conduct is intended to express a legal norm. It means that a state acts because it believes its actions are mandated by a norm, or that the conduct is intended to give rise to a new norm. In colloquial terms, *opinio juris* exists when a state acts in order to follow precedent set by other actions, or to set a new precedent which will be followed in the future. This was confirmed by the ICJ in the Nicaragua case; see further *Nicaragua v. USA* (Merits), ICJ Report, 1986, 14, at 97. In the Continental Shelf (*Libya v. Malta*) case, the ICJ further stated that the substance of customary law must be looked for primarily in the actual practice and *opinio juris* of states. See further ICJ report, 1985, 29; see also Advisory Opinion on the Legality of the Threat or Use of Nuclear Weapons, ILM 35 (1996), 809, at 826, paragraph 64; L. Condorelli, Custom, in M. Bedjaoui (Ed.), *International Law: Achievements and Prospects*, 189 (Dordrecht-Boston-London, 1991); L.J. Gibbons, No Regulation, Government Regulation, or Self-Regulation: Social Enforcement or Social Contracting For Governance in Cyberspace, 6 *Cornell J.L. & Pub. Policy* 475, 505 (1997).

[178] See, for example, R. Axelrod, *The Evolution of Cooperation* 11–19 (1984).

[179] Groups such as the Whole Earth 'Lectronic Link (known as the WELL) do resemble the small-town, restricted-entry communities. See generally R.C. Ellickson, *Order Without Law: How Neighbors Settle Disputes* (1991); L. Bernstein, Merchant Law in a Merchant Court: Rethinking the Code's Search for Immanent Business Norms, 144 *U. Pa. L. Rev.* 1765 (1996); L. Bernstein, Opting Out of the Legal System: Extralegal Contractual Relations in the Diamond Industry, 21 *J. Legal Stud.* 115 (1992); H. Rheingold, *The Virtual Community: Homesteading on the Electronic Frontier* 17–38 (1993); K. Hafner, The World's Most Influential Online Community (and It's Not AOL), Wired, May 1997, at 98.

[180] See, for example, Commission of the European Communities, Communication from the Commission to the Council and the European Parliament: On "Standardization and the Global Information Society: The European Approach", COM(96)359 (final) at 4, available at *Standardization and the Global Information Society*, at <http://www.ispo.cec.be/infosoc/legreg/docs/96359.html>. Committee T1 is a privately sponsored organization accredited by the American National Standards Institute, which develops technical standards and reports regarding interconnection and interoperability of telecommunications networks at interfaces with end-user systems, carriers, information and enhanced-service providers, and customer premises equipment. See further Standards Comm., T1 Telecomm., T1 Overview, at <http://www.t1.org/html/intro.html>.

[181] For the association's by-law, see general G.D. Webster, *The Law of Association*, Section 2.03 (1)(b), (1993).

rules are geared to the reality of a constantly evolving cyberspace in terms of speed, flexibility, and operation.[182]

Furthermore, users can create their own rules collectively through daily practice. Parties can specify in a contract not only their behavior toward one another,[183] but also which set of laws will resolve their future disputes.[184] Service providers can specify behaviors in their "part" of cyberspace through contracts. Other guides include the writings of scholars, like publications of customary international practice, and model codes and recommendations by various international bodies,[185] which could prove extremely influential in future legal disputes.[186] They, of course, could all be posted on an electronic bulletin board.[187]

Though not obligatory, these rules are made for the benefit of users and thus are voluntarily observed by users. Since they reflect customs and provide a greater opportunity for users to interact with and create rules than physical world law does, users recognize them as more legitimate than jurisdictional law. Users are unlikely break

[182] The primary source of *lex informatica* is the technology developer and the social process by which customary uses evolve. See further L. Lessig, Reading the Constitution in Cyberspace, 45 *Emory L.J.* 897 (1996).

[183] For example, a telephone subscriber's choice between per line and per call blocking of caller identification information creates a default rule applicable to all users of the particular telephone line. The fact that contracts between two parties over the use of intellectual property rights have significant effects on third parties is the central problem with the idea that private parties ought to be able to set their own legal rules. Several scholars have offered examples of these external effects in private contracts. See, for example, J.E. Cohen, Lochner in Cyberspace: The New Economic Orthodoxy of "Rights Management", 97 *Mich. L. Rev.* 462 (1998); N. Elkin-Koren, Copyright Policy and the Limits of Freedom of Contract, 12 *Berkeley Tech. L.J.* 93 (1997); W.J. Gordon, On the Economics of Copyright, Restitution, and "Fair Use": Systemic Versus Case-by-Case Responses to Market Failure, 8 *J.L. & Info. Sci.* 7 (1997); Lemley, *supra* note 51, at 169–171; M.A. Lemley, The Economics of Improvement in Intellectual Property Law, 75 *Tex. L. Rev.* 989, 1057–1058 (1997); L.P. Loren, Redefining the Market Failure Approach to Fair Use in an Era of Copyright Permission Systems, 5 *J. Intell. Prop. L.* 1 (1997); D. McGowan, Free Contracting, Fair Competition, and Draft Article 2B: Some Reflections on Federal Competition Policy, Information Transactions, and "Aggressive Neutrality", 13 *Berkeley Tech. L.J.* 1173 (1998); M.J. Meurer, Price Discrimination, Personal Use and Piracy: Copyright Protection of Digital Works, 45 *Buff. L. Rev.* 845 (1997).

[184] See further R.H. Coase, The Problem of Social Cost, 3 *J.L. & Econ.* 1 (1960).

[185] Janis, *supra* note 176, at 42–45, 48.

[186] See, for example, W.L. Craig et al., J. Paulson, *International Chamber of Commerce Arbitration*, section 35.01 (2nd Ed. 1990).

[187] See further E. Katsh, Law in A Digital World: Computer Networks and Cyberspace, 38 *Vill. L. Rev.* 403 (1993).

customary procedure and go their own way because once they deviate from general practice, they might be punished, or even expelled from cyberspace.[188] Users in cyberspace regard common practice as enforceable as law, as when one user breaks the practice, they put certain enforcement mechanisms in place to force him back to the right path.[189] From a psychological point of view, the users in cyberspace are committed to those practices as law and abide by these practices with such a view. In short, those practices have acquired legal force without the backing of the sovereign.

Consequently, the external and internal elements leading to the existence of *lex informatica* have been sufficient. The idea for the custom may take its roots in a posting on a discussion group, followed by a posted response that criticizes and expands on that idea, and so on until the idea has been rehashed over and over again.[190] In this way, a clear custom shall come into being. Consequently, *lex informatica* co-existing with existing laws would be an eminently practical and efficient way of handling commerce in cyberspace.

3.2.3. Lex Informatica *and Dispute Resolution*

Making rules for cyberspace or specifically for electronic commerce is a conceptually distinct process, different from the process of dispute resolution. However, these two different procedures can be combined in practice.[191] As we discussed, a new ADR mechanism shall be formulated to resolve disputes in electronic commerce.[192] Just like in the Middle Ages, the mechanism shall function in ways that rec-

---

[188] Technology allows automated and self-executing rule enforcement, which could prevent actions from taking place without the proper permissions or authority. See, for example, M. Blaze et al., Decentralized Trust Management, *in Proceedings of the IEEE Conference on Security and Privacy* (Oakland, Cal.) (May 1996).

[189] A group with a cohesive set of interests can punish individual members who act contrary to those interests and still claim some legitimacy. See further M.A. Lemley, Symposium on the Internet and Legal Theory: The Law and Economics of Internet Norms, 73 *Chi.-Kent. L. Rev.* 1270 (1998).

[190] See further T. Laquey, *The Internet Companion: A Beginner's Guide to Global Networking*, at 62–74 (2nd Ed., 1994). The arbitrators could establish a set of customs on a web page that would receive comment and criticism from academics and contract practitioners. This page could be updated constantly to reflect the current prevailing opinion of law for cyberspace. See further D.R. Johnson, *The New Case Law of Cyberspace*, at <http://www.eff.org/pub/Intellectualprop . . . ration_cyber_caselaw_johnson.article>.

[191] See further Perritt, *supra* note 8, at 349, 389.

[192] See, for example, Dunne, *supra* note 63.

ognize the needs of users in cyberspace;[193] arbitrators shall be selected from experts or esteemed specialists. The present mechanism also takes the same attitude.

Different from official adjudicative procedures, the new mechanism can rather flexibly accommodate the constantly evolving nature of customs.[194] Electronic commerce is replete with customary ways of doing things. As commerce increases, customs shall proliferate and develop on a larger commercial scale and may, in fact, conflict with "real world" customs.[195] The ability to respond and adapt rapidly to changes[196] in technical and legal environments[197] constitutes one of the most appealing aspects of *lex informatica*.[198] In adjudicating cases, the arbitrators shall make use of all existing rules and customs and other relevant principles to reach objective, justified decisions. They may make new rules just as a traditional common law court makes new rules to realize fairness in a particular case. Thus, dispute resolution processes in electronic commerce can range from a complete absence of pre-existing definite rules with a neutral party empowered to resolve disputes on some kind of general fairness basis[199] to a system in which the rules are highly specific and a fact-finder is

---

[193] The emphasis of these merchant courts and the law they applied was a speedy resolution of disputes, an important element when time is money. See further Hardy, *supra* note 139, at 1021.

[194] Conditions in cyberspace change rather rapidly and so many transactions occur that a well-established custom may only be weeks old.

[195] See Hardy, *supra* note 139, at 1009–1010.

[196] The rate of technological advances has outstripped the ability of the law, lurching from one precedent to another, to address new realities. L.H. Tribe, *American Constitutional Law*, Section 12–25, at 1007 (2nd Ed. 1988).

[197] Hardy, *supra* note 139, at 1021. As the Internet society has increased from less than a million scientists to more than one hundred million people from all walks of life, the rules have necessarily changed. Further changes in the character of Netizens and their sheer number shall push development of rules in cyberspace. See further K.S. Byford, Privacy in Cyberspace: Constructing a Model of Privacy for the Electronic Communications Environment, 24 *Rutgers Computer & Tech. L.J.* 1, 38, 63–64 (1998); L. Lessig, The Zones of Cyberspace, 48 *Stan. L. Rev.* 1403, 1407 (1996).

[198] Alternatively, a system can be envisioned in which the rules are flexible and easily changed and in which no one is given adjudicatory power and thus the rules have only some kind of moral force.

[199] For a general understanding of "fairness," we can refer to common law. For a custom to become enforceable, it has to be legal, notorious, ancient or immemorial and continuous, reasonable, certain, universal, and obligatory. See further J.H. Levie, Trade Usage and Custom Under the Common Law and Uniform Commercial Code, 40 *N.Y.U.L. Rev.* 1101, 1103 (1965).

empowered to apply them in a final and binding way.[200] And this shall become the origin of a new rule.[201] Further, *lex informatica* has the freedom of multiple jurisdictions, the deference to decisions of those who understand concepts best, and the enforceability required for effective cyberspace law.[202]

The application of *lex informatica* in dispute resolution and the final decision made by the new mechanism are inter-operative. On one hand, the ultimate decision regarding which customs should be applied rests with the decision-makers[203] and thus the application of the customs confirms their enforceability in cyberspace.[204] On the other hand, the decisions made could be a written form of evidence for those customs, which influences disputing parties as well as others. Concerns over the uncertainties of customs[205] can thus be resolved to a large extent by cumulative written decisions. Furthermore, the whole process of making decisions can further develop those customs. As the decision-makers are esteemed members of the Internet society, they are in the right position to understand how the laws or customs are or shall be evolving and accordingly and the decisions they made usually represent right ideas towards certain issues.[206] While considering the existing practices, they shall postulate further developments, which other members of the Internet shall respect.

---

[200] Perritt, *supra* note 8, at 390.

[201] The function is just that of the rulemakers. Since a case arises that seems anomalous under the preexisting rules, the rulemakers can simply make a new rule dealing with the case as they think appropriate.

[202] See Mefford, *supra* note 169, at 226.

[203] To maintain the stability and integrity of discretion based decisions, a judicial review process within the Net itself might be established. To ensure that the flexibility of the Net law does not lead to uncertainty, arbitrators who too easily recognize custom or who too often bow to popular pressure could simply be removed. See Mefford, *id.*, at 230.

[204] If cyberspace custom drives the decisions of cybercommunity-based dispute resolution, such decisions shall be recognized by the cyberspace community as proper and right. See, for example, B. Simpson, The Common Law and Legal Theory, in W. Twining (Ed.), *Legal Theory and Common Law*, 19 (1986).

[205] See further D.P. Fidler, Challenging the Classical Concept of Custom: Perspectives on the Future of Customary International Law, 39 *German Yearbook of International Law*. 198–208 (1996).

[206] Empirical studies have also demonstrated that arbitrators often do not apply the existing law to accommodate the specific situation in the case. See, for example, H. Kronstein, Arbitration Is Power, 38 *N.Y.U.L. Rev.* 661, 669–679 (1963); S. Mentschikoff, Commercial Arbitration, 61 *Colum. L. Rev.* 846, 865–867 (1961).

The information highway is now developing into a legal territory of its own, a territory for which no uniform legislator is in sight. While devising a mechanism for electronic commerce, the mechanism's potential contribution to the development of the law must be taken into consideration.[207] The dispute resolution process itself is not only an application of the existing rules, but also a process of formulating new rules, which could become customs once applied extensively in the future practices. In other words, the function of dispute resolution *per se* is not merely to resolve disputes but a way to formulate rules for future use. As regards its latter function, current dispute resolution, ADR in particular, is of momentous and far-reaching historical significance. It is especially suitable where expertise in a specific area is needed. The theory of *lex informatica* rightly affords this opportunity and proceeds in this direction.

3.3. *Comments*

Technology's intersection with the political or normative issues reshapes everything we as international lawyers do.[208] The inquiry into virtual law provides repeated confirmation of the longstanding hypothesis that individual and community identity requires the development of a body of law that defines and distinguishes communities.[209] As Galanter has observed, "Law usually works not by exercise of force, but by information transfer, by communications of what's expected, what's forbidden, what's allowable, what are the consequences of acting in certain ways."[210] Cyberspace is a very distinctive space, with its own set of rules. Difficulties faced in regulating the Internet through conventional state-oriented means encourage exploration of new kinds of public international law matrices for private self-ordering.[211] Set in the broad field of international law, its position is like that of international space. Though different in many ways, cyberspace retains

---

[207] Schneider, *supra* note 36, at 10.

[208] See J.G. Ruggie, International Responses to Technology: Concepts and Trends, 29 *Int'l Org.* 557–558 (1975).

[209] See further P. Giordano, Invoking Law as a Basis for Identity in Cyberspace, *Stan. Tech. L. Rev.* P8 (1998), at <http://stlr.stanford.edu/STLR/Articles/98_STLR_1/>.

[210] M. Galanter, The Legal Malaise: Or, Justice Observed, 19 *Law and Society Review*, 537, 545 (1985).

[211] See further Perritt, *supra* note 126, at 931.

the basic nature of international space. According to the theory of international space, the law of the state to which relevant cyber-activities belong should govern online activities.

However, in substance, as applicable law was rarely designed with the Internet in mind, there is a today a practice of 'hotchpotch' rather than a codified set of rules.[212] The present problem is that there are no national laws to regulate the activities in cyberspace[213] and regulation is requisite at the international level. A distinct body of law for cyberspace at the national level is unwarranted. It has been suggested that centralized law is not even plausible for a technologically advanced society; to be efficient, complex economies require decentralized law.[214] Tracing back to the Middle Ages, *lex mercatoria* provides a nice example for cyberspace. *Lex informatica* could be formulated to meet the Internet's demands. Throughout history, in almost all judicial systems, law has followed societal customs.[215]

Lex informatica is a complete set of independent rules that reaches across borders and does not face the same jurisdictional, choice of law problems that legal regimes encounter when networks cross territorial or state jurisdictional lines.[216] Representing the sum total of opinions of those who have expertise in the legal aspects and needs of the Internet, it meets many of the challenges faced by physical world law when it deals with cyberspace.

Clearly, there was until now no consensus on what rules should be adopted for electronic commerce or in cyberspace. However, the current view is that these budding cybercommunities should be given the chance to develop and test their own rules before the external authorities exert too heavy a hand to bring them into conformity

---

212 L. Edwards & C. Waelde, *Law and the Internet* 9 (Hart Publishing, Oxford, 1997).

213 Historically, law and government regulation have established default rules for information policy, including constitutional rules on freedom of expression and statutory rights of ownership of information. However, these rules are not specifically aimed at cyberspace. See generally J. Boyle, *Shamans, Software and Spleens* (1996); M.E. Katsh, *Law in a Digital World* (1995); D.L. Burk, Federalism in Cyberspace, 28 *Conn. L. Rev.* (1996).

214 Cooter, *supra* note 153, at 141, 148 (1996).

215 For example, early American Indian tribal courts recognized that customary underlying beliefs and conduct provided a contemporary foundation for tribal governance and regulation. See further G. Valencia-Weber, Tribal Courts: Custom and Innovative Law, 24 *N.M.L. Rev.* 225, 244 (1994).

216 See Reidenberg, *supra* note 174, at 578.

with real-world rules.[217] We are happy to see that a new mechanism for resolving disputes in cyberspace has been put in the agenda. As online opportunities prompt the appearance of general practices accepted by Internet society, the mechanism can both affirm those practices as customs and occasion the birth of further customs.

Of course, we would not deny the necessity of national and international efforts in formulating rules for electronic commerce.[218] Once conditions ripen, certain rules can be put in place to stabilize legal relationships. The potential exists for treaty or national rules and *lex informatica* to regulate electronic commerce concurrently.[219] Governments and organizations should not rush to legislation. The law for electronic commerce should reflect the current demands of Internet society and future developments.

One last thing to remember is that any forum for resolving disputes in electronic commerce should be viewed as credible by the inhabitants of the Internet.[220] This whole new system and the future of electronic commerce largely depend on Internet society's confidence in them.

4. *Epilogue*

As pointed out above, a bottom-up, flexible method of dispute resolution is much more suitable to the dynamic realm of cyberspace than a top-down statutory or judicial authority is in that it would not stifle the development of either custom or technology.[221] A formalized

[217] A.W. Branscomb, Anonymity, Autonomy, and Accountability: Challenges to the First Amendment in Cyberspaces, 104 *Yale L.J.*, 1667 (1995).

[218] For an argument concerning the appropriateness of the combination of new customary rules and a treaty or national rules, see A. Endeshaw, The Proper Law of Electronic Commerce, 7 *Information and Communications Technology Law*, No. 1, 11–12 (March 1998).

[219] The successful ICAO and ITU regimes rest on treaty obligations but also greatly depend on industry input for the development and enforcement of the rules. See further H.H. Perritt, Jr., The Internet as a Threat to Sovereignty? Thoughts on the Internet's Role in Strengthening National and Global Governance, 5 *Ind. J. Global Leg. Stud.* 433–434 (Spring, 1998).

[220] A.E. Almaguer & R.W. Baggott III, Shaping New Legal Frontiers: Dispute Resolution for the Internet, 13 *Ohio St. J. on Disp. Resol.* 717 (1998).

[221] E.C. Lide, ADR and Cyberspace: The Role of Alternative Dispute Resolution in Online Commerce, Intellectual Property and Defamation, 12 *Ohio St. J. on Disp. Resol.* 216 (1996).

ADR mechanism, grounded in customs, is a logical and natural step for the resolution of dispute in electronic commerce. Applying an online system applied to dispute resolution is not new. What is new is the extension of such a system to the whole body of electronic commerce. Disputes arising out of electronic commerce take various forms. Ensuring the new mechanism accommodates all those disputes is vital. The demands of the market and the unique circumstances of electronic commerce shall be considered in realizing the mechanism's initial purposes.

Considering the growth rate of electronic commerce, more disputes are expected to arise. Such an online mechanism shall need to stand the test of time. To make possible an objective assessment of the new mechanism, feedback and evaluation tools should be built into the mechanism. After one year of operation, all participants in the new mechanism should be surveyed. Three criteria should be considered in determining its worth: efficiency, effectiveness and the public's satisfaction with its process, outcome, and its relationship with them.[222] This mechanism should always remain responsive to the changing nature of cyberspace and the needs of its habitants, making corresponding modifications when necessary.[223]

Given the success of most ongoing online projects, we optimistically anticipate the development of the new mechanism. When more complaints are brought to the center, a heavy case-burden shall obstruct efficient resolution. Thus, independent sub-centers working under the general guidance of the international center could then be developed according to the standard of region or specialization. Further development could include a two-level arbitration system. While the sub-centers act as courts, the international center could receive appeals.

Again, while the present topic is to devise a mechanism for electronic commerce, there has been interest in possibilities for extending such an online mechanism beyond electronic commerce. The University of Maryland Project took the initiative concerning this issue.

---

[222] See Costantino, *supra* note 37, at 221–222.

[223] See further Bordone, Electronic Online Dispute Resolution: A Systems Approach-Potential, Problems, and a Proposal, 3 Harv. Negotiation L. Rev. 209–210 Spring 1998).

The NCAIR donated a grant for the initiation of the project, which began in the fall of 1996. In it, the University of Maryland School of Law and the Center for Online Mediation take the administrative job. A list of mediators is maintained and could be selected for mediation.

The project differs widely from other projects discussed in Chapter Five in that its concern is not with targeting disputes arising out of online activities, but rather with bringing new methods and sets of tools to bear on various other disputes that are currently being handled in a traditional manner.[224] This project has several limitations. It shall only deal with disputes coming out in the State of Maryland under Maryland law. Two types of disputes are defined: domestic disputes such as custody, visitation, child support and property division; and health care disputes between either consumers and insurance companies, or consumers and health care device manufacturers.[225]

One prominent aspect of the project is that it chooses mediation over arbitration to deal with such disputes. This arrangement appears appropriate for the time being. In family law disputes, emotional issues are more important than financial issues in most cases. The physical and psychological distance created by forms of communication other than face-to-face communication reduces the amount of emotional hostility between two parties. Agreements are reachable with less time and energy.

Furthermore, as such disputes arise out of many divergent circumstances, mediating on a case by case basis is appropriate. The project intends to make a wide array of tools available for mediators: besides online communication tools, non-network modes of communications are to be on hand for information exchange in appropriate situations. Additionally, network options should yield new perspectives on analyzing the dispute and monitoring performance after settlement is reached.[226]

Thus far, this project has been fairly successful, which suggests that applying the online mechanism to disputes outside electronic

---

[224] See further R. Granat, *Creating An Environment for Mediating Disputes on the Internet* (May, 1996), <http://www.law.vill.edu/ncair/disres/granat.htm>.

[225] Granat, *id.*

[226] M.E. Katsh, Dispute Resolution in Cyberspace, 28 *Connecticut Law Review*, 966 (1996).

commerce is feasible. In modern society, the volume of disputes is expected to rise, particularly when easily accessible online systems are made available. Such systems can in the future be adapted to handle off and online disputes. Our present goal is to formulate a complete and viable structure for disputes in electronic commerce, making modifications to allow for the structure's possible extension.

CHAPTER SEVEN

CONCLUSION

> The Key to the Internet's extraordinary innovation is that it doesn't allow a term like 'allow'. It's architected to disallow it.[1]

The world is undergoing a technical revolution.[2] Rapid technological development has made business online realistic and thus served as a catalyst for a new globalization system.[3] Its application in businesses has accelerated the convergence of national and regional market forces towards a truly global economy.[4]

As the world becomes an increasingly interwoven place, your opportunities and threats increasingly derive from those you are connected to, and those you are connected to exhibit radically different interests and traits. Behind computer screens, there are people of all nationalities, all ethnic-cultural groups, all social classes, all professions, all religions, all political convictions, all ages, all life-styles, and both sexes who together, but also among themselves, show a rich diversity of preferences, dislikes, expectations for the future and fears.[5]

In this global world, international cooperation and harmonization shall be valued and pursued, but conflicts shall continue to exist,

---

[1] L. Lessig, *Architecting Innovative, The Standard* (Intelligence for the Internet Economy), November 14, 1999, at <http://www.thestandard.com/article/display/0,1151,7430,00.html>. Every new developing technology brings challenges and opportunities which frighten people with power, and empower people without power. See further G. LaMarche, International Free Expression Principles in Cyberspace, 17 *Whittier L. Rev.* 279 (1995).

[2] For a discussion of the technical development, see J.E. Faucette, Note, The Freedom of Speech at Risk in Cyberspace: Obscenity Doctrine and a Frightened University's Censorship of Sex on the Internet, 44 *Duke L.J.* 1155, 1161–1162 (1995).

[3] F.H. Cate, Symposium: Sovereignty and the Globalization of Intellectual Property: Introduction Sovereignty and the Globalization of Intellectual Property, 6 *Ind. J. Global Legal Stud.* 1 (1998); F.H. Cate, Symposium: Data Protection Law and the European Union's Directive: The Challenge for the United States: The E.U. Data Protection Directive, Information Privacy, and the Public Interest, 80 *Iowa L. Rev.* 431, 441–442 (1995).

[4] J.W. Dellapenna, Law in a Shrinking World: The Interaction of Science and Technology with International Law, 88 *Ky. L.J.* 809, 837 (1999–2000).

[5] A. Benshop, *Peculiarities of Cyberspace "Building Blocks for an Internet Sociology"*, at <http://www.pscw.uva.nl/sociosite/WEBSOC/introE.html>.

and these conflicts shall exhibit even more complicated faces. Perhaps no set of issues appears more vexing than those associated with potential disputes arising out of electronic commerce, particularly between parties located in different parts of the world. Thus questions are raised concerning the nature of conflicts and conflict resolution. One particular hindrance to the growth of the electronic marketplace is, in fact, the lack of consumer confidence about being able to obtain a remedy if a complaint about a transaction, marketer, product or service cannot be settled amicably with a merchant. Rapid response from legal society is needed.

The fact that the legal world lags behind[6] and parties involved in electronic commerce feel rather insecure regarding the legal implications of their behavior has seriously impacted concerns over who shall take the responsibility to resolve a dispute once one arises and what rules shall help clarify the issue.[7] If these significant matters are not dealt with, the further development of electronic commerce may be limited. It is the purpose of the present study to tentatively address them.

This study explores a comprehensive legal environment for resolving disputes in electronic commerce. Chapter Two provides background information on electronic commerce, the Internet, cyberspace, disputes, and dispute resolution mechanisms. This overview of the present understanding among the public concerning disputes in electronic commerce serves as a starting point for further research.

Chapter Three discusses three policies important to resolving disputes in electronic commerce. Self-regulation affords Internet society the power and opportunity to define its position and express its own attitudes towards activities in cyberspace created by the application of the Internet. While electronic commerce is essentially a global, rather than a national issue,[8] the policy of international coop-

[6] M.I. Meyerson, Virtual Constitutions: The Creation of Rules for Governing Private Networks, *8 Harv. J.L. & Tech.* 129 (1994); J. Connellan, Regulators Face up to Ecommerce Uncertainty, *Telecommunications* (International Edition) 35–37 (January 2000); E.M. Landry, Scrolling Around the New Organization: The Potential for Conflict in the On-Line Environment, 16 *Negotiation Journal*, No. 2, 133–140 (April 2000).

[7] L. Margherio, *The Emerging Digital Economy*, at <http://www.ecommerce.gov/danintro.htm>.

[8] Building Confidence in Electronic Commerce: A Consultation Document, Department of Trade and Industry, UK, Unique Reference Number: URN 99/642.

eration is of consequence to all. Internet interactions recognize no territorial boundaries, inexorably forcing those with competing values and interests into conflicts in an environment outside exclusive domestic control.[9] With the trend of globalization well underway, this policy shall be increasingly and more broadly applied. Thirdly, the policy of consumer protection arises out of the fact that consumer transactions are becoming more and more important and extending further into our daily life. The specific position of consumers in electronic commerce justifies special treatment in such transactions. The way in which the former conception of consumer protection is reformulated in the present stage shall have vital effects on the fate of electronic commerce. These three policies are treated from a macro point of view and need to be further examined in detailed cases.

With the basic policy in hand, it is necessary to elaborate on dispute resolution in electronic commerce. Litigation, as the traditional main mechanism, shall still maintain its strong influence on disputes in electronic commerce. However, to accommodate recent technological developments the court system shall need to fundamentally change some theories, for example, those concerning adjudicative jurisdiction and choice of law, which are scrutinized in Chapter Four. Its discussion could provide a tentative guide for the future treatment of these issues.

Adjudicative jurisdiction, the entrance to court procedures, occupies an important position in litigation theory. A look into existing practices in the US and the EU serves to guide the present discussion. International efforts in realizing harmonization in adjudicative jurisdiction are also significant. The Draft Hague Convention provides a nice suggestion for change: the identification and localization of the parties to the contract could be one way to substitute the traditional territorial connection.

Choice of law arrives after the justification of adjudicative jurisdiction. Two issues are identified: contractual issues and tort. This study addresses ongoing practice in the US and the EU. Party autonomy is a very important theory for contractual disputes. In cases where autonomous choice is absent, we must make the choice of law with a view to certain connecting factors, for example, the place

[9] V. Chiappetta, The Impact of E-Commerce on the Laws of Nations Forward, 7 *Willamette J. Int'l L. & Dispute Resolution* 9 (2000).

of the delivery of goods or services, or the place of the merchant's residence or place of business. The location of the server could provide a point for deciding applicable law for tort.

Because of shortcomings in the litigation, ADR mechanisms are often valued. Several examples are discussed in Chapter Five. Pioneering the field of dispute resolution in electronic commerce, many of these experiments have achieved success, which suggests promise for future efforts. In particular, the successful WIPO mechanism for domain name disputes has received much attention, which caught the interest of the present study. But as an experiment, its reach is limited. Its success cannot justify its extension to other areas in electronic commerce. Without doubt, a more viable mechanism should be pursued further for disputes in electronic commerce in general.

Given the interconnection of trade with the Internet, it is easy to predict that the foreseeable expansion of electronic commerce shall lead involved parties to turn to the same media through which they do their business when it comes to their resolving disputes. While taking these media into account, Chapter Six undertakes to devise a permanent body to resolve disputes in electronic commerce. At first gloss, this body resembles other arbitration bodies, but its further elaboration requires us to acknowledge that our prior perceptions and assumptions about conflict and modes of resolving disputes may require further reorientation.

The difference between the present mechanism and traditional mechanisms concerns the use of online facilities, which has larger underpinnings for issues of maintenance, enforcement, and other ensuing procedures. This mechanism lies somewhere between a pure adjudicative one and a simple forum for the rule enforcement of a chosen legal system, incorporating expert neutrals to make determinations dependent on the unique nature of cyberspace.[10] It is a tentative one, the feasibility of which shall be tested in real commercial life. Cyberspace is an arena of experimentation and competition. It is not now and probably never will be a harmonious place. The emergence of effective justice systems will require considerable cre-

[10] E.C. Lide, ADR and Cyberspace: the Role of Alternative Dispute Resolution in Online Commerce, Intellectual Property and Defamation, 12 *Ohio St. J. on Disp. Resol.*, 220 (1996).

ativity, but the larger and more active cyberspace becomes, the more likely it is that demand for online ADR mechanism will grow.[11] In an age when law enforcement agencies are learning how to police a system in which they are unfamiliar, and the existing mechanisms are not rightly in the track of this new phenomenon, an alternative which has the potential to bring order on the new frontier should deserve considerable attention.

Closely related to this mechanism, the law for electronic commerce is discussed in a broad framework—the Internet. *Lex informatica* appears appropriate for electronic commerce for the time being. Reflecting self-regulation on the part of Internet society, a kind of "electronic federalism,"[12] *lex informatica* shall prelude formal harmonized rules for electronic commerce in the strict legal sense.

This study examines the legal system for resolving disputes in electronic commerce, and enthusiastically presents the probable mechanism for addressing such disputes. Whether the question is the protection of domain names, transnational security, the establishment and use of crypto-secured digital identities, or any other issue arising in the context of electronic commercial transactions, the need for efficient and effective dispute resolution cannot be overstated.[13] Fortunately, more and more timely attention is being paid to this topic. Many scholars have started researching it from different angles and various parties have already started projects offering dispute resolution services. Such efforts result from the initiative of the citizens of the Internet community at large. Its attitudes and activities rightly lead the way in this new exploration.

The efforts made by individual scholars and separate parties have aroused the attention of international society. Its interest led to the International Conference on Dispute Resolution in Electronic

[11] E. Katsh, J. Rifkin & A. Gaitenby, E-Commerce, E-Disputes, and E-Dispute Resolution: In the Shadow of "eBay Law", 15 *Ohio St. J. on Disp. Resol.* 733 (2000).

[12] See further G.S. Wood, Thomas Jefferson, Equality, and the Creatipon of a Civil Society, 64 *Fordham L. Rev.* 2133, 2135 (1996); J.R. Reidenberg, Governing Networks and Rule-Making in Cyberspace, in B. Kahin & C. Nesson (Eds.), *Borders in Cyberspace: Information Policy and the Global Information Infrastructure* 84 (Cambridge, MA: MIT Press, 1996); D.L. Burk, Federalism in Cyberspace, 28 *Conn. L. Rev.* 1095 (1996); D.G. Post, Anarchy, State, and the Internet, 1 *J. Online L.* 3, 20 (1995), at <http://www.law.cornell.edu/jol/post.html>.

[13] L. Yves Fortier, International Commercial Arbitration and E-Commerce: Plus ca Change, plus c'est La Meme Chose, October 27, 2000, International Conference on Dispute Resolution in Electronic Commerce, WIPO, ARB/ECOM/00/2.

Commerce organized by the WIPO Arbitration and Mediation Center on November 6 and 7, 2000. Besides individual participants, representatives from around 40 countries, intergovernmental organizations, non-governmental organizations also took part in this conference.[14] Various topics related to dispute resolution in electronic commerce were heatedly discussed. Discussions concerned new legal issues for dispute resolution, including issues of encryption and security, domain name dispute resolution, application service provider disputes, auction site disputes. Ostensibly, debates over such issues could provide the impetus for a new round of development in electronic commerce. Dispute resolution is not only an issue for the Internet society to deal with, but also the present focus of international scene.

The general consensus of ongoing projects and discussions is that e-commerce, or more generally, information technology, shall change the way of conducting dispute resolution by imposing specialized techniques, such as online arbitration. The need for fair, efficient, speedy and appropriate dispute resolution for electronic commerce has justified the online performance of dispute resolution. First of all, this causes no technological difficulties. The issues of security, confidentiality and encryption could be well resolved through technical improvements and legal implementation. The greatest practical hurdle could be dealing with heavy documentary evidence but, in the end, papers can be scanned. The minds of those arbitrators not keen to abandon well-proven methods in favor of untried methods[15] must be changed. Arbitration, a millennium-old dispute resolution mechanism, has always demanded innovation. This has in turn required arbitrators to be both aware of and responsive to the needs of its users.

As discussed in Chapter Six, legal problems such as the arbitration agreement, the seat of arbitration, final award, shall not become obstacles for the new mechanism. International society has launched efforts to provide a legal environment for electronic commerce. Several states in the US enacted versions of the Uniform Electronic Transactions Act (UETA); however, many states modified this model act, thus rendering interstate enforcement inconsistent. In 2000, the federal government enacted the Electronic Signature Act, leading to

[14] WIPO, ARB/ECOM/00/INF/1 Prov. 2, November 6, 2000.

[15] R. Hill, Institutional Perspectives and Responses, International Conference on Dispute Resolution in Electronic Commerce, November 3, 2000, WIPO, ARB/ECOM/00/32.

some consistency among states but still leaving gaps for those states that did not enact UETA. The European Commission and other government and non-governmental organizations have promulgated a series of directives.[16] UNCITRAL, for instance, presented a model law. None of these promises to create a universally recognized legal framework for electronic commerce in the near term. But though there is at present no complete set of national legislation or generally accepted international rules concerning electronic commerce, a new ADR mechanism seems appropriate.

Electronic commerce is reshaping and adopting new techniques and rules of dispute resolution to cope with its very nature. It opens the door for practitioners in arbitration to advocate and market a uniquely flexible and well-established dispute resolution mechanism to a new generation of people in cyberspace. An online dispute resolution mechanism should be the right choice for you when you need the assistance of a capable, experienced ADR professional; when you do not want to go to court; when you want to hold down costs and fees; and when you want to use an asynchronous process that allows you to participate when you have time. It is the obligation of global providers to build user confidence in electronic commerce and ensure protection in online transactions.[17]

It might be a bit too early to envisage a perfect and complete dispute resolution mechanism for electronic commerce that would have no gaps, uncertainties, or difficulties, even in developed parts of the world. The development of a mechanism for dealing with disputes in electronic commerce shall depend on electronic commerce's further development. The present study offers a few introductory suggestions that may aid others in their steps forward to a more perfect realization of dispute resolution in electronic commerce.

---

[16] See further M.I.M. Aboul-Enein, An Outline on "Dispute Resolution in Electronic Commerce" in the Arab Countries: Institutional Perspectives and Responses, International Conference on Dispute Resolution in Electronic Commerce, November 2000, WIPO, ARB/ECOM/00/29.

[17] L.E. Teitz, Providing Legal Services for the Middle Class in Cyberspace: The Promise and Challenge of On-Line Dispute Resolution, 70 *Fordham L. Rev.* 1016 (December 2001).

BIBLIOGRAPHY

1. *Treaties and Other Instruments*

A European Initiative in Electronic Commerce COM (97) 157

A Global Action Plan for Electronic Commerce (Prepared by Business with Recommendations for Governments)

American Bar Association, Achieving Legal and Business Order in Cyberspace: A Report on Global Jurisdiction Issues Created by the Internet (2000)

Antarctic Treaty BRIE Working Paper, Tools for Thought: What is New and Important About the "E-conomy"? (2000)

Appliance for Global Business, A Global Action Plan for Electronic Commerce (2nd Ed., 1999)

Brussels Convention on Jurisdiction and Enforcement of Judgments in Civil and Commercial Matters (1968)

Commission Green Paper on Guarantees for Consumer Goods and After-Sales Services, COM (93) 509

Convention on Jurisdiction and Foreign Judgments in Civil and Commercial Matters (Hague Conference on Private International Law)

Draft Code of Conduct for Electronic Commerce

Draft Swiss Act on Telecommunication

Electronic Fund Transfer Act, 15 U.S.C. (1994)

European Directive on Data Protection (24 October 1995)

European Parliament and Council Directive on Certain Legal Aspects of Electronic Commerce in the Internal Market

European Parliament and Council Directive on the Sale of Consumer Goods and Associated Guarantees, COM (95) 520

Fair Credit Billing Act, 15 U.S.C. (1994)

Federal Communications Decency Act

Final Report of the WIPO Internet Domain Name Process

Finnish Consumer Protection Act (1978)

General Usage for International Digitally Ensured Commerce (GUIDEC)

Hague Convention on the Law Applicable to Contracts of International Sales of Movable Goods

ICANN Uniform Domain-Name Dispute-Resolution Policy

Mail or Telephone Order Merchandise Rule, 16 C.F.R. (1997)

OECD Working Papers, Dismantling the Barriers to Global Electronic Commerce (1997)

——, Global Information Infrastructure—Global Information Society (1997b)

——, Measuring Electronic Commerce (1997)

——, Gateways to the Global Market Consumers and Electronic Commerce (1998)

——, Guidelines for Consumer Protection in the Context of Electronic Commerce (2000)

——, E-Commerce: Impacts and Policy Challenges (2000)

ONP Leased Line Directive (92/44/EEC, 5 June 1992)

Restatement (2nd) of Conflict of Laws (1971)

Restatement (3rd) of Foreign Relations Law of the US (1987)

Restatement (2nd) of Judgments (1982)

Three Year Action Plan of Consumer Policy in the EC (1990–1992), COM (90) 98

UNCITRAL Model Law on Electronic Commerce
Uniform Computer Information Transactions Act (2000)
Uniform Electronic Transaction Act
The European Telecommunications Platform, Inventory of Dispute Resolution Mechanisms: What are the Choices for the Telecommunications Sector? (1998)
WIPO Worldwide Symposium on the Impact of Digital Technology on Copyright and Neighboring Rights (1993)
WTO, A Quantitative Assessment of Electronic Commerce (September, 1999)

2. *Books*

Akdeniz, Y., Walker, C. & Wall, D. (Eds.), *The Internet, Law and Society* (Pearson Education Limited, 2000)
Allison, G.B., *The Lawyer's Guide to the Internet* (Chicago, The American Bar Association, 1995)
Anderson, B., *Imagined Communities: Reflections on the Origin and Spread of Nationalism* (London: Verso Editions/NLB, 1983)
Asch, P. & Seneca, R., *Government and the Marketplace* (Chicago: Dryden Press, 1985)
Axelrod, R., *The Evolution of Cooperation* (Basic Books, New York, 1984)
Ayres, I. & Braithwaite, J., *Responsive Regulation: Transcending the Deregulation Debate* (Oxford University Press, 1992)
Bacard, A., *The Computer Privacy Handbook* (Peachpit Press, 1995)
Bachetta, M. et al., *Electronic Commerce and the Role of the WTO* (Geneve: WTO Publications, 1998)
Barin, B. (Ed.), *Carswell's Handbook of International Dispute Resolution Rules* (Carswell, 1999)
Bedjaoui, M. (Ed.), *International Law: Achievements and Prospects* (Dordrecht-Boston-London, 1991)
Bekkers, V. et al. (Eds.), *Emerging Electronic Highways: New Challenges for Politics and Law* (Kluwer, 1996)
Bermann, G.A. et al., *Cases and Materials on European Community Law* (St. Paul, Minn.: West Publishing, 1993)
Berners-Lee, T. & Fischetti, M., *Weaving the Web: The Original Design and Ultimate Destiny of the World Wide Web by Its Inventor* (Harper San Francisco, 1999)
Bewes, W.A., *The Romance of the Law Merchant* (London: [s.n.], 1923)
Boele-Woelki, K. & Kessedjian, C. (Eds.), *Internet: Which Court Decides? Which Law Applies?* (Kluwer Law International, 1998)
Born, G. & Westin, D., *International Civil Litigation in the United States Courts* (Deventer [etc.]: Kluwer Law and Taxation Publishers, 1993)
Born, G., *International Commercial Arbitration in the United States: Commentary & Materials* (Deventer [etc.]: Kluwer Law and Taxation Publishers, 1994)
——, *International Civil Litigation in the United States Courts* (3rd Ed., Kluwer, 1996)
Boss, A.H. & Ritter, J.B., *Electronic Data Interchange Agreements: A Guide and Sourcebook* (Paris: ICC Publishing, 1993)
Boyle, J., Shamans, *Software and Spleens: Law and the Construction of the Information Society* (Cambridge, MA [etc.]: Harvard University Press, 1996)
Branscomb, A.W. (Ed.), *Toward a Law of Global Communications Networks* (New York: Longman, 1986)
Brilmayer, L., *Conflict of Laws: Foundations and Future Directions* (Boston [etc.]: Little, Brown & Co., 1991)
——, *Conflict of Laws: Cases and Materials* (4th Ed., Aspen, 1995)
Brown, L., *The Reluctant Reformation: On Criticizing the Press in America* (New York, McKay, 1974)

Brownlie, I., *Principles of Public International Law* (5th Ed., Oxford [etc.]: Clarendon Press, 1998)
Cairncross, F., *The Death of Distance: How the Communications Revolution Will Change Our Lives* (Boston, MA: Harvard Business School Press, 1997)
Campbell, D. & Summerfield, P. (Eds.), *Effective Dispute Resolution for the International Commercial Lawyer* (Deventer [etc.]: Kluwer Law and Taxation, 1989)
Carbonneau, T.E., *Alternative Dispute Resolution: Melting the Lances and Dismounting the Steeds* (University of Illinois Press, 1989)
—— (Ed.), *Lex Mercatoria and Arbitration* (Kluwer, 1990)
Cavazos, E.A. & Morin, G., *Cyberspace and the Law: Your Rights and Duties in the On-Line World* (Cambridge, Mass., [etc.]: MIT Press, 1994)
Cavers, D.F., *The Choice-of-Law Process* (University of Michigan Press, Ann Arbor, 1965)
Conley, J. & O'Barr, W., *Just Words: Law, Language, and Power* (Chicago: University of Chicago Press, 1998)
Cook, W.W., *The Logical and Legal Bases of the Conflict of Laws* (Cambridge, Mass., 1942)
Cooper, J. (Ed.), *Liberating Cyberspace* (Pluto Press, London, 1998)
Costantino, C.A. & Merchant, C.S., *Designing Conflict Management Systems: A Guide to Creating Productive and Healthy Organizations* (San Francisco: Jossey Bass 1996)
Craig, W.L. & Paulson, J., *International Chamber of Commerce Arbitration* (2nd Ed., New York: Oceana Publications, 1990)
Currie, B., *Selected Essays on the Conflict of Laws* (Durham, N.C.: Duke University Press, 1963)
De Ly, F., *International Business Law and Lex Mercatoria* (Amsterdam [etc.]: North-Holland, 1992)
Delta, G.B. & Matsuura, J.H., *Law of the Internet* (Aspen Law & Business, New York, 1998)
Dertouzos, M.L., *What Will Be: How the New World of Information Will Change Our Lives* (London: Piatkus, 1997)
Dhokalia, R.P., *The Codification of Public International Law* (Manchester etc.: Manchester University Press etc.; [Dobbs Ferry, N.Y.]: Oceana Publications, 1970)
Dickie, J., *Internet and Electronic Commerce Law in the European Union* (Oxford [etc.]: Hart, 1999)
Diederiks-Verschoor, I.H.Ph., *An Introduction to Space Law* (Kluwer, 1999)
Dyson, E., *Release 2.0: A Design for Living in the Digital Age* (New York: Broadway Books, 1997)
Edwards, L. & Waelde, C., *Law and the Internet* (Hart Publishing, Oxford, 1997)
Ellickson, R.C., *Order Without Law: How Neighbors Settle Disputes* (Cambridge, MA. [etc.]: Harvard University Press, 1991)
Firestone, C.M. & Garmer, A.K. (Eds.), *Digital Broadcasting and the Public Interest: Reports and Papers of the Aspen Institute Communications and Society Program* (The Aspen Institute, Aspen, COL., 1998)
Fuller, L., *The Morality of Law* (New Haven [etc.]: Yale University Press, 1964)
Gates, B., *The Road Ahead* (London: Viking, 1995)
Gelernter, D.H., *Mirror Worlds, or, the Day Software Puts the Universe in a Shoebox . . . How It Will Happen and What It Will Mean* (Oxford University Press, 1991)
Gibson, W., *Neuromancer* (Berkeley Publishing Group, 1984)
Glannon, J.W., *Civil Procedure Examples and Explanation* (2nd Ed., Boston: Little, Brown, 1992)
Goldberg, S.B., Green, E.D. & Sander, F.E.A. (Eds.), *Dispute Resolution* (Little, Brown & Company (Canada) Limited, 1985)
Goodrich, H.F., *Handbook of the Conflict of Laws* (3rd Ed., St. Paul, Minn.: West Publishing Co., 1949)

Grewlich, K.W., *Governance in 'Cyberspace': Access and Public Interest in Global Communications* (Kluwer, 1999)

Grotius, H., *Mare Liberum: Sive, de Iure Quod Batavis Competit ad Indicana Commercia Dissertio* (Lvgdvni Batavorvm: ex officinâ Elzeviriana, 1609)

Hafner, K. & Lyon, M., *Where Wizards Stay Up Late: the Origins of the Internet* (New York: Simon & Schuster, 1996)

Hanley, P., *Internet Regulation: The Way Forward?* (ITC, London, 2000)

Harasim, L.M. (Ed.), *Global Networks: Computers and International Communication* (Cambridge, MA [etc.]: MIT Press, 1993)

Hartley, T.C., *The Foundations of European Community Law: An Introduction to the Constitutional and Administrative Law of the European Community* (Oxford Clarendon Press, 1994)

Henkin, L. et al., *International Law: Cases and Materials* (3rd Ed., St. Paul, MN: West, 1993)

Horwitz, M.J., *The Transformation of American Law* (Cambridge, MA: Harvard University Press, 1977)

Hsu, C. & Pant, S., *Innovative Planning for Electronic Commerce and Enterprises: A Reference Model* (Kluwer, 2000)

Huber, P., *Law and Disorder in Cyberspace* (Oxford University Press, New York, 1997)

Huleatt-James, M. & Gould, N., *International Commercial Arbitration: A Handbook* (2nd Ed., LLP Asia, 1999)

Hunter, M., Marriot, A. & Veeder, (Eds.), *The Internationalization of International Arbitration: The LCIA Centenary Conference* (London: Graham & Trotman, 1995)

Janis, M.W., *An Introduction to International Law* (Boston [etc.]: Little, Brown and CO, 1988)

Jones, T. & Newburn, T., *Private Security and Public Policing* (Clarendon Press, Oxford, 1998)

Jordan, T., *Cyberpower* (Routledge, London, 1999)

Juenger, F.K., *Choice of Law and Multistate Justice* (Dordrecht [etc.]: Nijhoff, 1993)

Kahin, B. & Keller, J.H. (Eds.), *Coordinating the Internet* (Cambridge, MA: The MIT Press, 1997)

Kahin, B. & Nesson, C., *Borders in Cyberspace: Information Policy and the Global Information Infrastructure* (MIT Press, Cambridge, MA, 1997)

Kalakota, R. & Whinston, A.B. (Eds.), *Readings in Electronic Commerce* (Reading, MA [etc.]: Addison-Wesley, 1997)

Katsh, M.E., *The Electronic Media and the Transformation of Law* (Oxford University Press, 1989)

——, *Law in a Digital World* (Oxford University Press, 1995)

Kendall, V., *EC Consumer Law* (London [etc.]: Wiley Chancery, 1995)

Lafleur, E., *The Choice of Laws in the Province of Quebec* (Montreal, 1898)

Laquey, T., *The Internet Companion: A Beginner's Guide to Global Networking* (2nd Ed., Addison-Wesley Publishing Company, 1994)

Lee, J.D. & Lindahl, *Modern Tort Law: Liability & Litigation* (Willmette, IL Callaghan, 1994)

Leflar, R.A., *American Conflict of Law* (3rd Ed., Indianapolis: Bobbs-Merrill Co., 1977)

Lessig, L., *Code and Other Laws of Cyberspace* (New York. Basic Books, 1999)

Levine, J.R. & Baroudi, C., *The Internet for Dummies* (2nd Ed., San Mateo, CA: IDG Books Worldwide, 1994)

Litan, R.E. & Niskanen, W., *Going Digital!* (London: Profile Books, 1998)

Lowenfeld, A.F., *International Litigation and the Quest for Reasonableness* (Oxford: Clarendon Press, 1996)

Mackaay, E., Poulin, D. & Basque, G. (Eds.), *The Electronic Superhighway* (The Hague [etc.]: Kluwer Law International, 1995)

Malanczuk, P., *Akehurst's Modern Introduction to International Law* (Routledge, 7th Ed. 1997)

Mann, C.L., Eckert, S.E. & Knight, S.C., *A Policy Primer: Global Electronic Commerce* (Institute for International Economics, 2000)
Moore, J.W. et al., *Moore's Federal Practice* (3rd Ed., Matthew Bender, 1999)
Nash, T. (Ed.), *Electronic Commerce: Directors and Opportunities for Electronic Business* (London [etc.]: Director Publications [etc.], 1998)
Nathanson, N., *The Law of the Internet* (Butterworths, 1997)
Negroponte, N.P., *Being Digital* (London: Hodder & Stoughton, 1995)
Pallot, M. & Sandoval, V., *Concurrent Enterprising: Toward the Concurrent Enterprise in the Era of the Internet and Electronic Commerce* (Boston: Kluwer Academic Publishers, 1998)
Pennock, J.R. & Chapman, J.W. (Eds.), *Markets and Justice* (New York University Press, 1989)
Penz, G.P., *Consumer Sovereignty and Human Interests* (Cambridge University Press, 1986)
Perritt, Jr., H.H., *Law and the Information Superhighway* (New York [etc.]: John Wiley, 1996)
Petersmann, E.U. & Jaenike, G., *Adjudication of International Trade Disputes in International and National Economic Law* (University Press Fribourg, Switzerland, 1992)
Pike, M.A., *Using the Internet* (2nd Ed., Indianapolis, IN: Que, 1995)
Prechal, S., *Directives in European Community Law* ([S.l.]: Brouwer Uithof, 1995)
Rahman, S.M. & Raisinghani, M.S. (Eds.), *Electronic Commerce: opportunity and Challenges* (IDEA Group Publishing, 2000)
Raisch, M.J. & Shaffer, R.I., *Introduction to Transnational Legal Transactions* (New York 1995)
Reese, W.L.M., et al., *Cases and Materials on Conflict of Laws* (9th Ed., Westbury, New York: Foundation Press, 1990)
Redfern, A. & Hunter, M., *Law and Practice of International Commercial Arbitration* (London, 1991)
Reimann, M., *Conflict of Laws in Western Europe: A Guide Through the Jungle* (Irvington, NY: Transnational Publishers, 1995)
Rheingold, H., *The Virtual Community: Homesteading on the Electronic Frontier* (Reading, Mass. [etc.]: Addison-Wesley, 1993)
Richardson, J. (Ed.), *European Union Power and Policy-Making* (London and New York, Routledge, 1996)
Richman, W.M. & Reynolds, W.L., *Understanding Conflict of Laws* (Matthew Bender & Co., 1984)
Robin, B., Keeler, E. & Miller, R., *Educator's Guide to the Web* (New York: Henry Holt and Company, 1997)
Rosener, J., *Cyberlaw: The Law of the Internet* (London, 1997)
Sanford, B.W., *Libel and Privacy* (2nd Ed., Aspen Law & Business, 1997)
Schott, J. (Ed.), *The WTO after Seattle* (Institute for International Economics, July 2000)
Scoles, E.F. & Hay, P., *Conflict of Laws* (2nd Ed., West Group, 1992)
Shaw, M.N., *International Law* (3rd Ed., Grotius/Cambridge University Press, 1991)
——, Blanning, R., Strader, T. & Whinston, A. (Eds.), *Handbook on Electronic Commerce* (Springer-Verlag, 2000)
Shapiro, A.L., *The Control Revolution: How the Internet is Putting Individuals in Charge and Changing the World We Know* (New York, N.Y.: Public Affairs, 1999)
Shreve, G.R. (Ed.), *A Conflict-of-Laws Anthology* (Cincinnati: Anderson Publishing Co., 1997)
Siebel, T.M. & House, P., *Cyber Rules, Strategies for Excelling at E-Business* (New York [etc.]: Currency/Doubleday, 1999)
Silbey, S.S. & Sarat, A. (Eds.), *Studies in Law, Politics, and Society*, No. 12, (Greenwich, Conn. [etc.]: JAI Press, 1992)
Singer, L.R., *Settling Disputes: Conflict Resolution in Business, Families, and the Legal System* (Boulder, CO: Westview Press, 1994)

Smith, G.J.H., *Internet Law and Regulation* (FT Law and Tax, London, 1996)
Smith, P. & Swann, D., *Protecting the Consumer* (McGraw-Hill, 1979)
Smith, R. (Ed.), *Achieving Civil Justice: Appropriate Dispute Resolution for the 1990s* (Legal Action Group, 1996)
Spanogle, J.A. et al., *Consumer Law: Cases and Materials* (2nd Ed., West, 1991)
Stone, P., *The Conflict of Laws* (London: Longman, 1995)
Storme, M. & de Ly, F. (Eds.), *The Place of Arbitration* (Mys & Breesch, Gent, 1993)
Story, J., *Commentaries on Conflict of Laws* (2nd Ed., London: A. Maxwell, 1841)
Stourzh, G., *Alexander Hamilton and the Idea of Republican Government* (Stanford: Stanford University Press, 1970)
Swire, P. & Litan, R., *None of Your Business: World Data Flows, Electronic Commerce, and the European Privacy Directive* (International Economics/Technology Brookings Institution Press, 1998)
The International Bureau of the Permanent Court of Arbitration (Ed.), *Internationla Alternative Dispute Resolution: Past, Present and Future* (Kluwer, 2000)
Thirlway, H.W.A., *International Customary Law and Codification* (Kluwer, 1972)
Thomsen, H.B. & Wheble, B.S., *Trading with EDI—The Legal Issues* (IBC Financial Books: London, 1989)
Trakman, L.E., *The Law Merchant: The Evolution of Commercial Law* (Littleton, Colo.: Fred B. Rothman & Co., 1983)
Tribe, L.H., *American Constitutional Law* (2nd Ed., Mineola, NY: The Foundation Press, 1988)
Twining, W. (Ed.), *Legal Theory and Common Law* (Basil Blackwell, Oxford, 1986)
Ulmer, E., *Intellectual Property Rights and the Conflict of Laws* (Deventer, Kluwer, 1978)
Ury, W.L., Brett, J.M. & Goldberg, S.B., *Getting Disputes Resolved: Designing Systems to Cut the Costs of Conflict* (Jossey-Bass, Inc., 1988)
Utton, M.A., *The Economics of Regulating Industry* (Basil Blackwell Ltd., Oxford, 1986)
Van den Berg, A.J., *The New York Convention of 1958—Towards a Unification Judicial Interpretation* (Asser/Kluwer-The Hague Deventer, 1981)
Whaley, D.J., *Problems and Materials on Consumer Law* (Little, Brown, 1991)
Wiener, J., *Globalization and the Harmonization of Law* (Pinter: London and New York, 1999)
Wood, G.S., *The Radicalism of the American Revolution* (Knopf, 1992)
Wright, B. & Winn, J.K., *The Law of Electronic Commerce* (3rd Ed., Aspen Publishers, 1999)
Wright, C.A. & Graham, Jr., K.W., *Federal Practice and Procedure: Federal Rules of Evidence* (St. Paul: West, 1980)
Wriston, W., *The Twilight of Sovereignty* (Charles Scribner's Sons, New York, 1992)

3. *Articles*

Aaron, M.C., The Value of Decision Analysis in Mediation Practice, 11 *Negotiation Journal*, 123 (1995)
Abeyratne, R.I.R., Auctions on the Internet of Airline Tickets, 4 *Trolley's Communications Law*, No. 1, 22 (1999)
Acker, R.H., Choice-of-Law Questions in Cyberfraud, *The University of Chicago Legal Forum* 437–469 (1996)
Adam, N.R. et al., The Development and Practice of Law in the Age of the Internet: April 12, 1996, 46 *Am. U.L. Rev.* 327–475 (December 1996)
Adams, J.M., Controlling Cyberspace: Applying the Computer Fraud and Abuse Act to the Internet, 12 *Santa Clara Computer & High Tech. L.J.* 403–434 (August 1996)
Aguilar, J.R., Over the Rainbow European and American Consumer Protection

Policy and Remedy Conflicts on the Internet and a Possible Solution, 4 *Int'l J. Comm. L. & Pol'y* 1–57 (Winter 1999/2000)
Alboukrek, K., Adapting to a New World of E-commerce: The Need for Uniform Consumer Protection in the International Electronic Marketplace, 35 *George Washington International Law Review* 425 (2003)
Allard, N.W. & Kass, D.A., Law and Order in Cyberspace: Washington Report, 19 *Hastings Comm. & Ent. L.J.* 563 (1997)
Allen, W.H. & O'Hara, E.A., Second Generation Law and Economics of Conflict of Laws: Baxter's Comparative Impairment and Beyond, 51 *Stan. L. Rev.* 1011–1048 (May 1999)
Almaguer, A.E. & Baggott III, R.W., Shaping New Legal Frontiers: Dispute Resolution for the Internet, 13 *Ohio St. J. on Disp. Resol.* 711–748 (1998)
Arsic, J., International Commercial Arbitration on the Internet: Has the Future Come Too Early?, 14 *Journal of International Arbitration*, No. 3, 209–221 (1997)
Ashton, P., Using E-Commerce, 3 *Compuship*, No. 7, 32 (January 2000)
Baratta, O.M. & Hanaman, D.L., A Global Update on the Domain Name System and The Law: Alternative Dispute Resolution for Increasing Internet Competition-Oh, the Times They Are a-Changin'!, 8 *Tul. J. Int'l & Comp. L.* 325–390 (Spring 2000)
Barlow, J.P., Crime and Puzzlement: Desperados of the Datasphere, 68 *Whole Earth Rev.* 44–57 (Fall 1990)
Barnett, R., The Sounds of Silence: Default Rules and Contractual Consent, 78 *Va. L. Rev.* 821–911 (May 1992)
Bauchner, J.S., State Sovereignty and the Globalizing Effects of the Internet: A Case Study of the Privacy Debate, 26 *Brooklyn J. Int'l L.* 689–722 (2000)
Baxter, W.F., Choice of Law and the Federal System, 16 *Stanford Law Review* 1 (1963)
Beall, C.P., The Scientological Defenestration of Choice-of-Law Doctrines for Publication Torts on the Internet, 15 *J. Marshall J. Computer & Info. L.* 361–390 (Winter 1997)
Benkler, Y., Internet Regulation: A Case Study in the Problem of Unilateralism, 11 *EJIL* No. 1, 171–185 (2000)
Benson, B.L., The Spontaneous Evolution of Commercial Law, 55 Southern Econ. J. 644 (1989)
Berman, H.J. & Kaufman, C., The Law of International Commercial Transactions (*Lex Mercatoria*), 19 *Harv. Int'l L.J.* 221 (1978)
Berman, P.S., The Globalization of Jurisdiction, 151 *U.Pa. L. Rev.* 422–423 (December 2002)
Bermann, G.A., Taking Subsidiarity Seriously: Federalism in the European Community and the United States, 94 *Columbia Law Review*, 332–456 (March 1994)
Bernstein, L., Opting Out of the Legal System: Extralegal Contractual Relations in the Diamond Industry, 21 *J. Legal Stud.* 115 (1992)
——, Merchant Law in a Merchant Court: Rethinking the Code's Search for Immanent Business Norms, 144 *U. Pa. L. Rev.* 1765–1821 (May 1996)
Bing, J., The Legal Infrastructure for the Trade in networks of Information Services Related to Intellectual Property, 3 *Telecommunications and Space Journal* 83–101 (1996)
Blum, J., The Deep Freeze: Torts, Choice of Law, and the Antarctic Treaty Regime, 8 *Emory Int'l L. Rev.* 667–699 (Fall 1994)
Boddie, II, N.J. et al., A Review of Copyright and the Internet, 20 *Campbell Law Review*, 193–272 (Spring 1998)
Borchers, P.J., The Choice-of-Law Revolution: An Empirical Study, 49 *Wash. & Lee L. Rev.* 357 (1992)
Bordone, R.C., Electronic Online Dispute Resolution: A Systems Approach-Potential, Problems, and a Proposal, 3 *Harv. Negotiation L. Rev.* 175–211 (Spring 1998)

Born, G.B., Reflections on Judicial Jurisdiction in International Cases, 17 *Ga. J. Int'l & Comp. L.* 1 (1987)

Boss, A.H., Electronic Data Interchange Agreements: Private Contracting Toward a Global Environment, 13 *Nw. J. Int'l & Bus.* 31–70 (Spring/Summer 1992)

——, & Winn, J.K., The Emerging Law of Electronic Commerce, 52 *Business Lawyer* 1469 (August 1997)

——, Electronic Commerce and the Symbiotic Relationship Between International and Domestic Law Reform, 72 *Tulane L. Rev.* 1931–1984 (June 1998)

——, The Jurisdiction of Commercial Law: Party Autonomy in Choosing Applicable Law and Forum Under Proposed Revisions to the Uniform Commercial Code, 32 *International Lawyer* 1067 (1998)

——, The Internet and the Law: Searching for Security in the Law of Electronic Commerce, 23 *Nova L. Rev.* 583–624 (Winter 1999)

Bovenzi, G., Liabilities of System Operators on the Internet, 11 *Berkeley Tech. L.J.*, No. 1, 93 (Spring 1996)

Boyle, J., Foucault in Cyberspace: Surveillance, Sovereignty, and Hardwired Censors, 66 *U. Cin. L. Rev.* 177–205 (Fall 1997)

Bradley, C.A., Territorial Intellectual Property Rights in an Age of Globalism, 37 *Va. J. Int'l L.* 505–585 (Winter 1997)

Brady, G.T., Consumer Protection in the European Community: Hope for the Consumer or Unfulfilled Promises?, 23 *N.C.J. Int'l Law & Com. Reg.* 155–199 (Fall 1997)

Brand, R.A., Intellectual Property, Electronic Commerce and the Preliminary Draft Hague Jurisdiction and Judgments Convention, 62 *University of Pittsburgh Law Review*, No. 4, 581–603 (2001)

Branscomb, A.W., Anonymity, Autonomy, and Accountability: Challenges to the First Amendment in Cyberspace, 104 *Yale L.J.* 1639–1679 (May 1995)

Breen, M.N., Personal Jurisdiction and the Internet: "Shoehorning" Cyberspace into International Shoe, 8 *Seton Hall Const. L.J.* 763–814 (Summer 1998)

Brilmayer, L., Interest Analysis and the Myth of Legislative Intent, 78 *Michigan Law Review*, 392 (1980)

——, Consent, Contract, and Territory, 74 *Minn. L. Rev.* 1–35 (October 1989)

——, The Role of Substantive and Choice of Law Policies in the Formation and Applicable of Choice of Law Rules, 252 *Recueil des Cours* 9 (1995)

Brown, J.E., New Law for the Internet, 28 *Ariz. St. L.J.* 1243–1258 (Winter 1996)

——, Jurisdiction to Prosecute Crimes Committed by Use of the Internet, 38 *Jurimetrics Journal* 611–616 (Summer 1998)

Budnitz, M.E., Arbitration of Disputes Between Consumers and Financial Institutions: A Serious Threat to Consumer Protection, 10 *Ohio St. J. on Disp. Resol.* 267–342 (1995)

Burk, D.L., Patents in Cyberspace: Territoriality and Infringement on Global Computer Networks, 68 *Tulane Law Review*, 1–24 (1993)

——, Transborder Intellectual Property Issues on the Electronic Frontier, 6 *Stan. L. & Pol'y Rev.* 9–15 (1994)

——, Trademarks Along the Infobahn: A First Look at the Emerging Law of *Cybermarks, 1 Rich. J.L. & Tech.* 1 (1995)

——, Federalism in Cyberspace, 28 *Conn. L. Rev.* 1095–1136 (Summer 1996)

——, Jurisdiction in a World Without Borders, 1 *Va. J.L. & Tech.* 3 (Spring 1997)

——, Trademark Doctrines for Global Electronic Commerce, 49 *S.C.L. Rev.* 733 (1998)

——, Virtual Exit in the Global Information Economy, 73 *Chi-Kent L. Rev.* 943–995 (1998)

Burmeister, K., Jurisdiction, Choice of Law, Copyright, and the Internet: Protection Against Framing in an International Setting, 9 *Fordham I.P., Media & Ent. L.J.* 625–723 (Winter 1999)

Burnstein, M.R., Conflicts on the Net: Choice of Law in Transnational Cyberspace, 29 *Vand. J. Transnat'l L.* 75–116 (1996)
Byford, K.S., Privacy in Cyberspace: Constructing a Model of Privacy for the Electronic Communications Environment, 24 *Rutgers Computer & Tech. L.J.* 1–74 (1998)
Campbell, A.J., Self-Regulation and the Media, 51 *Federal Communications Law Journal* 711–772 (May 1999)
Carbonneau, T.E., Arbitral Adjudication: A Comparative Assessment of Its Remedial and Substantive Status in Transnational Commerce, 19 *Tex. Int'l L.J.* 33 (1984)
Carrington, P.D., Regulating Dispute Resolution Provisions in Adhesion Contracts, 35 *Harv. J. on Legis.* 225 (1998)
——, Virtual Civil Litigation: A Visit to John Bunyan's Celestial City, 98 *Colum. L. Rev.* 1516–1537 (October 1998)
Casey, T.D., & Magenau, J., A Hybrid Model of Self-Regulation and Governmental Regulation of Electronic Commerce, 19 *Santa Clara Computer & High Technology Law Journal* 1 (December 2002)
Cate, F.H., The Challenge for the United States: The E.U. Data Protection Directive, Information Privacy, and the Public Interest, 80 *Iowa L. Rev.* 431–443 (March 1995)
——, Law in Cyberspace, 39 *How. L.J.* 565–579 (Winter 1996)
——, Sovereignty and the Globalization of Intellectual Property, 6 *Ind. J. Global Legal Stud.* 1–9 (Fall 1998)
Cavers, D.F., A Critique of the Choice of Law Problem, 47 *Harv. L. Rev.* 173 (1933)
Caviedes, A.A., International Copyright Law: Should the European Union Dictate Its Development?, 16 *B.U. Int'l L. J.* 165–229 (Spring 1998)
Chase, A., A Primer on Recent Domain Name Disputes, 3 *Va. J.L. & Tech.* 3, (Spring 1998)
Cheatham, K., Negotiating a Domain Name Dispute: Problem Solving v. Competitive Approaches, 7 *Willamette J. Int'l L. & Dispute Resolution* 33–100 (2000)
Chiappetta, V., The Impact of E-Commerce on the Laws of Nations Forward, 7 *Willamette J. Int'l L. & Dispute Resolution* 1–9 (2000)
Chon, M., Internet Law Symposium: Introduction, 20 *Seattle Univ. L.Rev.* 613–618 (Spring 1997)
Chow, S.Y., UCITA: A 1990's Vision of E-Commerce, 18 *J. Marshall J. of Computer & Info. Law,* No. 2, 323–364 (2000)
Clift, J., Electronic Commerce: the UNCITRAL Model Law and Electronic Equivalents to Traditional Bills of Lading, 27 *International Business Lawyer*, No. 7, 311–316 (July/August 1999)
Coase, R.H., The Problem of Social Cost, 3 *Journal of Law & Economics* 1 (1960)
Cobb, S. & Rifkin, J., Practice and Paradox: Deconstructing Neutrality in Mediation, 16 *Law & Social Inquiry*, No. 1, 25–63 (1991)
Cohen, B., A Proposed Regime for Copyright Protection on the Internet, 22 *Brooklyn J. Int'l L.* 401–435 (1996)
Cohen, J.E., Lochner in Cyberspace: The New Economic Orthodoxy of "Right Management", 97 *Mich. L. Rev.* 462–563 (November 1998)
Cohen, S., Jurisdiction over Cross Border Internet Infringements, 20 *European Intellectual Property Review* 294–297 (1998)
Cona, F.A., Application of Online Systems in Alternative Dispute Resolution, 45 *Buff. L. Rev.* 975–999 (Fall 1997)
Connellan, J., Regulators Face up to Ecommerce Uncertainty, *Telecommunications (International Edition)*, 35–37 (January 2000)
Conner, C.L., *Compuserve v. Patterson*: Creating Jurisdiction through Internet Contacts, 4 *Rich. J.L. & Tech.* 9 (Spring 1998)
Cooter, R.D., Against Legal Centrism, 81 *Cal. L. Rev.* 417–429 (January 1993)

——, The Theory of Market Modernization of Law, 16 Int'l Rev. L. & Econ. 141 (1996)

——, Decentralized Law for a Complex Economy: The Structural Approach to Adjudicating the New Law Merchant, 144 *U. Pa. L. Rev.* 1643–1696 (May 1996)

Craig, W.L., Some Trends and Developments in the Laws and Practice of International Commercial Arbitration, 30 *Tex. Int'l L.J.* 1–58 (Winter 1995)

Craswell, R., Offer, Acceptance, and Efficient Reliance, 48 *Stan. L. Rev.* 481–553 (February 1996)

Currie, On the Displacement of the Law of the Forum, 58 *Columbia Law Review* 964 (1958)

Dane, P., Vested Rights, "Vestedness", and Choice of Laws, 96 *Yale L.J.* 1191–1275 (May 1987)

Danilenko, G.M. & Lauterpacht, H., Codification and Development of International Law, 49 *AJIL* 16 (1955)

Danilenko, G.M., The Concept of the "Common Heritage of Mankind" in International Law, 13 *Annals of Air & Space Law* 247 (1988)

David, R., The International Unification of Private Law 2 *International Encyclopedia of Comparative Law* 8 (1969)

Davis, C.N., Personal Jurisdiction in Online Expression Cases: Rejecting Minimum Contacts in Favor of Affirmative Acts, 14 *International Review of Law Computer & Technology*, No. 1, 43–54 (2000)

Davis, E.B., A Look at One of the Most Popular Services in Cyberspace: Usenet, 42 *Federal Lawyer* 15 (July 1995)

Delacourt, J.T., The International Impact of Internet Regulation, 38 *Harvard International Law Journal*, No. 1, 207–235 (Winter 1997)

Delaume, G., Comparative Analysis as a Basis of Law in State Contracts: The Myth of the *Lex Mercatoria*, 63 *Tulane Law Review*, 575–611 (February 1989)

Dellapenna, J.W., Law in a Shrinking World: The Interaction of Science and Technology with International Law, 88 *Ky. L.J.* 809–883 (Summer 1999/Summer 2000)

Dennis, E.E., Internal Examination: Self-Regulation and the American Media, 13 *Cardozo Arts & Ent. L.J.* 697–704 (1995)

DeSaussure, H. & Haanappel, P.P.C., A Unified Multinational Approach to the Application of Tort and Contract Principles to Outer Spaces, 6 *Syracuse J. International L. & Com.*, No. 1, 12 (Summer 1978)

Donahey, M.S., Dispute Resolution in Cyberspace, 15 *Journal of International Arbitration*, No. 4, 127–168 (1998)

Dreben, R.N. & Werbach, J.L., Top 10 Things to Consider in Developing an Electronic Commerce Web Site, 16 *Computer Lawyer*, No. 5, 17 (1999)

Driscoll, J.M., It's a Small World After All: Conflict of Laws and Copyright Infringement on the Information Superhighway, 20 *U. Pa. J. Int'l Econ. L.* 939–986 (Winter 1999)

Dunne, R.L., Deterring Unauthorized Access to Computers: Controlling Behavior in Cyberspace through a Contract Law Paradigm, 35 *Jurimetrics Journal*, No. 1, 2 (Fall 1994)

Easterbrook, F.H., Cyberspace and the Law of the Horse, *U. Chi. Legal F.* 207 (1996)

Edelstein, J.I., Anonymity and International Law Enforcement in Cyberspace, 7 *Fordham Intell. Prop. Media & Ent. L.J.* 231–294 (Fall 1996)

Eisenberg, M.A., Expression Rules in Contract Law and Problems of Offer and Acceptance, 82 *Cal. L. Rev.* 1127–1180 (October 1994)

Elkin-Koren, N., Copyright Law and Social Dialogue on the Information Superhighway: the Case Against Copyright Liability of Bulletin Board Operators, 13 *Cardozo Arts & Ent. L.J.* 3445 (1995)

——, Copyright Policy and the Limits of Freedom of Contract, 12 *Berkeley Tech. L.J.* 93 (1997)
Eltman, J., A Peace Zone on the High Seas: Managing the Commons for Equitable Use, 5 *Int'l Legal Persp.* 47 (1993)
Ely, J.H., Choice of Law and the State's Interest in Protecting Its Own, 23 *Wm. & Mary L. Rev.* 173 (1981)
Endeshaw, A., The Proper Law of Electronic Commerce, 7 *Information and Communications Technology Law*, No. 1, 5–14 (March 1998)
Epstein, K.J. & Tancer, B., Enforcement of Use Limitations By Internet Services Providers: "How to Stop that Hacker, Cracker, Spammer, Spoofer, Flamer, Bomber", 9 *Hastings Comm/Ent. L.J.* 661 (1997)
Evans, R., Time for Action: EU Consumer Policy, 4 *Consumer Policy Review* 18 (1994)
Faucette, J.E., The Freedom of Speech at Risk in Cyberspace: Obscenity Doctrine and a Frightened University's Censorship of Sex on the Internet, 44 *Duke L.J.* 1155–1182 (April 1995)
Faucher, J.D., Let the Chips Fall Where They May: Choice of Law in Computer Bulletin Board Defamation Cases, 26 *U.C. Davis L. Rev.* 1045–1078 (Summer 1993)
Feeley, M.J., EU Internet Regulation Policy: The Rise of Self-Regulation, 22 *B.C. Int'l & Comp. L. Rev.* 159–174 (Winter 1999)
Fidler, D.P., Challenging the Classical Concept of Custom: Perspectives on the Future of Customary International Law, 39 *German Yearbook of International Law* 198 (1996)
Fischer, J.C., Policing the Self-Help Legal Market: Consumer Protection or Protection of the Legal Cartel?, 34 *Ind. L. Rev.* 121–153 (2000)
Fitzmaurice, K.M. & Mody, R.N., International Shoe Meets the World Wide Web: Whither Personal Jurisdiction in Florida in the Age of the Internet?, 71 *Fla. B.J.* 22 (1997)
Flaming, T.H., The Rules of Cyberspace: Informal Law in a New Jurisdiction, 85 *Ill. B.J.* 174 (April, 1997)
Flint, D., Much Confusion in Cyberspace—A Personal View of the Proposals for Internet Regulation, 19 *Business Law Review*, No. 5, 112–115 (May 1998)
——, European Initiatives—A Progress (?) Report, 20 *Business Law Review*, No. 7, 184–186 (July 1999)
Fraser, S., The Copyright Battle: Emerging International Rules and Roadblocks on the Global Information Infrastructure, 15 *J. Marshall J. Computer & Info. L.* 759–818 (Summer 1997)
Frendo, M., Legal Aspects of E-Commerce, 32 *Law/Technology, The World Jurist Association*, No. 4, 1–30 (1999)
Frieden, R., Does a Hierarchical Internet Necessitate Multilateral Intervention?, 26 *N.C.J. Int'l Law & Com. Reg.* 361–405 (Spring 2001)
Friedman, G., & Gellman, R., An Information Superhighway "On Ramp" for Alternative Dispute Resolution, 68 *N.Y. St. Bus. J.* 38–39 (May-June 1996)
Froomkin, A.M., The Essential Role of Trusted Third Parties in Electronic Commerce, 75 *Oregon L. Rev.* 49 (1996)
——, The Legal and Policy Framework for Global Electronic Commerce: A Progress Report of Governments and Governance, 14 *Berkeley Tech. L.J.* 617 (Spring 1999)
——, Wrong Turn in Cyberspace: Using ICANN to Route Around the APA and the Constitution, 50 *Duke L.J.* 17–157 (October 2000)
——, Habermas@Discourse.net: Toward a Critical Theory of Cyberspace, 116 *Harvard Law Review* 749 (January 2003)
Fulton, A.M., Cyberspace and the Internet: Who Will be the Privacy Policy?, 3 *Commlaw Conspectus* 63 (1995)
Gaillard, E., Resolution of Consumer Disputes: A New Trend?, *New York Law Journal* (December 4, 1997)

Galanter, M., The Legal Malaise: Or, Justice Observed, 19 *Law and Society Review*, 537 (1985)

Gale, J.S., Service Over the "Net": Principles of Contract Law in Conflict, 49 *Case Western Reserve Law Review* 567 (Spring 1999)

Gamble, J.K., International Law and the Information Age, 17 *Mich. J. Int'l L.* 747 (1996)

Gassman, G.L., Internet Defamation: Jurisdiction in Cyberspace and the Public Figure Doctrine, 14 *J. Marshall J. of Computer & Info. L.* 563–593 (1996)

Gaumer, C.P., Conflicts, the Constitution, and the Internet, 86 *Ill. B.J.* 502 (September 1998)

Gautier, K., Electronic Commerce: Confronting the Legal Challenge of Building E-Dentities in Cyberspace, 20 *Miss. C.L. Rev.* 117–163 (Fall 1999)

Gaylord, J.E., State Regulatory Jurisdiction and the Internet: Letting the Dormant Commerce Clause Lie, 52 *Vand. L. Rev.* 1095–1130 (May 1999)

Geist, M.A., The Reality of Bytes: Regulating Economic Activity in the Age of the Internet, 73 *Wash. L. Rev.* 521–574 (July 1998)

Gibbons, L.J., No Regulation, Government Regulation, or Self-Regulation: Social Enforcement or Social Contracting for Governance in Cyberspace, 6 *Cornell J.L. & Pub. Pol'y* 475–551 (Spring 1997)

——, Rusticum Judicium? Private "Courts" Enforcing Private Law and Rights: Regulating Virtual Arbitration in Cyberspace, 24 *Ohio N.U. L. Rev.* 769–794 (1998)

Gibson, C., Digital Dispute Resolution: Internet Domain Names and WIPO's Role, *Computer Und Recht International*, No. 2, 33–39 (2001)

Gigante, A., Blackhole in Cyberspace: The Legal Void in the Internet, 15 *Journal of Computer & Information Law*, No. 3, 413–436 (1997)

Ginsburg, J.C., Global Use/Territorial Rights: Private International Law Questions of the Global Information Infrastructure, 42 *J. Copyright Society U.S.A.* 318 (1995)

——, Copyright Without Borders? Choice of Forum and Choice of Law for Copyright Infringement in Cyberspace, 15 *Cardozo Arts & Entertainment Law Journal* 153 (1997)

——, The Cyberian Captivity of Copyright: Territoriality and Authors' Rights in a Networked World, 15 *Santa Clara Computer & High Technology Law Journal* 347–361 (May 1999)

Giordano, P., Invoking Law as a Basis for Identity in Cyberspace, *Stanford Technology Law Review* 1 (1998)

Gliniecki, J.Y. & Ogada, C.G., The Legal Acceptance of Electronic Documents, Writings, Signatures, and Notices in International Transportation Conventions: A Challenge in the Age of Global Electronic Commerce 13 *J. Int'l. L. & Bus.* 117–158 (Spring/Summer, 1992)

Goldsmith, J.L., Regulation of the Internet: Three Persistent Fallacies, 73 *Chi.-Kent L. Rev.* 1119–1131 (1998)

——, Against Cyberanarchy, 65 *University of Chicago Law Review* 1199–1250 (Fall 1998)

——, The Internet and the Abiding Significance of Territorial Sovereignty, 5 *Ind. J. Global Legal Stud.* 475–491 (Spring 1998)

——, Unilateral Regulation of the Internet: A Modest Defence, 11 *EJIL* No. 1, 135–148 (2000)

Golsong, H., A Guide to Procedural Issues in International Arbitration, 18 *International Lawyer* 633 (1984)

Gordon, W.J., On the Economics of Copyright, Restitution, and "Fair Use": Systematic Versus Case-by-Case Responses to Market Failure, 8 *J.L. & Info. Sci.* 7 (1997)

Gore, A., Bringing Information to the World: The Global Information Infrastructure, 9 *Harv. J.L. & Tech.* 1 (Winter 1996)

Gorove, S., Interpreting Article II of the Outer Space Treaty, 37 *Fordham L. Rev.* 349 (1969)

Gotts, I.K. & Rutenberg, A.D., Navigating the Global Information Superhighway: A Bumpy Road Lies Ahead, 8 *Harvard Journal of Law and Technology* 275–344 (Spring, 1995)

Greenwood, D.J. & Campbell, R.A., Electronic Commerce Legislation: From Written on Paper and Signed in Ink to Electronic Records and Online Authentication, 53 *Bus. Lawyer*, No. 1, 307–338 (November, 1997)

Gregoire, C., Law Enforcement Challenges in Cyberspace, 34 *Prosecutor* 29 (September-October 2000)

Grosso, A., The National Information Infrastructure, 41 *Fed. B. News & J.* 481 (1994)

Grundfest, J., Internationalization of the World's Securities Markets: Economics Causes and Regulatory Consequences, 4 *J. Fin. Svcs. Res.* 349 (1990)

Guibault, I., Canada: New Legislation on E-commerce Underway, *Computer Und Recht International*, No. 1, 25–26 (2001)

Gurry, F., The Dispute Resolution Services of the World Intellectual Property Organization, 2 *Journal of International Economic Law*, No. 2, 385–398 (1999)

Guthrie, N., A Good Place to Shop: Choice of Forum and the Conflict of Laws, 27 *Ottawa Law Review* 201 (1995)

Hachigian, N., Essential Mutual Assistance in International Antitrust Enforcement, 29 *International Lawyer* 117 (Spring 1995)

Hang, L.Q., Online Dispute Resolution Systems: the Future of Cyberspace Law, 41 *Santa Clara L. Rev.* 837–866 (2001)

Hanley, S.M., International Internet Regulation: A Multinational Approach, 16 *J. Marshall J. of Computer & Info. L.*, No. 4, 997–1024 (1998)

Hardy, I.T., Electronic Communications and Legal Change: Electronic Conferences: The Report of an Experiment, 6 *Harv. J. Law and Tech.* 213–235 (Spring 1993)

——, The Proper Legal Regime for "Cyberspace", 55 *University of Pittsburgh Law Review* 993–1055 (1994)

——, Property (and Copyright) in Cyberspace, *U. Chi. Legal F.* 217–260 (Fall 1996)

Harper, F.V., Policy Bases of the Conflict of Laws: Reflections on Rereading Professor Lorenzen's Essays, 56 *Yale L.J.* 1155 (1947)

Hauser, H. & Wunsch-Vincent, S., A Call for a WTO E-Commerce Initiative, 6 *Int'l J. Comm. L. & Pol'y* 1–30 (Winter 2000/2001)

Hayford, S.L., Commercial Arbitration in the Supreme Court 1983–1995: A Sea Change, 31 *Wake Forest L. Rev.* 1–39 (Spring 1996)

Heim, B.E., Exploring the Last Frontiers for Mineral Resources: A Comparison of International Law Regarding the Deep Seabed, Outer Space, and Antarctica, 23 *Vand. J. Transnat'l L.* 819 (1990)

Heiskanen, V., Dispute Resolution in International Electronic Commerce, 16 *Journal of International Arbitration*, No. 3, 29–44 (1999)

Herscha, L.A., Is There a Doctor in the House? Licensing and Malpractice Issues Involved in Telemedicine, 2 *B.U.J. Sci. & Tech. L.* 8 (1996)

Highet, K., The Enigma of the *Lex Mercatoria*, 63 *Tulane Law Review* 613–628 (February 1989)

Hill, J.S. & Brazier, J.E., Constraining Administrative Decisions: A Critical Examination of the Structure and Process Hypothesis, 7 *Journal of Law, Economics & Organization*, No. 2, 373–400 (1991)

Hill, R. & Walden, I., The Draft UNCITRAL Model Law for Electronic Commerce: Issues and Solutions, 13 *Computer Lawyers*, No. 3, 18 (March 1996)

Hill, R., Electronic Commerce, The World-Wide Web, Minitel, and EDI, 13 *The Information Society*, No. 1, 33–41 (January-March 1997)

——, The Internet, Electronic Commerce and Dispute Resolution: Comments, 14 *Journal of International Arbitration*, No. 4, 103–110 (1997)

Hoegle, R.L. & Boam, C.P., The Internet and Jurisdiction: International Principles

Emerge but Confrontation Looms, 3 *Journal of World Intellectual Property*, No. 1, 31–50 (January 2000)

Horlick, G., Dispute Resolution Mechanism: Will the United States Play by the Rules?, 29 *JWT*, No. 2, 163–171 (1995)

Hughes, J., The Internet and the Persistence of Law, 44 *B.C.L. Rev.* 359 (March 2003)

Hunter, D., Cyberspace as Place and the Tragedy of the Digital Anticommons, 91 *California Law Review* 439 (March 2003)

Ingrim, C.L., Choice-of-Law Clauses: Their Effect on Extraterritorial Analysis-A Scholar's Dream, A Practitioner's Nightmare, 28 *Creighton Law Review* 663–682 (April 1995)

Jacques, S.C., *Reno v. ACLU*: Insulating the Internet, the First Amendment, and the Marketplace of Ideas, 46 *Am. U. L. Rev.* 1945 (1997)

Jasentuliyana, N., Space Law and the United Nations, 17 *Annals of Air & Space Law* 137 (1992)

Johns, M., The First Amendment and Cyberspace: Trying to Teach Old Doctrines New Tricks, 64 *U. Cin. L. Rev.* 1383–1437 (Summer 1996)

Johnson, D.R. & Marks, K.A., Mapping Electronic Data Communications onto Existing Legal Metaphors: Should We Let Our Conscience (and Our Contracts) Be Our Guide?, 38 *Vill. L. Rev.* 487–515 (1993)

Johnson, D.R. & Post, D.G., Law and Borders—The Rise of Law in Cyberspace, 48 *Stanford Law Review* 1357–1402 (May 1996)

Johnson, D.R., Due Process and Cyberjurisdiction, 2 *J. Computer-Mediated Comm.* (June 1996)

Johnson-Laird, A., The Anatomy of the Internet Meets the Body of Law, 22 *University of Dayton Law Review*, No. 3, 465–509 (1997)

Joseph, J.A., The Law at Your Fingertips: Practical Applications of the Law on the Internet, 18 *T. Jefferson L. Rev.* 53–60 (Spring 1996)

Joyner, C.C., Legal Implications of the Concept of the Common Heritage of Mankind, 35 *Int'l & Comp. L.Q.* 190 (1986)

Jueneman, R.R. & Robertson, Jr., R.J., Biometrics and Digital Signatures in Electronic Commerce, 38 *Jurimetrics Journal* 427 (1998)

Juenger, F.K., Choice of Law in Interstate Torts, 118 *U. Pa. L. Rev.* 202 (1969)

——, Conflict of Laws: A Critique of Interest Analysis, 32 *American Journal of Comparative Law* 48 (1984)

——, Mass Disaster and the Conflict of Laws, *University of Illinois Law Review*, No. 1, 105 (Spring 1989)

Kaplan, L.G.C. & Bankoff, J.R., Of Satellites and Copyrights: Problems of Overspill and Choice of Law, 7 *Emory International Law Review* 727 (1993)

Kaplan, N., Is the Need for Writing as Expressed in the New York Convention and the Model Law out of Step with Commercial Practice?, 12 *Arbitration International* 27 (1996)

Karamon, M.C., ADR on the Internet, 11 *Ohio St. J. on Disp. Resol.* 537–548 (1996)

Katsh, E., Law in a Digital World: Computer Networks and Cyberspace, 38 *Vill. L. Rev.* 403 (1993)

——, Dispute Resolution in Cyberspace, 28 *Conn. L. Rev.* 953–980 (Summer 1996)

——, Rifkin, J. & Gaitenby, A., E-Commerce, E-Disputes, and E-Dispute Resolution: In the Shadow of "eBay Law", 15 *Ohio St. J. on Disp. Resol.* 705–734 (2000)

——, The New Frontier: Online ADR Becoming a Global Priority, *Disp. Resol. Mag.*, 6–8 (Winter 2000)

——, Online Dispute Resolution: Some Lessons from the E-Commerce Revolution, 28 *N. Ky. L. Rev.* 810–821 (2001)

Katz, A., The Strategic Structure of Offer and Acceptance: Game Theory and the Law of Contract Formation, 89 *Mich. L. Rev.* 215–295 (November 1990)

Katz, L., Jurisdiction and E-Commerce Disputes, 3 *Journal of World Intellectual Property*, No. 2, 289–306 (March 2000)

Kaufman, I.J., The Domain Name System: Dispute Resolution and the Nice Classification System, 28 *International Business Lawyer*, No. 1, 35–41 (January 2000)

Kay, H.H., Theory into Practice: Choice of Law in the Courts, 34 *Mercer Law Review* 521 (1983)

Kay, J., Sexuality, Live Without a Net: Regulating Obscenity and Indecency on the Global Network, 4 *S. Cal. Interdisciplinary L.J.* 355–389 (Winter 1995)

Keefe, H., Making the Final Frontier Feasible: A Critical Look at the Current Body of Outer Space Law, 11 *Santa Clara Computer & High Tech. L.J.* 345–371 (July 1995)

Kelly & Hieber, Untangling a Web of Minimum Contacts: The Internet and Personal Jurisdiction in Trademark and Unfair Competition Cases, 18 *The Trademark Reporter*, No. 5, 576 (1997)

Kidd, Jr., D.L., Casting the Net: Another Confusing Analysis of Personal Jurisdiction and Internet Contacts in Telco Communications v. An Apple a Day, 32 *University of Richmond Law Review*, 505–543 (March 1998)

Kirby, M., Legal Aspects of Transborder Data Flows, 9 Computer/L. J. 233 (1991)

Kleinwaechter, W., ICANN Governance: From Self-Governanceto Public-Private Partnership: The Changing Role of Governments in the Management of the Internet's Core Resources, 36 *Loyola of Los Angeles Law Review* 1103 (Spring 2003)

Knoll, A., Any Which Way But Loose: Nations Regulate the Internet, 4 *Tul. J. Int'l & Comp. L.* 275–301 (Summer 1996)

Kohona, P.T.B., Dispute Resolution under the World Trade Organization: An Overview, 28 *JWT*, No. 2, 23–47 (1994)

Komuro, N., The WTO Dispute Settlement Mechanism: Coverage and Procedures of the WTO Understanding, 29 *JWT*, No. 4, 5–95 (1995)

Korn, H.L., Development of Judicial Jurisdiction in the United States, 65 *Brooklyn L. Rev.* 935–1001 (Winter 1999)

Kozyris, P.J., Values and Methods in Choice of Law for Products Liability: A Comparative Comment on Statutory Solutions, 38 *American Journal of Comparative Law* 475 (1990)

Kramer, L., Rethinking Choice of Law, 90 Colum. L. Rev. 277–345 (1990)

Krasner, S.D., Global Communications and National Power: Life on the Pareto Frontier, 43 *World Politics*, No. 3, 336–366 (April 1991)

Krasovec, J., Cyberspace: The Final Frontier, for Regulation? 31 *Akron L. Rev.* 101–145 (1997)

Kreimer, S.F., The Source of Law in Civil Rights Actions: Some Old Light on Section 1988, 133 *U. Pa. L. Rev.* 601–633 (March 1985)

Kronstein, H., Arbitration Is Power, 38 *N.Y.U.L. Rev.* 661 (1963)

Krueger, R.T., Traditional Notions of Fair Play and Substantial Justice Lost in Cyberspace: Personal Jurisdiction and On-Line Defamatory Statements, 51 *Cath. U.L. Rev.* 301–334 (Fall 2001)

Kuklin, B., On the Knowing Inclusion of Unenforceable Contract and Lease Terms, 56 *U. Cin. L. Rev.* 845–918 (1988)

Lachs, M., Views from the Bench: Thoughts on Science, Technology and World Law, 86 *AJIL* 673 (October 1992)

LaMarche, G., International Free Expression Principles in Cyberspace, 17 *Whittier L. Rev.* 279–284 (Winter 1995)

Landry, E.M., Scrolling Around the New Organization: The Potential for Conflict in the On-Line Environment, 16 *Negotiation Journal*, No. 2, 133–142 (April 2000)

Lazzaretti, A., Internet Regulation and On-Line Gambling: A Brief Study of the US and EU Legal Systems, 31 *Law/Technology, World Jurist Association*, No. 4, 1–30 (1998)

Lee, C.S., The Development of Arbitration in the Resolution of Internet Domain Name Disputes, 7 *Rich. J.L. & Tech.* 2 (Fall 2000)
Lee, T.R., In *Rem* Jurisdiction in Cyberspace, 75 *Washington Law Review*, No. 1, 97–145 (2000)
Lehmann, M., Electronic Commerce and Consumer Protection in Europe, 17 *Santa Clara Computer & High Tech. L.J.* 101–114 (December 2000)
Lemley, M.A., Dealing With Overlapping Copyrights on the Internet, 22 *U. Dayton L. Rev.* 547–585 (Spring 1997)
——, The Economics of Improvement in Intellectual Property Law, 75 *Tex. L. Rev.* 989–1084 (April 1997)
——, The Law and Economics of Internet Norms, 73 *Chi.-Kent. L. Rev.* 1257–1294 (1998)
——, Beyond Preemption: The Law and Policy of Intellectual Property Licensing, 87 *Calif. L. Rev.* 111–172 (January 1999)
——, Standardizing Government Standard-Setting Policy for Electronic Commerce, 14 *Berkeley Tech. L.J.*745–758 (Spring 1999)
Lessig, L., The Path of Cyberlaw, 104 *Yale Law Journal* 1743–1755 (1995)
——, The Zones of Cyberspace, 48 *Stan. L. Rev.* 1403–1411 (May 1996)
——, Reading the Constitution in Cyberspace, 45 *Emory L.J.* 869–910 (Summer 1996)
——, The Law of the Horse: What Cyberlaw Might Teach, 113 *Harvard Law Review* 501–549 (1999)
——, The Limits in Open Code: Regulatory Standards and the Future of the Net, 14 *Berkeley Tech. L.J.* 759–769 (Spring 1999)
Lester, T.P., Globalized Automatic Choice of Forum: Where Do Internet Consumers Sue?: Proposed Article 7 of the Hague Convention on International Jurisdiction and Foreign Judgments in Civil and Commercial Matters and its Possible Effects on e-Commerce, 9 *New England Journal of International and Comparative Law* 431–488 (2003)
Levie, J.H., Trade Usage and Custom Under the Common Law and Uniform Commercial Code, 40 *N.Y.U.L. Rev.* 1101 (1965)
Li, C., Tentative Discussion on the Challenge of the Internet Against Traditional Conflict of Laws, 11 *Legal Science* 52–54 (1999)
Lide, E.C., ADR and Cyberspace: The Role of Alternative Dispute Resolution in Online Commerce, Intellectual Property and Defamation, 12 *Ohio St. J. on Disp. Resol.* 193–222 (1996)
Litan, R.E., Law and Policy in the Age of the Internet, 50 *Duke L.J.* 1045–1085 (February 2001)
Litman, J., The Exclusive Right to Read, 13 *Cardozo Arts & Ent. L.J.*, 29–54 (1994)
Lock, D., Toll-Free Vanity Telephone Numbers: Structuring a Trademark registration And Dispute Settlement Regime, 87 *Calif. L. Rev.* 371–419 (March 1999)
Long, III, G.P., Who are You?: Identity and Anonymity in Cyberspace, 55 *U. Pitt. L. Rev.* 1177–1213 (Summer, 1994)
Loren, L.P., Redefining the Market Failure Approach to Fair Use in an Era of Copyright Permission Systems, 5 *J. Intell. Prop. L.* 1–58 (Fall 1997)
Loundy, D.J., A Primer on Trademark Law and Internet Addresses, 15 *J. Marshall J. Computer & Info. L.* 465–491 (Spring 1997)
Love, M., International Jurisdiction over the Internet: A Case Analysis of Yahoo!, Inc. v. La Ligue Contre le Racisme et L'antisemitisme, 17 *Temple International and Comparative Law Journal* 261–275 (Spring 2003)
Lubitz, M., Jurisdiction and Choice of Law for Electronic Contracts: an English Perspective, *Computer Und Recht International*, No. 2, 39–45 (2001)
Lucas, J.B., IAHC Announces New Top-Level Domains: Recommends New Challenge Procedures, 2 *BNA's Elec. Info. Pol'y & L. Rep.* 152 (February 7, 1997)

Lui-Kwan, K. & Opsahl, K., The Legal and Policy Framework for Global Electronic Commerce: A Progress Report, 14 *Berkeley Tech. L.J.* 503–518 (Spring 1999)

Macduff, I., Flames on the Wires: Mediating from an Electronic Cottage, 10 *Negotiation Journal* 5–13 (January 1994)

Macintosh, K.L., The New Money, 14 *Berkeley Tech. L.J.* 659–673 (Spring 1999)

Madden, R., Developments in the Electronic Courtroom, 6 *International Yearbook of Law Computer and Technology* 203–208 (1992)

Maggs, G.E., Internet Solutions to Consumer Protection Problems, 49 *S.C. L. Rev.* 887–902 (Summer 1998)

Maltz, E.M., Unraveling the Conundrum of the Law of Personal Jurisdiction: A Comment on *Asahi Mental Industry Co. v. Superior Court of California, Duke Law Journal* 669 (September 1987)

Mann, C.L., The Uniform Computer Information Transactions Act and Electronic Commerce: Balancing Issues and Overlapping Jurisdiction in the Global Electronic Marketplace: The UCITA Example, 8 *Washington University Journal of Law & Policy* 215 (2002)

Marcus, R.L., Completing Equity's Conquest? Reflections on the Future of Trial Under the Federal Rules of Civil Procedure, 50 *U. Pitt. L. Rev.* 725–788 (Spring 1989)

Margiano, R., The Ninth Circuit Holds that Internet Domain Name E-mail And Web Service Provider is not a Cybersquatter for Trademark Dilution Purposes, *Avery Dennison Corp. v. Sumpton, The Journal of Information, Law and Technology*, No. 3 (1999)

Mayer, F.C., Europe and the Internet: The Old World and the New Medium, 11 *EJIL* No. 1, 149–169 (2000)

Mayer-Schonberger, V., The Shape of Governance: Analysing the World of Internet Regulation, 43 *Va.J.Int'l L.* 605 (Spring 2003)

McGowan, D., Free Contracting, Fair Competition, and Draft Article 2B: Some Reflections on Federal Competition Policy, Information Transactions, and "Aggressive Neutrality", 13 *Berkeley Tech. L.J.* 1173–1238 (Fall 1998)

McGregor, H., Law on a Boundless Frontier: The Internet and International Law, 88 *Ky. L.J.* 967–986 (Summer 1999/Summer 2000)

McManis, C., Taking TRIPS on the Information Superhighway: International Intellectual Protection and Emerging Computer Technology, 41 *Vill. L. Rev.* 207–288 (1996)

Mefford, A., *Lex Informatica*: Foundations of Law on the Internet, 5 *Ind. J. Global Leg. Stud.* 211–237 (Fall 1997)

Menkel-Meadow, C., Do the "Haves" Come Out Ahead in Alternative Judicial Systems?: Repeat Players in ADR, 15 *Ohio St. J. on Disp. Resol.* 19–61 (1999)

Menthe, D., Jurisdiction in Cyberspace: A Theory of International Spaces, 4 *Mich. Telecomm. Tech. L. Rev.* 69 (1998)

Mentschikoff, S., Commercial Arbitration, 61 *Colum. L. Rev.* 846 (1961)

Meurer, M.J., Price Discrimination, Personal Use and Piracy: Copyright Protection of Digital Works, 45 *Buff. L. Rev.* 845–898 (Fall 1997)

Mewes, H.N., Memorandum of Understanding on the Generic Top-Level Domain Name Space of the Internet Domain Name System, 13 *Berkeley Tech. L.J.* 235–247 (1998)

Meyerson, M.I., Efficient Consumer Form Contracts: Law and Economics Meet the Real World, 24 *Ga. L. Rev.* 583–627 (Spring 1990)

——, Virtual Constitutions: The Creation of Rules for Governing Private Networks, 8 *Harvard Journal of Law and Technology* 129–153 (Fall 1994)

Michael, D.C., Federal Agency Use of Audited Self-Regulation as a Regulatory Technique, 47 *Administrative Law Review* 171–253 (1995)

Micklitz, H.W. & Weatherill, S., Consumer Policy in the European Community, 16 *Journal of Consumer Policy* 285 (1993)

Mirzaian, Esquire, A.G., Y2K . . . Who Cares? We Have Bigger Problems: Choice of Law in Electronic Contracts, 6 *Rich. J.L. & Tech.* 20 (Winter 1999–2000)
Mnookin, R.H., Why Negotiations Fail: An Exploration of Barriers to the Resolution of Conflict, 8 *Ohio St. J. on Disp. Resol.*, No. 2, 235–249 (1993)
Mullenix, L.S., Another Easy Case, Some More Bad Law: Carnival Cruise Lines and Contractual Personal Jurisdiction, 27 *Tex. Int'l L.J.* 323 (1992)
——, Resolving Aggregate Mass Tort Litigation: The New Private Law Dispute Resolution Paradigm, 33 *Val. U.L. Rev.* 413–447 (Spring 1999)
Muth, R.T., Old Doctrines on a New Frontier: Defamation and Jurisdiction in Cyberspace, 68 *Wisconsin Lawyer* 11 (September, 1995)
Nathenson, I.S., Showdown at the Domain Name Corral: Property Rights and Personal Jurisdiction Over Squatters, Poachers and Other Parasites, 58 *University of Pittsburgh law Review* 991 (1997)
Netanel, N.W., Cyberspace Self-Governance: A Skeptical View from Liberal Democratic Theory, 88 *Cal. L. Rev.* 395–498 (March 2000)
Newman, J.O., "Rethinking Fairness": Perspectives on the Litigation Process, 94 *Yale L.J.* 1643 (1985)
Nimmer, R.T. & Krauthaus, P.A., The Global Information Superhighway Challenges Virtually All of the Premises of Copyright Law, 6 *Stanford Law & Policy Review* 25–39 (1994)
Nimmer, R.T., Licensing on the Global Information Infrastructure: Disharmony in Cyberspace, 16 *Nw. J. Int'l L. Bus.* 224 (1995)
——, Electronic Contracting: Legal Issues, 14 *J. Marshall J. Computer & Info. L.* 211–246 (Winter 1996)
——, Article 2B: An Introduction, 16 *J. Marshall J. Computer & Info. L.* 211–253 (Winter 1997)
Noonan, M.F., Civil Procedure—Personal Jurisdiction: Evolution and Current Interpretation of the Stream of Commerce Test in the Third Circuit, 40 *Villanova Law Review* 779–802 (1995)
Nunziato, D.C., Freedom of Expression, Democratic Norms, and Internet Governance, 52 *Emory Law Journal* 187 (Winter 2003)
Okolie, C.C., International Law Principle of Jurisdiction in Regard to Settlements of Humankind on the Moon and Mars, *Proc. Thirty-Fourth Colloquium L. Outer Space* 64 (1991)
Oppedahl, C., Analysis and Suggestions Regarding NSI Domain Name Trademark Dispute Policy, 7 *Fordham Intellectual Property, Media & Entertainment Law Journal*, No. 1, 73 (Autumn 1996)
——, Remedies in Domain Name Lawsuits: How is a Domain Name Like a Cow?, 15 *J. Marshall J. of Computer & Info. L.* 437–464 (1997)
Orange, A., Developments in the Domain Name System: For Better or for Worse?, *The Journal of Information, Law and Technology*, No. 3 (1999)
O'Rourke, M.A., Fencing in Cyberspace: Drawing Borders in a Virtual World, 82 *Minn. L. Rev.* 609 (1998)
——, Progessing Towards a Uniform Commercial Code for Electronic Commerce or Racing Towards Nonuniformity?, 14 *Berkeley Tech. L.J.* 635–658 (Spring 1999)
Park, W.W., The *Lex Loci Arbitri* and International Commercial Arbitration, 32 *Int'l & Comp. L.Q.* 21 (1983)
——, Judicial Control in the Arbitral Process, 5 *Arbitration International*, No. 3, 230 (1989)
Patchel, K., Choice of Law and Software Licenses: A Framework for Discussion, 26 *Brooklyn J. Int'l L.* 117–186 (2000)
Paul, J.R., Comity in International Law, 32 *Harv. Int'l L.J.* 1–44 (1991)
Paulsson, J., Arbitration Unbound: Award Detached from the Law of the Country of Origin, 30 *Int'l & Comp. L.Q.* 358 (1981)

——, Delocalization of International Commercial Arbitration: When and Why It Matters?, 32 *Int'l & Comp. L.Q.*, 53 (1983)
Perritt, Jr., H.H., Dispute Resolution in Electronic Network communities, 38 *Vill. L. Rev.* 349–401 (1993)
——, President Clinton's National Information Infrastructure Initiative: Community Regained?, 69 *Chi.-Kent L. Rev.* 991–1022 (1994)
——, Property and Innovation in the Global Information Infrastructure, *U. Chi. Legal F.* (Fall 1996)
——, The Internet as a Threat to Sovereignty? Thoughts on the Internet's Role in Strengthening National and Global Governance, 5 *Ind. J. Global Leg. Stud.* 423–442 (Spring 1998)
——, The Internet is Changing International Law, 73 *Chi.-Kent L. Rev.* 997–1054 (1998)
——, The Internet is Changing the Public International Legal System, 88 *Ky. L.J.* 885–955 (Summer 1999/Summer 2000)
——, Dispute Resolution in Cyberspace: Demand for New Forms of ADR, 15 *Ohio St. J. on Disp. Resol.* 675–703 (2000)
Pollack, R.F., Creating the Standards of a Global Community: Regulating Pornography on the Internet—An International Concern, 10 *Temp. Int'l & Comp. L.J.* 467–492 (Fall 1996)
Ponte, L.M., Boosting Consumer Confidence in E-Business: Recommendations for Establishing Fair and Effective Dispute Resolution Programs for B2C Online Transactions, 12 *Albany Law Journal of Science & Technology* 441 (2002)
Posner, E.A., Law, Economics and Inefficient Norms, 144 *U. Pa. L. Rev.* 1697–1744 (May 1996)
Post, D.G., Anarchy, State, and the Internet, 1 *J. Online L.* 3 (1995)
——, Governing Cyberspace, 43 *Wayne L. Rev.*, 155–171 (Fall 1996)
—— & Johnson, D.R., "Chaos Prevailing on Every Continent": Towards a New Theory of Decentralized Decision-Making in Complex Systems, 73 *Chi.-Kent L. Rev.* 1055–1099 (1998)
Pridgen, D., How Will Consumers Be Protected on the Information Superhighway?, 32 *Land & Water Law Review* 237–255 (1997)
Pruner, M., The Internet and the Practice of Law, 19 *Pace L. Rev.* 69–93 (Fall 1998)
Puurunen, T., The Legislative Jurisdiction of States Over Transactions in International Electronic Commerce, 18 *J. Marshall J. Computer & Info. L.* 689–753 (Spring 2000)
Radin, M.J., Property Evolving in Cyberspace, 15 *J.L. & Com.* 509 (1996)
——, & Wagner, R.P., The Myth of Private Ordering: Rediscovering Legal Realism in Cyberspace, 73 *Chi.-Kent L. Rev.* 1295–1317 (1998)
Rakoff, T., Contracts of Adhesion: An Essay in Reconstruction, 96 *Harv. L. Rev.* 1173–1283 (April 1983)
Rana, H.S., The "Common Heritage of Mankind" & The Frontier: A Revaluation of Values Constituting the International Legal Regime for Outer Space Activities, 26 *Rutgers L.J.* 225–250 (Fall 1994)
Raysman, R. & Brown, P., Dangerous Liasons: The Legal Risks of Linking Web Sites, *N.Y.L.J.* 3 (April 8, 1997)
Redish, M.H., Of New Wine and Old Bottles: Personal Jurisdiction, the Internet, and The Nature of Constitutional Evolution, 38 *Jurimetrics Journal* 575–610 (Summer 1998)
Reese, W.L.M., The Law Governing Airplane Accidents, 39 *Washington & Lee Law Review* 1303 (1982)
Reeves, H.S., Property in Cyberspace, 63 *U.Chi L. Rev.* 761–799 (Spring 1996)
Reidenberg, J.R. & Gamet-Pol, F.O., The Fundamental Role of Privacy and Confidence in the Network, 30 *Wake Forest L. Rev.* 105–125 (Spring 1995)

Reidenberg, J.R., Governing Networks and Rule-Making in Cyberspace, 45 *Emory L.J.* 911–930 (Summer 1996)

——, *Lex Informatica*: The Formulation of Information Policy Rules Through Technology, 76 *Texas Law Review*, No. 3, 553–593 (February 1998)

Reindl, A.P., Choosing Law in Cyberspace: Copyright Conflicts on Global Networks, 19 *Mich. J. Int'l L.* 799–871 (Spring 1998)

Rice, D.T., Jurisdiction in Cyberspace: Which Law and Forum Apply to Securities Transactions on the Internet? Appendix, 21 *U. Pa. J. Int'l Econ. L.* 585–653 (Fall 2000)

Ritter, J. & Gliniecki, J., International Electronic Commerce and Administrative Law: The Need for Harmonized National Reforms, 6 *Harv. J.L. & Tech.* 263–285 (Spring 1993)

Robertson, R.J., Electronic Commerce on the Internet and the Statute of Frauds, 49 *S.C.L. Rev.* 787–845 (Summer 1998)

Roew, M.P., Options, Functions, and Skills: What an Organizational Ombudsperson Might Want to Know, 11 *Negotiation Journal*, 103 (April 1995)

Rogers, J.M., The Internet and International Law, 88 *Ky. L.J.* 803–808 (Summer 1999/Summer 2000)

Rosen, K.T. & Howard, A.L., E-Retail: Gold Rush or Fool's Gold?, 42 *California Management Review*, No. 3, 72–99 (Spring 2000)

Rothchild, J., Protecting the Digital Consumer: The Limits of Cyberspace Utopianism, *74 Indiana Law Journal*, 893–989 (Summer 1999)

Rowe, Jr., T.D., American Law Institute Study on Paths to a "Better Way": Litigation, Alternatives, and Accommodations: Background Paper, 38 *Duke L.J.* 824–902 (September 1989)

Ruggie, J.G., International Responses to Technology: Concepts and Trends, 29 *Int'l Org.* 557 (1975)

Rustad, M., Legal Resources for Lawyers Lost in Cyberspace, 30 *Suffolk U.L. Rev.* 317–352 (1996)

—— & Eisenschmidt, L., The Commercial Law of Internet Security, 10 *High Tech. L.J.* No. 2, 213 (1995)

Salaun, A., Consumer Protection—Proposals for Improving the Protection of Online Consumers, 15 *Computer Law & Security Report*, No. 3, 159–167 (1999)

Salbu, S.R., Who Should Govern the Internet?: Monitoring and Supporting a New Frontier, 11 *Harv. J. Law & Tech.* 429–480 (Winter 1998)

Saltzer, J.H. et al., End-to-End Arguments in System Design, 2 *ACM Transactions in Computer Systems* 277 (1984)

Schachter, O., International Law in Theory and Practice, 178 *Recueil des Cours* 9 (1982)

——, Philip Jessup's Life and Ideas, 80 *AJIL* 878–895 (1986)

Schack, J., Cost Containment, 33 *Institutional Investor* 43–49 (1999)

Schneiderman, E. & Kornreich, R., Personal Jurisdiction and Internet Commerce, *New York Law Journal* (June 4th, 1997)

Schuck, P.H., Legal Complexity: Some Causes, Consequences, and Cures, 42 *Duke L.J.* 1–52 (October 1992)

Schneider, M.E., Lean Arbitration, 10 *Arbitration International*, No. 2, 119 (1994)

—— & Kuner, C., Dispute Resolution in International Electronic Commerce, 14 *Journal of International Arbitration*, No. 3, 5–37 (1997)

Schwartz, A. & Scott, R.E., The Political Economy of Private Legislatures, 143 *U. Pa. L. Rev.* 595–654 (January 1995)

Schwartz, P.M., European Data Protection Law and Restrictions on International Data Flows, 80 *Iowa L. Rev.* 471–496 (March 1995)

Selin, S., Governing Cyberspace: The Need for an International Solution, 32 *Gonz. L. Rev.* 365–388 (1996/1997)

Shapiro, A.L., The Disappearance of Cyberspace and the Risk of Code, 8 *Seton Hall Const. L.J.* 703 (1998)
Shilston, A.W., The Evolution of Modern Commercial Arbitration, 4 *Journal of International Arbitration*, 45 (1987)
Shin, H., Oh, I have Slipped the Surly Bonds of Earth: Multinational Space Stations and Choice of Law, 78 *Cali. L. Rev.* 1375–1414 (October 1990)
Shreve, G.R., Choice of Law and the Forgiving Constitution, 71 *Indiana Law Review*, No. 2, 271 (Spring 1996)
Silbey, S.S. & Merry, S.E., Mediator Settlement Strategies, 8 *Law & Policy* 7 (1986)
Smit, H., A-national Arbitration, 63 *Tulane Law Review* 629–645 (February 1989)
Solimine, M.E., An Economic and Empirical Analysis of Choice of Law, 24 *Ga. L. Rev.* 49–93 (Fall 1989)
Solomon, L. & Corso, L., The Impact of Technology on the Trading of Securities: The Emerging Global Market and the Implications for Regulation, 24 *J. Marshall L. Rev.* 299 (1991)
Sommer, J.H., Against Cyberlaw, 15 *Berkeley Tech. L.J.* 1145–1232 (Fall 2000)
Spector, P.L., The Internet and Intellectual Property: Toward a New Model for the Economics of Content, 4 *Telecommunications and Space Journal* 155–175 (1997)
Staerk, III, R.B. & Rozell, L.M., A Cyberspace Perspective: The Federal Trade Commission's Commitment to On-Line Consumer Protection, 15 *J. Marshall J. Computer & Info. L.* 679–702 (Summer 1997)
Stefik, M., Shifting the Possible: How Trusted Systems and Digital Property Rights Challenge Us to Rethink Digital Publishing, 12 *Berkeley Tech. L.J.*, No. 1, 137 (Spring 1997)
Stein, A.R., The Unexceptional Problem of Jurisdiction in Cyberspace, 32 *International Lawyer* 1167 (1998)
Sterling, S.B., New Age Bandits in Cyberspace: Domain Names Held Hostage on the Internet, 17 *Loy. L.A. Ent. L.J.* 733–330 (1997)
Sternlight, J.R., Panacea or Corporate Tool?: Debunking the Supreme Court's Preference for Binding Arbitration, 74 *Wash. U.L.Q.* 637–712 (Fall 1996)
Stoll, P. & Goller, B., Electronic Commerce and the Internet, 41 *German Yearbook of International Law* 128–169 (1998)
Stott, D.L., Personal Jurisdiction in Cyberspace: The Constitutional Boundary of Minimum Contacts Limited to a Web Site, 15 *Journal of Computer & Information Law* 819–854 (1997)
Sunstein, C.R., Legal Interference with Private Preferences, 53 *U. Chi. L. Rev.* 1129–1174 (Fall 1986)
Suzan, K.D., Tapping to the Beat of a Digital Drummer: Fine Tuning U.S. Copyright Law for Music Distribution on the Internet, 59 *Alb. L. Rev.* 789–829 (1995)
Swanson, S.R., Comity, International Dispute Resolution Agreements, and the Supreme Court, 21 *Law & Policy in International Business*, 333 (1990)
Swindells, C. & Henderson, K., Legal Regulation of Electronic Commerce, 3 *The Journal of Information, Law and Technology* 30 (1998)
Swire, P.P., Of Elephants, Mice, and Privacy: International Choice of Law and the Internet, 32 *International Lawyer* 991 (1998)
Symeonides, S.C., Choice of Law in the American Courts in 1993 (and in the Six Previous Years), 42 *American Journal of Comparative Law* 599 (1994)
——, Choice of Law in the American Courts in 1994: A View "From the Trenches", 43 *American Journal of Comparative Law* 1 (1995)
Szasz, P.C., The Role of the U.N. Secretary-General: Some Legal Aspects, 24 *N.Y.U.J. Int'l L. & Pol.* 161 (1991)
Tamayo, Y.A., Who? What? When? Where? Personal Jurisdiction and the World Wide Web, 4 *Rich. J.L. & Tech.* 7 (Spring 1998)
Tavakol, S., Digital Value Units, Electronic Commerce and International Trade:

An Obituary for State Sovereignty over National Markets, 17 *Journal of Computer & Information Law* 1197–1233 (1999)
Taitz, A.B., Removing Road Blocks Along the Information Superhighway: Facilitating the Dissemination of New Technology by Changing the Law of Contributory Copyright Infringement, 64 *George Washington Law Review* 133–171 (1995)
Teitz, L.E., Providing Legal Services for the Middle Class in Cyberspace: the Promise and Challenge of On-line Dispute Resolution, 70 *Fordham L. Rev.* 985–1016 (December 2001)
Tetley, W., The Law of the Flag, "Flag Shopping", and Choice of Law, 17 *Maritime Lawyer* 139–184 (Spring 1993)
Thomas, S.K., The Protection and Promotion of E-Commerce: Should There Be a Global Regulatory Scheme for Digital Signatures?, 22 *Fordham Int'l L.J.* 1002–1063 (March 1999)
Thornburg, E.G., Sanctifying Secrecy: The Mythology of the Corporate Attorney-Client Privilege, 69 *Notre Dame L. Rev.* 157 (1993)
——, Going Private: Technology, Due Process, and Internet Dispute Resolution, 34 *U.C. Davis L. Rev.* 151–220 (Fall 2000)
Tien, L., Who's Afraid of Anonymous Speech? McIntyre and the Internet, 75 *Or. L. Rev.* 117–189 (Spring 1996)
Tiersma, P.M., The Language of Offer and Acceptance: Speech Acts and the Question of Intent, 74 *Cal. L. Rev.* 189–232 (January 1986)
Tita, S. & Scamby, G., The "Effects Test": Unifying Personal Jurisdiction Case law in Internet Defamation Cases, 33 *Law/Technology, World Jurist Association*, No. 1, 1–30 (2000)
Toth, A.G., The Principle of Subsidiarity in the Maastricht Treaty, 29 *Common Market Law Review* 1079 (1992)
Towle, H.K., Electronic Transactions and Contracting, 520 *PLI/Pat*, 515 (1998)
Trachtman, J.P., Conflict of Laws and Accuracy in the Allocation of Government Responsibility, 26 *Vand. J. Transnational L.* 975 (1994)
Trakman, L.E., From the Medieval Law Merchant to E-Merchant Law, 53 *University of Toronto Law Journal* 265 (Summer 2003)
Trangsrud, R.H., The Federal Common Law of Personal Jurisdiction, 57 *Geo. Wash. L. Rev.* 849–906 (March 1989)
Trimble, P.R., A Revisionist View of Customary International Law, 33 *UCLA L. Rev.* 665–732 (February 1986)
Trubow, G.B., Regulating Transactions of the Internet, 24 *Ohio N.U.L. Rev.* 831–841 (1998)
Uyttendaele, C. & Dumortier, J., Free Speech on the Information Superhighway: European Perspectives, 16 *J. Marshall J. of Computer & Info. L.*, No. 4, 905–936 (1998)
Valdivia, D.C., Panel I: Report on the E-Commerce Activities of the OAS, ICC, ABA, and UNCITRAL, 17 *Ariz. J. Int'l & Comp. Law* 109–117 (Winter 2000)
Valencia-Weber, G., Tribal Courts: Custom and Innovative Law, 24 *N.M.L. Rev.* 225–263 (Spring 1994)
Vermulst, E. & Driessen, B., An Overview of the WTO Dispute Settlement System and Its Relationship with the Uruguay Round Agreements: Nice on Paper but Too Much Stress for the System?, 29 *JWT*, No. 2, 131–161 (1995)
Vermut, R.S., File Caching on the Internet: Technical Infringement or Safeguard for Efficient Network Operation, 4 *J. Intell. Prop. L.* 273 (1997)
Victorio, R.M., Internet Dispute Resolution (IDR): Bringing ADR into the 21st Century, 1 *Pepp. Disp. Resol. L.J.* 279–300 (2001)
Wai, R., Transnational Liftoff and Juridical Touchdown: The Regulatory Function of Private International Law in an Era of Globalization, 40 *Columbia Journal of Transnational Law* 209 (2002)

Waldrop, M.M., Cultural Shock on the Networks, 265 *Science* 879–883 (1994)
Wall, D.S., Catching Cybercriminals: Policing the Internet, 12 *International Review of Law Computers & Technology*, No. 2, 201–218 (1998)
Wang, L., Some Observations on the Dispute Settlement System in the World Trade Organization, 29 *JWT*, No. 2, 173–178 (1995)
Ware, S.J., Default Rules from Mandatory Rules: Privatizing Law Through Arbitration, 83 *Minn. L. Rev.* 703–754 (February 1999)
Weinberg, J., ICANN and the Problem of Legitimacy, 50 *Duke L.J.* 187–260 (October 2000)
Weintraub, R.J., Methods for Resolving Conflict-of-Laws Problems in Mass Tort Litigation, *U. Ill. L. Rev.* 129 (1989)
Weiswasser, G., Domain Names, the Internet, and Trademarks: Infringement in Cyberspace, 13 *Santa Clara Computer & High Tech. L.J.* 137–180 (February 1997)
White, Jr., H.M. & Lavria, R., The Impact of New Communication Technologies on International Telecommunication Law and Policy: Cyberspace and the Restructuring of the International Telecommunication Union, 32 *Cal. W.L. Rev.* 1–30 (Fall 1995)
Wiley, R. & Butler, R., National Information Infrastructure: Preserving Personal Space in Cyberspace, 12 *Communications Lawyer* No. 3, 1–29 (Fall 1994)
Williams, N.G., Offer, Acceptance, and Improper Considerations: A Common-Law Model for the Prohibition of Racial Discrimination in the Contracting Process, 62 *Geo. Wash. L. Rev.* 183–229 (January 1994)
Wilske, S., Conflict of Laws in Cyber Torts, *Computer Und Recht International*, No. 3, 68–74 (2001)
—— & Schiller, T., International Jurisdiction in Cyberspace: Which States May Regulate the Internet?, 50 *Fed. Comm. L.J.* 117–178 (December 1997)
Wilson, D., Viewing Computer Crime: Where Does the Systems Error Really Exist?, 11 *Computer/L.J.*, No. 2, 265–286 (1991)
Wilson, Jr., P.E., Barking Up the Right Tree: Proposals for Enhancing the Effectiveness of the International Tropical Timber Agreement, 10 *Temp. Int'l & Comp. L.J.* 229–253 (Spring 1996)
Winn, J.K., Open Systems, Free Markets and Regulation of Internet Commerce, 72 *Tul. L. Rev.* 1177–1259 (March, 1998)
Winship, P., Private International Law and the U.N. Sales Convention, 21 *Cornell International Law Review*, No. 3, 487 (1988)
Wittow, M.H., U.S. District Court for the Northern District of California: Personal Jurisdiction over Nonresidents, *Computer Und Recht International*, No. 4, 111–117 (2001)
Wood, G.S., Thomas Jefferson, Equality, and the Creation of a Civil Society, 64 *Fordham L. Rev.* 2133–2147 (April 1996)
Wu, S.S., Incorporation by Reference and Public Key Infrastructures: Moving the Law Beyond the Paper-Based World, 38 *Jurimetrics Journal*, No. 3, 317–344 (Spring 1998)
Wu, T.S., Cyberspace Sovereignty?—The Internet and the International System, 10 *Harv. J. Law & Tech.* 647–666 (Summer 1997)
——, Application-Centered Internet Analysis, 85 *Va. L. Rev.* 1163–1204 (September 1999)
——, When Law & the Internet First Met, 3 *Green Bag 2d* 171–177 (Winter 2000)
Yates, J.C., Recent Legal Issues in Electronic Commerce and Electronic Data Interchange, *PLI/Pat* 271 (1996)
Yeo, M.S. & Berliri, M., Conflict Looms Over Choice of Law in Internet Transactions, 4 *Electronic Commerce & Law Report* 85 (1998)
Yntema, H.E., The Comity Doctrine, 65 *Mich. L. Rev.* 9 (1966)
Young, A.R., Towards a More Vigorous European Consumer Policy?, 7 *European Business Journal*, No. 4, 34 (1995)

Zain, S., Regulation of E-Commerce by Contract: Is It Fair to Consumers?, 31 *U. West. L.A. L. Rev.* 163–186 (2000)
Zanghi, J.S., "Community Standards" in Cyberspace, 21 *U. Dayton L. Rev.* 95 (1995)
Zaphiriou, G.A., Basis of the Conflict of Laws: Fairness and Effectiveness, 10 *Geo. Mason U.L. Rev.* 301 (1988)
Zembek, R.S., Jurisdiction and the Internet: Fundamental Fairness in the Networked World of Cyberspace, 6 *Alb. L.J. Sci. & Tech.* 339–381 (1996)
Zhao, Y., Internet Service Providers and their Liability, 34 *Law/Technology, World Jurist Association*, No. 1, 1–19 (2001)
Zittrain, J., ICANN: Between the Public and the Private—Comments Before Congress, 14 *Berkeley Tech. L.J.* 1071–1093 (1999)
Zollers, F.E., Hurd, S.N. & Shears, P., Consumer Protection in the European Union: An Analysis of the Directive on the Sale of Consumer Goods and Associated Guarantees, 20 *U. Pa. J. Int'l Econ. L.* 97–131 (Spring 1999)

4. *Miscellaneous*

A Consultative Document of Department of Trade and Industry of the U.S. Antitrust & Trade Reg. Rep. (BNA)
Black's Law Dictionary (6th Ed. 1990)
Business Horizon
Business Lawyer
Business Times (Singapore)
Business Week
Canada NewsWire
Commercial Communications
Computer Lawyer
Computer Weekly
Computer World
Consumer International
Cyberspace Lawyer
Electronic Information Policy & Law Report (BNA)
Electronic Messaging Services Task Force
European Report
Federal Register
Financial Times
Forrester Research
Global Internet Summit 2000
Information Week
International Communications Round Table
International Conference on Dispute Resolution in Electronic Commerce (WIPO)
International Conference on Electronic Commerce and Intellectual Property (WIPO)
Journal of Computer-Mediated Communication
Journal of Internet Law
Journal of Online Law
Legal Infosoc News Kiosk (the l.i.n.k.)
Litigation News
Los Angeles Times
Minnesota Journal of Global Trade
National Law Journal
Negotiation Journal
Network Magazine
New York Times

Newsweek
OECD Policy Brief
OECD Economics Department Working Papers
RAPID
Reuter European Community Report
Spicers Center for Europe
Sunday Times
Tech Law Journal
Toronto Star
Trans Atlantic Consumer Dialogue
Uniform Law Conference of Canada
USA Today
Wall Street Journal (Europe)
World Arbitration & Mediation Report
World Internet Law Report
World Telecom Law Report
WTO Staff Working Paper

5. *Internet Sources*

A Brief History of the Internet, by B.M. Leiner et al., <http://www.isoc.org/internet/history/brief.html>

A Brief history of the Virtual Magistrate Project: The Early Months, by R. Gellman, <http://mantle.sbs.umass.edu/vmag/gellman.htm>

A Declaration of the Independence of Cyberspace, by J.P. Barlow, <http://www.eff.org/pub/Publications/John_Perry_Barlow/barlow_0296.declaration>

A European Initiative in Electronic Commerce, <http://www.ispo.cec.be/ecommerce/answers/what.html>

A Framework for Global Electronic Commerce, by W.J. Clinton & A. Gore, Jr., <http://www.iitf.nist.gov/eleccomm/ecomm.htm>

A Global Approach to the Laws of Jurisdiction in Cyberspace, by T.P. Vartanian, <http://www.kentlaw.edu/cyberlaw/housetestimony.html>

A Separate Jurisdiction for Cyberspace?, by J.M. Oberding & T. Norderhaug, <http://www.ascusc.org/jcmc/vol2/issue1/juris.html>

A Survey of the Current Cases of Personal Jurisdiction and the Internet, by M. D'Amico, <http://www.madcapps.com/~Writings/asurvey.htm>

American Bar Association <http://www.abanet.org>

An Introduction to Internet Legal and Regulatory Issues, by D.N. Lampert et al., <http://www.mintz.com>

Anti-Cybersquatting Act: Federal Protection for Trademarks and Personal names on the Internet, by S.D. Littlepage, <http://www.dickinson-wright.com>

Arbitration in International Computer contracts, by R.M. Lucash, Esq., <http://www.lgu.com/in43.htm>

Australian Domain Name Allocation Policy <http://www.davies.com.au>

Avoid Domain Name Conflicts form the Start, by B.J.E. van Gils, <http://www.ideasiteforbusiness.com/bert.htm>

Better Business Bureau <http://www.bbb.org>

BitLaw <http://www.bitlaw.com>

British & Irish Legal Education Technology Association <http://www.bileta.ac.uk>

Center for democracy & Technology <http://www.cdt.org>

Changes in Domain-Name Rules Could Result in Ownership Loss, by C. Oppedahl, <http://www.patents.com/nylj4.sht>

Computer Law Tip of the Week <http://www.mgrossmanlaw.com>

Consumer Protection Principles in Electronic Commerce <http://www.accc.gov.au/ecomm/principles.htm>
Coudert Brothers Practice Groups <http://www.coudert.com>
Creating an Environment for Mediating Disputes on the Internet, by R.S. Granat, <http://mantle.sbs.umass.edu/vmag/granat.htm>
Customer Privacy on the Web—Self-regulation or Government Enforcement <http://mcgraw-hill.govtservices.com/speech/forum1.html>
Cybercourt: A Virtual Resolution of Differences or An Alternative Proposal for Law and Order in Cyberspace, by C.L. Mudd, <http://www.mudd.org/professional/articlesclm/cybercourt.htm>
Cyberspace Law Institute, <http://www.11.georgetown.edu/lc/cli.html>
Deeth Williams Wall <http://www.dww.com>
Determination of Jurisdiction in a Digital Environment, by W. Ginn, <http://www.willamette.edu/law/ilc/hackerpaper.html>
Dispute Resolution and Arbitration for Electronic Commerce, by A. Williams, <http://www.dww.com/articles/ec_adr.htm>
Dispute Resolution in Cyberspace: Engineering a Virtual Magistrate System, by D.G. Post (1996), <http://mantle.sbs.umass.edu/vmag/DGP2.htm>
Doing Business On-line in the Digital Millennium: the Law Looks Ahead <http://www.chapmantripp.co.nz/publish/c040500.htm>
Domain Names, Globalization, and Internet Governance, by M. Leaffer, <http://www.law.indiana.edu/glsj/vol6/no1/leaffer.html>
Domain Names: ICANN and New Remedies Against Cybersquatting, <http://www.gcwf.com/articles/interest/interest_32.html>
Domain Name Resolutions: CPSR Proposals for the New Corporation, <http://cpsr.vacia.is.tohoku.ac.jp/dns_resolutions.html>
eBay <http://www.ebay.com>
E-Commerce: A Choice of Laws?, by J. Warchus, <http://www.wiredsussex.org.uk/ecommerce/ecomm11.htm>
E-Commerce for Development: Prospects and Policy Issues, by A. Goldstein & D. O'Connor, <http://www.oecd.org/dev>
E-Commerce Times <http://www.ecommercetimes.com>
Electronic Arbitration Tribunal an Alternative Dispute Resolution for SMEs (E-Arbitration-T), <http://www.diritto.it/articoli/informatica/arbitration.htm>
Electronic Commerce <http://www.uscib.org/trade/eleccomm.htm>
Electronic Commerce and Consumer Protection Group <http://www.ecommercegroup.org>
Electronic Commerce Contract, by R. Hill (1995), <http://www.batnet.com/oikoumene/arbcont2.html>
Electronic Commerce in the NII <http://www.xiwt.org/documents/Ecommerce.html>
Electronic Commerce, the World-Wide Web, Minitel, and EDI, by R. Hill (1996) <http://www.batnet.com/oikoumene/arbecom.htm>
Electronic Dispute Resolution: an NCAIR Conference, by W.J. Olmstead, <http://mantle.sbsumass.edu/vmag/olmst.htm>
Electronic Frontier Foundation <http://www.eff.org>
Establishing Personal Jurisdiction for Internet transactions, by J.C. Henry, <http://www.law.stetson.edu/courses/computerlaw/papers/jhenryf97.htm>
Esther Dyson's Monthly Report <http://www.edventure.com>
EU Committee Position Paper on the Millennium Round <http://www.eucommittee.be/pop/pop1999/tra/trade%2023.htm>
European Commission <http://europa.eu.int>
Europe's Way to the Information Society: An Action Plan, <http://www.echo.lu/eudocs/en/com-asc.html>

Feasibility Studies for New Standards Relating to Consumers and Electronic Commerce, by A. McChesney, <http://strategis.ic.gc.ca/ssg/ca01275e.html>
Federal Trade Commission <http://www.ftc.gov>
FICPI Domain Name Meeting <http://www.regisgroup.com/domainname.html>
Foreign Domain Name Disputes 2000, by D. Cabell, Esq., <http://www.mama-tech.com/foreign.html>
Global Internet Project <http://www.gip.org>
Grounding the Virtual Magistrate, by J. Goldsmith & L. Lessig, <http://mantle.sbs.umass.edu/vmag/groundvm.htm>
gTLD-MoU Policy Oversight Committee <http://www.gtld-mou.org>
Hague Conference on Private International law <http://www.hcch.net>
ICC <http://www.iccwbo.org>
International Ad Hoc Committee <http://www.iahc.org>
Internet Governance Information Service <http://www.intgov.apdip.net>
Internet Jurisdiction, by P.J. Whalen, <http://www.spencerfane.com>
Internet Jurisdiction: The SEC "Opts Out", by M. Geist <http://lawschool.mtcibs.com/lawtech/archive/199705.htm>
Internet Law & Policy Forum <http://www.ilpf.org>
Internet Self-Regulation, <http://www.endispute.co.uk/isr/cirb.htm>
Internet Use and Personal Jurisdiction: Have Mouse, Will Travel, by S.D. Jones, <http://www.ralaw.com/frame8118.html>
Is the InterNIC's Dispute Policy unconstitutional?, by M. Barry, <http://www.mids.org/legal/dispute.html>
ITEC Law Alert <http://www.mbc.com/newsletters/itec/itec999.htm>
Joint EU-US Statement on Electronic Commerce, <http://www.qlinks.net/comdocs/eu-us.htm>
Jurisdiction in Cyberspace: User Beware, by G.R. Cummins, Esp., & C.M. Cerasale, <http://www.gcwf.com/articles/interest/interest_23.html>
Jurisdiction over Web Sites, or "Where Will I be Sued Next?", by W.E. Agin, <http://www.agin.com/aigc/tic84.html>
Litigation in Cyberspace: Jurisdiction and Choice of Law: A United States Perspective, by J.P. Donohue, <http://www.abanet.org/buslaw/cyber/initiatives/usjuris.html>
Local and International Jurisdiction on the Internet, by A.H. Ravia, <http://www.law.co.il/articles/juris1.htm>
Major Flaws in the WIPO Domain Name Proposal—A Quick Guide, by A.M. Froomkin, <http://www.law.miami.edu/~amf/quickguide.htm>
Name Conflicts in Cyberspace, by D. Cabell, <http://www.mama-tech.com/ali-aba.htm>
National Fraud Information Center <http://www.fraud.org>
National Information Infrastructure <http://ww.nap.edu>
Network Solutions, Inc. Domain Name Registration Agreement, <http://quick-start.rccis.com/internic.htm>
New Global Rules for E-Commerce: Moving the Dialogue Beyond the G-8, by C. Charles, <http://usinfo.state.gov/journals/ites/0500/ijee/giic3.htm>
Note on Personal Jurisdiction, by H.H. Perritt, Jr., <http://mantle.sbs.umass.edu/vmag/PJ2.htm>
NSI Domain Name Dispute Policy Puts Owners at Significant Risk, <http://www.patents.com/nylj6.sht>
OECD <http://www.oecd.org>
Onine Alternative Dispute Resolution: The "Write" Forum for the Right Parties, by K. Withrow, <http://www.mttlr.org/forum/withrow_art.html>
Out-of-Court Dispute Settlement For Trans-Border Electronic Commerce <http://dsa-isis.jrc.it/ADR/consumer.htm>

Out-of-State Jurisdiction Over Web Site Operators and Junk E-Mail: Legal Developments on the Internet, by E.S. Freibrun, Esq., <http://www.cl.ais.net/lawmsf/articl25.htm>

Personal Jurisdiction and the Internet <http://www.escm.com/new/art/jurisdiction.html>

Personal Jurisdiction in Cyberspace: Where can You be sued, and Whose Laws Apply?, by G.M. Perry, <http://www.llgm.com/firm/artilce14.htm>

Personal Jurisdiction Issues in Conducting Business Over the Internet, by E.G. Gunnells & A.G. Mersereau, <http://www.hicksmaloof.com/In7.html>

Principles of Consumer Protection for Electronic Commerce: A Canadian Framework <http://strategis.ic.gc.ca/oca>

Privacy and Self-Regulation in the Information Age, by US Department of Commerce, <http://www.ntia.doc.gov/reports/privacyprivacy_rpt.htm>

Settling Differences Through Interactive Multimedia Networks, by M., Lauritsen, <http://mantle.sbs.umass.edu/vmag/LAURIT.HTM>

Some Legal and Ethical Issues of the Access to Electronic Information, by V. Montviloff, <http://ksgwww.harvard.edu/iip/montpap.html>

Substantive Guidelines Concerning Administrative Domain Name Challenge Panels, <http://www.gtld-mou.org/docs/racps.htm>

Tensions Promote Discussions on a Code of Conduct, by C.A. Thayer, <http://www.csis.org/pacfor/cc/001Qchina_asean.html>

The Bureau of National Affairs Inc. <http://www.bna.com>

The Domain Name System-Act Now or Regret Later, by I.J. Kaufman, <http://ladas.com>

The Draft UNCITRAL Model Law for Electronic Commerce: Issues and Solutions, by R. Hill & I. Walden, <http://www.batnet.com/oikoumene/arbunc.html>

The Electronic Frontier: The Challenge of Unlawful Conduct Involving the Use of the Internet <http://www.usdoj.gov/criminal/cybercrime/unlawful.htm>

The Emerging Digital Economy, by L. Margherio, <http://www.ecommerce.gov/danintro.htm>

The First Annual Report, US Government's Working Group on Electronic Commerce, <http://www.ecommerce.gov/whatsnew.htm>

The Future of Domain Name, by S. Niyogi, <http://www.siliocnindia.com>

The Internet Society of New Zealand <http://www.isocnz.org.nz>

The Online Ombuds Office: Adapting Dispute Resolution to Cyberspace, by E. Katsh, <http://mantle.sbs.umass.edu/vmag/katsh.htm>

"The Only Way to Fully Protect your Domain Name under Our Current "Dispute Policy" is with a Federal Trademark!", <http://blaze.net/search/internic.html>

The Promise of Online Dispute Resolution, by D.R. Johnson, <http://www.toolbox.org/Tvtools/app-onlinedr.html>

The Richmond Journal of Law & technology <http://www.urich.edu>

The Standard Intelligence for the Internet Economy <http://www.thestandard.net>

The State of the Law on Cyberjurisdiction and Cybercrime on the Internet, by G. Zeviar-Geese, <http://www.law.gonzaga.edu/borders/documents/cyberlaw.htm>

The Top Ten Cyber-Commandments of Web Site Domain Names, by L.M. Hertz, <http://www.hedgero.com/domain.html>

The White House <http://www.whitehouse.gov>

The World Reports <http://www.hg.org>

Throwing Rocks at ICANN, by K. Perine, <http://www.thestandard.net/article/display>

Time <http://www.time.com>

Trademark Dispute Online—ICANN's New Uniform Dispute Resolution Policy, by D. Cabell, <http://www.mama-tech.com/udrp.html>

Trademarks and Domain Names: Property Rights and Institutional Evolution in Cyberspace, by M. Mueller, <http://istweb.syr.edu/Emueller/study.html>
TransAtlantic Business Dialogue <http://www.tabd.org>
Transnational Issues in Cyberspace: A Project on the Law Relating to Jurisdiction, <http://www.abanet.org/buslaw/cyber/initiatives/prospect.html>
TRUSTe <http://www.truste.com>
United States Council for International Business <http://www.uscib.org>
Why Censoring Cyberspace is Dangerous and Futile, by H. Rheingold, <http://www.well.com/user/hlr/tomorrow/tomorrowcensor.html>
WIPO <http://www.wipo.org>
World Information Technology and Services Alliance <http://www.wista.org>
WTO <http://www.wto.org>

INDEX

STUDIES AND MATERIALS ON THE SETTLEMENT OF INTERNATIONAL DISPUTES

Series Editor

PROFESSOR PETER MALANCZUK
School of Law, City University of Hong Kong

ISSN: 1387-2990

1. Kazazi, M. *Burden of Proof and Related Issues.* A Study on Evidence Before International Tribunals. 1996. ISBN 90 411 0142 X
2. Wellens, K.C. *Economic Conflicts and Disputes Before the World Court (1922-1995).* A Functional Analysis. 1996. ISBN 90 411 0195 0
3. Kokott, J. *The Burden of Proof in Comparative and International Human Rights Law.* Civil and Common Law Approaches with Special Reference to the American and German Legal Systems. 1998. ISBN 90 411 0570 0
4. Maluwa, T. *International Law in Post-Colonial Africa.* 1999. ISBN 90 411 1089 5
5. Magliveras, K.D. *Exclusion from Participation in International Organisations.* The Law and Practice Behind Member States' Expulsion and Suspension of Membership. 1999. ISBN 90 411 1239 1
6. Kaikobad, K. Homi *The International Court of Justice and Judicial Review.* A Study of the Court's Powers with Respect to Judgements of the ILO and UN Administrative Tribunals. 2000. ISBN 90 411 1471 8
7. Kamminga, M.T. & S. Zia-Zarifi (eds.). *Liability of Multinational Corporations under International Law.* 2001. ISBN 90 411 1504 8
8. Schweigman, D. *The Authority of the Security Council under Chapter VII of the UN Charter.* Legal Limits and the Role of the International Court of Justice. 2001. ISBN 90 411 1641 9
9. Zhao, Y. *Dispute Resolution in Electronic Commerce.* 2005. ISBN 90 04 14383 1